—*The Unofficial Guide*
to Washington, D.C. —

Also available from Prentice Hall Travel

The Unofficial Guide to Atlanta, by Bob Sehlinger
and Fred Brown
The Unofficial Guide to Disneyland, by Bob Sehlinger
The Unofficial Guide to Euro Disneyland,
by Bob Sehlinger
The Unofficial Guide to Las Vegas, by Bob Sehlinger
The Unofficial Guide to Walt Disney World,
by Bob Sehlinger

The Unofficial Guide to
Washington, D.C.

Bob Sehlinger and
Joe Surkiewicz
with Eve Zibart

PRENTICE HALL TRAVEL

New York · London · Toronto · Sydney · Tokyo · Singapore

Published by Prentice Hall General Reference
A division of Simon & Schuster Inc.
15 Columbus Circle
New York, New York 10023

Produced by Menasha Ridge Press

ISBN 0-671-79829-4

ISSN 1071-6440

Manufactured in the United States of America

10 9 8 7 6 5 4 3 2 1

First Edition

For Tom Nugent, writer and teacher

J. S.

To Dick Wood, who infected
me with this strange contagion
we call book publishing

B. S.

To D.

E. Z.

Contents

PART THREE: Hotels

PART FOUR: Getting Around Washington: Cabs, Cars, and the Metro

PART FIVE: Entertainment and Night Life

PART SIX: Exercise and Recreation

PART SEVEN: Visiting Washington on Business

PART EIGHT: Sight-Seeing Tips and Tours

PART NINE: Washington's Attractions

PART TEN: *Shopping in Washington*

Mall Shopping

Great Neighborhoods for Window-Shopping

Specialty Shops

PART ELEVEN: *Dining and Restaurants*

A Comment on Washington Cuisine

The Restaurants

APPENDIX

Hotel Information Chart

Index

List of Illustrations

Acknowledgments

Washingtonians are schizophrenic about their town: Most complain about its extremes of weather, the horrible traffic, and the high cost of real estate . . . but are rapturous about D.C.'s unique mix of the cultural, the political, and the ethnic. So we made every effort to reflect the city's mind-numbing range of attractions when putting this book together—tempered with an honest attempt to be realistic about the problems visitors face on a Washington sojourn. We got a lot of help along the way.

Tom Murphy at the Washington Convention and Visitors Association was unstinting in his labors, whether it was fulfilling a last-minute request for maps, offering suggestions on how to divide the town into zones, or finding the names of D.C.'s best freelance writers.

Eve Zibart, the *Washington Post*'s "Doctor Nightlife" columnist, drew on her intimate knowledge of D.C.'s diverse after-hours scene and the area's vast array of dining spots when writing our entertainment and restaurant sections.

For the inside scoop on the best deals in D.C., we thank Sherri Dalphonse for writing our section on shopping; she's a senior editor at *Washingtonian* magazine. And thanks to Officer Rod Ryan of the Washington Metropolitan Police, who gave us the straight skinny on how to avoid street crime in Washington.

B.J. Davis at the National Museum of American History offered invaluable insights on the best ways to tour the labyrinthine Smithsonian Institution, while Peter and Irna Jay supplied names of local contacts from their *Washington Post* days.

Metro's Phil Portlock provided photos of the subway system; Gary Barton supplied his detailed knowledge of Washington's streets and spent a Saturday chauffeuring us to suburban Metro stations; renown bicycling writer (and D.C. resident) Arlene Plevin shared suggestions on cycling around town; and mega-boater Steve Garrison blessed our section on white-water canoeing.

To fulfill their task, the hotel inspection team, Molly Burns and Leslie Cummins endured cold winds, sore feet, a Washington slush storm, evenings at ethnic eateries, and too many nights at a crummy hotel.

Finally, many thanks to Barbara Williams, Deborah Wong, Mary Caviness, Marjorie Hudson, Tim Krasnansky, Ann Cassar, Christi Stanforth, Alexa Dilworth, and Tseng Information Systems, the pros who managed to transform all this effort into a book.

INTRODUCTION

Washington Without the Hassle

Before we begin rhapsodizing about the joys of visiting Washington, D.C., we have a small confession to make: Sometimes we hate being visitors in D.C.

It's not that we are immune to the spell of this beautiful city on the Potomac. We've done our share of gaping in patriotic awe from the top of the Washington Monument, and have witnessed in utter fascination the histrionics of long-winded U.S. senators ramrodding a pork barrel project through Congress. For us, as for others, the locus of government is intoxicating. We thrive on the constant tension arising from the polarity of powerful people and ideas. Washington, unquestionably, is one of the most exciting cities on the planet.

Where else but in Washington can you watch fire-and-brimstone politicians debate the rights of men and women on the floor of the U.S. Senate or marvel at the eloquence of barristers arguing a case before the Supreme Court . . . or discover, perhaps, how politics really works by eavesdropping on a couple of veteran lobbyists as they plot strategy over dry martinis in a hip Georgetown pub.

Then, of course, there is the beauty, the magnificence, the majesty of the city. America's capitol city boasts some of the most stunning monuments ever created, as well as world-class museums and lush, verdant parks. Broad, shaded boulevards, meticulously laid out by Pierre-Charles L'Enfant, radiate like spokes from the heart of the city, punctuated by stately plazas, ornate bridges, and breathtaking sculpture.

Our problem with D.C. is simple: We cannot stand the peculiarly Washingtonian hassles that routinely get in the way of enjoying this extraordinary city — the sweltering summer heat and humidity, the Rube Goldberg street plan, the agonizing lack of legal parking, the elbow-to-elbow crowds that can wipe out your high spirits before lunch.

In response, we've become absolute *fanatics* when it comes to warning Washington visitors away from Washington's worst torments. Here's the short list: long lines that never seem to move, lousy food (when

D.C. boasts some of the finest restaurants on earth!), industrial-strength traffic jams, outrageous prices for mediocre hotel rooms, bored tour guides that herd tourists like sheep. . . .

We do get *quite* grumpy when things go wrong on a Washington visit. It doesn't have to be this way for you.

This book is the reason why. Its primary purpose can be expressed in exactly ten words: *We're going to take the misery out of touring Washington!*

While we can't guarantee great weather and small crowds, we'll tell you when you've got the best chances of encountering both, and we'll give you tons of information that will save your feet and your wallet, not to mention your temper.

You'll also find suggestions for things to do and see off the beaten track on hot August afternoons when a stroll on the Mall invites heat stroke and when crowds mob the best-known attractions. At the same time, we'll introduce the best of what D.C. has to offer after the museums close, places the people who live and work in Washington like to go after hours: the great ethnic restaurants, theaters, and nightspots. We'll also tell you about the best places around to shop, walk, take a hike, get a workout, or ride a bike.

This guide is designed both for folks planning a family trip to Washington to see its famous monuments, halls of government, historic places, and museums, and for business travelers who want to avoid the city's worst hassles. *The Unofficial Guide* also shows how you can see a side of Washington that most visitors miss: a re-creation of a Roman catacomb, $65 million worth of antiques in one place, and the mansion and gardens of a fabulously rich heiress, among others.

The bottom line: We'll help you see Washington like a native. Of course, we can't promise that your D.C. visit will be perfect. But this guidebook *can* help you eliminate most of the needless irritations that so frequently spoil the fun for Washington tourists.

And who knows? Maybe you'll discover, as we did while researching this book, that there's nothing left to "hate" about being a Washington visitor!

About This Guide

Most "official" guides to Washington, D.C., tout the well-known sights, promote the local restaurants and hotels indiscriminately, and leave out a lot of good stuff. This one is different.

Instead of pandering to the tourist industry, we'll tell you if the food is bad at a well-known restaurant, we'll complain loudly about D.C.'s notorious high prices, and we'll guide you away from the crowds and lines for a break now and then.

Visiting Washington requires wily strategies not unlike those used in the sacking of Troy. We've sent in a team of evaluators who toured each site, ate in the city's best restaurants, performed critical evaluations of its hotels, and visited Washington's wide variety of nightclubs. If a museum is boring, or standing in line for three hours to view a famous attraction is a waste of time, we say so—and, in the process, hopefully make your visit more fun, efficient, and economical.

We got into the guide-book business because we were unhappy with the way travel guides make the reader work to get any usable information. Wouldn't it be nice, we thought, if we could make guides that were easy to use?

Most guide books are compilations of lists. This is true regardless of whether the information is presented in list form or artfully distributed through pages of prose. There is insufficient detail in a list, and with prose the presentation can be tedious and contain large helpings of nonessential or marginally useful information. Not enough wheat, so to speak, for nourishment in one instance, too much chaff in the other. Either way, these guides provide little more than departure points from which readers initiate their own quests.

Many guides are readable and well researched, but they tend to be difficult to use. To select a hotel, for example, a reader must study several pages of descriptions with only the names of the hotels in bold type breaking up the text. Because each description essentially deals with the same variables, it is difficult to recall what was said concerning a particular hotel. Readers generally have no alternative but to work through all the write-ups before beginning to narrow their choices. The listings of restaurants, clubs, and attractions are similar, except that even more reading is usually required. To use such a guide is to undertake an exhaustive research process that requires examining nearly as many options and possibilities as starting from scratch. Recommendations, where made, lack depth and conviction. These guides compound rather than solve problems by failing to narrow travelers' choices down to a thoughtfully considered, well-distilled, and manageable few.

Readers care about the author's opinion. The author, after all, *is* supposed to know what he is talking about. This, coupled with the fact that the traveler wants quick answers (as opposed to endless alternatives), dictates that authors should be explicit, prescriptive, and, above all, direct. The *Unofficial Guide* tries to be just that. It spells out alternatives and recommends specific courses of action. It simplifies complicated destinations and attractions and allows the traveler to feel in control in the most unfamiliar environments. The *Unofficial Guide* makes no attempt to have the most information or all of the information; it aims to have the most accessible, useful information, unbiased by affiliation with any organization or industry.

An *Unofficial Guide* is a critical reference work that focuses on a travel destination that appears to be especially complex. Our authors and research team are completely independent from the attractions, restaurants, and hotels we describe.

The Unofficial Guide to Washington is designed for individuals and families traveling for the fun of it, as well as for business travelers and convention-goers, especially those visiting Washington for the first time. The guide is directed at value-conscious, consumer-oriented adults who seek a cost-effective, though not spartan, travel style.

—— *Special Features*

The *Unofficial Guide* offers the following special features:

- Friendly introductions to Washington's most fascinating neighborhoods.

- "Best of" listings giving our well-qualified opinions on things ranging from bagels to baguettes, four-star hotels to 12-story views.

- Listings that are keyed to your interests, so you can pick and choose.

- Advice to sight-seers on how to avoid the worst of the crowds; advice to business travelers on how to avoid traffic and excessive costs.

- Recommendations for lesser-known sights that are away from the huge monuments of the Mall, but are no less spectacular.

- A zone system and maps to make it easy to find places you want to go to and avoid places you don't.

- Expert advice on avoiding Washington's notorious street crime.

- A Hotel Chart that helps you narrow down your choices fast, according to your needs.

- Shorter listings that include only those restaurants, clubs, and hotels we think are worth considering.

- A detailed index and table of contents to help you find things fast.

- Insider advice on crowds, lines, best times of day (or night) to go places, and, our secret weapon, Washington's stellar subway system.

What you *won't* get:

- Long, useless lists where everything looks the same.

- Information that gets you somewhere you want to go at the worst possible time.

- Information without advice on how to use it.

A Modest, Good Faith Effort

We believe travel guides as a genre are evolving, and we would like to take a crack at contributing to the process, particularly by supplying more practical information and making guides easier to use. This book, one of eight in the *Unofficial Guide* series, makes a good faith effort toward that end.

— Letters, Comments, and Questions from Readers

We expect to learn from our mistakes, as well as from the input of our readers, and to improve with each new book and edition. Many of those who use the *Unofficial Guides* write to us asking questions, making comments, or sharing their own discoveries and lessons learned in Washington. We appreciate all such input, both positive and critical, and encourage our readers to continue writing. Readers' comments and observations will be frequently incorporated in revised editions of the *Unofficial Guide,* and will contribute immeasurably to its improvement.

How to Write the Authors:

Bob, Joe, Eve
The Unofficial Guide to Washington, D.C.
P.O. Box 43059
Birmingham, AL 35243

When you write, be sure to put your return address on your letter as well as on the envelope—sometimes envelopes and letters get separated. And remember, our work takes us out of the office for long periods of time, so forgive us if our response is delayed.

Reader Survey

At the back of the guide you will find a short questionnaire that you can use to express opinions about your Washington visit. Clip the questionnaire out along the dotted line and mail it to the above address.

— How This Guide Was Researched and Written

While a lot of guide books have been written about Washington, D.C., very little has been evaluative. Some guides come close to regurgitating the hotels' and tourist offices' own promotional material. In preparing this work, nothing was taken for granted. Each museum, monument, federal building, hotel, restaurant, shop, and attraction was visited by a team of trained observers who conducted detailed evaluations and rated each according to formal criteria. Team members conducted interviews with tourists of all ages to determine what they enjoyed most *and least* during their Washington visit.

While our observers are independent and impartial, they did not claim to have special expertise. Like you, they visited Washington as tourists or business travelers, noting their satisfaction or dissatisfaction.

The primary difference between the average tourist and the trained evaluator is the evaluator's skills in organization, preparation, and observation. The trained evaluator is responsible for much more than simply observing and cataloging. While the average tourist is gazing in awe at stacks of $20 bills at the Bureau of Engraving and Printing, for instance, the professional is rating the tour in terms of pace, how quickly the line moves, the location of rest rooms, and how well children can see the exhibits. He or she also checks out things like other attractions close by, alternate places to go if the line at a main attraction is too long, and the best local lunch options. Observer teams used detailed checklists to analyze hotel rooms, restaurants, nightclubs, and attractions. Finally, evaluator ratings and observations were integrated with tourist reactions and the opinions of patrons for a comprehensive quality profile of each feature and service.

In compiling this guide, we recognize that a tourist's age, background, and interests will strongly influence his or her taste in Washington's wide array of attractions and will account for a preference for one sight or museum over another. Our sole objective is to provide the reader with sufficient description, critical evaluation, and pertinent data to make knowledgeable decisions according to individual tastes.

HOW INFORMATION IS ORGANIZED:
By Subject and by Geographic Zones

In order to give you fast access to information about the *best* of Washington, we've organized material in several formats.

Hotels. Since most people visiting Washington stay in one hotel for the duration of their trip, we have summarized our coverage of hotels in charts, maps, ratings, and rankings that allow you to quickly focus your decision-making process. We do not go on page after page describing lobbies and rooms which, in the final analysis, sound much the same. Instead, we concentrate on the specific variables that differentiate one hotel from another: location, size, room quality, services, amenities, and cost.

Restaurants. We provide a lot of detail when it comes to restaurants. Since you will probably eat a dozen or more restaurant meals during your stay, and since not even *you* can predict what you might be in the mood for on Saturday night, we provide detailed profiles of the best restaurants in and around Washington.

Entertainment and Night Life. Visitors frequently try several different clubs or nightspots during their stay. Since clubs and nightspots, like restaurants, are usually selected spontaneously after arriving in Washington, we believe detailed descriptions are warranted. The best nightspots and lounges in Washington are profiled by category under night life in the same section (see pages 125–70).

Geographic Zones. Once you've decided where you're going, getting there becomes the issue. To help you do that, we have divided the city into geographic zones:

- Zone 1. The Mall
- Zone 2. Capitol Hill
- Zone 3. Downtown
- Zone 4. Foggy Bottom
- Zone 5. Georgetown
- Zone 6. Dupont Circle/Adams-Morgan
- Zone 7. Upper Northwest Washington

- Zone 8. Northeast Washington
- Zone 9. Southeast Washington
- Zone 10. Maryland Suburbs
- Zone 11. Virginia Suburbs

All profiles of hotels, restaurants, and nightspots include zone numbers. If you are staying at the Carlyle Suites, for example, and are interested in Japanese restaurants within walking distance, scanning the restaurant profiles for restaurants in Zone 6 (Dupont Circle/Adams-Morgan) will provide you with the best choices.

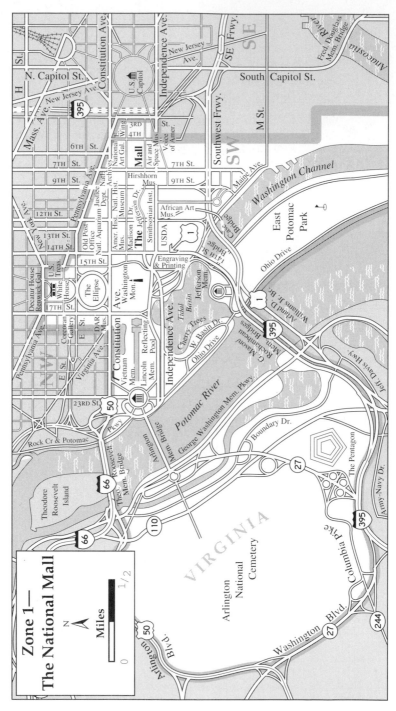

Zone 1—
The National Mall

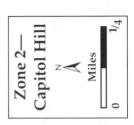

Zone 2— Capitol Hill

N

Miles

0   1/4

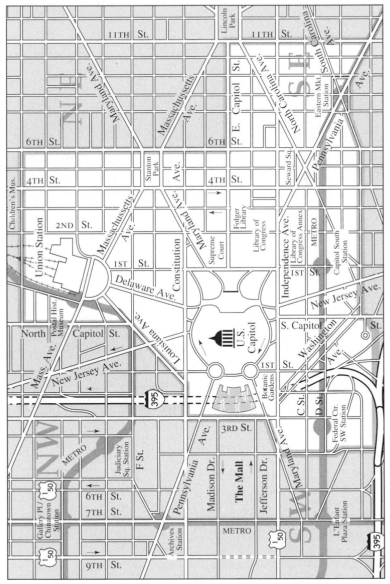

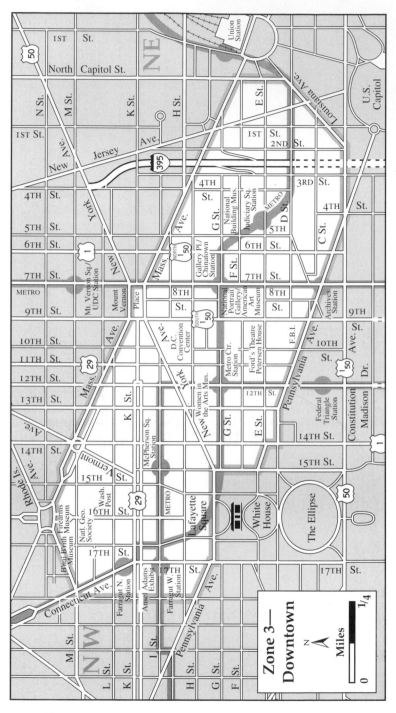

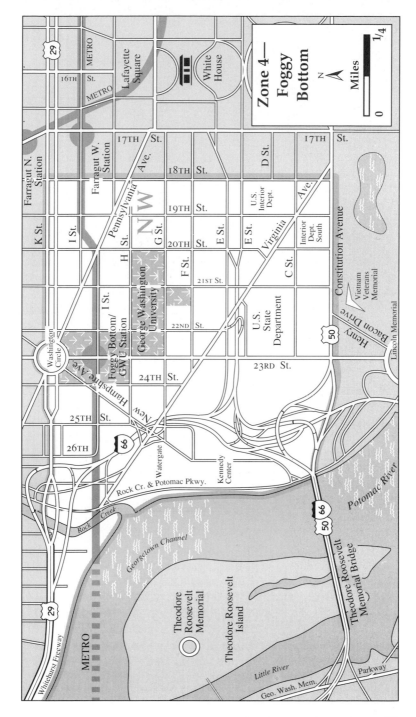

15

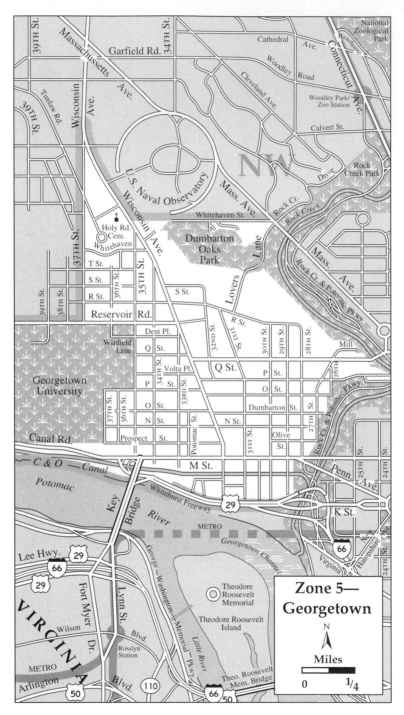

Zone 5—
Georgetown

N

Miles

0   1/4

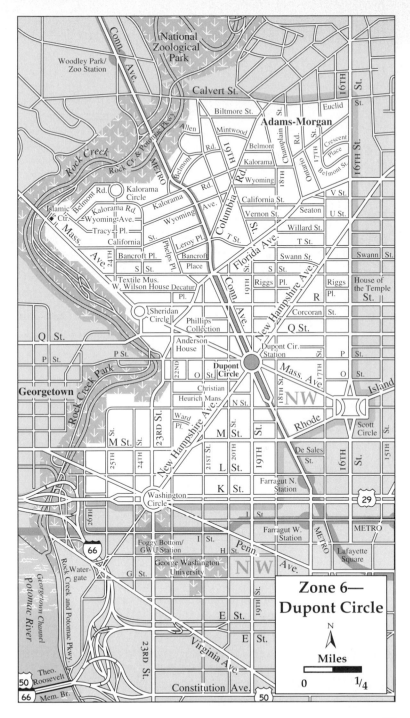

Zone 6—
Dupont Circle

N

Miles

0   1/4

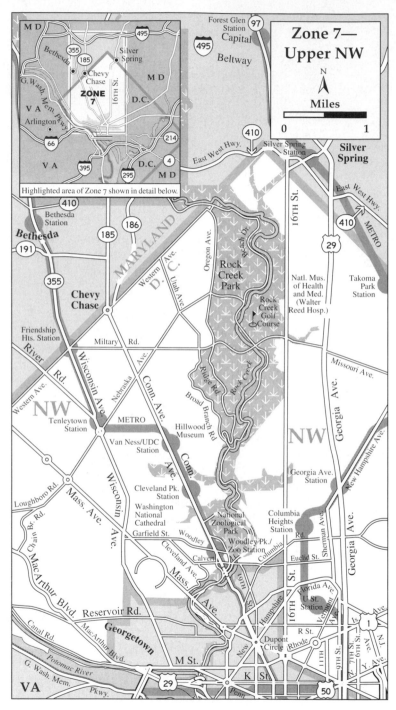

Zone 7—
Upper NW

N

Miles

0   1

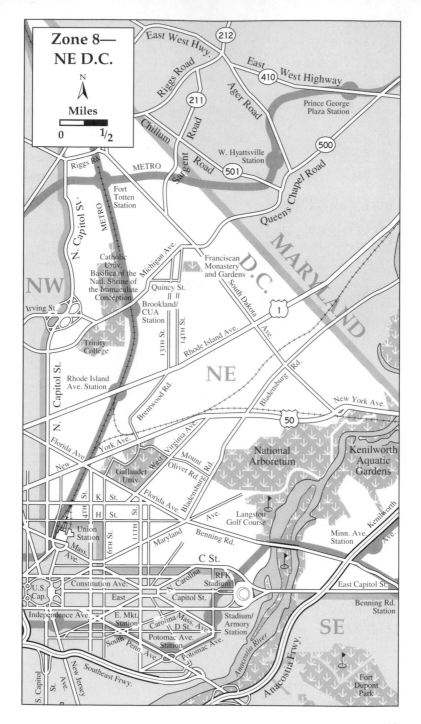

Zone 8—
NE D.C.

N

Miles

0   1/2

East West Hwy.   212

East   410   West Highway

Riggs Road   Ager Road   Prince George Plaza Station

211   W. Hyattsville Station   500

Chillum   Sargent Road   501   Queens Chapel Road

Riggs Rd.   METRO   MARYLAND

N. Capitol St.   Fort Totten Station   METRO

NW   Catholic Univ. Basilica of the Natl. Shrine of the Immaculate Conception   Michigan Ave.   Franciscan Monastery and Gardens   D.C.

Irving St.   Quincy St.   South Dakota Ave.   1

Brookland/ CUA Station   13TH St.   14TH St.   Rhode Island Ave.   NE

Capitol St.   Trinity College

Rhode Island Ave. Station   Brentwood Rd.   Bladensburg Rd.   New York Ave.

N.   50

Florida Ave.   York Ave.   West Virginia Ave.   National Arboretum   Kenilworth Aquatic Gardens

New   Gallaudet Univ.   Mount Olivet Rd.   Bladensburg Rd.

4TH St.   K St.   Florida Ave.   Ave.   Langston Golf Course   Kenilworth

H St.   6TH St.   11TH St.   Maryland   Benning Rd.   Minn. Ave. Station   Ave.

Union Station   Mass. Ave.   C St.

U.S. Cap.   Constitution Ave.   N. Carolina   RFK Stadium   East Capitol St.

East   Capitol St.   Benning Rd. Station

Independence Ave.   E. Mkt. Station   Carolina   Mass. Ave.   Stadium/ Armory Station   SE

South   Penn. Ave.   D St.   Potomac Ave.   Anacostia Frwy.

S. Capitol St.   New Jersey Ave.   Southeast Frwy.   Potomac Ave. Station   Anacostia River   Fort Dupont Park

19

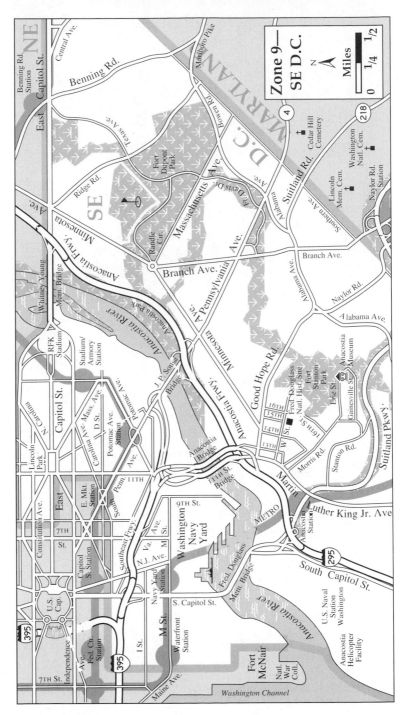

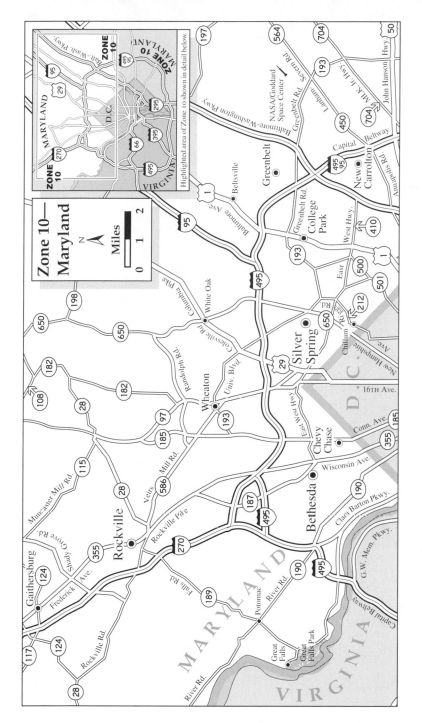

Zone 10—
Maryland

N

Miles

0   1   2

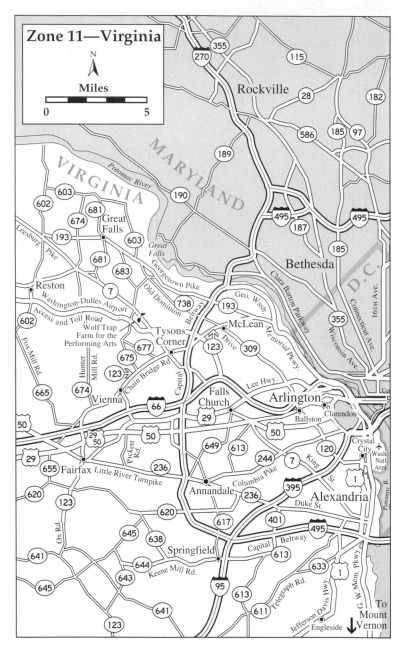

Zone 11—Virginia

N

Miles

0   5

(See pages 44–45 for maps showing all zones combined).

PART ONE:
Timing Your Visit to Washington

Going When the Weather Is Good

The best times to visit Washington are in the spring and fall, when the weather is most pleasant and nature puts on a show. The city's fabled cherry blossoms bloom in late March or early April, while fall brings crisp, cool weather and, by mid-October, a spectacular display of gold, orange, and red leaves.

The summers—mid-June through September—can be brutally hot and humid. Visitors in July and August not only contend with the heat as they sprint from building to building, but also must endure the city's overreliance on air conditioning that often reaches meat-locker chill. August, with its predictably oppressive heat, is the month when Washingtonians leave town in droves.

Washington's winter weather, on the other hand, is erratic. Balmy, mid-60s days are possible through December. While it often gets into the teens in January and February, midday temperatures can climb into the 40s and 50s. This is the season to beat the crowds.

March is tricky. While warm daytime temperatures are frequent, sometimes a large, moist air mass moving north from the Gulf of Mexico will collide with a blast of frigid air from Canada. The result is a big, wet snowfall that paralyzes the city for days. (It should be noted, in all fairness, that the *prediction* of snow can paralyze D.C.)

Washington weather can run the gamut from subzero (rarely) to mild (most of the winter, some of the summer, and most of the spring and fall) to scorchingly hot and unbearably humid (most of July and August). Here are the city's average monthly temperatures, in degrees Fahrenheit:

	High	*Low*
January	42	27
February	44	28
March	53	35
April	64	44
May	75	54
June	83	64

	High	*Low*
July	87	68
August	84	66
September	78	60
October	67	48
November	55	38
December	45	30

—— Avoiding Crowds

In general, popular tourist sites are busier on weekends than weekdays, and Saturdays are busier than Sundays, and summer is busier than winter. During the busiest tourist seasons, spring and summer, major Washington tourist attractions are always crowded between 9:30 and 3:00. For people in town on business, this tourist influx means heavier traffic, congested airports, a packed Metro . . . and a tough time finding a convenient hotel room.

Driving in weekday rush hours, featuring 100,000 frantic, short-tempered bureaucrats clawing their way to office or home, should be avoided at all costs. On weekends, the same government workers and their families become tourists, often creating midday traffic snarls during the warmer months.

If you're driving to Washington, try to time your arrival on a weekend or during a non–rush hour time — before 7 A.M. or during a rather narrow window that opens around 9:30 A.M. and starts to close quickly around 3 P.M. Afternoon traffic doesn't begin to clear up until at least 6:30. Friday afternoon rush hours are the worst: Don't even think of driving near D.C. until after 8 P.M.

The best time to avoid crowds entirely is in winter. On weekdays especially, the Mall is nearly deserted and museums, monuments, and normally crowd-intensive hot spots like the U.S. Capitol are virtually empty — except for the people who work there. Furthermore, the relative scarcity of tourists in the off-season eliminates the worst of D.C.'s traffic gridlock, except during peak rush hours.

—— Choosing a Time to Visit

Whether you're in town on business or pleasure, it's a good idea to be aware of when the big crowds of tourists are likely to be jamming up the Metro, the sidewalk, or the place you've picked for lunch.

After the winter doldrums, crowds begin picking up in late March and peak in early April, when the Japanese cherry trees along the Tidal Basin bloom and Washington is flooded with visitors. Mammoth throngs pack the Mall, the line for the Washington Monument wraps around the base three times (signaling a three-hour wait), and it's elbow to elbow in the National Air and Space Museum. Because of the crowded conditions, we do not recommend touring Washington in the early spring.

Instead, if at all possible, *delay your visit until late May or early June.* Crowds are more manageable for a few weeks and the weather is usually delightful.

The tourist pace begins picking up again in mid-June as schools let out. July through mid-August are very crowded—and usually the weather is brutally hot and humid. Popular museums such as the Museum of Natural History, the National Air and Space Museum, and the National Museum of American History fill up with masses of elbow-to-elbow people, eating in restaurants becomes a stress-inducing ordeal, and the entire experience becomes exhausting. Driving conditions, never good in Washington, degenerate into gridlock—even on weekends—and the Metro is packed to rush-hour levels all day.

The throngs begin to thin during the last two weeks of August, when kids start returning to school. After Labor Day, the volume of visitors drops off significantly during the week, but weekends remain packed through October—though not as packed as in spring and summer. In November, tourist activity slows down dramatically.

After May and June, the best time to visit Washington is in the late fall and winter. While Thanksgiving Day brings hordes of visitors to popular sights on the Mall, car traffic is light and getting around town from November through March is easy. Winter visitors can't count on balmy weather, but crowds are virtually nonexistent and Washington's elaborate cultural season kicks into full swing. Plays, music, opera, and ballet fill the city's theaters and halls—the Kennedy Center, Arena Stage, the Shakespeare Theater at the Folger, the National Theater, Ford's Theatre, and the Library of Congress. Both business visitors and folks in town to tour the sights will find Washington a lot easier to get around in during the late fall and winter.

The Longest Lines

Unlike in Disney World, a tourist destination with which Washington shares some similarities, in D.C. only a handful of attractions require enduring long queues. Among these are the Bureau of Engraving and Printing (before Easter and after Labor Day; otherwise a "time ticket" system is in effect that virtually eliminates lines), the Washington Monument, the White House, and the FBI. Even at these, a little judicious planning can virtually guarantee you won't spend hours standing in line.

If your visit to Washington must coincide with the heavy tourist season, read on: There are ways to make it more tolerable, in spite of the record crowds jamming the Mall, the popular museums, eateries, public transportation, and highways. And check Part Four for detailed information on transportation; Part Eight for pages of sight-seeing tips.

Which Day of the Week to Arrive

If you're driving to Washington, try to arrive on a weekend—Sunday is best. While tourist attractions are the most crowded on weekends, at least you won't have to deal with the worst of Washington's horrendous traffic.

The best days for avoiding big crowds at Washington's most popular attractions are Monday through Wednesday. Crowds begin to increase as the week progresses, with the volume of visitors peaking on Saturday. If you're visiting D.C. on business, try to schedule your appointments early in the week to avoid the worst congestion.

—— A Calendar of Special Events

Washington hosts a variety of special events throughout the year: fairs, celebrations, parades, shows, festivals, tours, film and jazz festivals, and ceremonies. For exact dates, times, locations, and admission fees, call the phone numbers provided before your visit.

January

Opening of Congress.   The first week of January.

Martin Luther King, Jr., Birthday Observance.   Wreath-laying ceremony at the Lincoln Memorial accompanied by his "I Have a Dream" speech. Local choirs, guest speakers, and military color guard salute King's memory. Free. (202) 619-7222.

Robert E. Lee Birthday Celebration.   Celebration held at the Arlington House in Arlington National Cemetery. The open house features

19th-century music, samples of period food, and exhibitions of restoration work. Free. (703) 557-0613.

Chinese New Year Parade. Traditional firecrackers, plus lions, drummers, and dragon dancers marching through Chinatown to celebrate the Chinese lunar New Year. Free. (202) 724-4091.

February

African-American History Month. Special events, various Smithsonian museum exhibits, and cultural programs celebrate the contributions of African-Americans to the quality of American life. Free. (202) 357-2700.

Abraham Lincoln's Birthday. (February 12) Lincoln's birthday is commemorated with an elaborate wreath-laying ceremony and a reading of the Gettysburg Address at the Lincoln Memorial. Free. (202) 619-7222.

Mount Vernon Open House. A wreath-laying ceremony at Washington's tomb is followed by a fife and drum corps performance on the green. Free. (703) 838-4200.

George Washington's Birthday Parade. The nation's largest parade celebrating our first president takes place in Old Town Alexandria. Free. (703) 838-4200.

Washington Boat Show. The latest in pleasure craft and equipment at the Washington Convention Center. Admission fee required. (202) 789-1600.

March

American Classic Antiques Show. Features more than 185 dealers from 20 states, Canada, and Europe displaying their goods at the D.C. Armory. Admission fee required. (301) 738-1966.

Festival of St. Patrick. Annual Irish cultural festival featuring Irish craftspeople, musicians, dancers, books, and media. Free. (202) 347-1450.

St. Patrick's Day Parade/Old Town Alexandria. Begins at noon. Free. (703) 549-4535.

St. Patrick's Day Parade/Downtown Washington. The parade goes down Constitution Avenue, with dancers, bands, bagpipes, and floats, at 1 P.M. Free. (301) 424-2200.

Washington Flower and Garden Show.   At the Washington Convention Center. Admission fee required. (202) 789-1600.

U.S. Botanic Garden's Spring Flower Show.   Free. (202) 225-7099.

Smithsonian Kite Festival.   Kite makers and flyers of all ages gather at the Washington Monument grounds to compete for prizes and trophies. Free. (202) 357-3244.

U.S. Army Band Annual Concert.   Musical and choral selections in an annual concert at the Kennedy Center. Free. (202) 467-4600.

National Cherry Blossom Festival.   More than 6,000 Japanese cherry trees bloom in late March to early April, bringing springtime splendor to Washington. The Cherry Blossom Festival Parade features princesses, floats, and VIPs. Other events include free concerts, the Japanese Lantern Lighting Ceremony, the Cherry Blossom Ball, and an annual Marathon. For parade ticket information, call (202) 728-1137. For general information, call (202) 737-2599 or (202) 789-7000.

April

Imagination Celebration.   An annual festival of the performing arts for young people that brings some of the best national children's theater companies to the Kennedy Center. Free and moderately priced events. (202) 416-8000.

John Wilkes Booth Escape Tour.   A trip through time from Ford's Theatre to Garrett's Farm in rural Maryland. Call six months in advance to get on the mailing list; tour reservations are taken from the mailing list only. Admission fee required. (301) 868-1121.

White House Spring Garden Tours.   Tour the beautiful gardens of the presidential home. Free. (202) 456-2200.

White House Easter Egg Roll.   For children eight and under accompanied by an adult. Eggs and entertainment provided. Enter at the southeast gate of the White House on East Executive Avenue. Free. (202) 456-2200.

Thomas Jefferson's Birthday.   The author of the Declaration of Independence is commemorated with military drills and a wreath-laying ceremony at the Jefferson Memorial. Free. (202) 619-7222.

Smithsonian's Washington Craft Show. One hundred exhibitors display and sell fine handcrafted objects of original design. Admission fee required. (202) 357-2700.

Filmfest D.C. Premieres of dozens of international and American films held at theaters across the city. Tickets required. (202) 727-2396.

Earth Day. Various events and displays on the National Mall. Free. (202) 619-7222.

Duke Ellington Birthday Celebration. Commemorating this native Washingtonian's contribution to American music. Free. (202) 331-9404.

Old Town Alexandria Tour of Homes and Gardens. A tour of the city's oldest and most elegant homes and gardens. Admission fee required. (703) 838-4200.

William Shakespeare's Birthday. (April 24) A day of music, theater, children's events, food, and exhibits at the Folger Shakespeare Library. Free. (202) 544-7077.

Georgetown House Tour. Private homes in the city's oldest neighborhood are open for viewing. Admission fee required. (202) 338-1796.

May

Annual Georgetown Garden Tour. The walking tour features 14 private gardens, tea, and self-guided tours. Admission fee required. (202) 333-4953.

Gross National Parade. A zany, unorthodox parade to benefit the Police Boys and Girls Club of D.C. From M and 18th streets to M Street and Wisconsin Avenue. Free. (202) 686-3215.

Air Force Service. A service honoring the anniversary of the U.S. Air Force at Washington National Cathedral. Free. (202) 537-6247.

Washington National Cathedral Flower Mart. Each year is a salute to a different country, with flower booths, entertainment, and decorating demonstrations. Free. (202) 537-6247.

American Classic Antiques Show. Devoted to Americana and Country antiques, 18th- and 19th-century furniture, quilts, woodenware, folk art, prints, and crystal. At the D.C. Armory. Admission fee required. (301) 738-1966.

Goodwill Embassy Tour. Various Washington embassies open their doors to the public. Tour tickets include free shuttle bus. Admission/ reservations required. (202) 636-4225.

Alexandria's Annual Cook's Tour of Homes. Showcases renovated and unusual private kitchens in Old Town Alexandria. Admission/ reservations required. (703) 838-4200.

Capitol Hill House and Garden Tour. See charmingly restored homes in this popular annual tour. Admission fee required. (202) 543-0425.

Greek Spring Festival. Celebrate spring with Greek food, music, dance, games, clowns, and arts and crafts. Free. (202) 829-2910.

Malcolm X Day. Celebrations honoring the life of the slain civil rights leader and orator. Free. (202) 543-3939.

Kemper Open Pro-Am Golf Tournament. Amateurs compete with pros at local courses in this major golf event. Admission fee required. (301) 469-3737.

Memorial Day Weekend Concert. The National Symphony Orchestra performs on the West Lawn of the U.S. Capitol, kicking off the summer season. Free. (202) 619-7222.

Memorial Day Jazz Festival. (May 31) Annual jazz festival in Old Town Alexandria featuring big band music performed by local bands. (703) 838-4200.

Memorial Day Ceremonies at Arlington National Cemetery. (May 31) Wreath-laying ceremonies at the Kennedy grave site, a presidential wreath-laying at the Tomb of the Unknowns, and services at the Memorial Amphitheater featuring military bands and a presidential keynote address. Free. (202) 475-0856.

Memorial Day Ceremonies at the Vietnam Veterans Memorial. (May 31) Wreath-laying, speeches, military bands, and a keynote address. Free. (202) 619-7222.

Memorial Day Ceremonies at the U.S. Navy Memorial. (May 31) Wreath-laying ceremonies and an evening concert by the U.S. Navy Band. Free. (202) 737-2300.

June

Alexandria Red Cross Waterfront Festival. Family-oriented weekend featuring tall ships, ethnic food, entertainment, fireworks, arts and crafts, a 10K run, and the blessing of the fleet. Admission fee required. (703) 549-8300.

Dupont-Kalorama Museum Walk Day. Celebration of collections by seven institutions in the area. Activities include textile demonstrations, video programs, interactive tours, hands-on art programs, historic house tours, food, and crafts. Shuttle service provided. Free. (202) 387-2151.

Dance Africa D.C. Folk dances at Dance Place, 3225 8th Street, NE. Free. (202) 269-1600.

Flag Day. (June 14) Each year, the "Great American Flag," the largest U.S. flag in America, is displayed on the grounds of the Washington Monument. (202) 619-7222.

Marathon Reading of "Ulysses." (June 15–16) This annual reading of James Joyce's classic starts around 11 A.M. on the weekend nearest June 15 or 16 and ends in the early morning of the next day — the same days as the setting of the novel. Held at the Irish Times Pub, 14 F Street, NW. Free. (202) 543-5433.

July

Festival of American Folklife. More than one million people attend this festival of American music, crafts, and ethnic foods on the Mall each year. Free. (202) 357-2627.

Children's Festival. Day-long festival featuring live music, performing arts, and hands-on activities sponsored by the Capital Children's Museum and the National Park Service. Carter Barron Amphitheater, 16th and Colorado Avenue, NW. Free for adults, $3 for children. (202) 619-7226.

D.C. Free Jazz Festival. A series of concerts featuring top national and international jazz performers at Freedom Plaza, 1300 Pennsylvania Avenue, NW. Free. (202) 783-0360.

National Independence Day Celebration. (July 4) A full day of dramatic readings, a parade, a demonstration of colonial military maneuvers, entertainment at the Sylvan Theatre, a star-studded concert by the National Symphony Orchestra, and a spectacular fireworks display over the Washington Monument. Free. (202) 452-1132.

Hispanic-American Festival. Food, crafts, music, dance, and theater from 40 Latin-American countries. Free. (202) 269-0101.

August

U.S. Army Band's "1812 Overture." A concert and pageant at the Sylvan Theatre on the Washington Monument grounds. Free. (703) 696-3718.

Navy Band Children's Lollipop Concert. A special program geared to children of all ages at the Sylvan Theatre. Free. (202) 433-2525.

Summer-long Activities

Marine Corps Tuesday Evening Sunset Parades. (every Tuesday evening at 7 P.M.) At the Iwo Jima Memorial. Free shuttle bus service from the Arlington Cemetery Visitors Center at 6 P.M. Free. (202) 433-4173.

Marine Corps Friday Evening Parades. At the Marine Barracks, 8th and I streets, SE. Begins promptly at 8:45 P.M. Reservations required. Free. (202) 433-6060.

Carillon Saturday Evening Recitals. At the Netherlands Carillon on the grounds of the Iwo Jima Memorial. 6:30 P.M. to 8:30 P.M. Free. (703) 285-2598.

"Music under the Stars" Wednesday Evening Concerts. (every Wednesday night) Big band sounds at the Sylvan Theatre on the grounds of the Washington Monument, 7 P.M. to 9 P.M. Free. (202) 619-7222.

Washington National Cathedral's Summer Festival of Music. (June and July) Concert series. Most concerts at 7:30 P.M. Free. (202) 537-6200.

Sunday Polo. (every Sunday afternoon) Matches on the field east of the Lincoln Memorial: 2 P.M. in May; 3 P.M. in June; 4 P.M. in July; 3 P.M. September and October. Free. (202) 619-7222.

C & O Canal Barge Rides. (mid-April through mid-October) Mule-drawn barge rides in Georgetown. Costumed Park Service guides accompany each 90-minute trip, telling the canal's history through stories and song. Admission required. (202) 472-4376.

U.S. Botanic Garden's Summer Terrace Show.   (June–August)   A series of summer gardens in various themes. Free. (202) 225-7099.

Military Band Summer Concert Series.   Outdoor concerts held every summer evening, from Memorial Day through Labor Day, beginning at 8 P.M. Free. Army Band: (703) 696-3399; Marine Band: (202) 433-4011; Navy Band: (202) 433-2525; Air Force Band: (202) 767-5658.

Monday:	U.S. Navy Band, U.S. Capitol, east side
Tuesday:	U.S. Army Band, Sylvan Theatre
	U.S. Air Force Band, U.S. Capitol, east side
	U.S. Navy Band, Navy Memorial Plaza
Wednesday:	U.S. Marine Band, U.S. Capitol, east side
Thursday:	U.S. Navy Band, Sylvan Theatre
Friday:	U.S. Army Band, U.S. Capitol, east side
	U.S. Air Force Band, Sylvan Theatre
Saturday:	Rotating branches, Navy Memorial Plaza
Sunday:	U.S. Marine Band, Sylvan Theatre

"The American Sailor."   (every Wednesday evening, May through August)   At the Washington Navy Yard waterfront, a multimedia presentation showcasing the history and character of the U.S. Navy. Events begin at 6:30 P.M., pageant begins at 9 P.M. Free, but reservations required. (202) 433-2218.

Twilight Tattoo Series.   (every Wednesday evening, mid-July through August)   A traditional military parade on the Ellipse, between the White House and the Washington Monument, featuring the 3rd U.S. Infantry and the U.S. Army Band. Begins at 7 P.M. Free. (703) 696-3570.

September

National Frisbee Festival.   The largest noncompetitive Frisbee festival in the United States, featuring world-class Frisbee champions and disc-catching dogs. On the Mall near the National Air and Space Museum. Free. (202) 645-5043.

International Children's Festival.   A three-day, outdoor arts celebration at the Wolf Trap Farm Park for the Performing Arts in Vienna, Virginia. Admission fee required. (703) 642-0862.

African Cultural Festival. Authentic cuisine, music, dance, and crafts. At Freedom Plaza, 14th Street and Pennsylvania Avenue, NW. Free. (202) 667-5775.

D.C. Blues Festival. Features top blues performers at Anacostia Park in Southeast Washington. Free. (301) 483-0871.

Black Family Reunion. A weekend-long celebration of the African-American family offers headline performers, fun, food, and exhibits on the Mall. Free. (202) 659-2372.

Labor Day Weekend Concert. The National Symphony Orchestra closes the summer season with an evening concert on the West Lawn of the U.S. Capitol. Free. (202) 619-7222.

Elderfest. A day-long celebration featuring food, crafts, and entertainment. At Freedom Plaza, 1300 Pennsylvania Avenue, NW. Free. (202) 724-4091.

Adams-Morgan Day. D.C.'s most culturally diverse neighborhood celebrates with live music, crafts, and cuisine. 18th Street and Columbia Road, NW. Free. (202) 332-3292.

Kalorama House and Embassy Tour. Tour selected homes and embassies, and the Woodrow Wilson House. Admission fee required. (202) 387-4062.

Constitution Day Commemoration. (September 17) The original U.S. Constitution is displayed in its entirety at the National Archives. Free. (202) 501-5215.

Old Town Alexandria's Annual Tour of Homes. A tour of privately owned homes. Admission fee required. (703) 838-4200.

Rock Creek Park Day. International and national music, children's activities, food, arts and crafts, exhibits, and demonstrations. Free. (202) 426-6832.

Annual Croquet Tournament. On the 17th Street side of the Ellipse. Everyone over 16 invited; equipment provided. Free. (202) 463-0880.

October

Supreme Court in Session. First Monday of October. Free. (202) 479-3000.

U.S. Army Band Fall Concert Series. Tuesdays and Thursdays during October and November. Bruckner Hall at Fort Myer in Arlington, Virginia. Free. (703) 696-3399.

Decorator's Show House. Tour a selected Washington residence that's been redecorated by local interior designers. Admission fee required. (202) 416-8100.

Fall D.C. Antiques Fair. More than 185 dealers from 20 states, Canada, and Europe at the D.C. Armory. Admission fee required. (301) 738-1966.

American Discoveries Festival. Top performers, unique music, and the cuisine of a selected American city highlight this annual festival at Freedom Plaza, 1300 Pennsylvania Avenue, NW. Free. (202) 783-0360.

Annual "Taste of D.C." Festival. The best of D.C.'s vast array of restaurant food and ethnic cuisine, plus three stages with entertainment, a special children's area, and arts and crafts. Free admission; purchase tickets for food tastings. (202) 724-4093.

Columbus Day Ceremonies. An annual tribute at the Columbus Memorial Plaza in front of Union Station. Free. (202) 619-7222.

U.S. Navy Birthday Concert. The U.S. Navy Band plays the Concert Hall of the Kennedy Center. Free, but tickets must be picked up in advance. (202) 433-2525.

White House Fall Garden Tours. See the Rose Garden and the South Lawn to the sounds of a military band. Free. (202) 456-2200.

Theodore Roosevelt's Birthday Celebration. Festivities are held at Theodore Roosevelt Island in the Potomac, reached by car from the George Washington Memorial Parkway. Free. (703) 285-2702.

November

Annual Seafaring Celebration. Maritime lore, history, food, arts and crafts, storytelling, and performances at Building 76 in the Washington Navy Yard. Free. (202) 433-4882.

Marine Corps Marathon. Thousands of world-class runners compete at this race beginning at the Iwo Jima Marine Corps Memorial. Registration fee required. (703) 690-3431.

Armistice Day Celebration. (November 11) A special tour of the Woodrow Wilson House, featuring food from World War I. Admission/tickets required. (202) 673-4034.

Veterans Day Ceremonies. (November 11) Military bands, services at the Memorial Amphitheater at Arlington National Cemetery, and a wreath-laying ceremony at the Tomb of the Unknown Soldier. Additional services at the Vietnam Veterans Memorial on the Mall. Free. (202) 475-0843.

Alexandria Antiques Show. At the Old Colony Inn in Old Town Alexandria. Admission fee required. (703) 838-4200.

"A Christmas Carol." Dickens' holiday classic returns each year to Ford's Theatre. Admission fee required. (202) 347-4833.

December

Georgetown's Gift of Light. (all month) Beautiful holiday decorations and lights, including illuminated 6-foot snowflakes on street lamps and two 42-foot trees. Free.

"Holidays at Mount Vernon." A re-creation of the authentic 18th-century holiday season. Visitors may tour the mansion's third floor, which is usually closed to the public. Admission fee required. (703) 780-2000.

Winter D.C. Antiques Fair. At the D.C. Armory. Admission fee required. (301) 738-1966.

Alexandria Community Y Scottish Christmas Walk. Featuring a parade through Old Town, bagpipes, highland dancers, old homes tours, and children's events. Free. (703) 838-4200.

"An American Holiday Celebration." A holiday music show by the U.S. Army Band at DAR Constitution Hall. Free, but tickets are required to assure seating. (703) 696-3399.

Annual Woodlawn Plantation Christmas. (early December) Carolers, musicians and costumed actors, wagon rides, a burning yule log, and refreshments re-create an old Virginia Christmas. At Woodlawn Plantation, 9000 Richmond Highway, Alexandria, Virginia. Admission fee required. (703) 780-4000.

People's Christmas Tree Lighting. Military bands play as the magnificent Christmas tree on the west side of the U.S. Capitol is lighted the day before the Pageant of Peace begins. Free. (202) 224-3069.

National Christmas Tree Lighting/Pageant of Peace. The president lights the giant National Christmas Tree near the White House. Through the end of the year, the Ellipse is the site of nightly choral performances, a Nativity scene, a burning yule log, and a spectacular display of lighted Christmas trees representing each state and territory. Free. (202) 619-7222.

Old Town Christmas Candlelight Tours. Visit Ramsey House, Gadsby's Tavern Museum, the Lee-Fendall House, and the Carlyle House in Old Town Alexandria. Music, colonial dancing, period decorations, and light refreshments. Admission fee required. (703) 838-4200.

"Bringing in Christmas." Period decorations and music from the 1850s at Arlington House, the plantation home of Robert E. Lee, in Arlington Cemetery. Admission fee required. (703) 557-0613.

"The Nutcracker." (mid- to late December) The Washington Ballet performs this Christmas classic at the Warner Theater. Tickets required. (202) 362-3606.

U.S. Navy Band Holiday Concert. A concert of holiday music at DAR Constitution Hall. Tickets required. (202) 433-2525.

U.S. Botanic Garden's Christmas Poinsettia Show. More than 3,000 red, white, and pink flowers and other plants in a holiday setting of Christmas wreaths and trees. Free. (202) 226-4082.

Washington National Cathedral Christmas Celebration and Services. (December 24 and 25) Choral performances are part of the special services. Dec. 24: 4 P.M. pageant and 10 P.M. service. Dec. 25: 9 A.M. service. Free. (202) 537-6200.

White House Christmas Candlelight Tours. Evening tours of the White House Christmas decorations. Free. (202) 456-2200.

PART TWO: Arriving and Getting Oriented

A Geographic Overview of Washington

— A City and Two States

Washington, D.C., is a city of about 600,000 people located near the southern end of the East Coast megalopolis stretching from Boston to Richmond. George Washington chose the city's site, where the Anacostia River flows into the Potomac, upriver from his Mount Vernon plantation. Maryland and Virginia donated wedges of land from both sides of the Potomac to make the 100-square-mile diamond called "the District of Columbia." In 1846, Virginia snatched its lands back; today, the planned city of Washington sits on the former Maryland acreage on the river's east bank.

Washington proper is surrounded by bustling, congested suburbs. Across the Potomac, Arlington County, the town of Alexandria, and Fairfax County crowd D.C. from the south and west, while the Maryland counties of Montgomery and Prince George's surround Washington's northwestern and eastern borders. All the suburbs surrounding D.C. are experiencing exponential growth. Rockville, for example, a few miles north of the D.C. line, has become Maryland's second-largest city, after Baltimore.

Washington's most important geographical feature, the Potomac River, is a natural impediment to both tourists and suburban commuters. The few bridges that cross the river from Virginia to Washington are rush-hour bottlenecks. While driving across the border to the Maryland suburbs is nominally easier, D.C.'s intense traffic and concentration of government and tourist sites near the river makes for a long trek into Maryland.

— D.C.'s Street Plan

While Washington's reputation as a tough city to get around in is well deserved — at least for first-time visitors — the city's layout is

43

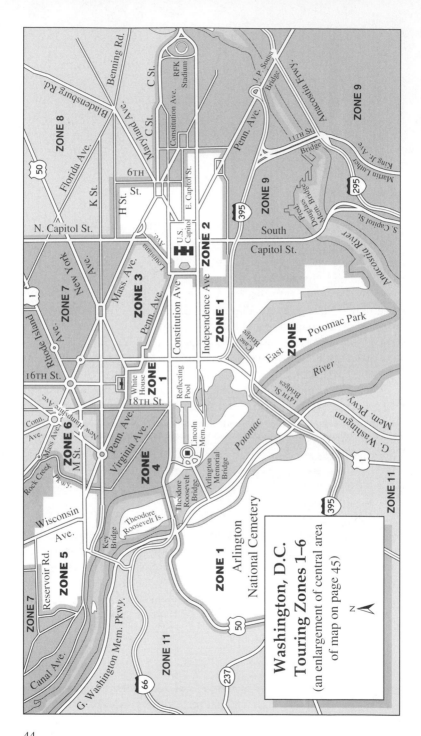

Washington, D.C.
Touring Zones 1–6
(an enlargement of central area
of map on page 45)

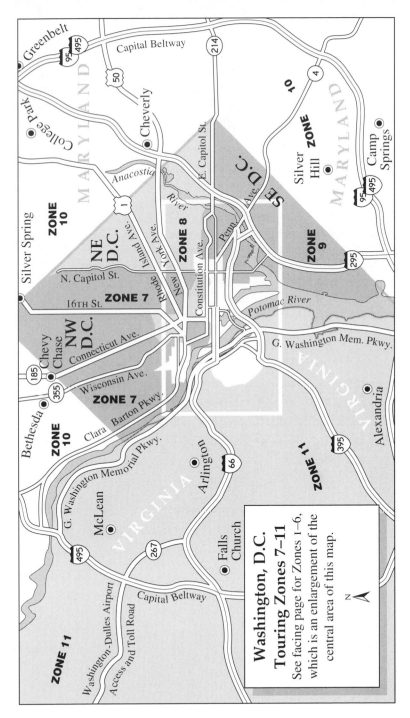

**Washington, D.C.
Touring Zones 7–11**

See facing page for Zones 1–6, which is an enlargement of the central area of this map.

N

actually fairly logical. Downtown streets are arranged in a grid, with numbered streets running north/south and lettered streets going east/ west. The loose cannons in the scheme are streets named after states, which cut across the grid diagonally and meet in traffic circles that are the nemesis of Washington drivers.

Our advice: Ignore the state-named streets on your map and you'll discover the underlying logic of the system. If your destination is, in fact, on a street named after a state, the underlying grid of number- and letter-named streets will get you there and can even help you locate your block. An example: A popular destination for both tourists and power seekers is 1600 Pennsylvania Avenue, NW. Since this well-known street snakes a course from the poor neighborhoods of Southeast Washington through downtown and into Georgetown, pinpointing an exact address is tough. The clue, however, is in the street address: The White House is near the intersection of Pennsylvania Avenue and 16th Street.

Coming into the City

If you drive, you will most likely come in from one of three directions: Interstate 95 from the north or south, or I-70 from the northwest. Other routes that converge in Washington are I-66 from the west (which links up with I-81 in Virginia's Shenandoah Valley), US 50 (which hooks up with Annapolis, Maryland, US 301, and Maryland's Eastern Shore), and the Baltimore-Washington Parkway, which parallels I-95 between the two cities' beltways.

All these routes have one common link: They connect with Washington's Capital Beltway, a ribbon of concrete encircling the city. Now for an introduction to how un–user-friendly D.C. is to unsuspecting motorists: Part of the Beltway is numbered both I-95 *and* I-495.

Why? Since I-95 doesn't cut directly through Washington (the way it does in Richmond to the south and Baltimore to the north), it's rerouted along the southern half of the Beltway. It's quite confusing to visitors — and it's only the first of many Washington driving horrors you'll encounter.

Drivers coming from the north and I-70 and headed downtown should take the Beltway to the Baltimore-Washington Parkway and exit south. Bear right onto New York Avenue where the Parkway splits; it goes straight to downtown, near Union Station.

From the south and west, motorists can take either I-66 or I-395 (what I-95 becomes after it crosses inside the Beltway). Both get you across the Potomac and into D.C. near the center of the tourist hubbub.

Our advice to drivers unfamiliar with Washington is to sit down with a map before you leave home and carefully trace out the route to your destination. If you need to make a phone call or two for directions, do it then. And don't try to fight the weekday rush hour traffic (between 6:30 and 9:30 A.M. or 3 and 7 P.M.).

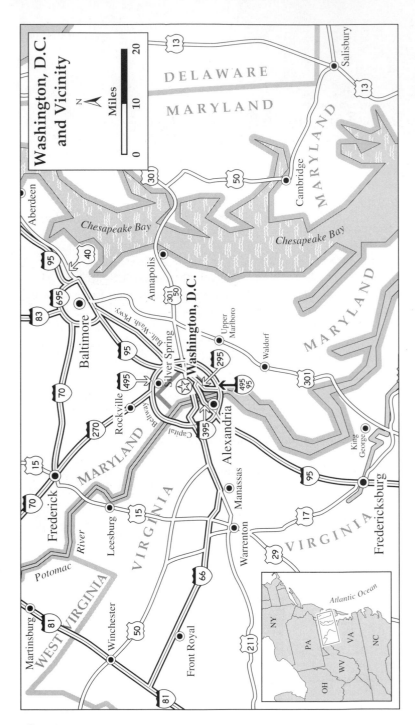

Washington, D.C. and Vicinity

— By Plane

Washington National Airport. While Washington officially has three major airports, this is the most convenient by far for domestic flyers, just a few miles south of the city on the Virginia side of the Potomac. Don't ask a friend to pick you up: Parking is terrible at this cramped airport. A courtesy van service can whisk you from the terminal to the Metro station, but if you're hauling a lot of baggage, consider taking a cab or a shuttle bus to your hotel. If you're unburdened by luggage and want to stretch your legs, it's about an eight-minute walk to the station.

Washington National is a small, well-designed facility with good, clear signs that get you from your gate to the baggage claim area and out the front doors to ground transportation. If someone is picking you up by car, you should proceed on ground level through the baggage claim area and out the doors to the curb. Short-term hourly parking is immediately across the street ($2 per half hour). Rental car courtesy buses are available at shelters on the lower roadway (down the stairs after you exit the terminal). For hotel/motel courtesy transportation, call from the courtesy boards located inside the terminal.

Cab fares to nearby downtown Washington are reasonable (around $10). The Washington Flyer express bus service shuttles every 30 minutes between National and its terminal on K Street, NW, in downtown Washington. Fares are $8 one-way, $14 round trip; call (703) 685-1400 for pickup times. From K Street, a free shuttle will take you to any of eight downtown hotels: the Sheraton Washington, Omni Shoreham, Washington Hilton, Mayflower, Ramada Renaissance Techworld, Grand Hyatt, J. W. Marriott, and Harrington. You can purchase shuttle tickets at the U.S. Air ticket counter (convenient if your gate is on the lower level) or from the Washington Flyer ticket office at the end of the terminal (to your right as you come out the doors of the terminal).

Dulles International Airport. Dulles is where foreign flights arrive and is the least convenient of the three airports serving Washington. Located in the rolling Virginia countryside beyond the suburbs, Dulles is about a 40-minute drive from downtown—longer during rush hour. Use the Dulles Access Road, which connects with the Capital Beltway and I-66.

From the gate, go to the lower level and claim your baggage at the baggage carousels. Then proceed out of the terminal on the ground level to the curb, where you can meet someone picking you up or find

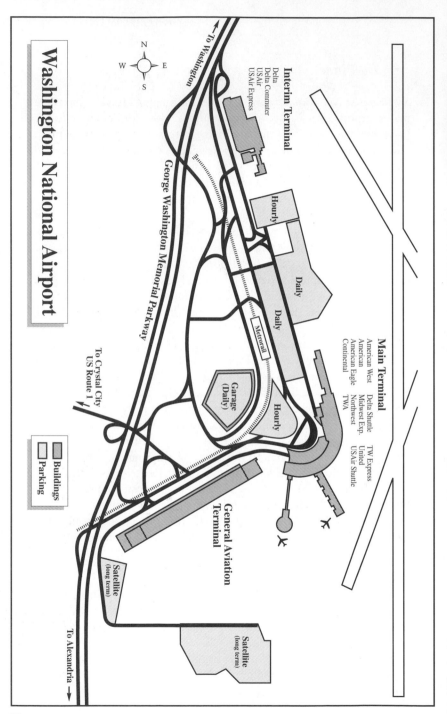

Washington National Airport

Interim Terminal
Delta
Delta Commuter
USAir
USAir Express

N
W — E
S

To Washington

George Washington Memorial Parkway

Hourly

Daily

Daily

Metrorail

Garage
(Daily)

Hourly

Main Terminal
American West
American
American Eagle
Continental

Delta Shuttle
Midwest Exp.
Northwest
TWA

TW Express
United
US Air Shuttle

To Crystal City
US Route 1

☐ Buildings
☐ Parking

General Aviation Terminal

Satellite
(long term)

Satellite
(long term)

To Alexandria →

ground transportation out of the airport. A shuttle to the West Falls Church Metro station leaves about every 20 minutes ($8 one-way). The Washington Flyer express bus will take you downtown for $16 one-way and $26 round trip; the ticket office is on the ground level adjacent to the baggage claim area. They leave every 30 minutes. Children six and under ride free; family rates are for three members of the same family traveling together. Cab fare to D.C. can run more than $40 one-way.

Baltimore-Washington International. BWI, 10 miles south of Baltimore's Inner Harbor, is about a 50-minute drive from downtown Washington; allow lots more time during rush hour. From the gate area, descend to the luggage pick-up belts, which are located next to the ground-level doors. If someone is picking you up, they can meet you outside the baggage claim area at the curb. The Airport Connection shuttles to and from BWI and its K Street terminal in downtown Washington every 90 minutes; call (301) 441-3108 for a schedule. One-way is $13 and round trip is $23; kids under seven ride free.

—— *By Train*

Union Station. Located near Capitol Hill, Union Station is the central Amtrak connecting point in Washington. From here, trains go out all over the country. For most routes you can choose either a speedy Metroliner or a regular train. Once inside the newly restored train station, you can jump on the Metro, located on the lower level. But, not so fast! The station itself is full of delights—small shops, cafes, and even a theater complex. To reach cabs, limousines, buses, and open-air tour trolleys, walk through Union Station's magnificent Main Hall to the main entrance.

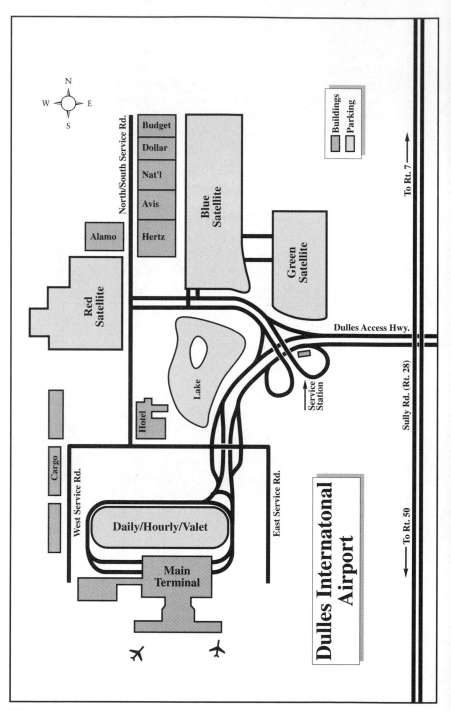

Dulles Internatonal Airport

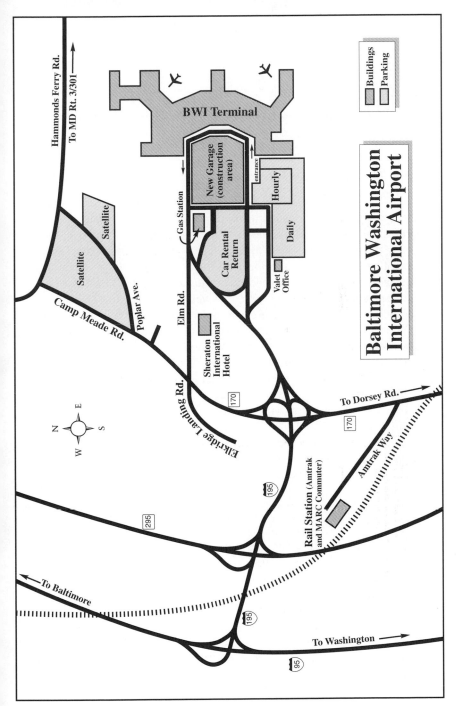

Baltimore Washington International Airport

Things the Natives Already Know

―― The Metro: An Introduction

The first section of Washington's clean, modern, safe, and efficient subway system opened in 1976, just in time for the nation's bicentennial celebrations. As the five-line system has expanded over the years, the rave reviews keep coming. The stations all follow the same brown-and-beige color scheme, with high, curved ceilings made of square concrete panels that fade into the distance. Monotonous, maybe, but the stations are safe and make the lives of visitors infinitely easier.

The trains themselves are clean, quiet, carpeted, virtually crime-free, and air-conditioned. They run so often that carrying a schedule isn't necessary. With two notable exceptions (trendy Georgetown and hip Adams-Morgan), the Metro delivers visitors within easy walking distance of everywhere they might want to go inside the city and into the suburbs.

Even if, like a lot of Americans, you're not comfortable with the idea of relying on public transportation, Washington provides a strong argument for seriously reconsidering your love affair with your car. The Metro system is easy, even fun, to ride. There's really no excuse not to use it. Later, in Part Four, we include a chapter on how.

―― Taxis

Washington's cab fares are low, but the fare system is weird: Fares are based on zones, not a meter. You can go 2 blocks from one zone to another, and be charged more than for a 12-block ride within one zone. It helps to know the zones.

Washington has more cabs per capita than any other American city. But other than for schlepping your luggage to and from National Airport or Union Station, or dining out in subway-free Georgetown and Adams-Morgan, cabs are superfluous, thanks to the Metro. Take the train instead.

If you do take a cab, from our experience, Washington cabbies are polite and friendly. Yet it's a good idea to ask for a receipt at the beginning of the ride, just to let the driver know that you're not some inexperienced out-of-towner and you won't tolerate being charged for a roundabout route through many zones. Most sight-seeing attractions and hotels are in Zone 1. (The strange hows, whats, and wheres of taxi travel in D.C. are discussed in more detail in Part Four.)

— Traffic

If at all possible, avoid driving during your stay in Washington. If you arrive by car, make sure your hotel has parking and is either within walking distance to a Metro station (more on that in Part Four) or offers convenient shuttles to one. Park your car and, with few exceptions, don't plan on moving it until you leave.

Here's why: Driving in Washington is infuriating, and trying to park your car near major tourist sites and government buildings is usually hopeless. The city is a bewildering mix of traffic circles, diagonal boulevards, and one-way streets that change direction depending on the time of day. To make matters worse, some avenues change names for no apparent reason. And the volume of traffic? The *Washington Post* doesn't call its regular traffic column "Dr. Gridlock" for nothing.

One last note: You'll see a lot of cars with cute red, white, and blue license plates imprinted with the word "Diplomatic." The driver of such a car is associated with a foreign embassy and has diplomatic immunity from many local laws—including traffic violations. Give these cars a wide berth. (We cover driving in more detail in Part Four.)

— Finding Your Way

Once you get the hang of it, finding your way around Washington is a snap. You'll have a head start if you know the basics of how D.C. is arranged. The roughly diamond-shaped city's four corners point north, south, east, and west. Inside the diamond, Washington is laid out in a rectilinear gridlike plan and divided into four pie-wedge-shaped quadrants: Northwest (NW), Northeast (NE), Southwest (SW), and Southeast (SE); the center of the pie is the U.S. Capitol building. Separating the quadrants and running in compass directions from the Capitol are North Capitol Street, East Capitol Street, and South Capitol

Street. What happened to "West Capitol Street"? It's the Mall, which runs west from the Capitol to the Potomac River.

Within each quadrant, numbered streets run north-south, and lettered streets run east-west. Addresses on lettered streets give a clue to the numbered cross street at the end of the block. For example, the National Building Museum at 401 F Street, NW, is located on F Street between 4th and 5th streets, NW.

Surprise: Washington has four 1st streets, four E streets and so on, one for each quadrant. As a result, addresses must bear designations such as "NW" to prevent utter confusion. The good news for short-term visitors is that they can virtually ignore the quadrants: Almost all tourist sights, hotels, restaurants, and night life are in Northwest Washington. Northeast and Southeast Washington, with the exception of the middle-class enclave of Capitol Hill, are predominantly poor and less commercially developed, while tiny Southwest is mostly middle-class.

Avenues are named after states (Connecticut, Massachusetts, Wisconsin, etc.) and cut diagonally across the street grid. Some are major thoroughfares and do a good job of disrupting the traffic pattern. Downtown, the avenues meet at circles and squares, the most noteworthy of which are:

- *Dupont Circle* (Connecticut, Massachusetts, and New Hampshire avenues)
- *Washington Circle* (New Hampshire and Pennsylvania avenues)
- *Scott Circle* (Massachusetts and Rhode Island avenues, and 16th Street) and
- *Mount Vernon Square* (Massachusetts and New York avenues).

Here's a run-down of some major roads that visitors will encounter in the city:

- *Pennsylvania Avenue* runs from Southeast and Capitol Hill through downtown and into Georgetown
- *Wisconsin Avenue* starts in Georgetown and leads north to the Maryland suburbs
- *Connecticut Avenue* runs from Lafayette Square, in front of the White House, through Dupont Circle, past the National Zoo, and into Chevy Chase, Maryland
- *16th Street, NW* heads due north from the White House through Adams-Morgan and merges with Georgia Avenue in the Maryland suburbs

- *K Street, NW* is a major east-west downtown business artery
- *Constitution and Independence avenues* run east-west along the Mall
- *New York Avenue* is a major artery that runs from the White House to Northeast Washington and turns into US 50 and the Baltimore-Washington Parkway
- *14th Street, SW* is a major point of egress to and from the Virginia suburbs, and
- *Massachusetts Avenue* runs from Union Station through Dupont Circle, up Embassy Row, and past Washington National Cathedral and American University on its way to Maryland.

The Neighborhoods

Arguably, Washington is the most important city in the world. When most people think of D.C., they conjure up an image of the Mall, anchored by the U.S. Capitol at the east end and the Lincoln Memorial on the other. On its east end alone, the Mall features at least 11 major museums and attractions. In the center is the Washington Monument, with the White House just to the north.

While there's much to see and do on the Mall, visitors who don't get beyond the two-mile strip of green are missing a lot of what this vibrant, international city has to offer: brick sidewalks in front of charming colonial-era row houses in Georgetown, the bohemian Adams-Morgan cafes, stately town houses and mansions near Dupont Circle, the glitter and overflowing street life in the "new" downtown along K Street. At the very least, a foray off the Mall can elevate your trip beyond the level of an educational grade-school field trip and give you a taste of the lively city itself. All the neighborhoods that follow are safe for visitors to explore on foot, except where noted. For more detail on zones, see page 000, "Geographic Zones."

Adams-Morgan (in Zone 6)

An ethnic neighborhood with a heavy emphasis on the Hispanic and African, Adams-Morgan is where young and cool bohemians migrated after the price of real estate zoomed around Dupont Circle in the 70s and 80s. While it doesn't offer much in the way of large museums or monuments, the neighborhood is full of ethnic restaurants, eclectic shops, and nightclubs. Parking, alas, is a severe problem:

Adams-Morgan isn't served by Metro. Don't let that stop you; take a cab.

Dupont Circle (in Zone 6)

Dupont Circle is the center of one of the city's most fashionable neighborhoods, where you'll find elegantly restored town houses, boutiques, restaurants, cafes, bookstores, and art galleries. A stroll down Embassy Row (along Massachusetts Avenue) leads past sumptuous embassies and chancelleries, as well as some of Washington's best visitor attractions: Anderson House, the Phillips Collection, Woodrow Wilson House, and the Islamic Center. You can recognize an embassy by the national coat-of-arms or flag; a pack of reporters and TV cameras may indicate international unrest has erupted somewhere in the world.

Capitol Hill (in Zone 2)

The neighborhood surrounding the Capitol is a mix of residential and commercial, with plenty of restored town houses and trendy bars. Called "The Hill" by natives, here congressional staffers, urban homesteaders, and an element of poor people commingle — sometimes not so successfully: Street crime can be a problem. Blocks can change character abruptly from one end to the other, but if you don't wander far from the Capitol itself you'll be okay.

Downtown (in Zone 3)

Directly north of the Mall is "old downtown," full of department stores, government office buildings (including the FBI), shops, street vendors, hotels, restaurants, two Smithsonian museums, Ford's Theatre, a tiny Chinatown, and the Washington Convention Center. To the west is "new" downtown, the glittery glass and steel office buildings where D.C.'s legions of lobbyists and lawyers do their thing. Both areas offer visitors plenty of choices for shopping, dining, and sight-seeing.

Foggy Bottom (in Zone 4)

Located west of the White House, Foggy Bottom got its name from the swampy land on which it was built. Today, it's home to George Washington University, the U.S. Department of State ("Foggy Bottom" is journalese for State), and the Kennedy Center. Closer to the Mall, massive government office complexes such as the Department of the Interior and the Federal Reserve crowd the White House.

Georgetown (in Zone 5)

A river port long before Washington was built, Georgetown is now the epitome of swank. From the distance, Georgetown is immediately identifiable by its skyline of spires. The neighborhood of restored town houses is filled with crowded bars and shops, and the streets pulse with crowds late into the night. An overflow of suburban teenagers on weekends makes for traffic congestion that's intense, even by Washington standards; lack of a Metro station only makes it worse. Georgetown University marks the neighborhood's western edge. (The Jesuit institution points with pride to its alumnus in the White House.) The Chesapeake and Ohio Canal and its famous towpath begin in Georgetown and follow the Potomac River upstream for 184 miles to Cumberland, Maryland. When you've had enough of the city, rent a bike and see how far you can get.

Upper Northwest (in Zone 7)

Here's where the Washington National Cathedral, the National Zoo, the Hillwood Museum, the city's best private schools, and its wealthiest citizens are found. Without clear boundaries to separate them, Tenleytown, Glover Park, Woodley Park, and Cleveland Park are full of Victorian houses that are homes to members of Congress, rich lobbyists, and attorneys. Attention, joggers: This is where you go for a nighttime run.

Rock Creek Park (in Zone 7)

It's not a neighborhood, but a managed forest in the heart of Washington well worth knowing about. Hikers, joggers, in-line skaters, equestrians, mountain bikers, and anyone wishing an escape from the city can escape here. In the summer, it's ten degrees cooler than the rest of the city.

The Southwest Waterfront (in Zone 1)

A fascinating array of private yachts is on view in Washington's waterfront area, a stretch along Maine Avenue that features marinas, seafood restaurants, and the Wharf Seafood Market, where visitors can sample fresh fish and Chesapeake Bay delicacies such as oysters on the half shell. Here's where you can take a scenic river cruise, on the *Spirit of Washington* or the *Spirit of Mount Vernon.* It's easy to get to the waterfront: Take the subway to the Waterfront Metro station.

Anacostia (in Zone 9)

The city's first suburb today sits in the midst of a war zone of drive-by shootings, drug dealing, and random violence. When Washington is called "Murder Capital of the U.S.," the reference is usually to a large swath of Northeast and Southeast Washington across the Anacostia River from downtown. While Anacostia is well off the beaten tourist path, there are two attractions visitors should take the time to explore: Cedar Hill, the home of 19th-century abolitionist Frederick Douglass, and the Smithsonian's Anacostia Museum. Either drive or ride special tourist buses (not public transportation) to visit these attractions.

— Customs and Protocol

In spite of its status as a world capital, Washington is a fairly relaxed town under the surface. The city's laid-back Southern heritage and the vestiges of an inferiority complex relative to older East Coast cities mean that Washingtonians, by the way they dress and socialize, aren't an ostentatious crowd. For men, suits and ties remain the uniform of work, while most women stick to power suits with padded shoulders in neutral colors for office wear.

Tourists have diplomatic immunity from this dreary dress code, however. In daytime and around the major tourist areas, it's perfectly okay to look the part: If it's hot, wear a T-shirt and bermudas as you stroll the Mall with three cameras around your neck. You won't be alone.

For forays up Connecticut Avenue and into Georgetown, though, leave the cameras and loud Hawaiian print shirts in your hotel room. The crowds are better dressed and hipper, and if you don't follow suit, you'll really stand out in the crowd.

Washington, we're glad to report, is quite informal after 5 P.M. — which makes it easy on visitors. With few exceptions, men needn't worry about going out to a restaurant without a tie, and women can feel comfortable wearing slacks. If there's a casual, after-work uniform in this city, it's probably the preppie look: chinos, Docksiders, and an Izod shirt for men and similar attire for women.

Eating in Restaurants. Washington, as an international city, is full of inexpensive ethnic restaurants — Ethiopian, Thai, Vietnamese, Lebanese, Greek, Afghani . . . the list goes on. Most are casual and you needn't feel intimidated about unfamiliar menus — just ask the waiter or waitress for a recommendation. Since Washington doesn't take itself as seriously as, say, New York, you won't be made to feel uncomfortable in a Japanese restaurant if you request a spoon for your miso soup. Expect to be elbow to elbow with other diners in the crowded eateries, since dining out seems to be a full-time activity for a lot of Washingtonians.

Tipping. Is the tip you normally leave at home appropriate in Washington? The answer is yes. Just bear in mind that a tip is a reward for good service. Here are some guidelines:

Porters and Redcaps. At least 50 cents per bag and $2–3 for a lot of baggage.

Cab Drivers. 15% of the fare. Add an extra dollar if the cabby does a lot of luggage handling.

Valet Parking. A dollar.

Bellmen. At least 50 cents per bag and $2–3 for a lot of baggage.

Waiters. 15–20% of the pretax bill.

Bartenders. 10–15% of the pretax bill.

Chambermaids. A dollar a day.

Checkroom Attendants in Restaurants and Theaters. A dollar per garment.

Going Where the Locals Go. During the week, you'll have to get away from the Mall or the Washington Convention Center if you want to rub shoulders with native Washingtonians. But not too far — Capitol Hill bars and restaurants are crowded with congressional aids, lobbyists, secretarial staff, and even the odd congressperson or two. During the lunch hour, L'Enfant Plaza is jammed with bureaucrats from the myriad concrete-enclosed agencies located south of Independence Avenue.

North of the White House, the "new" downtown (roughly from 15th Street, NW, west to Rock Creek Park) is an area of glass-enclosed office buildings where lawyers, lobbyists, and other professionals ply their trades — and take their clients to lunch. Dupont Circle, formerly Washington's bohemian quarter, remains headquarters to Washington's artists, international, and gay communities.

How Not to Look Like a Tourist. If it's important to you not to look like A Visitor on Holiday in Our Nation's Capital, we offer the following advice:

1. Never say "Washington"—it's "D.C." to the natives. If you *must* say the full name of the city, pronounce it "Worshington."
2. Be obsessive, if not maniacal, about the Redskins.
3. For men, wear a coat and tie, and carry a briefcase at all times. For women, wear power suits with padded shoulders.
4. Tuck a *Washington Post* under your arm and march up Connecticut Avenue with a determined stride.
5. Be blasé about Washington's tourist attractions: Deny ever going to the Mall except in the company of small children.
6. Clutch an espresso, latte, or cappuccino in one hand and a just-baked, multigrain olive loaf in the other: The natives are wild about fresh bread and coffee bars.

Tips for the Disabled

Washington is one of the most accessible cities in the world for the disabled. The White House, for example, has a special entrance on Pennsylvania Avenue for visitors arriving in wheelchairs, and White House guides usually allow visually handicapped visitors to touch some of the items described on tours. Each Metro station is equipped with an elevator, complete with Braille number plates.

All Smithsonian museum buildings are accessible to wheelchair visitors, as are all museum floors. For a copy of the Smithsonian's *A Guide for Disabled Visitors,* call (202) 357-2700. The Lincoln and Jefferson memorials and the Washington Monument are equipped to accommodate disabled visitors. Most sight-seeing attractions have elevators for others who want to avoid a lot of stair climbing. See our section on visitors to Washington with special needs on page 123–24 in Part Four for more information.

The Local Press

Washington is a city of news junkies, and the *Washington Post* is the opiate of choice. Visitors should make a point of picking up Friday's editions, which include the paper's "Weekend" section. It's loaded with information on things to do in and around Washington; if you can, grab a copy of a Friday *Post* before you come to town.

The *Washington Times,* Washington's other daily newspaper, offers a more conservative slant on world events.

City Paper, a free weekly "alternative" newspaper, is another good source of information on arts, theater, clubs, popular music, and movie reviews. It's available from street-corner vending machines and stores all over town.

Washingtonian, a monthly magazine, is strong on lists (top 10 restaurants, etc.), and provides a calendar of events, dining information, and feature articles.

Where/Washington is one of several free publications that list popular things to do around town.

Visitors looking for the latest information on Washington theater, night life, restaurants, special exhibitions, and gallery shows in advance of their trip should call or write:

Where/Washington Magazine, 1625 K Street, NW, Suite 1290, Washington, D.C. 20006. Phone (202) 463-4550.

The Washingtonian, 1828 L Street, NW, Suite 200, Washington, D.C. 20036. Phone (202) 331-0715.

—— *Telephones*

The Washington area is served by three area codes: (202) inside the District, (703) in the Northern Virginia suburbs across the Potomac River, and (301), which connects you with the Maryland suburbs. To dial out of D.C. to suburbs beyond the city's limits, it's necessary to dial the right area code. While calls to Arlington, Alexandria, and most of Fairfax County in Virginia, and Montgomery and Prince George's counties in Maryland are dialed as if they're long distance, they are charged as local calls (free).

—— *Rest Rooms*

Field researchers for the *Unofficial Guide* are selected for their reporting skills, writing ability . . . and small bladders. When we enter a marble edifice, you can be sure we're not just scrutinizing the layout, the flow of the crowd, and the aesthetics: We're also nervously eyeing the real estate for the nearest public facility where we can unload that second cup of coffee.

So how does Washington rate in the bathroom department? Actually, pretty good. That's because of the huge number of museums, monuments, federal office buildings, restaurants, bars, department stores, and hotels that cover the city. Most bathrooms are clean and conveniently located.

Leading any list of great rest room locations should be the National Air and Space Museum on the Mall. For women who claim there's *no* justice in the world when it comes to toilet parity, consider this: There are three times as many women's rest rooms as there are men's restrooms. "And the men don't seem to notice," says a female Smithsonian employee who works at the information desk.

Other facilities of note on the Mall include those at the National Gallery of Art, the Arthur M. Sackler Gallery, the Hirshhorn Museum and Sculpture Garden, and the National Museum of African Art. The rest rooms in the National Museum of Natural History are inconveniently located on a lower level. At the Arts and Industries Building, facilities are located far away from the front entrance. On the other hand, the bathrooms in The Castle, the Smithsonian's visitor center, are easy to find and usually not very crowded.

Virtually all the monuments are rest room equipped, including the Lincoln and Jefferson memorials and the Washington Monument. One notable exception is the White House, a place infamous for long lines. Downtown, hotels, restaurants, and bars are good bets. Avoid the few public rest rooms located in parks, such as the ones on the grounds of the Washington Monument and at Dupont Circle; they're usually dirty. Nor will you find rest rooms in Metro stations, although a few stations are located in complexes that *do* provide rest rooms, including Union Station, Metro Center, Farragut North, and L'Enfant Plaza.

How to Avoid Crime and Keep Safe in Public Places

—— Crime in Washington

The combination of a widespread crack epidemic and the availability of high-powered weaponry put Washington on the map for a very dubious distinction: "Murder Capital of the United States." Anyone who watches the evening news or reads a newspaper knows about Washington's grim murder rate. So the question arises, as you contemplate a trip to D.C.: Just how safe is Washington anyway? Am I going to end up just another statistic?

"It's very safe [as long as you stay in proscribed areas]," says Officer Rod Ryan of D.C.'s Metropolitan Police Department, a three-year veteran of the force, who has worked special anticrime details around the Mall and popular tourist sites. "Washington patrols its main visitor areas very strongly, because tourism is all the city has for income."

To get an idea of how much protection the average tourist or business visitor gets, consider this fact: It's not just Officer Ryan and the rest of D.C.'s finest patrolling the city. Contributing to the task are a number of other law enforcement agencies whose jobs include protecting visitors: The U.S. Park Police patrols the monuments, the U.S. Capitol Police protects the Capitol and the 20-square-block area around it, and the Secret Service patrols the area around the White House. Plus, the Metro has its own police force for protecting people riding public transportation.

"Police are patrolling on bicycles, on horseback, on small motorcycles, on foot, and in unmarked cars," explains Officer Ryan. "And the Smithsonian has its own police force — highly trained federal officers — who patrol inside the buildings and around the grounds. Anyone who knows what he's looking for can spot five police patrols from anywhere on the Mall."

Statistics support his claim: D.C.'s overall crime rate, as defined by the FBI, is actually fairly low. In the summer of 1991, FBI statistics ranked Washington 21st in overall rate of crime among major U.S. cities.

So, who's on the receiving end of all that automatic weapons fire? Most of the victims are young drug dealers in shootouts with competitors, and people involved in violent domestic disputes. Random murders are rare events in D.C., despite its reputation, and police say the odds here are about the same as anywhere else. Furthermore, the mayhem usually occurs in sections of the city visitors do not normally frequent: low-income, residential areas that are removed from the city center and business/tourist districts. The worst areas are in Northeast and Southeast Washington across the Anacostia River from downtown and the major visitor areas. You'd have to go to quite an effort to get there, even by mistake.

"Tourists should never wander across the bridge over the Anacostia River," says Officer Ryan, who should know: He leads a newly formed mountain bike patrol that has helped reduce street crime by 75% in one of the worst sections of Southeast Washington. "Visitors should stay within the boundaries of the Mall, Georgetown, Upper Northwest, Dupont Circle, Adams-Morgan, and downtown."

Even Capitol Hill, which gained notoriety when a legislative aide was murdered on the street a few years ago, is as safe for visitors as any other area that out-of-towners frequent. Ryan explains: "Too many powerful congressmen live in Capitol Hill for it not to be well patrolled."

—— *Having a Plan*

Random violence and street crime are a fact of life in any large city. You've got to be cautious and alert, and plan ahead. Police are rarely able to actually foil a crime in progress. When you are out and about you must work under the assumption that you must use caution because you are on your own; if you run into trouble, it's unlikely that police or anyone else will be able to come to your rescue. You must give some advance thought to the ugly scenarios that might occur, and consider both preventive measures that will keep you out of harm's way, and an escape plan just in case.

Not being a victim of street crime is sort of a survival of the fittest thing. Just as a lion stalks the weakest member of the antelope herd, muggers and thieves target the easiest victim. Simply put, no matter where you are or what you are doing, you want potential felons to think of you as a bad risk.

On the Street. For starters, you always present less of an appealing target if you are with other people. Secondly, if you must be out alone, act alert, be alert, and always have at least one of your arms and hands free. Felons gravitate toward preoccupied folks, the kind found plodding along staring at the sidewalk, with both arms encumbered by briefcases or packages. Visible jewelry (on either men or women) attracts the wrong kind of attention. Men, keep your billfolds in your *front* trouser or coat pocket, or in a fanny pack. Women, keep your purses tucked tightly under your arm; if you're wearing a coat, put it on *over* your shoulder bag strap.

Here's another tip: Carry two wallets, including one inexpensive one, carried in your hip pocket, containing about $20 in cash and some expired credit cards. This is the one you hand over if you're accosted. Your real credit cards and the bulk of whatever cash you have should be in either a money clip or a second wallet hidden elsewhere on your person. Women can carry a fake wallet in their purse, and keep the real one in a pocket or money belt.

If You're Approached. Police will tell you that a felon has the least amount of control over his intended victim during the few moments of his initial approach. A good strategy, therefore, is to short-circuit the crime scenario as quickly as possible. If a felon starts by demanding your money, for instance, quickly take out your billfold (preferably your fake one), and hurl it as far as you can in one direction while you run shouting for help in the opposite direction. The odds are greatly in your favor that the felon will prefer to collect your silent billfold rather than pursue you. If you hand over your wallet and just stand there, the felon will likely ask for your watch and jewelry next. If you're a woman, the longer you hang around, the greater your vulnerability to personal injury or rape.

Secondary Crime Scenes. Under no circumstance, police warn, should you ever allow yourself to be taken to another location — a "secondary crime scene" in police jargon. This move, they explain, provides the felon more privacy and consequently more control. A felon can rob you on the street very quickly and efficiently. If he tries to remove you to another location, whether by car or on foot, it is a certain indication that he has more in mind than robbery. Even if the felon has a gun or knife, your chances are infinitely better running away. If the felon grabs your purse, let him have it. If he grabs your coat, come out of the coat. Hanging onto your money or coat is not worth getting mugged, raped, or murdered.

Another maxim: Never believe anything a felon tells you, even if he's telling you something you desperately want to believe, for example, "I won't hurt you if you come with me." No matter how logical or benign he sounds, assume the worst. Always, always, break off contact as quickly as possible, even if that means running.

In Public Transport.   When riding a bus, always take a seat as close to the driver as you can; never ride in the back. Likewise, on the subway, sit near the driver's or attendant's compartment. These people have a phone and can summon help in the event of trouble.

In Cabs.   While it is possible to hail a cab on the street in Washington, you are somewhat vulnerable in the process. Particularly after dusk, call a reliable cab company and stay inside while they dispatch a cab to your door. When your cab arrives, check the driver's certificate, which must, by law, be posted on the dashboard. Address the cabbie by his last name (Mr. Jones or whatever) or mention the number of his cab. This alerts the driver to the fact that you are going to remember him and/or his cab. Not only will this contribute to your safety, it will keep your cabbie from trying to run up the fare.

If you are comfortable reading maps, familiarize yourself with the most direct route to your destination ahead of time. If you can say, "Georgetown via Wisconsin Avenue, please," the driver is less likely to run up your fare by taking a circuitous route so he can charge you for three zones instead of two.

If you need to catch a cab at the train station or at one of the airports, always use the taxi queue. Taxis in the official queue are properly licensed and regulated. Never accept an offer for a cab or limo made by a stranger in the terminal or baggage claim. At best, you will be significantly overcharged for the ride. At worst, you may be abducted.

—— *Personal Attitude*

While some areas of every city are more dangerous than others, never assume that any area is completely safe. Never let down your guard. You can be the victim of a crime and it can happen to you anywhere. If you go to a restaurant or night spot, use valet parking or park in a well-lighted lot. Women leaving a restaurant or club alone should never be reluctant to ask to be escorted to their car.

Never let your pride or sense of righteousness and indignation imperil your survival. This is especially difficult for many men, particularly for men in the presence of women. It makes no difference whether you are approached by an aggressive drunk, an unbalanced street person, or an actual felon, the rule is the same: Forget your pride and break off contact as quickly as possible. Who cares whether the drunk insulted you, if everyone ends up back at the hotel safe and sound? When you wake up in the hospital with a concussion and your jaw sewn shut, it's too late to decide that the drunk's filthy remark wasn't really all that important.

Felons, druggies, some street people, and even some drunks play for keeps. They can attack with a bloodthirsty hostility and hellish abandon that is beyond the imagination of most people. Believe me, you are not in their league (nor do you want to be).

—— *Self-Defense*

In a situation where it is impossible to run, you'll need to be prepared to defend yourself. Most policemen insist that a gun or knife is not much use to the average person. More often than not, they say, the weapon will be turned against the victim. Additionally, concealed firearms and knives are illegal in most jurisdictions. The best self-defense device for the average person is Mace. Not only is it legal in most states, it is nonlethal and easy to use.

When you shop for Mace, look for two things: It should be able to fire about eight feet, and it should have a protector cap so it won't go off by mistake in your purse or pocket. Carefully read the directions that come with your device, paying particular attention to how it should be carried and stored, and how long the active ingredients will remain potent. Wearing a rubber glove, test-fire your Mace, making sure that you fire downwind.

When you are out about town, make sure your Mace is someplace easily accessible, say, attached to your keychain. If you are a woman and you keep your Mace on a keychain, avoid the habit of dropping your keys (and the Mace) into the bowels of your purse when you leave your hotel room or your car. *The Mace will not do you any good if you have to dig around in your purse for it.* Keep your keys and your Mace in your hand until you have safely reached your destination.

— More Things to Avoid

When you do go out, walk with a minimum of two people whenever possible. If you have to walk alone, stay in well-lit areas that have plenty of people around. And don't walk down alleys. It also helps not to look like a tourist when venturing away from the Mall. Don't wear a camera around your neck, and don't gawk at buildings and unfold maps on the sidewalk. Be careful about who you ask for directions. (When in doubt, shopkeepers are a good bet.) Don't count your money in public, and carry as little cash as possible. At public phones, if you must say your calling card number to make a long-distance call, don't say it loud enough for strangers around you to hear. And, with the exception of the Mall, avoid public parks after dark. In particular, don't go to Rock Creek Park at night.

Carjackings. With the recent surge in carjackings, drivers also need to take special precautions. "Keep alert when you're driving in D.C. traffic," Officer Ryan warns. "Keep your doors locked, with the windows rolled up and the air conditioning or heat on. In traffic, leave enough space in front of you so that you're not blocked in and can make a U-turn. That way, if someone approaches your car and starts beating on your windshield, you can drive off." Store your purse or briefcase under your knees when you are driving, rather than on the seat beside you.

— Help May Be Nearer Than You Think

While walking in Washington, try to be aware of public and federal facilities. If, despite your precautions, you are attacked, head for any federal office building for help. The entrances are all patrolled by armed guards who can offer assistance.

While this litany of warnings and precautions may sound grim, it's really common-sense advice that applies to visitors in any large American city. Keep in mind that Washington's reputation for crime is enhanced by the worldwide media attention the city gets: Local news in Washington is really national news. Finally, remember that 19 million visitors a year still flock to the nation's capital, making it one of the most-visited destinations in the United States. The overwhelming majority encounter no problems with crime during their Washington visit.

Ripoffs and Scams. First-time visitors to the Mall stepping off the escalator at the Smithsonian Metro are often confronted by fast-talking men who try to sell them museum brochures. Don't fall for it; the brochures are free in Smithsonian museums — and the fast-talkers are trying to rip you off.

Another scam that visitors need to watch out for is the well-dressed couple who claim their car broke down and they need $5 for train fare. Refer them to a cop for help and move on.

Though most police officials offer similar advice when it comes to personal safety on the streets, Detective J. J. Bittenbinder of the Chicago Police Department has consolidated professional opinion on the subject in an instructional audio cassette titled *Street Smart: How to Avoid Being a Victim.* In this logical and forceful presentation, Bittenbinder offers practical suggestions for safeguarding your body, possessions, and sanity in the city. The cassette can be ordered from the J Marc Group, (800) 888-5176, for about $15 (worth every penny in our opinion).

— *Other Tourist Concerns*

The Homeless. If you're not from a big city or haven't visited one in a while, you're in for a shock when you come to Washington. It seems that every block in the city is filled with shabbily dressed people asking for money. Furthermore, along the Mall, near the national monuments, on downtown sidewalks and in parks and gardens, you will see people sleeping in blankets and sleeping bags, their possessions piled up next to them.

On crowded Georgetown streets filled with opulent shops, homeless women with small children beg for money. Drivers in cars are approached at stoplights by men carrying Magic-Marker-on-cardboard signs reading "Homeless — Will Work for Food." Virtually every Metro exit is choked with clusters of people begging for money.

Who Are These People? "Most are lifelong D.C. residents who are poor," according to Joan Alker, assistant director of the National

Coalition for the Homeless, an advocacy group headquartered in Washington. "The people you see on the streets are primarily single men and women. A disproportionate number of them are minorities and people with disabilities—they're either mentally ill, or substance abusers, or have physical disabilities."

Are They a Threat to Visitors? "No," Ms. Alker says. "Studies done in Washington show that homeless men have lower rates of conviction for violent crimes than the population at large. We know that murders aren't being committed by the homeless. I can't make a blanket statement, but most homeless people you see are no more likely to commit a violent crime than other people."

Should You Give the Homeless Money? "That's a personal decision," Ms. Alker says. "But if you can't, at least try to acknowledge their existence by looking them in the eye and saying, 'No, I can't.'" While there's no way to tell if the guy with the Styrofoam cup asking for a handout is really destitute or just a con artist, no one can dispute that most of these people are what they claim to be: homeless.

Ways to Help. It's really a matter for your own conscience. We confess to being both moved and annoyed by these unfortunate people: moved by their need and annoyed that we cannot enjoy the nation's capital without running a gauntlet of begging men and women. In the final analysis, we found that it is easier on the conscience and spirit to get a couple of rolls of quarters at the bank and carry an overcoat or jacket pocket full of change at all times. The cost of giving those homeless who approach you a quarter really does not add up to all that much, and it is much better for the psyche to respond to their plight than to deny or ignore their presence.

There is a notion, perhaps valid in some instances, that money given to a homeless person generally goes toward the purchase of alcohol or drugs. If this bothers you excessively, carry granola bars for distribution, or, alternatively, buy some inexpensive gift coupons that can be redeemed at a McDonald's or other fast food restaurant for coffee or a sandwich.

We have found that a little kindness regarding the homeless goes a long way, and that a few kind words delivered along with your quarter or granola bar brighten the day for both you and your friend in need. We are not suggesting a lengthy conversation or prolonged involvement, just something simple like, "Sure, I can help a little bit. Take care of yourself, fella."

Those moved to get more involved in the nationwide problem of homelessness can send inquiries—or a check—to the National Coalition for the Homeless, 1612 K Street, NW, Suite 1004, Washington, D.C. 20006.

Keep It Brief. Finally, don't play psychologist. All the people you encounter on the street are strangers. They may be harmless, or they may be dangerous. Either way, maintain distance and keep any contacts or encounters brief. Be prepared to handle street people in accordance with your principles, but mostly, just be prepared. If you have a druggie in your face wanting a handout, the last thing you want to do is pull out your wallet and thumb through the twenties looking for a one-dollar bill. As the sergeant used to say on "Hill Street Blues," be careful out there.

PART THREE: *Hotels*

Deciding Where to Stay

On weekdays, driving and parking in downtown Washington are nightmarish. On weekends, there is less traffic congestion, but parking is extremely difficult, particularly in the area of the Mall. Because the best way to get around Washington is on the Metro, we recommend a hotel within walking distance of a Metro station. With two rather prominent exceptions, all of Washington's best areas, as well as most of the Virginia and Maryland suburbs, are safely and conveniently accessible via this clean, modern subway system. Only historic Georgetown and the colorful, ethnic Adams-Morgan neighborhood are off-line.

Unless you plan to spend most of your time in Georgetown, we suggest that you pick a hotel elsewhere in the city. If you lodge in Georgetown, you will be relegated to driving or cabbing to get anywhere else. Adams-Morgan, a great neighborhood for dining and shopping, does not offer much in the way of lodging. If you go to Adams-Morgan, especially at night, take a cab.

Getting a Good Deal on a Room

Though Washington, D.C., is a major tourist destination, the economics of hotel room pricing is driven by business, government, and convention trade. This translates to high "rack rates" (a hotel's published room rate) and very few bargains. The most modest Econo Lodge or Days Inn in Washington charges upwards of $45 a night, and midrange chains, such as Holiday Inn and Ramada, ask from $75 to $150.

The good news is that Washington, D.C., and its Virginia and Maryland suburbs offer a staggering number of unusually fine hotels, including a high percentage of suite properties. The bad news, of course, is that you can expect to pay dearly to stay in them.

In most cities, the better and more expensive hotels are located close to the city center, with less expensive hotels situated farther out. There is normally a trade-off between location and price: If you are willing to stay out off the interstate and commute into downtown, you can expect to pay less for your suburban room than you would for a downtown room. In Washington, D.C., unfortunately, it very rarely works this way.

In the greater Washington area, every hotel is seemingly close to *something.* No matter how far you are from the Capitol, the Mall, and downtown, you can bank on your hotel being within spitting distance of some bureau, agency, airport, or industrial complex that funnels platoons of business travelers into guest rooms in a constant flow. Because almost every hotel and motel has its own captive market, the customary proximity/price trade-off doesn't apply. The Marriott at the Beltway and Wisconsin Avenue, for example, is 30 to 40 minutes away by car from the Mall, but stays full with visitors to the nearby National Institutes of Health.

Discounts

Getting Special Weekend Rates

While Washington hotels are tough for the budget-conscious, it's not impossible to get a good deal—relatively speaking. For starters, most hotels that cater to business, government, and convention travelers offer special weekend discount rates that range from 15% to 40% below normal weekday rates. You can find out about weekend specials by calling the hotel or by consulting your travel agent.

Getting Corporate Rates

Many hotels offer discounted corporate rates, too, at 5 to 20% off rack. Usually you do not need to work for a large company or have a special relationship with the hotel to obtain these rates. Simply call the hotel of your choice and ask for their corporate rates. Many hotels will guarantee you the discounted rate on the phone when you make your reservation. Others may make the rate conditional on your providing some sort of *bona fides,* for instance, a fax on your company's letterhead requesting the rate, or a company credit card or business card when you check in. Generally, the screening is not rigorous.

Half-Price Programs

The larger discounts on rooms (35 to 60%), in Washington or anywhere else, are available through half-price hotel programs, often called travel clubs. Program operators contract with an individual hotel to provide rooms at a deep discount, usually 50% off rack rate, on a "space available" basis. Space available, in practice, generally means that you can reserve a room at the discounted rate whenever the hotel expects to be at less than 80% occupancy. If you take the time to find out when the big conventions are, and are willing to arrange your visit around them, you may be able to get this kind of discount. (See our Schedule of Conventions, Part Seven.)

Most half-price programs charge a fee of $25 to $125 for an annual membership or directory subscription. Once enrolled, you are mailed a membership card and a directory listing all the hotels participating in the program. As you look at the directory, you will notice right away that there are lots of restrictions and exceptions. Some hotels, for instance, "black out" certain dates or times of year. Others may offer the discount only on certain days of the week, or require you to stay a certain number of nights to be eligible. Still others may offer a much smaller discount than 50%.

Some discount programs specialize in domestic travel, some in international travel, and some do both. The more established operators offer members between one and four thousand hotels to choose from in the United States. All of the programs have a heavy concentration of hotels in California and Florida, and most have a very limited selection of participating properties in New York City or Boston. Offerings in other cities and regions of the United States vary considerably.

The programs with the largest selection of hotels in Washington, D.C. (and in the surrounding Maryland and Virginia suburbs) are *Encore, Travel America at HalfPrice (Entertainment Publications), International Travel Card,* and *Privilege Card.* Each of these programs lists 22 to 50 hotels in the greater Washington area:

Encore	(800) 638-0930
Travel America at HalfPrice	(800) 285-5525
International Travel Card	(800) 342-0558
Privilege Card	(800) 359-0066

One problem with half-price programs is that not all hotels offer a full 50% discount. Another slippery problem is that the base rate against which the discount is applied may be jacked up. Some hotels figure the discount on an exaggerated rack rate that nobody would ever have to pay. A few participating hotels may deduct the discount from a supposed "superior" or "upgraded" room rate, even though the room you get is the hotel's standard accommodation.

Though base rates can be hard to pin down, the majority of participating properties base discounts on the published rate in the *Hotel & Travel Index* (a quarterly reference work used by travel agents) and work within the spirit of their agreement with the program operator. As a rule, if you travel several times a year, you will more than pay for your program membership in room rate savings.

A noteworthy addendum to this discussion is that rooms that are deeply discounted through half-price programs are not commissionable to travel agents. In practical terms this means that you must ordinarily make your own inquiry calls and reservations. If you travel frequently, however, and run a lot of business through your travel agent, he or she will probably do your legwork, even without a commission.

Preferred Rates

If you cannot book the hotel of your choice through a half-price program, you and your travel agent may have to search for a lesser discount, often called a preferred rate. A preferred rate could be a discount made available to travel agents to stimulate their booking activity, or a discount initiated to attract a certain class of traveler. Most preferred rates are promoted through travel industry publications and so are often accessible only through an agent.

We recommend sounding out your travel agent about possible deals. Be aware, however, that the rates shown on travel agents' computerized reservations systems are not always the lowest rates obtainable. Zero in on a couple of hotels that fill your needs in terms of location and quality of accommodations, and then have your travel agent call for the latest rates and specials.

Hotel reps are almost always more responsive to travel agents, because travel agents represent a source of additional business. There are certain specials that hotel reps will disclose *only* to travel agents. Travel agents also come in handy when the hotel you want is supposedly booked. A personal appeal from your agent to the hotel's director of sales and marketing will get you a room more than half of the time.

If you want to do your own research, Travelgraphics, in Norcross, Georgia, (800) 633-7918, will sell you a directory of preferred rates just like the one travel agents use. With the directory in hand, you can make your own arrangements or have your agent make them for you.

Wholesalers, Consolidators, and Reservation Services

If you do not want to join a program or buy a discount directory, you can take advantage of the services of a wholesaler or consolidator. Wholesalers and consolidators buy rooms, or options on rooms (room blocks), from hotels at a low, negotiated rate. They then resell the rooms at a profit through travel agents or tour packagers, or directly to the public. Most wholesalers and consolidators have a provision for returning unsold rooms to participating hotels, but are disinclined to do so. The wholesaler's or consolidator's relationship with any hotel is predicated on volume. If they return rooms unsold, the hotel might not make as many rooms available to them the next time around. Thus, wholesalers and consolidators often offer rooms at bargain rates, at anywhere from

15 to 50% off rack, occasionally sacrificing their profit margin in the process, to avoid returning the rooms to the hotel unsold.

When wholesalers and consolidators deal directly with the public, they frequently represent themselves as "reservation services." When you call, you can ask for a rate quote for a particular hotel, or, alternatively, ask for their best available deal in the area where you prefer to stay. If there is a maximum amount you are willing to pay, say so. Chances are, the service will find something that will work for you, even if they have to shave a dollar or two off their own profit. Sometimes you will have to pay for your room in advance, with a credit card, when you make your reservation. Other times you will pay at the usual time, when you check out. Listed below are several services that frequently offer substantial discounts:

Central Reservation Service	(800) 950-0232
Express Hotel Reservations	(800) 356-1123
Quikbook	(800) 221-3531
RMC Travel Centre	(800) 782-2674
Room Exchange	(800) 846-7000

—— *Making Your Own Reservations*

As you poke around trying to find a good deal, there are several things you should know. First, always call the hotel in question as opposed to the hotel chain's national 800 number. Quite often, the reservationists at the national 800 number are unaware of local specials. Always ask about specials before you inquire about corporate rates. Do not be reluctant to bargain. If you are buying a hotel's weekend package, for example, and want to extend your stay into the following week, you can often obtain at least the corporate rate for the extra days. Do your bargaining, however, before you check in, preferably when you make your reservations.

—— *Tips for Business Travelers*

Most business travelers want to stay near where their business will be transacted, and save money doing it. Identify the zone(s) where your business will take you, and then cross-reference the hotels in the Hotel Chart in Part Twelve that are situated there. Once you have developed a short list of hotels that are conveniently located, fit your budget, and offer the standard of accommodation you require, you (or your travel agent) can make use of the cost-saving suggestions discussed earlier to obtain the lowest rate.

If you are attending a major convention or trade show, it is probable that the meeting's sponsoring organization has negotiated "convention rates" with some number of hotels. Under this arrangement, hotels agree to "block" a certain number of rooms at an agreed-upon price for the use of convention attendees. Sometimes, as in the case of a small meeting, only one hotel is involved. In the event of a large "city-wide" convention at the Washington Convention Center, almost every downtown hotel will participate in the room block.

Because the convention sponsor is bringing a lot of business to the city and reserving a large number of rooms, it usually can negotiate a volume discount on the room rates, a rate that should be substantially below rack rate. The bottom line, however, is that some conventions and trade shows have more bargaining clout and negotiating skill than others. Hence, your convention sponsor may or may not have found a rate as low as the one you could negotiate on your own.

Once a convention or trade show sponsor has completed negotiations with participating hotels, it will send its attendees a list of all the hotels serving the convention, along with the special convention rate for each. If the negotiated convention rate doesn't sound like a good deal, you can try to reserve a room using a half-price club, a consolidator, or a tour operator, using the strategies suggested earlier, under "Discounts." Remember, however, that many of the deep discounts are available only when the hotel expects to be at less than 80% occupancy, a condition that rarely prevails when a big convention is in town.

Here are some tips for beating convention rates:

1. Reserve early. Most big conventions and trade shows announce meeting sites one to three years in advance. Get your reservation booked as far in advance as possible using a half-price club. If you book well before the convention sponsor sends out its hotel list, chances are much better that the hotel will have space available.

2. If you've already got your convention's housing list, compare it with the list of hotels presented in this guide. You might be able to find a different hotel that suits your needs better.

3. Use a local reservations agency or consolidator. This strategy is

useful even if, for some reason, you need to make reservations at the last minute. Local reservations agencies and consolidators almost always control some rooms, even in the midst of a huge convention or trade show. (See the list of travel clubs on page 80 and the list of wholesalers and consolidators on page 82.)

4. Book a hotel somewhat distant from the convention center, but situated close to the Metro. In addition to saving money on your room rate, your commuting time underground to the convention center will often be shorter than taking a cab or driving from downtown hotels.

5. Stay in a bed and breakfast, either downtown or near a Metro line. *Bed and Breakfast Accomodations Ltd.,* at (202) 328-3510, can help you locate one.

—— *Hotel/Motel Toll-Free 800 Numbers*

For your convenience, we've listed the toll-free numbers for the following hotel and motel chains' reservation lines:

Best Western	(800) 528-1234 U.S. & Canada
	(800) 528-2222 TDD (Telecommunication Device for the Deaf)
Comfort Inn	(800) 228-5150 U.S.
Courtyard by Marriott	(800) 321-2211 U.S.
Days Inn	(800) 325-2525 U.S.
Doubletree	(800) 528-0444 U.S.
Econo Lodge	(800) 424-4777 U.S.
Embassy Suites	(800) 362-2779 U.S. & Canada
Fairfield Inn by Marriott	(800) 228-2800 U.S.
Guest Quarters	(800) 424-2900 U.S. & Canada
Hampton Inn	(800) 426-7866 U.S. & Canada
Hilton	(800) 445-8667 U.S.
	(800) 368-1133 TDD
Holiday Inn	(800) 465-4329 U.S. & Canada
Howard Johnson	(800) 654-2000 U.S. & Canada
	(800) 654-8442 TDD
Hyatt	(800) 233-1234 U.S. & Canada

Loew's	(800) 223-0888 U.S. & Canada
Marriott	(800) 228-9290 U.S. & Canada
	(800) 228-2489 TDD
Quality Inn	(800) 228-5151 U.S. & Canada
Radisson	(800) 333-3333 U.S. & Canada
Ramada Inn	(800) 228-3838 U.S.
	(800) 228-3232 TDD
Residence Inn by Marriott	(800) 331-3131 U.S.
Ritz-Carlton	(800) 241-3333 U.S.
Sheraton	(800) 325-3535 U.S. & Canada
Stouffer	(800) 468-3571 U.S. & Canada
Westin	(800) 228-3000 U.S. & Canada
Wyndham	(800) 822-4200 U.S.

Hotels and Motels:
Rated and Ranked

—— What's in a Room?

Except for cleanliness, state of repair, and decor, most travelers do not pay much attention to their hotel rooms. There are, of course, discernable differences in quality and luxury between a Motel 6 and a Holiday Inn, a Holiday Inn and a Marriott, and so on. In general, however, hotel guests fail to appreciate that some rooms are better engineered than others.

Contrary to what you might suppose, designing a hotel room is (or should be) a lot more complex than picking a bedspread to match the carpet and drapes. Making the room usable to its occupants is an art, a planning discipline that combines form and function.

Decor and taste are important, certainly. No one wants to spend several days in a room where the decor is dated, garish, or even ugly. But beyond the decor, certain other variables determine how "livable" a hotel room is. In Washington, for example, we have seen some beautifully appointed rooms that are simply not well designed for human habitation. The next time you stay in a hotel, pay attention to the details and design elements of your room. Even more than decor, these are the things that will make you feel comfortable and at home.

It takes the *Unofficial Guide* researchers about 40 minutes to inspect a hotel room. Here are a few of the things we check:

Room Size.   While some smaller rooms are cozy and well designed, a large and uncluttered room is generally preferable, especially for a stay of more than three days.

Temperature Control, Ventilation, and Odor.   You should be able to control the temperature of the room. The best system, because it's so quiet, is central heating and air conditioning, controlled by the room's own thermostat. The next best system is a room module heater and air conditioner, preferably controlled by an automatic thermostat, but usually by manually operated button controls. The worst system is central heating and air without any sort of room thermostat or guest control.

The vast majority of hotel rooms have windows or balcony doors that have been permanently secured shut. Though there are some legitimate safety and liability issues involved, we prefer windows and balcony doors that can be opened to admit fresh air. Hotel rooms should be free of smoke or odors and not feel stuffy or damp.

Room Security. Better rooms have locks that require a plastic card instead of the traditional lock and key. Card and slot systems allow the hotel to change the combination or entry code of the lock with each new guest who uses the room. A burglar who has somehow acquired a room key to a conventional lock can afford to wait until the situation is right before using the key to gain access. Not so with a card and slot system. Though the largest hotels and hotel chains with lock and key systems usually rotate their locks once each year, their rooms remain vulnerable to hotel thieves much of the time. Many smaller or independent properties rarely rotate their locks.

In addition to the entry lock system, the door should have a deadbolt, and a chain that can be locked from the inside. A chain by itself is not sufficient. Doors should also have a peephole. If windows and balcony doors can be opened, they should have secure locks.

Safety. Every room should have a fire or smoke alarm, clear fire instructions, and, preferably, a sprinkler system. Bathtubs should have a nonskid surface, and shower stalls should have doors that either open outward or slide side to side. Bathroom electrical outlets should be high on the wall and not too close to the sink. Balconies should have sturdy, high rails.

Noise. Most travelers have been kept awake by the TVs, partying, or amorous activities of people in the next room, or by traffic on the street outside. Better hotels are designed with noise control in mind. Wall and ceiling construction are substantial, effectively screening routine noise. Carpets and drapes, in addition to being decorative, also absorb and muffle sounds. Mattresses mounted on stable platforms or sturdy bed frames do not squeak even when challenged by the most passionate and acrobatic lovers. Televisions enclosed in cabinets, and with volume governors, rarely disturb guests in adjacent rooms.

In better hotels, the air conditioning and heating system is well maintained and operates without noise or vibration. Likewise, plumbing is quiet and positioned away from the sleeping area. Doors to the hall, and to adjoining rooms, are thick and well fitted to better keep out noise.

Darkness Control. Ever been in a hotel room where the curtains would not quite come together in the middle? It's important to have a dark, quiet room where you can sleep late without the morning sun blasting you out of bed. We prefer thick, lined curtains that close completely in the center and extend beyond the dimensions of the window or door frame. In a well-planned room, the curtains, shades, or blinds should almost totally block light at any time of day.

Lighting. American hotel rooms often have poor lighting. The lighting is usually adequate for dressing, relaxing, or watching television, but not for reading or working. Lighting should be bright over tables and desks, and alongside couches or easy chairs. Since so many people read in bed, there should be a separate light for each side of any double bed. A room with two queen beds should have an individual light for four people. Better bedside reading lights illuminate a small area, so if you want to sleep and someone else prefers to stay up and read, you will not be bothered by the light. The worst lighting plan by far is a single lamp on a table between beds. In each bed, only the person next to the lamp will have sufficient light to read. This deficiency is often compounded by light bulbs of insufficient wattage.

In addition, closet areas should be well lit, and there should be a switch near the door that turns on lights in the room when you enter. A seldom seen, but desirable, feature is a bedside console that allows a guest to control all or most lights in the room from bed.

Furnishings. At bare minimum, the bed(s) must be firm. Pillows should be made with nonallergic fillers and, in addition to the sheets and spread, a blanket should be provided. Bed clothes should be laundered with a fabric softener and changed daily. Better hotels usually provide extra blankets and pillows in the room or on request, and sometimes use a second topsheet between the blanket and the spread.

There should be a dresser large enough to hold clothes for two people during a five-day stay. A small table with two chairs, or a desk with a chair, should be provided. The room should be equipped with a luggage rack and a three-quarter to full-length mirror.

The television should be color, cable-connected, and ideally have a volume governor and remote control. It should also be mounted on a swivel base, and preferably enclosed in a cabinet. Local channels should be posted on the set and a local TV program guide should be supplied.

The telephone should be touchtone, conveniently situated for bedside use, and should have, on or near it, easily understood dialing instructions and a rate card. Local white and yellow pages should be provided. Better hotels have phones in the bath and equip room phones with long cords.

Well-designed hotel rooms usually have a plush armchair or a sleeper sofa for lounging and reading and padded headboards for comfortable reading in bed. In addition, there should be a nightstand or table on each side of the bed(s). Nice extras in any hotel room include a small refrigerator, a digital alarm clock, and a coffeemaker.

Bathroom. Two sinks are better than one, and you cannot have too much counter space. A sink outside the bath is a great convenience when two people are bathing and dressing at the same time. Sinks should have drains with stoppers.

Better bathrooms have both tub and shower with a nonslip bottom. Tub and shower controls should be easy to operate. Adjustable shower heads are preferred. The bath needs to be well lit and should have an exhaust fan and a guest-controlled bathroom heater. Towels, hand towels, and washcloths should be large, soft, and fluffy, and provided in generous quantities. There should be a convenient and safely placed electrical outlet for each sink.

Complimentary shampoo, conditioner, and lotion are a plus, as are robes and bathmats. Better hotels supply their bathrooms with tissues and extra toilet paper. Luxurious baths feature a phone, a hair dryer, sometimes a small television, or even a jacuzzi.

Vending. There should be complimentary ice and a drink machine on each floor. Welcome additions include a snack machine and a sundries (combs, toothpaste) machine. The latter are seldom found in large hotels that have 24-hour restaurants and shops.

— Room Ratings

To separate properties according to the relative quality, tastefulness, state of repair, cleanliness, and size of their **standard rooms,** we have grouped the hotels and motels into classifications denoted by stars. Star ratings in this guide apply to Washington, D.C. properties only and do not necessarily correspond to ratings awarded by Mobil, AAA, or other travel critics. Because stars have little relevance when awarded in the absence of commonly recognized standards of comparison, we have tied our ratings to expected levels of quality established by specific American hotel corporations.

★★★★★	*Superior Rooms*	Tasteful and luxurious by any standard
★★★★	*Extremely Nice Rooms*	What you would expect at a Hyatt Regency, or Marriott
★★★	*Nice Rooms*	Holiday Inn or comparable quality
★★	*Adequate Rooms*	Clean, comfortable, and functional without frills — like a Motel 6
★	*Super Budget*	

Star ratings apply to *room quality only,* and describe the property's standard accommodations. For most hotels and motels a "standard accommodation" is a hotel room with either one king bed or two queen beds. In an all-suite property, the standard accommodation is either a one- or two-room suite. In addition to standard accommodations, many hotels offer luxury rooms and special suites that are not rated in this guide. Star ratings for rooms are assigned without regard to whether a property has restaurant(s), recreational facilities, entertainment, or other extras.

In addition to stars (which delineate broad categories), we also employ a numerical rating system. Our rating scale is 0–100, with 100 the best possible rating, and zero (0) the worst. Numerical ratings are presented to show the difference we perceive between one property and another that may be in the same star category. Rooms at One Washington Circle Hotel, Sheraton City Centre, and Holiday Inn Crowne Plaza Metro Center, for instance, are all rated as ★★★★ (four stars). In the supplemental numerical ratings, the Washington Circle and the Sheraton are rated 88 and 86, respectively, while the Holiday Inn Crowne Plaza is rated 83. This means that within the four-star category, One Washington Circle and the Sheraton are comparable, and that both have somewhat nicer rooms than the Holiday Inn Crowne Plaza.

—— *The Nicest Rooms in Town*

Cost estimates are based on the hotel's published rack rates for standard rooms, averaged between weekday and weekend prices. Each "$" represents $30. Thus a cost symbol of "$$$" means a room (or suite) at that hotel will average about $90 a night (it may be less on weekends or more on weekdays).

Here is a hit parade of the nicest rooms in town. We've focused strictly on room quality, and excluded any consideration of location, services, recreation, or amenities. In some instances, a one- or two-room suite can be had for the same price or less than that of a standard hotel room.

The Nicest Rooms in Town

Rank	Hotel	Room Quality Rating	Room Star Rating	Cost ($ = $30)
1	Ritz-Carlton Pentagon City	98	★★★★★	$$$$$+
2	Grand Hotel of Washington	96	★★★★★	$$$$$+
3	Park Hyatt (suites)	96	★★★★★	$$$$$$+
4	Watergate Hotel	95	★★★★½	$$$$$$+
5	Jefferson Hotel	94	★★★★½	$$$$$$$+
6	Four Seasons Hotel	93	★★★★½	$$$$$$$$$$−
7	Westin ANA Hotel	92	★★★★½	$$$$$$$−
8	Sheraton Premiere Tysons Corner	91	★★★★½	$$$$+
9	Sheraton Suites Alexandria	91	★★★★½	$$$+
10	St. James	91	★★★★½	$$$$−
11	Stouffer Mayflower Hotel	91	★★★★½	$$$$$+
12	Willard Inter-Continental	91	★★★★½	$$$$$$
13	Capitol Hilton	90	★★★★½	$$$$$$−
14	Loew's L'Enfant Plaza	90	★★★★½	$$$+
15	Morrison-Clark Inn	90	★★★★½	$$$+
16	Park Hyatt (standard rooms)	90	★★★★½	$$$$$+
17	Sheraton Carlton	90	★★★★½	$$$$+
18	Washington Vista Hilton	90	★★★★½	$$$$+
19	Embassy Suites Alexandria	89	★★★★	$$$$$$−
20	Hay-Adams Hotel	89	★★★★	$$$$$$$+
21	Georgetown Inn	88	★★★★	$$$$$$$
22	One Washington Circle Hotel	88	★★★★	$$$$+
23	Embassy Row Hotel	87	★★★★	$$$$$
24	Grand Hyatt Washington	87	★★★★	$$$$$$$+

The Nicest Rooms *(continued)*

Rank	Hotel	Room Quality Rating	Room Star Rating	Cost ($ = $30)
25	Guest Quarters Pennsylvania Ave.	87	★★★★	$$$$$–
26	Marriott Tysons Corner	87	★★★★	$$$$$–
27	Ritz-Carlton Hotel	87	★★★★	$$$$$$$$+
28	Washington Court Hotel	87	★★★★	$$$+
29	Canterbury Hotel	86	★★★★	$$$$+
30	Days Inn Alexandria	86	★★★★	$$$$–
31	Embassy Suites Chevy Chase	86	★★★★	$$$$$+
32	Embassy Suites Crystal City	86	★★★★	$$$$$+
33	Hyatt Regency Bethesda	86	★★★★	$$$$$+
34	J.W. Marriott Hotel	86	★★★★	$$$$$$+
35	Latham Hotel Georgetown	86	★★★★	$$$+
36	Marriott Crystal Gateway	86	★★★★	$$$$$$$–
37	Morrison House	86	★★★★	$$$$$
38	Sheraton City Centre	86	★★★★	$$$$$$+
39	Stouffer Concourse Hotel	86	★★★★	$$$$$+
40	Inn at Foggy Bottom	85	★★★★	$$$–
41	Marriott Crystal City	85	★★★★	$$$$$–
42	River Inn	85	★★★★	$$$+
43	Washington Marriott Hotel	85	★★★★	$$$$$–
44	Embassy Suites Downtown	84	★★★★	$$$$$$$–
45	Residence Inn Bethesda	84	★★★★	$$$$$
46	Sheraton Washington Hotel	84	★★★★	$$$$$$$
47	Doubletree Hotel Pentagon City	83	★★★★	$$$$–
48	Guest Quarters New Hampshire Ave.	83	★★★★	$$$$+
49	Henley Park Hotel	83	★★★★	$$$$$+
50	Holiday Inn Crowne Plaza Metro Center	83	★★★★	$$$$$$$–
51	Madison	82	★★★½	$$$$$$$$+
52	Ramada Renaissance	82	★★★½	$$$+
53	Ramada Renaissance Techworld	82	★★★½	$$$$$$–
54	Wyndham Bristol Hotel	82	★★★½	$$$$$+
55	Hyatt Regency Capitol Hill	81	★★★½	$$$$$$+
56	Pullman Highland Hotel	81	★★★½	$$$$$–
57	Channel Inn Hotel	80	★★★½	$$$$–
58	Courtyard Landover	80	★★★½	$$$–
59	Georgetown Dutch Inn	80	★★★½	$$$+
60	Holiday Inn Bethesda	80	★★★½	$$+
61	Radisson Plaza at Mark Center	80	★★★½	$$$$
62	Sheraton Crystal City	80	★★★½	$$$+

The Nicest Rooms (continued)

Rank	Hotel	Room Quality Rating	Room Star Rating	Cost ($ = $30)
63	Washington Hilton	80	★★★½	$$$$$$$$+
64	Courtyard Crystal City	79	★★★½	$$$$
65	Marriott Hotel Key Bridge	79	★★★½	$$$$$$–
66	Ramada Hotel Tysons Corner	79	★★★½	$$$–
67	Sheraton National Hotel	79	★★★½	$$$+
68	Courtyard Alexandria	78	★★★½	$$$+
69	Hotel Lombardy	78	★★★½	$$$
70	Hyatt Regency Crystal City	78	★★★½	$$$$$$–
71	Quality Hotel Central	77	★★★½	$$$+
72	Ramada Hotel Bethesda	77	★★★½	$$$–
73	Hotel Washington	76	★★★½	$$$$$$+
74	Hampshire Hotel	75	★★★½	$$$$
75	Radisson Park Terrace	75	★★★½	$$$$–
76	State Plaza Hotel	75	★★★½	$$+
77	Tabard Inn	75	★★★½	$$$$–
78	Holiday Inn Old Town	74	★★★	$$$+
79	Ramada Inn Downtown	74	★★★	$$+
80	Best Western Skyline Inn	73	★★★	$$$
81	Holiday Inn Chevy Chase	73	★★★	$$$
82	Hotel Anthony	73	★★★	$$$–
83	Hyatt Arlington	73	★★★	$$$$$+
84	Holiday Inn Ballston	72	★★★	$$$+
85	Omni Shoreham Hotel	72	★★★	$$$$+
86	Savoy Suites Hotel	72	★★★	$$$–
87	Embassy Square Suites	71	★★★	$$$+
88	Ramada Hotel Old Town	71	★★★	$$+
89	Best Western Old Colony Inn	70	★★★	$$–
90	DuPont Plaza Hotel	70	★★★	$$$+
91	Holiday Inn Capitol	70	★★★	$$$$$–
92	Kalorama Guest House	70	★★★	$$+
93	Marriott Hotel Bethesda	70	★★★	$$$$$–
94	Holiday Inn Central	68	★★★	$$$$$–
95	Holiday Inn Silver Spring	68	★★★	$$+
96	Carlyle Suites Hotel	67	★★★	$$$
97	Holiday Inn Governor's House	67	★★★	$$$+
98	Holiday Inn National Airport	67	★★★	$$$$–
99	Best Western New Hampshire Suites	66	★★★	$$$–
100	Comfort Inn Downtown	66	★★★	$$$$
101	Hampton Inn Alexandria	66	★★★	$$$–

The Nicest Rooms (continued)

Rank	Hotel	Room Quality Rating	Room Star Rating	Cost ($ = $30)
102	Holiday Inn Georgetown	66	★★★	$$$–
103	Holiday Inn Thomas Circle	66	★★★	$$$$–
104	Omni Georgetown Hotel	66	★★★	$$$$$+
105	Bellevue Hotel	65	★★★	$$$
106	Holiday Inn Eisenhower Metro	65	★★★	$$$+
107	Howard Johnson National Airport	65	★★★	$$$$–
108	Phoenix Park Hotel	65	★★★	$$$
109	Days Hotel Crystal City	64	★★½	$$$$–
110	Quality Hotel Downtown	64	★★½	$$$+
111	Days Inn Downtown	63	★★½	$$$–
112	Quality Inn Iwo Jima	63	★★½	$$$–
113	Best Western Rosslyn Westpark	62	★★½	$$$+
114	Comfort Inn Ballston	62	★★½	$$$–
115	Comfort Inn Landmark	62	★★½	$$
116	Days Inn Camp Springs	62	★★½	$$+
117	Holiday Inn Key Bridge	62	★★½	$$$+
118	Quality Inn College Park	62	★★½	$$
119	Days Inn Connecticut Ave.	60	★★½	$$+
120	Holiday Inn Camp Springs	60	★★½	$$+
121	Normandy Inn	60	★★½	$$$+
122	Quality Hotel Capitol Hill	60	★★½	$$$
123	Ramada Inn Alexandria	60	★★½	$$$$–
124	Best Western Tysons Westpark	59	★★½	$$$–
125	Quality Hotel Silver Spring	58	★★½	$$$–
126	Center City Hotel	57	★★½	$$$–
127	Comfort Inn Van Dorn	57	★★½	$$+
128	Econo Lodge West Arlington	57	★★½	$$+
129	Embassy Inn	57	★★½	$$$–
130	Manor Inn Bethesda	57	★★½	$$$–
131	Windsor Park Hotel	57	★★½	$$+
132	Adams Inn	55	★★	$$+
133	Econo Lodge National Airport	54	★★	$$
134	American Inn of Bethesda	53	★★	$$$–
135	Best Western Arlington Inn	53	★★	$$+
136	Harrington Hotel	53	★★	$$$–
137	Howard Johnson Downtown	52	★★	$$$–
138	Connecticut Woodley Guest House	31	★	$$+

— ## The Best Deals in Town

Having listed the nicest rooms in town, let's switch priorities and rank Washington's best rooms in terms of quality *and* value. As before, the rankings are made without consideration of location or the availability of restaurant(s), recreational facilities, entertainment, and/or amenities.

Listed below are the top room buys for the money, regardless of location or star classification, based on averaged rack rates. Note that sometimes a suite can cost less than a hotel room.

The Best Deals in Town

Rank	Hotel	Room Value Rating	Room Star Rating	Cost ($ = $30)
1	Inn at Foggy Bottom	99	★★★★	$$$–
2	Sheraton Suites Alexandria	80	★★★★½	$$$+
3	Loew's L'Enfant Plaza	79	★★★★½	$$$+
4	Morrison-Clark Inn	79	★★★★½	$$$+
5	Holiday Inn Bethesda	78	★★★½	$$+
6	Best Western Old Colony Inn	74	★★★	$$–
7	State Plaza Hotel	73	★★★½	$$+
8	St. James	69	★★★★½	$$$$–
9	Washington Court Hotel	68	★★★★	$$$+
10	Courtyard Landover	68	★★★½	$$$–
11	Ramada Hotel Tysons Corner	68	★★★½	$$$–
12	Latham Hotel Georgetown	67	★★★★	$$$+
13	River Inn	66	★★★★	$$$+
14	Ramada Hotel Bethesda	66	★★★½	$$$–
15	Ramada Inn Downtown	66	★★★	$$+
16	Sheraton Carlton	63	★★★★½	$$$$+
17	Washington Vista Hilton	61	★★★★½	$$$$+
18	Grand Hotel of Washington	60	★★★★★	$$$$$+
19	Ritz-Carlton Pentagon City	59	★★★★★	$$$$$+
20	Sheraton Premiere Tysons Corner	59	★★★★½	$$$$+
21	Hotel Lombardy	59	★★★½	$$$
22	Days Inn Alexandria	58	★★★★	$$$$–
23	Doubletree Hotel Pentagon City	58	★★★★	$$$$–
24	Ramada Renaissance	58	★★★½	$$$+
25	Georgetown Dutch Inn	55	★★★½	$$$+
26	Quality Hotel Central	55	★★★½	$$$+

The Best Deals in Town (continued)

Rank	Hotel	Room Value Rating	Room Star Rating	Cost ($ = $30)
27	Sheraton Crystal City	55	★★★½	$$$+
28	Hotel Anthony	54	★★★	$$$–
29	Kalorama Guest House	54	★★★	$$+
30	Sheraton National Hotel	53	★★★½	$$$+
31	Savoy Suites Hotel	53	★★★	$$$–
32	Courtyard Alexandria	52	★★★½	$$$+
33	Comfort Inn Landmark	51	★★½	$$
34	Quality Inn College Park	51	★★½	$$
35	Park Hyatt (suites)	50	★★★★★	$$$$$$+
36	Stouffer Mayflower Hotel	50	★★★★½	$$$$$+
37	Guest Quarters New Hampshire Ave.	50	★★★★	$$$$+
38	One Washington Circle Hotel	50	★★★★	$$$$+
39	Park Hyatt (standard rooms)	49	★★★★½	$$$$$+
40	Canterbury Hotel	49	★★★★	$$$$+
41	Channel Inn Hotel	49	★★★½	$$$$–
42	Hampton Inn Alexandria	49	★★★	$$$–
43	Marriott Tysons Corner	48	★★★★	$$$$$–
44	Best Western New Hampshire Suites	48	★★★	$$$–
45	Holiday Inn Georgetown	48	★★★	$$$–
46	Holiday Inn Silver Spring	48	★★★	$$+
47	Guest Quarters Pennsylvania Ave.	47	★★★★	$$$$$–
48	Best Western Skyline Inn	47	★★★	$$$
49	Holiday Inn Chevy Chase	47	★★★	$$$
50	Radisson Park Terrace	46	★★★½	$$$$–
51	Tabard Inn	46	★★★½	$$$$–
52	Days Inn Camp Springs	46	★★½	$$+
53	Capitol Hilton	45	★★★★½	$$$$$$–
54	Embassy Row Hotel	45	★★★★	$$$$$
55	Radisson Plaza at Mark Center	45	★★★½	$$$$
56	Holiday Inn Ballston	45	★★★	$$$+
57	Willard Inter-Continental	44	★★★★½	$$$$$$
58	Morrison House	44	★★★★	$$$$$
59	Residence Inn Bethesda	44	★★★★	$$$$$
60	Courtyard Crystal City	44	★★★½	$$$$
61	Carlyle Suites Hotel	44	★★★	$$$
62	DuPont Plaza Hotel	43	★★★	$$$+
63	Holiday Inn Old Town	43	★★★	$$$+
64	Watergate Hotel	42	★★★★½	$$$$$$+

The Best Deals in Town (continued)

Rank	Hotel	Room Value Rating	Room Star Rating	Cost ($ = $30)
65	Embassy Suites Crystal City	42	★★★★	$$$$$+
66	Hyatt Regency Bethesda	42	★★★★	$$$$$+
67	Hampshire Hotel	42	★★★½	$$$$
68	Bellevue Hotel	42	★★★	$$$
69	Embassy Square Suites	42	★★★	$$$+
70	Phoenix Park Hotel	42	★★★	$$$
71	Comfort Inn Van Dorn	42	★★½	$$+
72	Holiday Inn Camp Springs	42	★★½	$$+
73	Adams Inn	42	★★	$$+
74	Henley Park Hotel	41	★★★★	$$$$$+
75	Westin ANA Hotel	40	★★★★½	$$$$$$$−
76	Embassy Suites Chevy Chase	40	★★★★	$$$$$+
77	Stouffer Concourse Hotel	40	★★★★	$$$$$+
78	Marriott Crystal City	39	★★★★	$$$$$$−
79	Washington Marriott Hotel	39	★★★★	$$$$$$−
80	Holiday Inn Eisenhower Metro	39	★★★	$$$+
81	Holiday Inn Governor's House	39	★★★	$$$+
82	Days Inn Connecticut Ave.	39	★★½	$$+
83	Econo Lodge West Arlington	39	★★½	$$+
84	Embassy Suites Alexandria	39	★★★★	$$$$$$−
85	Pullman Highland Hotel	38	★★★½	$$$$$−
86	Quality Inn Iwo Jima	38	★★½	$$$−
87	Windsor Park Hotel	37	★★½	$$+
88	Jefferson Hotel	36	★★★★½	$$$$$$$+
89	Sheraton City Centre	36	★★★★	$$$$$$+
90	Best Western Tysons Westpark	36	★★½	$$$−
91	Days Inn Downtown	36	★★½	$$$−
92	Manor Inn Bethesda	36	★★½	$$$−
93	J. W. Marriott Hotel	35	★★★★	$$$$$$+
94	Wyndham Bristol Hotel	35	★★★½	$$$$$+
95	Holiday Inn National Airport	35	★★★	$$$$−
96	Comfort Inn Ballston	35	★★½	$$$−
97	Embassy Inn	35	★★½	$$$−
98	Quality Hotel Silver Spring	35	★★½	$$$−
99	Econo Lodge National Airport	35	★★	$$
100	Marriott Crystal Gateway	34	★★★★	$$$$$$$−
101	Holiday Inn Thomas Circle	34	★★★	$$$$−
102	Howard Johnson National Airport	33	★★★	$$$$−

The Best Deals in Town *(continued)*

Rank	Hotel	Room Value Rating	Room Star Rating	Cost ($ = $30)
103	Quality Hotel Capitol Hill	33	★★½	$$$
104	Quality Hotel Downtown	33	★★½	$$$+
105	Embassy Suites Downtown	32	★★★★	$$$$$$$–
106	Georgetown Inn	32	★★★★	$$$$$$$
107	Holiday Inn Crowne Plaza Metro Center	32	★★★★	$$$$$$$–
108	Marriott Hotel Key Bridge	32	★★★½	$$$$$$–
109	Ramada Renaissance Techworld	32	★★★½	$$$$$$–
110	Comfort Inn Downtown	32	★★★	$$$$
111	Omni Shoreham Hotel	32	★★★	$$$$+
112	Center City Hotel	32	★★½	$$$–
113	Grand Hyatt Washington	31	★★★★	$$$$$$$+
114	Hay-Adams Hotel	31	★★★★	$$$$$$$+
115	Sheraton Washington Hotel	31	★★★★	$$$$$$$
116	Hyatt Regency Crystal City	31	★★★½	$$$$$$–
117	Best Western Rosslyn Westpark	31	★★½	$$$+
118	Normandy Inn	31	★★½	$$$+
119	Hyatt Regency Capitol Hill	30	★★★½	$$$$$$+
120	Ramada Hotel Old Town	30	★★★	$$+
121	Holiday Inn Key Bridge	30	★★½	$$$+
122	Holiday Inn Capitol	29	★★★	$$$$$–
123	Best Western Arlington Inn	29	★★	$$+
124	Holiday Inn Central	28	★★★	$$$$$–
125	Marriott Hotel Bethesda	28	★★★	$$$$$–
126	Days Hotel Crystal City	28	★★½	$$$$–
127	Four Seasons Hotel	27	★★★★½	$$$$$$$$$$–
128	Ritz-Carlton Hotel	27	★★★★	$$$$$$$$+
129	Hotel Washington	27	★★★½	$$$$$$+
130	American Inn of Bethesda	27	★★	$$$–
131	Hyatt Arlington	26	★★★	$$$$$+
132	Ramada Inn Alexandria	26	★★½	$$$$–
133	Harrington Hotel	26	★★	$$$–
134	Howard Johnson Downtown	26	★★	$$$–
135	Omni Georgetown Hotel	24	★★★	$$$$$+
136	Madison	22	★★★½	$$$$$$$+
137	Washington Hilton	22	★★★½	$$$$$$$+
138	Connecticut Woodley Guest House	10	★	$$+

The Best Deals on Four- and Five-Star Rooms

Rank	Hotel	Room Value Rating	Room Star Rating	Cost ($ = $30)
1	Inn at Foggy Bottom	99	★★★★	$$$–
2	Sheraton Suites Alexandria	80	★★★★½	$$$+
3	Loew's L'Enfant Plaza	79	★★★★½	$$$+
4	Morrison-Clark Inn	79	★★★★½	$$$+
5	St. James	69	★★★★½	$$$$–
6	Washington Court Hotel	68	★★★★	$$$+
7	Latham Hotel Georgetown	67	★★★★	$$$+
8	River Inn	66	★★★★	$$$+
9	Sheraton Carlton	63	★★★★½	$$$$+
10	Washington Vista Hilton	61	★★★★½	$$$$+
11	Grand Hotel of Washington	60	★★★★★	$$$$$+
12	Ritz-Carlton Pentagon City	59	★★★★★	$$$$$+
13	Sheraton Premiere Tysons Corner	59	★★★★½	$$$$+
14	Days Inn Alexandria	58	★★★★	$$$$–
15	Doubletree Hotel Pentagon City	58	★★★★	$$$$–
16	Park Hyatt (suites)	50	★★★★★	$$$$$$+
17	Stouffer Mayflower Hotel	50	★★★★½	$$$$$+
18	Guest Quarters New Hampshire Ave.	50	★★★★	$$$$+
19	One Washington Circle Hotel	50	★★★★	$$$$+
20	Park Hyatt (standard rooms)	49	★★★★½	$$$$$+
21	Canterbury Hotel	49	★★★★	$$$$+
22	Marriott Tysons Corner	48	★★★★	$$$$$–
23	Guest Quarters Pennsylvania Ave.	47	★★★★	$$$$$–
24	Capitol Hilton	45	★★★★½	$$$$$$–
25	Embassy Row Hotel	45	★★★★	$$$$$
26	Willard Inter-Continental	44	★★★★½	$$$$$$
27	Morrison House	44	★★★★	$$$$$
28	Residence Inn Bethesda	44	★★★★	$$$$$
29	Watergate Hotel	42	★★★★½	$$$$$$+
30	Embassy Suites Crystal City	42	★★★★	$$$$$+
31	Hyatt Regency Bethesda	42	★★★★	$$$$$+
32	Henley Park Hotel	41	★★★★	$$$$$+
33	Westin ANA Hotel	40	★★★★½	$$$$$$$–
34	Embassy Suites Chevy Chase	40	★★★★	$$$$$+
35	Stouffer Concourse Hotel	40	★★★★	$$$$$+
36	Marriott Crystal City	39	★★★★	$$$$$$–
37	Washington Marriott Hotel	39	★★★★	$$$$$$–
38	Jefferson Hotel	36	★★★★½	$$$$$$$+

The Best Deals on Four- and Five-Star Rooms *(continued)*

Rank	Hotel	Room Value Rating	Room Star Rating	Cost ($ = $30)
39	Sheraton City Centre	36	★★★★	$$$$$$+
40	J. W. Marriott Hotel	35	★★★★	$$$$$$+
41	Marriott Crystal Gateway	34	★★★★	$$$$$$$–
42	Embassy Suites Downtown	32	★★★★	$$$$$$$–
43	Georgetown Inn	32	★★★★	$$$$$$$
44	Holiday Inn Crowne Plaza Metro Center	32	★★★★	$$$$$$$–
45	Grand Hyatt Washington	31	★★★★	$$$$$$$+
46	Hay-Adams Hotel	31	★★★★	$$$$$$$+
47	Sheraton Washington Hotel	31	★★★★	$$$$$$$
48	Four Seasons Hotel	27	★★★★½	$$$$$$$$$$$–
49	Ritz-Carlton Hotel	27	★★★★	$$$$$$$$+

The Best Deals on Three-Star Rooms

Rank	Hotel	Room Value Rating	Room Star Rating	Cost ($ = $30)
1	Holiday Inn Bethesda	78	★★★½	$$+
2	Best Western Old Colony Inn	74	★★★	$$–
3	State Plaza Hotel	73	★★★½	$$+
4	Courtyard Landover	68	★★★½	$$$–
5	Ramada Hotel Tysons Corner	68	★★★½	$$$–
6	Ramada Hotel Bethesda	66	★★★½	$$$–
7	Ramada Inn Downtown	66	★★★	$$+
8	Hotel Lombardy	59	★★★½	$$$
9	Ramada Renaissance	58	★★★½	$$$+
10	Georgetown Dutch Inn	55	★★★½	$$$+
11	Quality Hotel Central	55	★★★½	$$$+
12	Sheraton Crystal City	55	★★★½	$$$+
13	Hotel Anthony	54	★★★	$$$–
14	Kalorama Guest House	54	★★★	$$+
15	Sheraton National Hotel	53	★★★½	$$$+
16	Savoy Suites Hotel	53	★★★	$$$–
17	Courtyard Alexandria	52	★★★½	$$$+
18	Channel Inn Hotel	49	★★★½	$$$$–
19	Hampton Inn Alexandria	49	★★★	$$$–

The Best Deals on Three-Star Rooms (continued)

Rank	Hotel	Room Value Rating	Room Star Rating	Cost ($ = $30)
20	Best Western New Hampshire Suites	48	★★★	$$$–
21	Holiday Inn Georgetown	48	★★★	$$$–
22	Holiday Inn Silver Spring	48	★★★	$$+
23	Best Western Skyline Inn	47	★★★	$$$
24	Holiday Inn Chevy Chase	47	★★★	$$$
25	Radisson Park Terrace	46	★★★½	$$$$–
26	Tabard Inn	46	★★★½	$$$$–
27	Radisson Plaza at Mark Center	45	★★★½	$$$$
28	Holiday Inn Ballston	45	★★★	$$$+
29	Courtyard Crystal City	44	★★★½	$$$$
30	Carlyle Suites Hotel	44	★★★	$$$
31	DuPont Plaza Hotel	43	★★★	$$$+
32	Holiday Inn Old Town	43	★★★	$$$+
33	Hampshire Hotel	42	★★★½	$$$$
34	Bellevue Hotel	42	★★★	$$$
35	Embassy Square Suites	42	★★★	$$$+
36	Phoenix Park Hotel	42	★★★	$$$
37	Holiday Inn Eisenhower Metro	39	★★★	$$$+
38	Holiday Inn Governor's House	39	★★★	$$$+
39	Pullman Highland Hotel	38	★★★½	$$$$$–
40	Wyndham Bristol Hotel	35	★★★½	$$$$$+
41	Holiday Inn National Airport	35	★★★	$$$$–
42	Holiday Inn Thomas Circle	34	★★★	$$$$–
43	Howard Johnson National Airport	33	★★★	$$$$–
44	Marriott Hotel Key Bridge	32	★★★½	$$$$$$–
45	Ramada Renaissance Techworld	32	★★★½	$$$$$$–
46	Comfort Inn Downtown	32	★★★	$$$$
47	Omni Shoreham Hotel	32	★★★	$$$$+
48	Hyatt Regency Crystal City	31	★★★½	$$$$$$–
49	Hyatt Regency Capitol Hill	30	★★★½	$$$$$$+
50	Ramada Hotel Old Town	30	★★★	$$+
51	Holiday Inn Capitol	29	★★★	$$$$$–
52	Holiday Inn Central	28	★★★	$$$$$–
53	Marriott Hotel Bethesda	28	★★★	$$$$$–
54	Hotel Washington	27	★★★½	$$$$$$+
55	Hyatt Arlington	26	★★★	$$$$$+
56	Omni Georgetown Hotel	24	★★★	$$$$$+
57	Madison	22	★★★½	$$$$$$$$+
58	Washington Hilton	22	★★★½	$$$$$$$$+

The Best Deals on Two-Star Rooms

Rank	Hotel	Room Value Rating	Room Star Rating	Cost ($ = $30)
1	Comfort Inn Landmark	51	★★½	$$
2	Quality Inn College Park	51	★★½	$$
3	Days Inn Camp Springs	46	★★½	$$+
4	Comfort Inn Van Dorn	42	★★½	$$+
5	Holiday Inn Camp Springs	42	★★½	$$+
6	Adams Inn	42	★★	$$+
7	Days Inn Connecticut Ave.	39	★★½	$$+
8	Econo Lodge West Arlington	39	★★½	$$+
9	Quality Inn Iwo Jima	38	★★½	$$$–
10	Windsor Park Hotel	37	★★½	$$+
11	Best Western Tysons Westpark	36	★★½	$$$–
12	Days Inn Downtown	36	★★½	$$$–
13	Manor Inn Bethesda	36	★★½	$$$–
14	Comfort Inn Ballston	35	★★½	$$$–
15	Embassy Inn	35	★★½	$$$–
16	Quality Hotel Silver Spring	35	★★½	$$$–
17	Econo Lodge National Airport	35	★★	$$
18	Quality Hotel Capitol Hill	33	★★½	$$$
19	Quality Hotel Downtown	33	★★½	$$$+
20	Center City Hotel	32	★★½	$$$–
21	Best Western Rosslyn Westpark	31	★★½	$$$+
22	Normandy Inn	31	★★½	$$$+
23	Holiday Inn Key Bridge	30	★★½	$$$+
24	Best Western Arlington Inn	29	★★	$$+
25	Days Hotel Crystal City	28	★★½	$$$$–
26	American Inn of Bethesda	27	★★	$$$–
27	Ramada Inn Alexandria	26	★★½	$$$$–
28	Harrington Hotel	26	★★	$$$–
29	Howard Johnson Downtown	26	★★	$$$–

PART FOUR: Getting Around Washington: Cabs, Cars, and the Metro

Driving Your Car
A Really Bad Idea

—— Traffic Hot Spots

Here's some bad news for anyone considering driving to Our Nation's Capital: Washington is legendary for its epic traffic congestion. Let's start with the Capital Beltway (I-495 and I-95), which encircles the city through the Virginia and Maryland suburbs: It's guaranteed to be logjammed on weekdays from 7 A.M. to 9:30 A.M. and again from 3 P.M. to 7 P.M. Unremitting suburban growth and geography confound the best efforts of traffic engineers to alleviate the congestion.

Inside the Beltway, the situation only gets worse. The few bridges that connect Washington and Virginia across the Potomac River are rush-hour bottlenecks. Interstates 66 and 395 in Virginia have restricted car-pool lanes inbound in the morning and outbound in the evening. Inside the District, Rock Creek Parkway becomes one-way during rush hour, and major thoroughfares such as Connecticut Avenue switch the direction of center lanes to match the predominant flow of traffic at different times of day. Downtown, the city's traffic circles can trap unwary motorists and reduce drivers to tears or profanity. Pierre L'Enfant's 18th-century grand plan of streets and avenues that intersect in traffic circles is a nightmare for 20th-century motorists.

First-time drivers to Washington should map out their routes in advance, avoid arriving and departing during rush hour, and then leave the car parked throughout their stay. Lunch-hour traffic can be equally ferocious, and don't think that weekends are immune from traffic snarls: Washington's popularity as a tourist mecca slows Beltway traffic to a crawl on Saturdays and Sundays in warm weather.

If there's any good news about driving in Washington, it's this: After evening rush hour subsides, getting around town by car is pretty easy.

Parking

If you ignore our advice about driving in Washington (we repeat: don't) and battle your way downtown by car, you'll find yourself stuck in one of those good news/bad news scenarios. The good news: There are plenty of places to park. The bad news: Virtually all the spaces are in parking garages that charge an arm and a leg. Figure on $12 a day or $4 an hour, minimum.

Think you can beat the system by finding street parking? Go ahead and try, but bring a lot of quarters—and plenty of patience. Most metered parking is restricted to two hours—not a long time if you're intent on exploring a museum or attending a business meeting. And D.C. cops are quick to issue tickets for expired meters. Also, a lot of legal spaces turn illegal during afternoon rush hour.

In popular residential neighborhoods such as Georgetown and Adams-Morgan, parking gets even worse at night. Unless you've got a residential parking permit—not likely if you're an out-of-town visitor—street parking is limited to from two to three hours, depending on the neighborhood. The parking permits are prominently displayed in the cars of area residents.

If you're tempted to park illegally, be warned: D.C. police are grimly efficient at whisking away cars parked in rush-hour zones, and the fines are hefty. Incredibly, there's free parking along the Mall beginning at 10 A.M. weekdays; the limit is three hours. Needless to say, competition for the spaces is fierce.

Riding the Metro
A Really Good Idea

—— A Clean, Safe Alternative

It should be clear by now that visitors who would prefer to spend their time doing something productive other than sit in traffic jams shouldn't drive in or around Washington. Thanks to Metrorail, visitors can park their cars and forget them.

Five color-coded subway lines connect downtown Washington to the outer reaches of the city, and beyond to the Maryland and Virginia suburbs. It's a clean, safe, and efficient system that saves visitors time, money, and shoe leather as it whisks them around town. Visitors to Washington should use the Metro as their primary mode of transportation.

The trains are well maintained and quiet, with carpeting, cushioned seats, and air conditioning. The stations are modern, well lighted, and usually spotless, and are uniformly constructed with high, arching ceilings paneled with sound-absorbing, lozenge-shaped concrete panels. The wide-open look of the stations has been criticized as sterile and monotonous, but the design may explain why the Metro has maintained a crime-free reputation: There's no place for bad guys to hide. In addition, the entire system is monitored by closed-circuit TV cameras, and each car is equipped with passenger-to-operator intercoms, as are rail platforms and elevators. And cars and stations are nearly graffiti-free.

The Metro (nobody calls it Metrorail) transports more than half a million passengers a day along 90 miles of track and through 74 stations. When the system is completed early in the next century, the Metro will boast 83 stations connected by 103 miles of track. It's a world-class engineering marvel.

Trains operate so frequently that carrying a schedule is unnecessary. During peak hours (weekdays 5:30 A.M. to 9:30 A.M. and 3 P.M. to 7 P.M.), trains enter the stations every six minutes. During off-peak hours, the interval increases to an average of 12 minutes; it can go to 15 minutes on weekends. To maintain the intervals throughout the year, the Metro adds and deletes trains to compensate for holidays and peak tourist season. Hours of operation are 5:30 A.M. to midnight weekdays, and 8 A.M. to midnight on weekends and holidays.

How to Ride the Metro

Finding the Stations

Many (but, unfortunately, not all) street signs in Washington indicate the direction and number of blocks to the nearest Metro station. Station entrances are identified by brown columns or pylons with an "M" on all four sides and a combination of colored stripes in red, yellow, orange, green, or blue that indicate the line or lines serving that station. Since most stations are underground, users usually descend on escalators to the mezzanine or ticketing part of the station. At above-ground and elevated stations outside of downtown Washington, the mezzanine is most often on the ground level. At the kiosk located there, pick up a system map with quick directions on how to use the Metro.

Purchasing a Farecard

Next comes the tricky part: You must determine your destination and your fare ahead of time because the ticketing system is automated. Walk up to the color-coded map located in each mezzanine and locate the station nearest your ultimate destination. Then look on the bottom of the map, where an alphabetized list of stations reveals both the fare (peak and off-peak) and the estimated travel time to each. Peak fares, usually more expensive, are in effect from 5:30 A.M. to 9:30 A.M. and 3 P.M. to 7 P.M. weekdays. Unless you're traveling from a suburban station to downtown, or from one suburb to another, the one-way fare is typically a buck. One last note: Before you walk away from the map, make a mental note of the last station of the train that you plan to board, even though you're probably not traveling that far. The name of your train's final destination is the key to locating the right platform, the one whose trains are going the right direction.

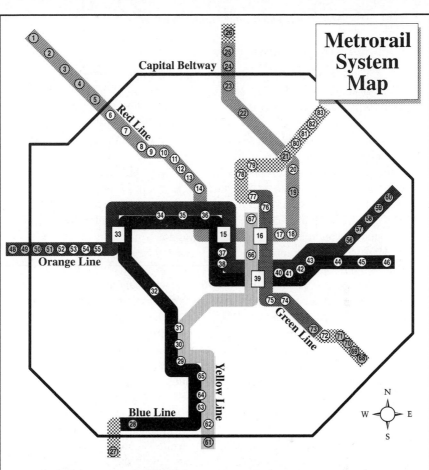

Metrorail System Map

Capital Beltway

N
W — E
S

Red Line
Orange Line
Green Line
Yellow Line
Blue Line

Red Line ▨▨▨
Wheaton/Shady Grove
1. Shady Grove
2. Rockville
3. Twinbrook
4. White Flint
5. Grosvenor
6. Medical Center
7. Bethesda
8. Friendship Heights
9. Tenleytown - AU
10. Van Ness - UDC
11. Cleveland Park
12. Woodley Park - Zoo
13. Dupont Circle
14. Farragut North
15. Metro Center
16. Gallery Place, Chinatown
17. Judiciary Square
18. Union Station
19. Rhode Island Ave
20. Brookland - CUA
21. Fort Totten
22. Takoma
23. Silver Spring
24. Forest Glen
25. Wheaton
26. Glenmont

Blue Line ▮▮▮
Addison Road/Van Dorn Street
27. Franconia - Springfield
28. Van Dorn Street
29. Pentagon City
30. Pentagon City
31. Pentagon
32. Arlington Cemetery
33. Rosslyn
34. Foggy Bottom - GWU
35. Farragut West
36. McPherson Square
37. Federal Triangle
38. Smithsonian
39. L'Enfant Plaza
40. Federal Center SW
41. Capitol South
42. Eastern Market
43. Potomac Ave
44. Stadium - Armory
45. Benning Road
46. Capitol Heights
47. Addison Road

Orange Line ▨▨▨
New Carrollton/Vienna
48. Vienna
49. Dunn Loring
50. West Falls Church
51. East Falls Church
52. Ballston
53. Virginia Square - GMU
54. Clarendon
55. Court House
56. Minnesota Ave
57. Deanwood
58. Cheverly
59. Landover
60. New Carrollton

Yellow Line ‖‖‖‖‖
Mt. Vernon Square - UDC/Huntington
61. Huntington
62. Eisenhower Ave
63. King Street
64. Braddock Road
65. National Airport
66. Archives - Navy Memorial
67. Mt. Vernon Square - UDC

Green Line ▮▮▮
U Street - Cardozo/Anacostia
68. Branch Ave
69. Suitland
70. Naylor Road
71. Southern Ave
72. Congress Heights
73. Anacostia
74. Navy Yard
75. Waterfront
76. Shaw - Howard University
77. U Street - Cardozo
78. Columbia Heights
79. Georgia Ave Petworth
80. West Hyattsville
81. Prince George's Plaza
82. College Park - U of Md
83. Greenbelt

▨▨ **Future**

◯ **Stations -** all day parking

◯ **Stations -** no all day parking

☐ **Transfer stations**

Farecard Vending Machines

Those big vending machines lining the walls of the mezzanine don't dispense sodas. Instead, they swallow your money and issue fare-cards with magnetic stripes that get you in and — *this is crucial* — *out* of Metro stations. Once you get your card, hang onto it.

Buying a farecard works like this: Walk up to the farecard vending machine and look for the numeral "1" on the left side at eye level. (We'll call this **Step 1**.) This is where you insert bills and/or coins. If your destination is, say, a $1 fare, and you're making a round trip, insert $2 into the machine. As the money slides in, look at the middle of the machine for the numeral "2" (**Step 2**), where a digital readout registers the amount you've shoved into the contraption.

Machines that accept paper money invariably screw up, and these machines are no exception. They often spit back bills they don't like, so try smoothing wrinkled bills before inserting them and choose new, unfrayed greenbacks over bills that are worn. Inserting coins is nearly foolproof, but not very practical if you're riding the Metro a lot.

Our advice is to cut down on using these infernal machines as much as possible by plugging in $5, $10, or even $20 at once, which means you're buying a ticket that can last several days or longer. The comput-erized turnstiles print the remaining value on the farecard after each use, which lets you know when it's time to buy a new one. A major drawback, of course, is the possibility of losing the farecard while it's still worth a few bucks. If you value your time at all, take the risk.

Below the digital readout at Step 2 are white "+" and "−" buttons that let you adjust the readout to the exact fare you wish to purchase. For example, if your round-trip fare is $2 and you inserted a $5 bill, toggle the readout from $5 down to $2 by repeatedly pushing the "−" button. (If you overshoot, push the "+" button to increase the value.) Then look to the right side of the machine and the numeral "3" (**Step 3**), and press the button that reads "Press for Farecard." If all goes well (and, in all fairness, it usually does), out pops your farecard and your change — in this case, three dollars in quarters; the machines don't dispense bills. We told you to buy a $5 farecard.

The farther out you get from downtown, the fewer number of fare-card machines line the walls of the mezzanines — which usually isn't a problem at these less-busy stations. However, many of these suburban machines will only accept coins, $1 bills, and $5 bills — a real pain if all you've got is twenties. But all is not lost: For a problem like this, or for balky machines that won't take your money, or any problem at all,

Bronze pylons *(top)* identify Metro stations; colored stripes at top show the line or lines served by that station.

Metro systems and neighborhood maps *(bottom)* are located in the mezzanine of each station.

Rush-hour and non-rush-hour fares are listed alphabetically at each station's kiosk (*(top)*).

Automated Farecard machines *(bottom)* are located in the mezzanine of each station.

Step 1 *(top):* To purchase a farecard, insert bills and/or coins.

Step 2 *(bottom left):* Use toggle switches to add or decrease the farecard's value. Plug in enough cash to buy at least a round-trip ticket (or more, if desired).

Step 3 *(bottom right):* Press the "Push for Farecard" button; the farecard appears at the "Used Farecard Trade-In" slot.

Automated faregates, which control access in and out of spacious Metro stations, are located near the kiosk. The woman pictured here is exiting the station.

When entering *or* exiting, insert the farecard (face up with the magnetic
stripe on the right) into the slot on the front of the faregate *(top)*.
The farecard reappears at the top of the faregate *(bottom)*; remove it and
the faregate opens.
Note: Remember to hang on to the farecard—you need it to exit the
system.

When the value of a farecard drops below $1, trade it
in for a new one at a Farecard machine *(top)*.
Emergency intercoms *(bottom)* are located on all
station platforms.

help is only a few steps away at the kiosk located at each station near the faregate. Inside is a breathing human being who will help. Don't be shy.

One last warning: If the farecard machine accepts $20 bills, keep in mind that the maximum amount of change the machine can spit out is $4.95—which means you're stuck buying a farecard with a minimum value of $15.05. Unfortunately, this information isn't printed on the vending machine. If that's a bit more than you planned to shell out, step over to the kiosk and ask for change.

Entering the Station

With your farecard firmly in hand, you are now authorized to enter the Metro system. Hold the card in your right hand with the brown magnetic stripe facing up and on the right. Walk up to one of the waist-high faregates with the green light and white arrow near the kiosk (*not* the faregates that read "Do Not Enter"—they are for passengers exiting the station) and insert your card into the slot, where it is slurped into the bowels of the Metro. As the gate opens, walk through and grab your card as it is regurgitated from the slot at the top of the gate. All this happens in less than a second. Place the farecard in a safe place; *if you lose it, you must pay the maximum fare when you exit.*

Finding the Train Platform

Once you're past the faregate, look for signs with arrows and the name of your intended line's end station that point toward the platform where your train will arrive. Depending on whether you're at an underground or above-ground station, either ascend or descend on an escalator or stairs to the train platform. You can reconfirm that you're on the correct side of the platform by reading the list of stations printed on the pylon located there and finding your destination. If you're at the last station on a line, this isn't a problem; departing trains go in one direction only. Stand in the red-tiled area to wait for the next train.

Boarding the Train

As a train approaches an underground station, lights embedded in the floor along the granite edge of the platform begin flashing. As the train comes out of the tunnel, look for a sign over the front windshield that states the train's destination and line (blue, red, green, orange, or yellow). The destination, but not the color, is also shown on the side of the train. Double-check to make sure the approaching train is the one you want.

If it's the right train, approach the doors, but stand clear to let departing passengers exit the train. Then move smartly; the train stops for only a few seconds, then chimes will indicate that the doors are about to close. If you're rushing to catch a train and hear the chimes, don't attempt to board. Wait for the next train.

Inside, take a seat, or if you're a first-time Metro user, study the system map located near the doors. The trains all have real operators who announce the next station over a PA system and give information for transferring to other lines (sometimes you can even hear them over the din). It's better to study the map and read the signs mounted on the cavernous station walls at each stop.

Exiting the Station

As the train enters your station, move toward the doors. When you step off the train, look for stairs or escalators on the platform and walk toward them. Some stations have two exits, but the signs on the walls of the stations aren't always clear about where each exit goes. If you know which exit you want (for example, most tourists want the Mall exit at the Smithsonian station, not Independence Avenue), look for that sign and follow the arrow.

At the top of the escalator or stairs, walk toward the mezzanine area, get your farecard ready, and repeat the same procedure you used to enter the Metro system (card in right hand, magnetic stripe up and on the right, insert in slot). If you bought exact fare, the gate will open and a little sign will flash "Exact Fare." You're on your way. If your farecard still has money left on it, it pops up as the gate opens and the sign flashes "Take Farecard." Do same; exit station.

If your farecard doesn't have enough value to cover your trip, the gate won't open and the card will pop back out. You need to take it to an "Exitfare" machine somewhere just behind you. (Invariably 10 people are lined up behind you when this happens, creating the equivalent of a minor Beltway backup.) The reddish-colored exitfare machines look like their brothers, the farecard machines. Insert your card and immediately the digital readout displays the exact amount of moolah it needs so you can exit the station. (Don't make my mistake: The machine asked for $.40 and I stuck a $5 bill into it. I got $4.60 in change back.) Plug in the coins; the farecard reappears; grab it; insert same into the faregate, which swallows it forever and sets you free.

Changing from One Line to Another

Sooner or later — probably sooner — you will need to transfer from one Metro line to another. Metro Center is the Big Enchilada of the transfer stations, where the red, orange, and blue lines converge in downtown Washington. Other transfer stations that tourists are likely to hit are Gallery Place (red, yellow, and green), L'Enfant Plaza (yellow, blue, orange, green), Rosslyn (orange and blue), and Pentagon (yellow and blue).

To transfer, you don't use your farecard. Simply exit your train, take the escalator to the correct platform, and reboard. Try to listen to the PA system as your train enters the station: The conductor recites where the different lines are located in the approaching station (for example, "Transfer to the red line on the lower level"). If you can't hear the conductor's instructions, look for the color-coded pylons with arrows that point toward the platforms, and look for the one with your destination listed on it.

The Gallery Place–Chinatown station is especially complicated. Frequently, you're routed down and up escalators to reach your platform. Keep your eyes up for signs overhead that state reassuring messages such as "Red line — Wheaton Straight Ahead."

—— Metro Foibles and How to Cope

Boarding the Wrong Train

Unless you're concerned about being 10 minutes or so late for your meeting with President Clinton, boarding a train going in the wrong direction isn't a big problem. Simply get off at the next station, and if the platform is located between the tracks, wait for the next train running in the opposite direction and board it. If both sets of tracks run down the center of the station, take the escalator or stairs and cross the tracks to the other side, where you can catch the next train going the other way.

If you belatedly realize you boarded the wrong *color* train (say, the orange train to Vienna, Virginia, instead of the blue train to Van Dorn

Street), just get off at the next station, stay on the same platform, and take the next blue line train.

What to Do with Farecards Worth 50 Cents

After a few days in Washington, you may start accumulating fare-cards that don't have enough value for even a one-way trip. Don't throw them away! Instead, go up to a farecard vending machine in the mez-zanine and insert the old farecard into the slot on the right side of the machine marked "Trade In Used Farecard." Its value will be displayed on the digital readout at Step 2. Feed the machine money at Step 1, futz with the "+" and "−" buttons, and press the white "Push for Farecard" button to get a new card that includes the value on your old card.

If, Like Joe, You're Color Blind

Joe's heart sank the first time he tried to figure out Washington's Metro system: Like gazillions of other men, he is afflicted with red-green color blindness. To his eyes, the Metro's red and green lines look nearly identical in color, and the orange line looks a lot redder than it ought to. The only lines on the system map he could distinguish by color were the blue and yellow ones.

The solution is to fixate on the names of the stations that terminate lines. That way, the red line becomes the "Wheaton/Shady Grove" line, while the green line is the "U Street–Cardoza/Anacostia" line. It's harder, at first, but you'll end up with a distinct advantage over those who blindly follow colored signs: Knowing a line's end station is helpful when you've got to make a split-second decision on whether or not to board a train that's almost ready to depart the station. For instance, if you enter the Dupont Circle Metro and want to go to Union Station, you need to board the red line train heading toward Wheaton — not Shady Grove. So, sooner or later, you'll get familiar with the end stations anyway.

⸺ Discounts and Special Deals

Children.   Up to two children under age five can ride free when ac-companied by a paying passenger.

Senior Citizens and People with Disabilities.   Reduced fares are avail-able for qualified senior citizens. Call (202) 637-7000 for more information. People with disabilities can call (202) 962-1245 for information on reduced fares.

The Metro is a tourist attraction in its own right, featuring the longest escalator in the Western Hemisphere: the 230-foot, mezzanine-to-platform-level behemoth at the Wheaton Metro in suburban Maryland. If that's a little out of the way, the Dupont Circle Metro's escalator is nearly as long. If escalators terrify you or you are wheelchair-bound, all stations are equipped with elevators. But it's a good idea to check at a station kiosk and confirm that the elevator at your destination station is in operation, or call the elevator hot line at (202) 962-1825. To find the elevator, look for the wheelchair symbol near the station entrance.

Fare Discounts. If you plan on using the Metro more than once or twice a day, call Metrorail at (202) 637-7000 to find out what discounts are in effect during your visit. Usually, high-value farecards of $20 or more garner a 10% bonus, while a farecard worth $10 kicks in 5%. A Metrorail One-Day Pass lets you ride from 9:30 A.M. till midnight for $5 weekdays, and all day on weekends and holidays. Commuters can save money by purchasing passes that let them ride anywhere, anytime, for two weeks. Most discount passes are available at the Metro Center sales office.

— A Note about Metrobus

Washington's extensive bus system, known as Metrobus, serves Georgetown, downtown, and the suburbs. With 400 routes and more than 1,500 buses, Metrobus is also an extremely complicated system to figure out how to use. As a result, we feel that visitors to Washington should leave Metrobus to the commuters and stick to the Metro. For the few places that the Metro doesn't reach — notably Georgetown and Adams-Morgan — we recommend taking a cab.

Bus Transfers

If, despite our advice, you plan to transfer from the Metro to a Metrobus, get a free transfer from the machine located next to the escalator in the mezzanine of the station that you entered. You also need to pick up a bus transfer at some suburban stations to qualify for reduced parking fees on weekdays; look for signs in the station.

Taxis

Washington taxis are plentiful and relatively cheap. They're also strange. Instead of a metered fare system, fares are figured on a map that splits the city into 5 zones and 27 subzones. A zone map and fare chart are posted in all legal cabs, but probably won't mean much to first-time visitors — or most residents, for that matter. If you're concerned about getting ripped off, request a receipt before you start the ride. That way the driver knows he's got no defense in an overcharging claim.

The cab system has other quirks. Drivers can pick up other fares as long as the original passenger isn't taken more than five blocks out of the way of the original destination. That's good news if you're the second or third rider and it's raining; it's not so hot if you're the original passenger and trying to catch a train.

To eliminate the possibility of a ride in a dirty cab driven by a recent immigrant, who is as unfamiliar with the city as you are, stick to the major cab companies, which include Yellow Cab, Diamond, and Capitol. Some of the independents are illegal, yet still carry the markings and roof light of a legit cab. One way to spot a fly-by-night taxi is to check for hubcaps. If there aren't any, pass that one by.

People with Special Needs

Washington is one of the most accessible cities in the world for folks with disabilities. With the equal-opportunity federal government as the major employer in the area, Washington provides a good job market for disabled people. As a result, the service sector—bus drivers, waiters, ticket sellers, retail clerks, cab drivers, tour guides, and so on— are somewhat more attuned to the needs of people with disabilities than service-sector employees in other cities. It doesn't hurt that a number of organizations that lobby for handicapped people are headquartered in Washington.

The Metro, for example, was designed to meet federal standards for accessibility. As a result, the stations and trains provide optimal services to a wide array of people with special requirements. Elevators provide access to the mezzanine or ticketing areas, platform, and street level; call the Metro's 24-hour elevator hot line at (202) 962-1825 to check if the elevators at the stations you plan to use are operating.

The edge of the train platform is built with a 14-inch, smooth, light gray, granite strip that's different in texture from the rest of the platform flooring so that visually impaired passengers can detect the platform edge with a foot or cane. Flashing lights embedded in the granite strip alert hearing-impaired passengers that a train is entering the station. Handicapped-only parking spaces are placed close to station entrances. While purchasing a farecard is a strictly visual process, visually impaired passengers can go to the nearby kiosk for assistance. Priority seating for senior citizens and passengers with disabilities is located next to doors in all cars.

Visitors with disabilities who possess a transit ID from their home city can pick up a courtesy Metro ID that provides substantial fare discounts; the ID is good for a month. Go to Metro Headquarters, 600 5th Street, NW, from 8 A.M. to 4:30 P.M. weekdays to pick one up; call (202) 637-7000 for more information. If you want to ride the Metro to get there the nearest station is Gallery Place.

The Smithsonian and the National Park Service, agencies that run the lion's share of popular sights in Washington, offer top-notch services to folks with disabilities. Designated handicapped parking spaces are located along Jefferson Drive on the Mall, and museums are equipped with entrance ramps, barrier-free exhibits, elevator service to all floors, and accessible rest rooms and water fountains. Visually impaired visitors can pick up large-print brochures, cassette tapes and recorders, and raised-line drawings of museum artifacts at many Smithsonian museums. The National Air and Space Museum offers special tours that let visitors touch models and artifacts; call (202) 357-1400 for information.

Hearing-impaired visitors to the National Air and Space Museum can arrange tours with an interpreter by calling (202) 357-1400 (voice) or (202) 357-1696 (TDD). Public telephones in the museum are equipped with amplification, and the briefing room is equipped with audio loop. For a copy of the Smithsonian's *A Guide for Disabled Visitors,* call (202) 357-2700.

The Lincoln and Jefferson memorials and the Washington Monument are equipped to accommodate disabled visitors. Most sight-seeing attractions have elevators for seniors and others who want to avoid a lot of stair climbing. The White House, for example, has a special entrance on Pennsylvania Avenue for visitors arriving in wheelchairs, and White House guides usually allow visually handicapped visitors to touch some of the items described on tours.

Tourmobile offers a special van equipped with a wheelchair and scooter lift for handicapped visitors. The van visits all the regular sites on the tour; in fact, visitors can usually specify what sites they want to see in any order and the van will wait until they are finished touring. The service is the same price as the standard Tourmobile rate, $10.50 for adults and $5 for children. Call (202) 554-7020 at least a day in advance to reserve a van.

In spite of all the services available to disabled visitors, it's still a good idea to call ahead to any facility you plan to visit and confirm that services are in place and that the particular exhibit or gallery you wish to see is still available.

Foreign visitors to Washington who would like a tour conducted in their native language can contact the Guide Service of Washington. See page 229 in our chapter on touring.

PART FIVE: *Entertainment and Night Life*

Washington Night Life
More Than Lit-Up Monuments

Washington after-hours used to be an oxymoron. Public transportation set its clock by the bureaucracy, commuters had too far to go (and come back next morning) to stay out late, and the big expense account money was lavished on restaurants and buddy bars. Besides, Washingtonians suffered from a persistent cultural inferiority complex that had them running to buy tickets for touring companies while not-so-benignly neglecting homegrown theatrical troupes.

Nowadays, though, the joke about "Washington after-hours" being an oxymoron is just that: a joke. It's not that there's too little night life around, it's that there's too much. Or too many. Washington is a polyglot of big-city bustlers, yuppies, diplomats, immigrants, CEOs, and college students; and every one of those groups is trying to create, and then integrate, their own circles. The fact that many overlap, and others evolve sequentially, means you can dabble in a little of everything.

Washington's legitimate theatrical community is underestimated but excellent; ballet, Broadway, and cabaret are almost constant presences, opera less so but increasingly frequent. At least some of the racetracks are open year-round; there are major- and minor-league sports teams in whatever season (see the recreation chapter). And nightclubs come in as many flavors as their patrons: discos, live music venues, comedy showcases, country dance halls, specialty bars, sports bars, espresso bars, singles scenes, and "second scenes" for re-entering singles. There are even a couple of strip joints around for boys' night sentimentalists and brewpubs for beer connoisseurs.

Live entertainment in Washington can be divided into three categories: legitimate theater, comedy, and live rock/pop/jazz/country music. The 30 profiles of clubs that follow focus on live music, comedy clubs, discos/dance clubs, and noteworthy after-hours scenes because they generally require no advance planning. (In some cases, live music venues might sell out particular performances, so call ahead.) Nightly schedules of live music clubs, comedy clubs, and theatrical productions, as well as listings of piano rooms, opera companies, movie showtimes, etc., are printed in the *Washington Post* Friday "Weekend" section and the free Washington *City Paper.*

— Legitimate Theater

Washington boasts six major theatrical venues (ten if you count the Kennedy Center's five stages separately) and more than a half-dozen smaller residential and repertory companies, plus university theaters, small special-interest venues, and itinerant troupes. The Big Six are where national touring companies, classical musicians, and celebrity productions are most apt to show up, and have the most complete facilities for handicapped patrons. They are also likely to be the most expensive.

On any given night at the **Kennedy Center for the Performing Arts,** you might see the resident National Symphony Orchestra under Mstislav Rostropovich or a visiting philharmonic in the 2,500-seat Concert Hall, a straight drama or classic farce in the 1,100-seat Eisenhower Theater, and a Broadway musical, kabuki spectacular, or premiere cru ballet company in the 2,300-seat Opera House. The two smaller arenas, Terrace Theater and Theater Lab, share the third floor with the restaurant (which has a nice view if you can get it), and archives. Philip Johnson's steeply canted and gracious Terrace, a gift from the nation of Japan, houses experimental or cult-interest productions, specialty concerts, and showcases; in the Theater Lab, designed to accommodate the avant and cabaret, the semi-improvisational murder farce "Sheer Madness" is safely ensconced in its tenth year. The Kennedy Center is at Virginia and New Hampshire avenues, NW next to the Watergate; the closest subway station is Foggy Bottom. For tickets and information, call (202) 467-4600. The Kennedy Center also houses the American Film Institute, which nightly screens films, usually double bills, of particular historical and aesthetic value.

The **National Theater,** which was thoroughly, if a little showily, restored in Miami heat pastels a few years ago, is managed by the Shubert Organization, which not only books its touring Broadway productions there but more and more often uses it for pre-Broadway tryouts. The National is at 1321 Pennsylvania Avenue, NW, near the Federal Triangle or Metro Center subway stop; for tickets and information call (202) 628-6161.

The **Shakespeare Theater,** which moved in 1992 from its beloved but cramped home at the Folger Shakespeare Library into new digs in the grandly renovated Lansburg Building, now seats about 450. Each season it produces four classic plays, three by Shakespeare, and corrals at least a couple of stage or screen stars. Shakespeare Theater is at 450 Seventh Street, NW near the Gallery Place subway stop; for information call (202) 393-2700.

Ford's Theatre, where the balcony box in which Abraham Lincoln was shot remains draped in black (and spectrally inhabited, according to rumor), is a smallish (750) but comfy venue that hosts primarily family fare such as the annual production of Dickens' "Christmas Carol" and musicals and revues. Ford's is at 511 10th Street, NW (Metro Center subway); call (202) 347-4833.

The **Warner Theater,** which recently reopened after a two-year restoration marathon, is now a rococo delight; although it is emphasizing more legitimate theatrical bookings and musicals, it still occasionally harkens back to the days when it was one of the nicer small-concert venues for popular music. The Warner is at 13th and E streets, NW near Federal Triangle or Metro Center; for information call (202) 783-4000.

The tripartite **Arena Stage** is the most prestigious of Washington resident companies and was a prime factor in the rebirth of American regional theater. The Fichandler theater-in-the-round seats a little over 800; the Kreeger holds more than 500, and the tiny, pubbish (now coffee bar-ish) Old Vat Room seats fewer than 200. Though it likes to show off its versatility (a dizzying re-enactment of the Marx Brothers' "Coconuts" and the Flying Karamazov Brothers acting in "The Brothers Karamazov," for example), Arena is dedicated and fearless, producing Athol Fugard as well as Tennessee Williams. The Arena is at Sixth and Maine, SW — on the waterfront, which is also the subway station; call (202) 488-3300.

Although as noted, many of these professional productions can be pricey, and nominally sold out, the Ticket Place office in the Lisner Auditorium building at 21st and H streets, NW sells half-price seats for same-day shows and concerts. Ticket Place is open Tuesday–Friday from noon until 4 P.M. and Saturday from 11 A.M. until 5 P.M., when it also sells tickets for Sunday and Monday shows; call (202) 842-5387 for a list of available tickets. The Kennedy Center also sells a limited number of same-day tickets at half price and offers half-price tickets for students, seniors, and those with permanent disabilities. For information call (202) 467-4600. A limited number of standing-room passes at reduced prices and occasional returned seats may be available as well.

Washington also has its own "off-Broadway" of theaters in a cluster along 14th Street, NW, specializing in new and cutting-edge works. Among the most intriguing are **Source Theater Co.** (1835 14th Street, NW; (202) 462-1073), **Woolly Mammoth Theatre Co.** (1401 Church Street, NW; (202) 393-3939), and the **Studio Theater** (14th and P streets, NW; (202) 332-3300). Not merely "off off" but literally down in the basement is the tiny but cheerfully unflustered **Tavern Stage Theater Co.** Located in the back room of Kelley's Irish Times belowground pub on Capitol Hill (14 F Street, NW; (202) 547-0188), the theater puts on everything from original one-act plays to cabaret warhorses ("Jacques Brel . . ."), all to benefit local charities.

There are a handful of dinner theaters in the Washington area, but all are in the suburbs; if you're interested, check the Guide to the Lively Arts in the *Washington Post*'s Friday "Weekend" or Sunday "Show" sections, or look for a copy of *Washingtonian* magazine.

In general, Washington audiences have loosened their ties when it comes to theater attire; to some extent, the more "serious" a production is, the dressier the crowd, although jeans have become ubiquitous, particularly at the smaller, avant companies. Opening nights are often black tie (or "creative black tie"), but you can go as you are. And incidentally, many of the nicer restaurants near the big-ticket venues offer pre-theater menues at fixed (and bargain) prices; be sure to inquire.

—— Comedy in Washington

Washington is full of jokes — and that's the first one. Capital comedians divide very roughly into three generations and styles: the cabaret performers, those "Washington institutions" whose satires are usually musical and relatively gentle; the sketch and improvisational troupes from the post-Watergate "Saturday Night Live" era; and the stand-up artists who are the anti-establishment baby-busters — in some cases, the urban guerillas. The first two groups are almost unavoidably political; the stand-up comedians range from political podium to locker room.

The most famous of the cabaret comedians is PBS irregular **Mark Russell,** whose residency at the Omni Shoreham lasted about four senatorial terms, and who still plays several weeks at a time at Ford's Theatre every year. His slot at the Shoreham is filled these days by **"Mrs. Foggybottom,"** a.k.a Joan Cushing, who performs weekends in the Marquee Lounge (above the Woodley Park Metro at 2500 Calvert Street, NW; (202) 745-1023).

The most loyal opposition is offered by the **Capitol Steps,** a group of former and current Hill staffers who roast their own hosts by rewriting familiar songs with pun-ishing lyrics. In addition to entertaining at semi-official functions (which may be one reason why their barbs are a tad blunter than some satirists'), the Capitol Steps are a popular tourist attraction (which may be another) and perform every Saturday at Chelsea's nightclub in Georgetown (1055 Thomas Jefferson Street, NW; (202) 298-8222).

The most successful sketch-humor troupe in Washington is **Gross National Product,** an underground resistance movement that went aboveground after Reagan's election. Politics, especially the executive power structure, is its obsession: It skewers snoops, creeps, and veeps with gusto and, despite its long tenure, a hint of childish glee. Revues have titles like "Clintoons: The First Hundred Daze." Shows are about 90 minutes long and, since topicality is the name of the game, skits rise and fall with the state of the world. Performances are a third to one-half improvisation. GNP's Saturday night shows at the Bayou in Georgetown (Wisconsin and K streets, NW; (202) 783-7212) have become required recreation not only for unreconciled rat race victims but the newer, looser White House staff as well. GNP also operates one of Washington's more unique tour services, Scandal Tours, which takes sight-seers past such political landmarks as Gary Hart's town house and Fanne Fox's bathtub, the Tidal Basin.

ComedySportz, which is both improvisational and interactive, is part Rorshak test, part parlor game, part contortionists' convention in which audience members select the topics, the characters, and all the particulars; and troupe members then ad-lib the skits. Actually, it's like a cross between American Gladiators and hockey: archetypes on thin ice. ComedySportz plays Thursday through Saturday at the Little Cafe near the Courthouse Metro stop in Arlington (2039 Wilson Boulevard; (703) 471-5212).

Another intriguing sketch improv troupe is **Dropping the Cow,** which from its Georgetown church-annex home, lampoons other Washington entertainers as freely as it does political figures (weekends in the Georgetown Lutheran Church, Wisconsin and Q streets, NW; (202) 829-0529). Check newspaper listings for appearances by other, part-time groups.

The stand-up/sit-down revolution that made comedy clubs the discos of the '80s is now the Energizer bunny of the '90s. The clubs keep opening and opening: a franchise of the star-circuit **Evening at the Improv,** the cable-comic showcases **Headliners** (both profiled below), and the **Comedy Cafe** (1520 K Street, NW; (202) 638-5653)—even a couple of spots that hope to specialize in booking national African-American comedians. Hip gay and straight comedians of both sexes— Kate Clinton, Paula Poundstone, Dennis Miller, Judy Tenuta—draw so well in Washington that many are regularly booked not into clubs but into mid-sized theatrical venues.

In general, all clubs now follow a standard lineup: the opener, usually a local beginner who patters about 10 minutes and also serves as emcee (and who, especially on open mike night, may mean the difference between a smooth production and a free-for-all); the "featured act," either an experienced journeyman or perhaps a second-rank national or cable TV performer, who does about 30 minutes; and the headliner, usually somebody with Letterman or Leno credits or at least a cable special, who plays about an hour. Among other comedy showcases are the **Bethesda Theatre Cafe,** a Deco-era moviehouse that offers pizza, first-run movies, and on weekends irregularly scheduled comedy, jazz, and even theatrical concerts (near the Bethesda Metro at 7719 Wisconsin Avenue, Bethesda, MD; (301) 656-3337), the **Soul of Comedy** in the Howard Inn, an offshoot of a Howard University public TV showcase of African-American comedians (2225 Georgia Avenue, NW; (202) 562-7685), and the semi-floating **Garvin's Comedy Clubs** at area hotels. Many other nightclubs or restaurants offer comedy one night a week; check newspapers for specific listings.

Live Pop/Rock/Jazz

Credit for the boom in live-music clubs in the Washington area is split between the booming third-world community, used to later hours and different music styles; the large college and twentysomething population looking for entertainment, along with the thirtysomethings who started looking 10 years ago; the increasing number of those twenty- and thirty- and even fortysomethings who are living in the suburbs and don't want to go downtown for a good time; the more assertive gay and faux-prole communities seeking accommodation; and the fair number of stubborn musicians and underground entrepreneurs who have established venues and support networks for themselves and one another.

Jazz, of course, has a long history in Washington — in the '30s and '40s, the U Street/Howard Theater corridor was known as the "Black Broadway" and rivaled Harlem — but after years of declining audiences and bankrupted clubs, jazz is reviving all around the area; and the number of young jazz musicians, black and white, classical and contemporary, is remarkable.

Among the best places to hear jazz are **Blues Alley, One Step Down, Takoma Station Tavern,** and **Cafe Lautrec** (all profiled in the next section); **City Blues Cafe** (facing the Woodley Park stop at 2651 Connecticut Avenue, NW; (202) 232-2300); **Twins** (5516 Colorado Avenue, NW; (202) 882-2523); **Busara** (2340 Wisconsin Avenue, NW; (202) 337-2340); **Tradewinds** (1775 Rockville Pike, Rockville, MD; (301) 881-8855); **Brewbaker's** (6931 Arlington Road, Bethesda, MD (301) 907-2602); the **Blue Bayou Bistro** (7945 MacArthur Blvd., Cabin John, MD (301) 229-9774); **The Saloon** in Georgetown (3239 M Street, NW; (202) 338-4900); **Eugertha's** (6817 Georgia Avenue, NW; (202) 829-3840); the **Evening Star** below Dupont Circle (1200 19th Street, NW; (202) 785-7827); **The Wharf** (119 King Street, Alexandria, VA; (703) 836-2834); **The Ice House Cafe** (760 Elden Street, Herndon, VA; (703) 471-4256); and **Normandie Farm Inn** (10710 Falls Road, Potomac, MD; (301) 983-8388). In addition, many hotels have fine jazz pianists in their lounges.

The mega-rock concert venues tend to be sports arenas doing double duty: the 20,000-seat **USAir Arena** (formerly the **Capital Centre**), home to the Washington Bullets basketball and Washington Capitals hockey teams; the 50,000-seat **RFK Stadium,** erstwhile home of the Redskins football team (which has the advantage of being accessible by subway to the Stadium/Armory stop); and the all-purpose 10,000-seat **Patriot Center** college arena at George Mason in Fairfax, which also tends to carry the big-name country concerts. Tickets for these shows are usually available by phone from TicketMaster at (202) 432-7328, but beware: "service charges" and handling fees have been known to reach $4.50 per person — not per order.

George Mason University Center for the Arts, which adjoins the Patriot Center, is a lovely new mid-sized venue for classical and jazz music and drama. Its phonecharge ticket service is (703) 993-8888.

The most popular outdoor music venue is **Wolf Trap Farm Park** off Route 7 in Vienna, VA, which offers almost nightly entertainment — pop, country, jazz and R&B, and MOR (middle of the road) rock — and picnicking under the stars during the summer at its Filene Center amphitheater. During the winter season, it has mostly weekend bookings in its small but acoustically magnificent Barns. Wolf Trap has started its own phonecharge service called ProTix, which charges lower fees than TicketMaster; call (703) 218-6500 for Wolf Trap shows. On summer nights, the Metro operates a $3 shuttle service from the West Falls Church station to the Filene Center, but watch your watch: The return shuttle leaves either 20 minutes after the final curtain or 11 P.M., whichever is earlier, in order to ensure riders don't miss the subway.

Carter Barron Amphitheatre, uptown in Rock Creek Park, hosts gospel, soul, jazz, and R&B concerts on summer weekends. **Merriweather Post Pavilion** in Columbia, MD, is the busiest pop/rock outdoor arena, but is some distance away and can only be reached by car. Both use the TicketMaster network as well; see newspapers for current listings.

The more progressive rock acts, which draw strong college and postgrad audiences, tend to be booked into college auditoriums such as George Washington University's **Lisner Auditorium** or **Smith Center,** and sometimes the old **WUST Radio Hall** at Ninth and V streets, NW. National acts with limited audiences — R&B, gospel, soul, folk — are often booked into **DAR Constitution Hall** alongside the Ellipse. Check the newspaper listings for entertainers and phone numbers while you're in town.

The most important club booking national alternative rock acts is the **9:30** club. The best college-circuit and area alternative-rock acts show up at **15 Mins.** The mainstream national and regional rock market belongs to the **Bayou.** All are profiled below. The most interesting techno and progressive bands play **Club Heaven** in Adams-Morgan (2327 18th Street, NW; (202) 667-4355).

For folk, country, and bluegrass music, the most important venue is the **Birchmere** in Alexandria, VA, which has the Seldom Scene as a house band (Thursdays) and Mary-Chapin Carpenter as favorite daughter. Traveling country performers with first albums under their belts, or a long way behind them, often play **Zed** in Alexandria. The major old R&B, blues, and rockabilly club is **Tornado Alley,** which offers both national cajun and deep-blues acts and front-line local groups. See profiles of these three clubs in the next section.

The best bets for acoustic or folk music just any old night are **Food for Thought** near the Dupont Circle Metro (1738 Connecticut Avenue, NW; (202) 797-1095) or **Dylan's** in Georgetown (3251 Prospect Street, NW; (202) 337-0593). Coffeehouses are flourishing — the folkie variety, not the cappuccino type, though they're booming too — but most are monthly events in area churches or schools; check the papers.

Irish bars do a flourishing business in Washington with the help of a resident community of performers. Among the pubs with live music — and almost always at least one fireplace — are the **Dubliner** (profiled below), **Ireland's Four Provinces** (by the Cleveland Park Metro at 3413 Connecticut Avenue, NW; (202) 244-0860), the **Old Brogue** (760-C Walker Road, Great Falls, VA; (703) 759-3309), **Murphy's** (near Woodley Park, at 2609 24th Street, NW; (202) 548-1717), **Ireland's Own** (132 North Royal Street, Alexandria, VA; (703) 549-4535), and **Flanagan's** (near the Bethesda station at 7637 Old Georgetown Road, Bethesda, MD; (301) 986-1007), which also hosts the semiannual appearances of Irish veterans Tommy Makem and the Furey Brothers.

For reggae and third-world music, the longtime champion is **Kilimanjaro** (profiled below), which brings in top Jamaican and African musicians, plus transplanted European world-music stars. The local reggae acts generally play the **Roxy** (18th Street at Connecticut Avenue, NW; (202) 296-9292) or **Grog & Tankard** (2408 Wisconsin Avenue, NW; (202) 333-3114), which is also local Deadhead Central.

Washington is also home to one other type of band: the **armed services bands.** In June, July, and August, ensembles from the four branches perform every evening at dusk, except Saturday, on the East Terrace of the Capitol and at the Sylvan Theatre at the foot of the Washington Monument. Programs include patriotic/martial numbers, country, jazz, pop, and some classical music. You're welcome to bring brown bags, but alcohol is not permitted.

— *Swing Your Partner*

Country and disco dancing have been big for years in Washington, but ethnic and folk dancing — klezmer, polka, contra, cajun — as well as swing dance and big-band boogie are also popular, especially in the suburbs. They're also non-threatening and hospitable spots for singles, even novices, since many have predance "workshops" for learning the steps and all seem well supplied with tolerant and deft "leaders."

For swing dancing, the best bets are the **Washington Swing Dance Committee,** which holds Saturday night dances in all but the coldest weather at the grand deco Spanish Ballroom in the old Glen Echo amusement park in Bethesda, MD (phone number: (301) 340-9732); and the **Rock Around the Clock Club,** which holds dances twice a month at the Cherry Hill Park clubhouse in College Park, MD (phone number: (301) 897-8724). Glen Echo also hosts folk, cajun, and contra dances every weekend; call the **Glen Echo** schedule hotline at (301) 492-6282 or the **Washington Area Folklore Society** hotline at (703) 281-2228.

And you can polka (and pile on the bratwurst) to your heart's content any Friday, Saturday, or Sunday at **Max Blob's Park,** a Bavarian-fantasy beer hall and polka pavilion that holds 1,000 and a five-man oompah band in Jessup, MD; call (301) 799-0155 for information.

For country and western dancing, check **Zed** and **Country Junction,** both profiled below; or if you can hitch a ride, **Latela's** (Route 175 and the Baltimore-Washington Parkway, Jessup, MD; (301) 799-7110) or **Cotton-Eyed Joe's** (5859 Allentown Way, Camp Springs, MD; (301) 449-7500).

— *Espresso and Eight-Ball*

The two biggest trends in Washington are coffee bars and billiards parlors. At either you can spend not merely hours but whole evenings, and in a few cases, hang out virtually round the clock.

Many of the espresso bars are tiny walk-ins; some are mere service windows. But a couple are among the most interesting after-hours hangouts in the city, even if the patrons are the only "entertainment." **Zig-Zag** (1524 U Street, NW; (202) 986-5949) is a fractured 50s-decor (mismatched dinettes, Chipmunks cut-outs, and queer collectibles) hangout for new grads, new greens, postgrads, unreconciled computer wonks, and bike couriers who write poetry all night over pints of mocha or the more substantial whim-of-the-day pasta specials, sandwiches, and boggling desserts. The **Pop Stop** (1513 17th Street, NW; (202) 328-0880) is a flamboyantly busy, bustling and hustling Dupont Circle sidewalk cafe that mixes smarts, gays, and straights with such spur-of-the-moment giggles as bingo and performance art. And just a few doors up, **Cafe Blanca** (1523 17th Street, NW; (202) 986-3476) is a "Casablanca" lovers' heaven, with stills and murals of the Bogey-man plastered on every surface that isn't already claimed by the espresso machine or sandwich.

The biggest billiards parlors around are **Georgetown Billiards** (3251 Prospect Street, NW; (202) 965-7665), **Babe's** (near the Tenleytown Metro at 4600 Wisconsin Avenue, NW; (202) 966-0082), **Shootz Cafe**

(4915 St. Elmo Street, Bethesda, MD; (301) 654-8288), **Champion Billiards** (1776 East Jefferson Street, Rockville, MD; (301) 231-4949), which also serves food 24 hours a day, **Breakers** (Rockville Metro Mall, Rockville, MD; (301) 762-1020), and **Pocket Billiards** (18925 Earhart Court, Gaithersburg, MD; (301) 869-2900).

For funkier decor and less formal atmosphere, try **Atomic Billiards** (3427 Connecticut Avenue, NW at the Cleveland Park Metro; (202) 363-7663), **Bedrock Billiards** (1841 Columbia Road, NW; (202) 667-7665), or **Julio's** in Adams-Morgan (15th and U streets, NW; (202) 483-8500). For the strangest decor of all, and bugs to snack on, try the **Insect Bar;** it only has a couple of tables, but between the decor — a psycho-mystical history of the world recreated in ant-farm dioramas and 50s schlock sci-fi mutants — and the insect hors d'oeuvres, it's a fly-by must (625 E Street, NW; (202) 347-8884).

⸺ *The Sex Thing*

Washington is not the singles capital of the world, but it does have many of the ingredients for a busy meet-market scene: frequent turnovers in power, a dozen colleges and universities, a continual influx of immigrants and corporate hires, and what until recently was considered a "recession-proof" economy.

The singles bars around Washington are relatively benign. Many of them are dance clubs as well, so there's something to do besides discuss astrological incompatibilities. The sports-bar habituees tend to be a little more flagrant in their appraisals of fresh talent, as do those that cater to the fortysomething crowd.

The busiest singles strip in the District is midtown just south and a bit west of Dupont Circle, especially around the intersection of 19th and M streets where the **Sign of the Whale, Rumours, Madhatter,** and **Mr. Day's** pack them in starting at happy hour. A few blocks west is the **Lulu's/Déjà Vu** complex (profiled below), and a few more blocks west is Georgetown, so you can have a sort of progressive singles party.

The busiest singles bars for the older and cash-flow confident crowd are the **Yacht Club of Bethesda** (profiled) and the **River Club** (3223 K Street, NW; (202) 333-8118); for divorced, disinherited, or just disoriented aristocrats the **Marquis de Rochambeau;** for Gold Coast types the **Zanzibar** and the five-room bouncing buppie **Ritz,** all profiled; or **Chelsea's** (1055 Thomas Jefferson Street, NW; (202) 298-8222).

Latin dancing is hottest at **Cafe Atlantico** (see dining guide) and **Brasil Tropical** (2519 Pennsylvania Avenue, NW; (202) 293-1773).

Suburban singles centers in the suburbs are easy to spot: Anything with a bar will do.

Although the District has been home to a strong gay community for many years, most clubs attract at least a slightly mixed crowd, albeit unobtrusive. However, there are many well-established gay nightspots, especially around Dupont Circle and Capitol Hill. Among the most popular are the Polo-label **JR's** (1519 17th Street, NW; (202) 328-0090) and the older-and-wiser piano bar **Friends** (2122 P Street, NW; (202) 822-8909), both near Dupont Circle; the boy-toy and cocktail chatter **French Quarter Cafe** (808 King Street, Alexandria, VA; (703) 683-2803), the pointy-toe and big-buckle **Remington's** (near the Eastern Market station at 639 Pennsylvania Avenue, SE; (202) 543-3113), and the softcore leather-with-rhythm **DC Eagle** (near Gallery Place at 639 New York Avenue, NW; (202) 347-6025). **El Faro** is a semi-reticent Adams-Morgan hangout for primarily Latino lovers (2411 18th Street, NW; (202) 387-6554). The classiest girls' nights out are at the woodgrain and glass **Hill Haven** (Eastern Market, 516 Eighth Street, SE; (202) 543-4242). The newest bars are **Wild Oats** (also Eastern Market at 539 Eighth Street, SE; (202) 547-9453) and the mixed businessman's happy hour **Green Lantern** near MacPherson Square (1335 Green Court, NW, in the alley off 14th and L; (202) 638-5133).

The hottest dance clubs are **Tracks,** which is a vast and mixed gay and straight disco of long standing (see profile below), **Badlands,** which has semi-steamy videos to go with the marathon mixes (Dupont Circle, 1415 22nd Street, NW; (202) 296-0505), and the predominantly lesbian **Hung Jury** (near Farragut West at 1819 H Street, NW; (202) 279-3212). **Ziegfeld's** is the most flamboyant of the hangouts, featuring uproarious and often astonishingly polished drag shows (1345 Half Street, SE; (202) 554-5141); although it's not the safest neighborhood to be in, Ziegfeld's will call you a cab when you're ready to leave.

If you can't dance, but hate to eat alone, try the **Paramount Steak House** (1609 17th Street, NW; (202) 232-0395), **Perry's** (1811 Columbia Road, NW; (202) 234-6218), or the **Pop-Stop** coffee bar, which has turned into the busiest yuppie-gay appraisal scene in town.

Finally, although the onetime red-light district around 14th Street was officially eradicated by redistricting and redevelopment, old habits die hard. North and east of the White House, and especially in the blocks around 13th and L, prostitutes not only parade past and proposition pedestrians but take advantage of traffic lights and stop signs to accost drivers.

A few reminders: Although most prostitutes try to protect themselves from disease, both drug use and AIDS are pervasive. Secondly, many dates are actually bait, fronts for drug dealers in town, who can be a more immediate danger to your health and safety. Besides, District police are fully familiar with the tricks of the trade, so we don't advise you to get involved. If you must look, don't touch—and keep your car doors locked.

For a somewhat less hands-on experience, there are a couple of relatively sedate strip joints downtown: **Archibald's,** which is on the ground floor of the Comedy Cafe building off MacPherson Square (1520 K Street, NW; (202) 737-2662) and the new and discreet gentlemen's-special **1720 Club** (Farragut West, 1720 H Street, NW; (202) 338-1774). And for the safest fantasy trips around, drop by Georgetown's funny/fantasy sex boutiques: the **Pleasure Place** (1063 Wisconsin Avenue, NW; (202) 333-8570), which offers videos, X-rated birthday cards, T-shirts, fishnet stockings and the like, and its across-the-street-rival **Dream Dresser,** a fancy-silly X-rated Victoria's Secret, which dispenses leather and latex as well as lighter-hearted souvenirs and accoutrements (1042 Wisconsin Avenue, NW; (202) 625-0373).

— *More on the Safety Thing*

There is only one safety tip to remember: You're never entirely safe. There is no guaranteed neighborhood in the area. In fact, we have left some otherwise deserving and successful clubs off the list because they're in questionable territory, even for savvy residents. The suburbs are generally okay, but even the ostensibly upscale areas of the District, such as Georgetown and Dupont Circle, are not immune to crime. It's best to leave nightclubs, especially after about 10 P.M., in company. Attach yourself to a group or ask the club management for an escort. It's also wiser to call a cab than to walk more than a block or so. (Mace, incidentally, is now legal in Maryland, Virginia, and the District of Columbia.)

And a final tip: If you believe in helping out the homeless, the staggering number of which you may find one of the less inspiring monuments to modern life in Washington, you might consider stashing your single dollar bills or change in an outside pocket, so that you can reach them without having to open your wallet or pocketbook.

The Bayou

Live national and regional pop, rock, reggae, deadhead, dinosaur, and zydeco bands showcase

Who Goes There: 21–45; locals and tourists; MOR radio addicts, yuppies, nongrads, metal lite dabblers

3135 K Street, NW
(202) 333-2897   Georgetown   Zone 5

Hours: Daily, 8 P.M.–2 A.M.
Cover: Varies with act; roughly $5–20
Minimum: None
Mixed drinks: $5.50
Wine: $2.85
Beer: $2.85–4.50
Dress: Match the act: jackboots, flannel shirts, jacket and tie, big hats, tie-dye
Specials: Occasional all-ages (18 and up) shows, usually semiheavy metal or arena rockers with area following
Food available: Basket food: pretzels, pizza

What goes on: This is the flagship club venue of a national concert promoter, Cellar Door, and serves to break both regional bands the agency has signed and bands on the up- or downturn who can't quite pull the big arena crowds. Local bands work their way from opening act to headliners.

Setting & atmosphere: It's not too pretty, but it's powerful. This 400-seat club has, as you'd expect, high-quality sound equipment and even a couple of obstructed-view TVs. A U-shaped balcony overlooks the main floor and elevated stage, with one bar downstairs, one upstairs, and table service. Rest rooms are upstairs.

If you go: Expect the show to start late; the Bayou is notoriously slow to get going (to let bar tabs accumulate a little first). You'll still need to get in line early to get good seats, but remember: front seats aren't necessarily the best seats; there's an informal dance floor just below the stage.

The Birchmere

Live national country-rock, newgrass, neo-folk, R&B, and blues showcase

Who Goes There: West Virginia flannel shirts, urban cowboys, unreconciled folkies, and lately, the Clintons and Gores

---

3901 Mount Vernon Avenue, Alexandria
(703) 549-5919   Virginia suburbs   Zone 11

Hours: Tuesday–Saturday,
7–11:30 P.M.
Cover: Varies with act; roughly $8–20
Minimum: None
Mixed drinks: None
Wine: $4.25
Beer: $3.25–3.75
Dress: Boots — cowboy, biker, hiking or fashion; jeans, tweeds, flannels
Food available: Mostly sandwich-basket fare

What goes on: This is one of the major clubs in town, the biggest for new acoustic and country acts especially, such as Rosanne Cash and hometown heroine Mary-Chapin Carpenter; plus cult regulars Jerry Jeff Walker and Delbert McClinton, old folk Tom Paxton and John Stewart; and new femme fronters Kristin Hersh and Christine Lavin.

Setting & atmosphere: The Birch, as it's called, has more reputation than ambience, and that's fair: it's just a long, slightly tiered barn of a room with big country manners and a ladies room in the basement where the graffiti swoons over gray-haired new-grasser Peter Rowan.

If you go: Go early: Parking is tight (but free), the line is long, and seating is first-come, closest-in. If you're trying to eat light, eat elsewhere. Remember to take off your big hat so the folks behind you can see. And take thankful note of the sign that asks for quiet during performances: This really is a listening club.

Blues Alley

National-circuit jazz dinner club

Who Goes There: 20–60; locals and tourists; other jazz pros; neo-jazz fans

1073 Wisconsin Avenue, NW (in the alley)
(202) 337-4141   Georgetown   Zone 5

Hours: Sunday–Thursday, 6 P.M.–
midnight; Friday and Saturday,
6 P.M.–2 A.M.
Cover: Varies with entertainment;
$12–20
Minimum: Two drinks or $7 food
Mixed drinks: $3.95–7.50
Wine: $3.50–5
Beer: $3–5
Dress: Jacket over jeans, business
attire, musician chic
Food available: Full menu of
semicreole food: gumbo, chicken, steak

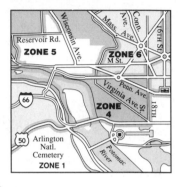

What goes on: When the big-name jazz performers come to town, this is where they play. And although many customers grumble about ticket prices, they pay anyway—partly because the acts require high guarantees, partly because Georgetown rents are high, and partly because so many other jazz clubs have folded.

Setting & atmosphere: A fairly simple lounge, with exposed brick walls, a platform at one end and the bar at the other, and smallish dinner tables scattered between.

If you go: Get there early; the line often goes all around the block, and seating is first-come and squeeze-'em-together, even with reservations. The old and cramped rest rooms that are barely accessible upstairs are one drawback, the ventilation can be another, but the acoustics are very good.

Brickskeller

Encyclopedic beer rathskeller

Who Goes There: 21–45; students, former students, home brewers, beer fanatics

1523 22nd Street, NW
(202) 293-1885   Dupont Circle/Adams-Morgan   Zone 6

Hours: Monday–Thursday,
11:30 A.M.–2 A.M.; Friday,
11:30 A.M.–3 A.M.; Saturday, 6 P.M.–
3 A.M.; Sunday, 6 P.M.–2 A.M.
Cover: None
Minimum: None
Mixed drinks: $3–4
Wine: $3.50
Beer: $2.75–65
Dress: Jackets, jeans, khakis
Specials: Monthly beer tastings,
often with guest speaker

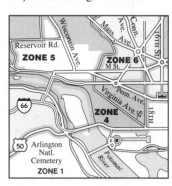

Food available: The house specialty is buffalo; good pub food in general.

What goes on: Thirty-five years ago, Maurice Coja put 50 kinds of beer, mostly bottled, in the basement of the Marifex Hotel and opened for business. Twenty years later, he had to give up kegs because room was so tight, and now, with 500 beers from all over the world offered at the same time, including over 100 microbrews, brands and cans are stuffed into every corner. The Brickskeller used to offer live music of the folk-rock variety, but eventually realized the beer was sufficient entertainment. There are dart boards and a jukebox instead.

Setting & atmosphere: A rabbit warren of rooms, with the main bar in the front and scuffed and hard-working tables snaking around between the dart boards. Feel free to strike up a conversation; the Brickskeller is unpretentious, college-bar friendly, and lively.

If you go: Don't be shy; consult the staff. Beer is serious business here—three-liter bottles of Corsondonk go for $60—and you can learn a lot if you go slowly. Start light and work your way up to Samiclaus, a potent by-the-fireside beer of 14% alcohol. Skip the mixed beer cocktails, or beer-tails; they're more novelty act than revelation.

Cafe Lautrec

Neo-Boho bistro and jazz bar

Who Goes There: 23–50; neighborhood jazz fans, postgrads, artistes

2431 18th Street, NW
(202) 265-6436   Dupont Circle/Adams-Morgan   Zone 6

Hours: Sunday–Thursday, 5 P.M.–
2 A.M.; Friday and Saturday,
5 P.M.–3 A.M.
Cover: None
Minimum: $6
Mixed drinks: $4–6
Wine: $3.50–5
Beer: $3–3.75
Dress: Jacket and jeans; black on
black, a touch of grunge, a bit of
cafe society leotard
Food available: Old-style bistro fare:
pasta, salads, trout meunière, lamb shanks, maybe sweetbreads

What goes on: As the night progresses, Lautrec evolves from early-offhours bar for neighborhood vegans to old-favorite cafe to Rive Gauche stage set, with live jazz nightly and old-style tap-dancing on the bar Thursdays through Sundays.

Setting & atmosphere: This comfortably careless wood and brick shoebox turns its age to atmospheric advantage, picking up the decadent posture along with the Moulin Rouge reproductions, which include a 20-foot Lautrec reproduction painted over the facade. Study the wait staff and their black leggings and you'll suddenly catch the kinship between bohemian Paris soul and post-punk flat soles.

If you go: Go late and get the whole show. Sundays, when longtime jazz grace Mary Jefferson sings, the trio plays, and dapper tapper Johne Forges croons a little, you get the full Folies. Don't bother to dress to impress this crowd: Cafe Lautrec's lack of attitude about your attitude is its most valuable asset. If you're a guy with a shy bladder, you may have to concentrate; the men's room is truly a water closet under the stairs.

Champions

Sports-memorabilia gallery and jock-groupie audition spot

Who Goes There: TV-game regulars; local pro-team fans, faded glory boys, B-ball boys, and big-eyed businessmen

---

1206 Wisconsin Avenue, NW
(202) 332-2211   Georgetown   Zone 5

Hours: Monday–Thursday, 5 P.M.–
2 A.M.; Friday, 5 P.M.–3 A.M.;
Saturday, 11:30 A.M.–3 A.M.; Sunday,
11:30 A.M.–2 A.M.
Cover: None
Minimum: Weekends after 10, one
drink
Mixed drinks: $3.25–4.95
Wine: $3.50–3.85
Beer: $2.35–3.65
Specials: Friday 5–8 P.M., $1.25
drafts, $2 rail drinks, and 30¢ buffalo
wings, etc.

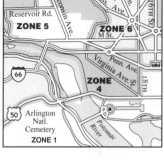

Food available: Ballpark franks, burgers, and also larger portioned pub fare for old athletic appetites

---

What goes on: Redskins fans and the braver adherents of other teams break bread, and often beer mugs, together over multiscreen satellite TV games; real pros from area teams and former pros–turned–sports announcers are common sightings. On any given night, some sort of promotion or "contest" may be going on, from wet T-shirt parades to faked-orgasm competitions.

Setting & atmosphere: Part sports bar, part meet market, this is simultaneously a sports-trivia master class and competitive escort parade—thanks to the guiding example of founder and professional bachelor Mike O'Harro, who never saw a beauty pageant contestant he didn't like. This is the flagship club of a coast-to-coast franchise, with a quarter-million dollars' worth of sports memorabilia, autographed photos, uniform shirts, etc.

If you go: Have a valid ID; O'Harro, having had plenty of opponents— business rivals and area residents—looking for reasons to shut down his bar, is very strict on legal drinking ages. He's even started requiring his dates to be 21. Don't expect to talk business unless you bring your client with you; although Champions is full of credit card customers, this is major playtime. Do not peer into the tinted windows of limos; these guys are paying for privacy so they can make a public spectacle. A safe bet for protective camouflage is either a Redskins or Georgetown U. sweatshirt, available on the streets. This is not a sanctuary for solo (or sensitive) women.

Country Junction

Country and western dance hall

Who Goes There: 21–55; serious C&W dancers,
some gentle barflies, and neighborhood regulars

11410 Rockville Pike, Rockville
(301) 231-5761

Maryland suburbs   Zone 10

Hours: Sunday–Thursday, 7 P.M.–
1 A.M.; Friday and Saturday,
7 P.M.–3 A.M.
Cover: $5 Friday and Saturday
Minimum: None
Mixed drinks: $3–5
Wine: $2–3
Beer: $1.50–3
Dress: After-work permanent press;
mostly boots, snap-button shirts,
and jeans with boots; flippy skirts
and pom-pom boots (no tank tops)

Specials: Free introductory dance classes Sundays; beginning to
advanced classes other nights with cover
Food available: Nachos, burgers, pizza

What goes on: Some fancy steppin'; CJ belongs to many-time national and
world country dance and swing dance champ Barry Durand, who's often on
hand for the warm-up lessons and dizzying exhibitions.

Setting & atmosphere: A big, loose tavern in a suburban motel; lots of
wooden tables and chairs that scrunch together at happy hour and move off
the big dance floor thereafter. Country DJ booth and good sound system. The
actual bar, set up for observers, is in a long, thin annex with look-through
panels.

If you go: Don't be self-conscious; everybody's a beginner, but the lessons
are fun and good exercise. Wear shoes with fairly smooth soles so you can
shuffle and spin. And try not to look down; you may trip somebody, because
this is a tightly packed and fast-moving circuit.

Dubliner

Classic Irish pub

Who Goes There: Hill workers, both upwardly mobile (staffers) and established (senators and lobbyists)

---

520 North Capitol Street, NW
(202) 737-3773   Capitol Hill   Zone 2

Hours: Monday–Thursday, 11 A.M.–2 A.M.; Friday, 11 A.M.–3 A.M.; Saturday, 7 P.M.–3 A.M.; Sunday, 11 A.M.–2 A.M.
Cover: None
Minimum: None
Mixed drinks: $3.25–5. Dubliner coffee is an Irish coffee with Bailey's added.
Wine: $2.75
Beer: $2.95–3.95
Dress: No cutoffs or tank shirts allowed.
Specials: Reduced light-fare prices, 11 P.M.–1 A.M.
Food available: Irish pub classics, from stew to hot sandwiches

---

What goes on: This is not the oldest Irish bar in town, but it has become the clan leader—centrally located, pol-connected, and providing the training ground for founders of a half-dozen other bars, including the semisibling rival Irish Times next door. Fittingly, the Dubliner also has one of the most colorful histories, filled with romantic intrigue, boom-and-bust bank troubles, and riotous St. Patrick's week parties.

Setting & atmosphere: Now part of the pricey and hunt-country gracious Phoenix Hotel complex, the Dubliner is filled with antiques, such as the 1810 hand-carved walnut bar in the back room. The front bar is louder and livelier, often populated by the surviving members of the Dubliner's Irish football and soccer teams; the snug is a discreet heads-together, take-no-names hideaway in the finest tradition; and the parlor is where the tweeds gather.

If you go: Be sure to have at least one Guinness on draft: The Dubliner pours an estimated quarter-million pints a year. Then brave the Gaelic Triangle, where many a fine stout imbiber has lost, if not his life, then several hours of unexplained time. If you're dressed nicely, slip upstairs to the Powerscourt restaurant and sip a wee one while gauging the Jesuit/politico connection. Drop by the Irish Times for a breather (the high ceilings carry smoke away) and the *Finnegans Wake* crazy quilt of literary and political conversation. Then call a cab. Please.

Fairfax Bar

A rich romantic piano bar with political connections

Who Goes There: 30–60; old Washington money and power and new-administration wannabes

Ritz-Carlton Hotel, 2100 Massachusetts Avenue, NW

(202) 293-2100   Dupont Circle/Adams-Morgan   Zone 6

Hours: Daily, 4 P.M.–1:30 A.M.
Cover: None
Minimum: None
Mixed drinks: $9.50
Wine: $6.50
Beer: $6.50
Dress: Casual, but "informal" is relative here — suggests resort hopping at best; jackets for men in the evening
Specials: Afternoon tea and fondues
Food available: Light fare, primarily sandwiches and dessert

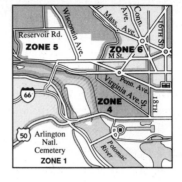

What goes on: Cocktail party chatter of the rich or famous (it's déclassé to be both, unless you're hereditarily obliged to serve your country).

Setting & atmosphere: The aristocrats' hideaway of your dreams: oriental rugs, gleaming wood, real fireplaces, and a great pianist — longtime lounge fave Peter Robinson. It's like some grand racing stable that's been hand-polished in and out; you see the other tables as if over stall doors. One's almost surprised it doesn't smell of saddle soap. (The rest rooms, on the other hand, are strictly Big House.)

If you go: Enjoy the history. This is an old pols' networking cradle, literally: Vice President Gore spent a lot of time here as a child when it belonged to the Republican side of his family. Besides, like any other vanishing breed, armchair clubs have a sentimental attraction.

Fatty's

Neighborhood tavern flowing against redevelopment tide; live local music

Who Goes There: Courthouse complex fugitives; data processors; minor press; area diehards

---

1M (One Metro) Building, 51 Monroe Street, Rockville
(301) 762-4630   Maryland suburbs   Zone 10

Hours: Monday–Thursday, 11 A.M.–midnight; Friday, 11 A.M.–1 A.M.; Saturday, 6 P.M.–1 A.M.; closed Sunday.

Cover: $3–5 on weekends, none on weekdays.

Minimum: None

Mixed drinks: $2.95–5.25

Wine: $2.95

Beer: $2.25–3.85

Dress: After-hours suits, jeans, even shorts, and nice sports garb

Specials: Happy hour 3–7 P.M. weekdays: $1.50 drafts, $2 rail drinks, cut-price appetizers

Food available: Beyond the valley of the bar food: fried chicken, meatloaf, catfish, pasta, ribs, steaks

---

What goes on: Doubling as office building lunchroom, happy-hour recovery room, and emergency meeting room, Fatty's is also a popular and lively novelty-rock and R&B venue seating well over 200. Its old roots as a hangout are most obvious in football season (Monday night television) or softball season (postgame nacho therapy).

Setting & atmosphere: Although Fatty's is on the first level of one of the ugliest, most penitential-looking county executive complexes ever constructed, and although it expanded and renovated into a dangerously predictable-looking middle-management and computer wonk lunch place, Fatty's still manages, by dint of personality (its earthy owners, Bob "Fatty" Wills and wife, Patty), to retain its old neighborhood tavern atmosphere.

If you go: Order either a draft, so you can enjoy the Mason-jar mugs with Fatty's visage printed on them, or a "tooter shooter," a primary-paint-colored concoction served in test tubes from a wire cage. Don't wear ornate headgear—there may be table surfing from the softball types after a bit. Sing along.

---

15 Mins.

Live alternative/roots rock and blues club

Who Goes There: Street culturati, bike couriers, real music addicts

---

1030 15th Street, NW
(202) 408-1855   Downtown   Zone 3

Hours: Monday–Thursday, 5 P.M.–
2 A.M.; Friday, 5 P.M.–3 A.M.;
Saturday, 9 P.M.–3 A.M.; Sunday,
5 P.M.–2 A.M.
Cover: None on Thursday; $5–6
after 9 P.M. on weekends; $2 for
the Monday poetry slams
Minimum: None
Mixed drinks: $3.50–4.50
Wine: $3.25
Beer: $2.30–3.50
Dress: Bicycle tights, happy-hour
suits, semigrunge, dance blacks, neo-'60s rococo
Specials: No cover charge Thursdays
Food available: Weekend late-night buffet

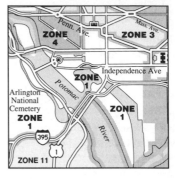

What goes on: This was the first in a series of cheap-chic bars opened in downtown office buildings scheduled for razing and thus low-rent. Hence the name, a play on Warhol's famous dictum about fame. An office workers' cafeteria by day, it turns into a bar at night with intentionally cheesy videos in the bar, DJs for dancing (on the tiniest dance floor in D.C.), live bands in the back, and maybe acoustic jazz or poetry at the same time.

Setting & atmosphere: A combination *Interview* magazine goof and salvage job, with hand-stenciled fish skeletons, new-south cactus jokes and skulls, and a few black-velvet idol paintings that seem to move when the UV lights come on. This being a cafeteria, nothing is too fragile; unfortunately, it can also be said that the vinyl booths are none too comfortable.

If you go: On weekends, especially after 10 P.M., you may have to wait outside. Go with the flow. The crowd is fluid — bike couriers, off-duty bartenders, artists, curiosity-seekers, postgrad literati, and slumming office captives from surrounding firms. You may see softcore moshing (although that's limited) or juggling or hula-hooping, which is a returning fad. The bands who play here are among the area's best, alternating with imported cult bands, cutting-edge groups from the college circuit, or independent labels. For women, this is hassle-free territory; for '60s survivors, it's junior high nostalgia.

Fifth Column

Techno/industrial rock disco

Who Goes There: 21–35; stylemongers, Hill
assistants, computer literati, leather lites

---

915 E Street, NW
(202) 393-3632   Downtown   Zone 3

Hours: Monday, 9 P.M.–2 A.M.;
Tuesday–Thursday, 10 P.M.–2 A.M.;
Friday and Saturday, 10 P.M.–
3 A.M.; closed Sunday.
Cover: $5 Wednesday, $8
Monday and Thursday through
Saturday
Minimum: None
Mixed drinks: $4.50–7
Wine: $4.25
Beer: $3.75–4.25
Dress: Italian shoulders, chica-chica

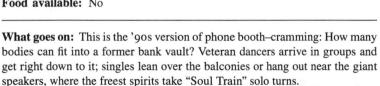

slingbacks, jackets with T-shirts, jeans with creases, black or "statement"
ties; no extremely casual wear after Wednesday
Specials: Name DJs imported from New York; open bar Monday
9–10:30 P.M.; and two-for-one Heinekens all night Monday; no
cover Tuesdays
Food available: No

What goes on: This is the '90s version of phone booth–cramming: How many
bodies can fit into a former bank vault? Veteran dancers arrive in groups and
get right down to it; singles lean over the balconies or hang out near the giant
speakers, where the freest spirits take "Soul Train" solo turns.

Setting & atmosphere: This really is a former bank building (as is the adjoining Vault, another bank-vault disco), with teller windows turned into bar
service. The art around is usually local, and often outré. Although there aren't
many chairs, there is a small talking lounge if you OT (over-techno).

If you go: Try the "smart bar," which offers concoctions said to improve your
memory, among other things. What can it hurt? Monday is Poseurs night,
almost a disco institution in D.C. This is usually a pretty friendly crowd, not
so competitive as that at Zei; but if the occasional clique of Armani fashion
victims gets too demonstrative, head next door, where the Vault usually has
a choice of mixes going: techno/industrial below, slightly more glide-friendly
stuff upstairs. On the other hand, nobody in the Vault seems to have vaulted
the 30-year barrier.

Galaxy Hut

Live original music and microbrew bar

Who Goes There: 22–45; area musicians, street-buzz connections, artists, unfrocked young professionals

---

2711 Wilson Boulevard, Arlington
(703) 525-8646   Virginia suburbs   Zone 11

Hours: Monday–Thursday,
11:30 A.M.–2:30 P.M., 5 P.M.–
2 A.M.; Friday and Saturday,
6 P.M.–2 A.M.; Sunday, 6 P.M.–
2 A.M.
Cover: None
Minimum: None
Mixed drinks: License pending
Wine: $2.50
Beer: $2–3.75
Dress: Anything goes; mostly
jeans with signals — bolo ties, worn
elbows, ironed collars, elkskin or motorcycle boots
Specials: Happy hour 5–8 P.M., with $5.50–7.25 pitchers
Food available: Burgers, pizza, pasta

What goes on: The most promising area and college-circuit independent bands, usually roots rock, neo-folk, or alternative rock — polish their material here; it's as much support group as audience. You'll know it when you see it: there's a Fiat Spyder sticking out of the roof. (Divorced former co-owner Bill Stewart's Amdo Rodeo and Bardo brewpub, both within mug-tossing distance, have very similar decors.)

Setting & atmosphere: Galaxy Hut may be small, but it's big on style, or rather, style as statement. It's half Southwest, half South Seas — a salvaged and custom-painted grille-toothed Caddy chassis does rehabilitated duty as the bar while its lesser half houses the jukebox, chili-pepper lites in the Tiki Room, assorted stuffed armadillos, etc.

If you go: Spend a little time reading the chalkboard, where more than five dozen microbrews, a dozen of them on tap, are listed. Bring money for the CD jukebox. If you don't smoke, expect to have to step outside every once in a while to revive your pulmonary system.

Hard Rock Cafe

Souvenir shop disguised as barbecue bar

Who Goes There: 12–55; tourists and locals; Hard Rock memorabilia collectors; air-guitar experts

999 E Street, NW
(202) 737-7625   The Mall   Zone 1

Hours: Sunday–Thursday, 11 A.M.–
midnight; Friday and Saturday,
11 A.M.–1 A.M.
Cover: None
Minimum: None
Mixed drinks: $3.25–5.25
Wine: $3.75–4.75
Beer: $3.25–3.50
Dress: To be seen: pony-print leather,
denim, sports or rock 'n' roll tour
jackets, business attire, creative black
tie, Bermuda shorts (on tourists)
Specials: Happy hour reduced prices, Wednesday 4–9 P.M.
Food available: Surprisingly good barbecue, burgers, nachos

What goes on: One of perhaps 30 Hard Rocks around the world, each of which takes its nickname from the site, this is the "Embassy" and sometimes the "Smithsonian of Rock 'n' Roll," taking its turn rotating the nearly 7,000 pieces of music history in the HRC collection. The souvenir shop, with its signature T-shirts, is as busy as the bar, which is often stand-in-line packed — a doorman passes inspection on the hopeful.

Setting & atmosphere: This is ersatz nostalgia for the second Rolling Stone generation — a bar designed like a piano, half a pink Cadillac (sort of a franchise signature) hanging from the ceiling, and a lot of fed suits from nearby buildings trying to look cool. Hard Rock also makes a point of being Lollapalooza-era PC, supporting the Walden Project and nuclear freezes and hosting radio-chic benefits and postconcert VIP receptions, usually without the star.

If you go: Pick up the guide book, formally known as the "Hard Rock Cafe Self-Motivating Non-Nuclear-Powered Memorabilia Tour of the World's Foremost Rock 'n' Roll Museum" and start circling the balcony. Look for such treasures as Bo Diddley's first jerry-rigged electric guitar, Michael Jackson's glittering kneepad, and a stained-glass triptych featuring Elvis, Jerry Lee Lewis, and Little Richard.

Headliners

Pro-circuit comedy club

Who Goes There: 18–50; suburban
singles, young marrieds, comedy groupies

Radisson Mark Plaza, I-395 and Seminary Road, Alexandria
(703) 379-4242   Virginia suburbs   Zone 11

Hours: Monday–Thursday, 5 P.M.–
midnight (no show Monday and
Tuesday); Friday, 5 P.M.–12:30 A.M.;
Saturday, 6 P.M.–12:30 A.M.; Sunday,
11 A.M.–3 P.M.
Cover: $13
Minimum: None
Mixed drinks: $3–6
Wine: $3–6
Beer: $2.50–3.75
Dress: Anything goes, except
cutoffs and sandals

Specials: Happy hour weekdays, 5–8, with free buffet and reduced drink
prices; Wednesday is all ages night (no alcohol served after 8); "Sunday
funnies" brunch isn't live, but does come with free *Post* comics
Food available: Burgers, sandwiches, big salads

What goes on: One of the better regional performers and comic writers, Chip
Franklin, books this club as well as doing feature duty; he brings in not only
cable-friendly names but sharp, cutting-edge "smart" comics. Like the Improv,
Headliners largely eschews novices for full-time pros.

Setting & atmosphere: A nice but undramatic convention hotel dining room:
a generous two-tiered space with semicircular bar on the upper level, tables
across the main floor, and a small elevated screen with TV remotes near
obstructed view sections. Good smoke retrieval system.

If you go: You can drive your car to get here; there's free, covered parking.

The Improvisation
National-circuit comedy club
Who Goes There: Visiting business types, 30ish suburbanites, 25-45 midlevel managers

---

1140 Connecticut Avenue, NW
(202) 296-7008

Downtown   Zone 3

Hours: Sunday–Thursday, 7–10:30 P.M.; Friday and Saturday, 7 P.M.–12:30 A.M.
Cover: $8 Sunday–Thursday, $10 Friday and Saturday
Minimum: None
Mixed drinks: $4–6
Wine: $3.50–5
Beer: $2.50–3.50
Dress: T-shirts with jackets, suits, casual yup attire
Specials: Tuesday free admission to anyone wearing an Improv T-shirt ($10 in the lobby)
Food available: Full menu described as being available before the 8:30 P.M. show, but light fare available whenever; standard one-size-fits-all menu with chicken cordon bleu, prime rib, catch of the day, Caesar salad, etc.

What goes on: Standard Improv franchise fare: A short opening act, often local; a semiestablished feature act; and a headliner from the national club/cable showcase circuit. Monday and Tuesday are "best of Washington" nights, i.e., minor-league tryouts.

Setting & atmosphere: Again, this goes with the franchise—a "brick wall" stage sentimentally recalling the original no-frills Improvisation, and the black-and-white checkerboard floor and trim that is practically a logo design. TV screens hang overhead for those with obscured views, but they're not big enough to be terribly useful. The wait staff wears tux-material bermuda shorts and slithers between tables at knee height.

If you go: Don't bother to come early, at least on weeknights, when being seated in order of arrival isn't apt to be a problem. Since latecomers are usually seated amongst the diners, you have no real reason to seek early reservations, despite what you might be told. Besides, nibbling through the appetizers list is a more satisfying experience than sitting down to dinner and then sitting through the show. The Improv, though below sidewalk level, has wheelchair access via the elevator in the building lobby. Check your check before tipping; a 15% gratuity is figured in automatically.

Kilimanjaro

Live Caribbean and African dance and dinner club

Who Goes There: 21–45; students,
musicians, embassy/Gold Coast imports

1724 California Street, NW

(202) 328-3839   Dupont Circle/Adams-Morgan   Zone 6

Hours: Monday–Thursday, 5 P.M.–
2 A.M.; Friday, 5 P.M.–3 A.M.;
Saturday, 8 P.M.–3 A.M.; Sunday,
8 P.M.–2 A.M.

Cover: Varies with act; from
about $8 to $10

Minimum: Two drinks

Dress: With an ethnic courtesy,
from batiks, African high collars, and
loose trousers to Caribbean flounced
and cocktail dress; no shorts

Specials: Happy hour 5–9 P.M.
weekdays with two-for-one drinks and no cover

Food available: Ethiopian/Jamaican menu, a little West African

---

What goes on: This is the Black Rock for live local and, on weekends, national and international reggae and world-beat music, with acts from Zaire, Ghana, Jamaica, Nigeria, Senegal, Haiti, etc. Tuesday is karaoke night, with two-for-one beer until 11.

Setting & atmosphere: Although it remains a rather weather-beaten brick warehouse on the outside, Kilimanjaro has spruced up its once dismal interior with new chairs, tables lacquered with its trademark giraffe, plentiful (plastic) greenery, and zebra skins on the walls.

If you go: Turn down your metabolic light. The pace is leisurely here — so leisurely that though the remarkably crisp meat-filled samosas are worth waiting for, it may mean setting your stomach alarm for 45 minutes. Also, the lighting is extremely dim, so don't bother to bring a magazine to read while you wait.

Lulu's/Déjà Vu

Mardi Gras singles bar/semioldies disco

Who Goes There: 25–45; office fugitives, knit collars, former college jocks

---

2121 M Street, NW
(202) 861-5858   Dupont Circle/Adams-Morgan   Zone 6

Hours: Monday–Thursday, 11:30 A.M.–11 P.M.; Friday and Saturday, 11 A.M.–2 A.M.; Sunday, 10 A.M.–10 P.M.

Cover: $2 Friday and Saturday after 9
Minimum: None
Mixed drinks: $3.75–5.50
Wine: $3.50
Beer: $2.75–3.50
Dress: Georgetown prep, after–office hours, cajun cowpunk
Specials: Sunday brunch includes complementary beignets and champagne
Food available: Gumbo, étouffé, po'boys, sometimes crawfish and half-shells

---

What goes on: This is a pack-'em-in lunch spot, catering to nearby office workers, but beginning at 4 P.M., when the Dixieland band "promenades" and the appetizer baskets begin to fry, it becomes a permanent party. In the DJ areas, the music is '60s–'80s; for the early boomers who used to patronize the bar nearly 20 years ago when it was called Déjà Vu, dancing here is really Déjà Vu all over again.

Setting & atmosphere: A re-created corner of Bourbon Street, with the restaurant area authentically accessorized with a wrought-iron balcony and the glittering carnival queen gown that the owner's mother, Lulu, wore in the 1962 Mardi Gras procession. There's a garden-style dining room reminiscent of Brennan's conservatory, and the multiple bar and informal dance rooms form a warren of exposed-brick walls, bare-board floors, and mahogany bars.

If you go: Try arriving at happy hour—a 22-ounce beer in a souvenir plastic cup is $1.25.

Marquis de Rochambeau

A combination cabaret, bistro, faux bordello, and white elephant sale

Who Goes There: 25–65; the titled, entitled, and entailed; rich and eccentric and fantasy-minded

---

3108 M Street, NW
(202) 333-0393

Georgetown   Zone 5

Hours: Monday–Thursday, 6 P.M.–
2:30 A.M.; Friday and Saturday,
5 P.M.–2:30A.M.
Cover: None
Minimum: None
Mixed drinks: $6–25
Wine: $6.50
Beer: $5.50
Dress: Almost anything, but make
it flamboyant — slinky draping, top
hat, cravat, big hair
Specials: Constant live entertainment,
from torch to tango
Food available: Expensive, old-line "Parisian" cuisine

What goes on: This is a fantastic, febrile re-creation of Moulin Rouge demi-mondo bizarro; bartending blonds in catsuits and berets, a Piaf-style vocaliste and her baritone partner; a little accordian music, a little samba, a little sax, just one riff after another. Upstairs is another whole club — a dance floor with DJ and wraparound bar for the less glittering conversationalists.

Setting & atmosphere: This is decor as stage set, and almost as fluid: antique Tabriz carpets as booth upholstery, old shawls as swags and lampshades, oil paintings, graffiti, rosaries, knickknacks, Remington replicas, silver and silverplate, chandeliers, and bowers of boas. The most whimsical touch: the incredible shrinking and expanding bar.

If you go: Be brave, be dashing, be anything but boring. Or pompous. If you're a woman, you'll be adored; if you're a man, you'll be expected to dip. Watch your footing; the carpets sometimes kick up. Go before 8:30 to get one of the romantic back booths, but don't be surprised when the rush comes about 10:30. This is not a place for anti–role playing; it's a libido's Disney World. Warning: Keep track of the high bar prices — they add up but they do subsidize the no-cover policy.

9:30

National-name live alternative, progressive, semipunk rock music club

Who Goes There: 18–35; new music hopefuls, precollege shoegazers, couriers, hard-core jackbooters, and cowpunks

930 F Street, NW
(202) 393-0930

Downtown   Zone 3

Hours: Sunday–Thursday, 8 P.M.–
2 A.M.; Friday and Saturday,
8 P.M.–3 A.M.
Cover: Varies with entertainment,
from $3 to as much as $20
Minimum: None
Mixed drinks: $3–4.25
Wine: $3.50
Beer: $3–3.75
Dress: Grunge, imitation grunge,
rhinestone cowboy, leftover
businesswear, knife-customized
athletic wear, black jersey, black spandex, black denim
Specials: Happy hour 4–8 Friday with half-price drinks; no cover for
DJ dancing Friday and Saturday after 12:30 A.M.

What goes on: "9:30" is the name, the address, and it used to be the show-time, but thanks to workday hangovers, midweek music now starts at 8:30. This is one of Washington's most important clubs, the loss-leader indulgence of major concert promoter Seth Hurwitz, who, with daring and eclectic booking of breaking acts, fosters loyalty from new bands as their reputations rise. Promising local bands fight to get work as first acts here; a headliner contract is a real prize.

Setting & atmosphere: A cavern club only the She-Wolf of London could love: black, concrete, chilly in winter, sweltering in summer, and dedicated to the premise that all paying customers are created equal—not dignified, perhaps, but equal. Seating is primarily limited to ledges upholstered with indoor-outdoor carpeting.

If you go: Find out who's playing: The crowd that pays up for Ice T isn't the same as the one for Marshall Crenshaw or Happy Mondays. Heads up around the stage; there's still a little moshing and stage-surfing going on in the "pit." Wear comfortable shoes; you'll be standing. Either go with friends or call a cab; the downtown location can be tricky for late-night walkers (though increasing redevelopment in the neighborhood is changing this).

One Step Down
Live national and local jazz club
Who Goes There: 18–65; students, novices, professional musicians, locals, jazz pilgrims

2517 Pennsylvania Avenue, NW
(202) 331-8864

Georgetown   Zone 4

Hours: Daily 10 A.M.–2 A.M.
Cover: Varies with act, roughly $5–15
Minimum: Two drinks
Mixed drinks: $3.75–4
Wine: $2.75
Beer: $2.25–2.75
Dress: Casual
Specials: Happy hour 3–7 P.M. weekdays, with $1.50 rail drinks and 90¢ drafts
Food available: Touch-all-bases lunchspot/bar menu, sandwiches to steak

What goes on: Less famous than Blues Alley but more purist, One Step Down books the sort of jazz performers described as musicians' musicians, as well as the more experimental artists. Imported headliners play Friday and Saturday. Sunday afternoon is the live jam session, which draws local pros as well as journeymen and students; Sunday night is a regular set by vibist Lenny Cuje.

Setting & atmosphere: This dark little shoebox pays homage to the old jazz faith, and it shows; most of the seats aren't seats, they're pews, salvaged from an old Sunday school in coal-town Cumberland, Maryland, along with the stained glass. The other tables are old-style booths with scratched-up tops and mini-flip jukebox controls (jazz standards, of course). Access is very tight; the rest rooms are at the far end of the squeezehall past the bar.

If you go: Wear comfortable clothes; after all, pews get hard. Seats fill up fast, and One Step Down doesn't take reservations. If you don't mind stools, sitting at the bar gives you both access to a great bartending staff and a good view of the pianist, but you'll have to stand the traffic to the rest rooms. It's well worth it if owner Joe Cohen or one of his family is working the bar; they know and can make almost any drink, and tell good stories, too. *Note:* Drink prices may increase during performances, since they're part of the cover.

The Ritz

House, R&B, and techno-buppie dance complex

Who Goes There: 24–44; black
professionals, artists, students, bankers

---

919 E Street, NW
(202) 638-2582

Downtown   Zone 3

Hours: Wednesday–Sunday 9 P.M.–
2 A.M.; Thursday, 5 P.M.–2 A.M.;
Friday, 5 P.M.–3 A.M.; Saturday,
9 P.M.–3 A.M.
Cover: $5 weekdays, $10 after
8:30 P.M. Friday, and after 10 P.M.
Saturday.
Minimum: None
Mixed drinks: $4–6
Wine: $4.25
Beer: $4
Dress: A mix of pinstripes,
draped lapels, and cocktail shimmer; no sneakers
Specials: Happy hour, 5–8:30, Thursday and Friday $1 off all drinks
Food available: No

What goes on: Five rooms on three floors, each decorated to match the music: jazz in the big "Matisse" jazz-stenciled room; house, hip-hop, and a touch of techno in the graffiti-strewn, Manhattan subway–style top floor; and reggae or soca or Top 40 in between.

Setting & atmosphere: From casual to classy, with local art, a mezzanine with conversation areas for more in-depth introductions, and bars galore.

If you go: Dress to express.

Studebaker's

Golden-oldies disco and sync tank
Who Goes There: 25–50; jitterbug
jocks, office partiers, off-duty waiters

8028 Leesburg Pike, Tysons Corner
(703) 356-9334   Virginia suburbs   Zone 11

1750 Rockville Pike (Holiday Inn/Crowne Plaza), Rockville
(301) 881–7340   Maryland suburbs   Zone 10

Hours: Tysons Corner: Monday, 7 P.M.–2 A.M.; Tuesday–Friday, 4:30 P.M.–2 A.M.; Saturday and Sunday, 7 P.M.–2 A.M. Rockville: Tuesday–Thursday, 5 P.M.–1 A.M.; Friday, 5 P.M.–2 A.M.; Saturday, 7 P.M.–2 A.M.; closed Sunday and Monday.
Cover: Tysons Corner: $6; Rockville: $1, $4 after 8 Friday and Saturday
Minimum: None
Mixed drinks: $3.25–5.25
Wine: $2.95–3.50
Beer: $3–3.75

Dress: Department-store prep and workday stuff, nothing much hipper than Gap; Spandex is a poor advertisement here, unless you're really advertising
Specials: All-you-can-eat buffet, 5–8 P.M. weekdays; Wednesday ladies' night with $1.50 rail drinks (Rockville only) or beer specials (Tysons Corner)
Food available: '50s diner updated; alcoholic ice cream sodas (Rockville)

What goes on: A staff of costumed, lip-synching, and choreographed (on the counters) sock-hoppers alternate performance with the DJ spinning music from the '60s to '80s and customers jiving and synchin'. Tuesdays in Rockville, boogie piano boss Daryl Davis swings for '50s and even '40s revivals.

Setting & atmosphere: *American Graffiti* comes to chrome-edged life, with glass bricks, red vinyl-topped soda counter stools, waitresses in poodle skirts, and round-bumpered service tables like car grilles. In Tysons Corner, a rock 'n' roll "wall of fame" salutes 20 of the late greats, from Elvis to Otis, but with plaques, not Hard Rock–style memorabilia. In Rockville, the secondary theme is sports souvenirs.

If you go: Prepare for some jostling; these are extremely popular after-office spots for middle-management and data-wonk types. The music is fun, if not fresh; and some of the dancers are really good. Don't cut in here, just wait for a break in the music — unless you're really good, then you grab a solo spotlight.

Takoma Station Tavern

Classically minded buppie jazz bar

Who Goes There: 25–55; mixed media
types, yuppies, buppies, other musicians

6914 4th Street, NW
(202) 829-1937

Upper Northwest   Zone 7

Hours: Sunday–Thursday, 4 P.M.–
1:30 A.M.; Friday and Saturday,
4 P.M.–2 A.M.
Cover: None
Minimum: Two drinks per table
Mixed drinks: Their Long Island
Iced Tea is strong enough to make
you confuse your geography
Dress: Suits and nice dresses; jeans,
but with a jacket; no cutoffs
Specials: Happy hour 4–8 P.M.
weekdays
Food available: Southern-style fried chicken, greens, meatloaf, ribs

What goes on: Cocktail conversation here is loud, but once the performers—
high-profile area pros and often national-rank musicians passing through who
drop in to jam—begin, the attention level is pretty good. A true neighborhood
joint owned by the taciturn Bobby Boyd, this bar was one of the nightspots
that helped revitalize the untrendy side of Takoma Park without changing its
character.

Setting & atmosphere: This building, a former boxing gym, wears its age
gracefully, with exposed brick, see-through room dividers that make the bar
an integral part of the stage area, and just a handful of hanging plants.

If you go: Don't be demonstrative, especially if you arrive early; the Boyds
live on the nightside schedule, and like to start mellow. Don't gawk at the
media types who come in after production hours. Sunday is change-up night,
with live reggae and a slightly younger crowd.

Tornado Alley

Live blues, zydeco, R&B, and rockabilly dance club

Who Goes There: 20–50; locals, swing and cajun dancers, electric-blues revival fans

11319 Elkins Avenue, Wheaton
(301) 929-0795

Maryland suburbs   Zone 10

Hours: Tuesday–Thursday and
Sunday, 5 P.M.–1 A.M.; Friday
and Saturday, 5 P.M.–2 A.M.; closed
Monday
Cover: Varies with entertainment,
roughly $7–12
Minimum: None
Mixed drinks: $3.25–4
Wine: $2–3.50
Beer: $2.25–3.50
Dress: Anything goes for
listeners; dancers tend toward

Western-swing with shiny boots and calico on rockabilly nights, sea o'
denim for blues and R&B, after-hours workboots and flannel shirts with
leather vests for longneck-sipping spectating
Specials: Occasional no-cover shows midweek
Food available: Ribs and barbecue-grilled chicken; andouille po'boys,
pulled pork, and Cajun specials such as crawfish étouffé and shrimp creole

What goes on: This is Yasgur's farm for children of the 50s. Owner Marc
Gretschel, whose original Twist & Shout blues-and-zydeco revival dances inspired the Mary-Chapin Carpenter hit, has an old blues habit that jumped him
to the front of the Delta revival and gave him an early in on booking acts
that blues labels are "rediscovering." Gretschel alternates lean, mean Chicago
blues with flashy cajun barnstorming and six-cylinder rockabilly, drawing both
a mom-and-pop crowd and a roots-rock second generation.

Setting & atmosphere: This is a carpet warehouse turned Louisiana roadhouse — big, open, and frankly cinderblock, with the bar at one end, the stage
at the other, and a couple of pool tables in the back. The only decorations
are old blues and Texabilly concert posters; the four ceiling fans make fair
headway against the smoke; and the sound system was a sound investment.

If you go: Wear washable clothes; the squeaky-polystyrene plates provide
slippery chicken parts with a launch pad. After 9, the room gets crowded and
chairs and tables get shoved together as the dance crowd expands beyond the
floor inset. Tornado Alley has exceptionally good wheelchair access.

Tracks
Mixed gay/straight, black/white/Asian disco
Who Goes There: 21–50; heterogeneous if not heterosexual; strong postgrad and dance-addicted elements

---

IIII 1st Street, SE
(202) 488-3320

Southeast   Zone 9

Hours: Thursday, 9 P.M.–4 A.M.;
Friday and Saturday, 8 P.M.–6 A.M.;
Sunday, 8 P.M.–4 A.M.; closed
Monday.
Cover: $5 Thursday; $5 Friday,
21 and over ($7 under 21); $5 Saturday
and Sunday, after 9 P.M.
Minimum: None
Mixed drinks: $3.50–6.75
Wine: $3.75
Beer: $1.75–3.75
Dress: Discreet, drag, denim,
grunge, sleek, Euro-trash, body-bar exercisewear
Specials: Ladies' Night on last Tuesday of the month; Thursday,
free drinks 9–10:30 P.M.; Saturday, $2 Stoly shooters till midnight;
Friday, $4 pitchers till midnight

What goes on: This is one of the greatest, most free-spirited dance clubs in town, having survived the periodic antigay upsurges with a becoming poise. It's also popular with some wheelchair athletes, as it has wide open spaces. The mix is harder hip, house, and industrial on weekends, a slightly softer soul mix midweek.

Setting & atmosphere: When we say wide open spaces, we mean 20,000 square feet: indoor-outdoor disco, volleyball court, and a half-dozen full bars. This is still The Place to dance, unless by dancing you mean ballet. It is frequently where the post-post-party party is, after which the post-post-post party munchie attack packs head off in cabs.

If you go: Take cash, but tuck it away; this is a rough part of town. Cabbing is best, and company is even better, if possible (at Tracks, anything is possible).

Whitey's

Old redneck tavern/good-eats joint with live blues

Who Goes There: Oldtimers, yuppie couples with
blues joneses, frathouse beer buddies

2761 North Washington Boulevard, Arlington
(703) 525-9825   Virginia suburbs   Zone 11

Hours: Sunday–Tuesday 10 A.M.–
12:30 A.M.; Wednesday–Saturday,
10 A.M.–1:30 A.M.
Cover: None
Minimum: None
Mixed drinks: $3.15–4.20
Wine: $3–4
Beer: $2.50–4
Dress: Jeans, with or without bolo;
motorcycle leathers; athletic uniforms
Specials: Happy hour 4–7 P.M.,
reduced prices
Food available: Legendary "broasted" chicken; home-style dinners,
sandwiches, bar food

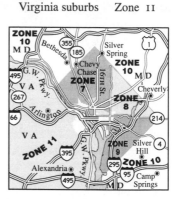

What goes on: Although Whitey's was for many years the best bar–blues
roadhouse in the region—Sunday night jams were bywords and drew national-
rank performers passing through town—neighborhood complaints about noise
and parking (and overindulged patrons) gutted their live-music permit, so that
now Whitey's is limited to karaoke on Thursdays, open mike (usually led by
an area pro) on Tuesdays, and top local bands on Saturdays. Pee Wee, the
Wednesday-night DJ, has been spinning golden oldies for nearly 15 years.

Setting & atmosphere: This is a real neighborhood tavern, whose neighborhood has upscaled around and past it, at least in some eyes. As neighbor and
harmonica godfather Mark Wenner of the Nighthawks says, "We plant one
bike outside and one official biker at the bar for atmosphere." It's a plain old
wood and beer-sign bar with booths, a game room in the rear with dart board,
pinball, shufflebowl, etc., and longneck regulars talking politics.

If you go: Don't go by appearances; if you strike up a conversation, you'll
discover this draws one of the most eclectic and politically opinionated crowds
around. If you like the Dallas Cowboys, don't admit it. Tip well; since the
kitchen keeps costs down, the waitresses don't always make what those at
pricier nightspots do. Park legally—after 7 at the Country Club Cleaners and
the law firm around the corner—and don't litter; Whitey's doesn't need your
help in alienating more neighbors.

Yacht Club of Bethesda

Second-chance singles bar and retro disco

Who Goes There: 28–55; platinum cards and platinum blondes, the monied and the alimonied

8111 Woodmont Avenue, Bethesda
(301) 654-2396   Maryland suburbs   Zone 10

Hours: Tuesday–Thursday, 5 P.M.–
1 A.M.; Friday, 5 P.M.–2 A.M.;
Saturday, 8 P.M.–2 A.M. Closed
Sunday and Monday.
Cover: None
Minimum: None
Mixed drinks: $3.95–4.50
Wine: $3.65
Beer: $3.65–4.25
Dress: Dress as class advertisement;
big earrings, gold chains — for women,
too; jacket and tie required for men
Food available: Entrees, appetizers, and sandwiches

What goes on: Upper, upper-middle, and upper-ambitious ring candidates in recession denial eye their conjugal options; more than 50 marital matches have been made here. This astonishingly successful mating pen is the brainchild of longtime singles-bar spinmaster, flatter-patter DJ, and trend-shift sacrificial lamb Tom Curtis.

Setting & atmosphere: A classy woodgrain, gray and burgundy deco style that in fact does suggest the master suite of a luxury cruiser. The name, and Curtis's use of the title "commodore," are metaphors for preferred rather than actual lifestyle, like wearing Polo sportswear. Or maybe it suggests the amount of booze that nightly goes down the hatch.

If you go: Either line up before 8, or wait till about 11. This is the sort of place that confuses Gloria Vanderbilt with Coco Chanel; you can be rich and thin enough, but your dress can never be too little or too black. The Yacht Club boasts the only black-tie waiting line in Bethesda, which is sort of a self-fulfilling prophecy. If you don't dance (and many who do, shouldn't), get in line at the pool table.

Zanzibar

Worldbeat disco

Who Goes There: 23–45; trade law, embassy, and import reps; black media; BAPs

1714 G Street, NW
(202) 842-4488

Foggy Bottom   Zone 4

Hours: Friday, 5 P.M.–3 A.M.;
Saturday, 9 P.M.–3 A.M.; dark
Sunday–Thursday.
Cover: $7 before 10:30; $10 after
Minimum: None
Mixed drinks: $4.50–7
Wine: $4.50
Beer: $3.50–4.50
Dress: Dress to impress or advertise
success: European lapels, dresses with
hip flounces, aerobic wear disguised as
cocktail Spandex; no T-shirts, jeans, or
sneakers

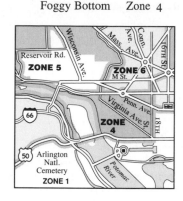

Specials: Free hors d'oeuvres and double-sized drinks, 5–8 P.M. Friday
Food available: Appetizers

What goes on: Salsa, soca, soukous, samba, and so on circulate under a disco
inferno mirror ball. This is an expansively, expensively stylish singles bar, with
potentially valuable networking as the undertone. The serious action starts
after midnight; the visiting amateurs tend to turn pumpkin at 12 A.M.

Setting & atmosphere: A sometime bureaucrats' business lunch spot, Zanzibar is a long, underground wood and brick setup divided into larger and smaller
areas, with a mahogany bar facing both and a lighted patio fountain outside
the window.

If you go: Be prepared to dance if you want to meet people; there's very little
chatter at the bar unless you prove yourself (or are extremely well-dressed).
To go with the flow, move up and down both sides of the room; there is an
unspoken tidal wave of unattached partners. Note that tax and tip are included
in drink prices.

Zed Restaurant and Public House

Live country & western music club and dance hall

Who Goes There: 28–60; studs and rustlers; reformed aerobics users

---

6151 Richmond Highway, Alexandria
(703) 768-5558

Virginia suburbs   Zone 11

Hours: Daily, 11 A.M.–1:45 A.M.
Cover: None; dinner reservations
required for some special concert
shows
Minimum: None
Mixed drinks: $3.50–5
Wine: $3–3.50
Beer: $2.75–3.25
Dress: Boots and bolos, collar tips
for the coolest, swirly skirts
Specials: Free dance lessons Sunday–
Wednesday; at happy hour (4–7 P.M.),
domestic draft beers are $1, domestic bottled beers and rail drinks, $1.25
Food available: Pub food plus; real sandwiches for real folks

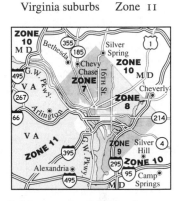

What goes on: About twice a month, Zed books just-breaking (or older and coming down) country acts, most often those whose first albums are getting lots of label support. The other nights, popular area C&W bands play for dancing.

Setting & atmosphere: Zed is sui generis — half British pub, half country saloon. (The old country came first, but the new country has sort of taken over.) Zed stocks upwards of 30 beers, more than 20 of them imported and most of them British. The most popular piece of decor is the fully operational wrought-iron English phone box (carried in by tractor, at the temporary expense of the front doors).

If you go: Use a little hairspray; neat is the national look in two-step country.

Zei

State-of-the-techno disco

Who Goes There: 22–35; Manhattan wannabes,
fashion-mag victims, drug-and-power pretenders

1415 Zei Alley, NW (half-block south of I Street between 14th and 15th)
(202) 842-2445   Downtown   Zone 3

Hours: 9 P.M.–2 A.M. Wednesday–
Saturday; closed Sunday–Tuesday
Cover: $5 weekdays, $10 weeknights
Minimum: None
Mixed drinks: $4.25–6.25
Wine: $4.25–5.25
Beer: $3.50–4
Dress: Alphabet soup
Food available: No

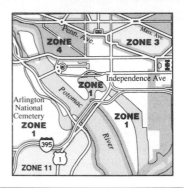

What goes on: The trendiest resident techno-rave in town, Zei manages to play up to the remnants of Republican class consciousness (by offering $750 private memberships and restricted access to the third floor) and also to neo-liberals through a meritocracy of fashion and physical fitness.

Setting & atmosphere: This $1.55-million re-creation of a floating ware-house club turns the thrift-shop ethic on its head: Oversized Mad Tea Party furniture with shoulder-pad silhouettes (on the elite third floor area), a 24-screen video-mix wall, aerobically correct house dancers, and a burnished steel mirror above the bar that turns the whole dance floor into a living video. The DJ, often a visiting dance-hall celeb from New York, works from an overhead catwalk like a starship bridge. There's an artsy steel "curtain" gathered to one side that's almost as heavy as the smoke screen from the cigarettes.

If you go: Polish up a shorthand version of cocktail conversation, because even in the "quiet zones," the 22-speaker sound system will reduce you to body language. Zei has particularly good wheelchair access. If for some reason the action here is a little too loud and attitudinal, step across the alley to the less frenetic, more landed-class Spy Club, a morning-in-America singles bar-cum-disco that draws late boomers, BMW tailgate partiers, and the prematurely jaded plastic riche.

PART SIX: *Exercise and Recreation*

Working Out

Most of the folks on our *Unofficial Guide* research team work out routinely. Some bike, some run, some lift weights or do aerobics. While visiting Washington during the hot summer months, it didn't take long to figure out that exercising in the city's fearsome heat and humidity presented some problems.

The best months for outdoor exercise are March through June and October through December. In July and August, you must get up very early to beat the heat. January and February can bring very cold weather, although snow isn't usually a problem. During the summer months, unless you get up very early, we recommend working out indoors.

—— Walking

With its wide open spaces, Washington is made for walking. Security is very good along the Mall and Potomac Park, making for a safe walking environment at all hours of the day and night.

A long walk down the Mall and through East and West Potomac parks offers grand views of the Lincoln and Jefferson memorials and the Washington Monument, as well as the Tidal Basin and the Potomac River. For a really long excursion, cross Arlington Memorial Bridge and explore Arlington National Cemetery. You can also walk north along the river past the Kennedy Center and the Thompson Boat Center and into Georgetown.

North of the Mall, downtown is not particularly interesting or aesthetically pleasing—and not too safe above New York Avenue. North of the White House, Connecticut Avenue offers unlimited window-shopping at the city's ritziest shops. South of the Capitol, Fort McNair is open to anyone who would like to stroll through well-kept grounds on a narrow peninsula where the Washington Channel and the Anacostia River meet the Potomac: Take the Metro to the Waterfront Station and walk straight down 4th Street, SW, to Fort McNair (not recommended after dark). Afterwards, you can stroll the waterfront marinas on Maine Avenue.

Although you must drive to get there, the U.S. National Arboretum in Northeast Washington offers walkers three and a half miles of easy trails winding through 444 acres of trees and flowers. In late April and May, fields of azaleas, flowering dogwood, and mountain laurel are in bloom.

The Mall and surrounding areas are fairly flat and distances can be deceiving there, making it easy to overextend yourself. Carry enough money to buy refreshments en route and for cab or Metro fare back to your hotel in case you get too tired to complete your walk.

— *Running*

Washington's wealth of parks offers plenty of options to both casual and serious joggers. Most of the better running areas are relatively flat but visually stunning. Many of the best paths are centrally located, close to major in-town hotels and other attractions, making either a morning or late afternoon run easy to fit into a busy business or touring schedule. We don't recommend jogging at night; see our chapter on "How to Avoid Crime and Keep Safe in Public Places."

The heart of Washington and its most popular running location is the **Mall,** featuring packed-dirt paths. Nearby, the **Ellipse** (behind the White House) and the **Tidal Basin** offer paved pathways to run on.

Tree-shaded **Rock Creek Park** is a better bet during hot weather. A good starting point is where Connecticut Avenue crosses over Rock Creek Parkway in Northwest Washington. Run north to Pierce Mill and retrace your steps for a four-mile jog.

In Georgetown, the **Chesapeake and Ohio Canal** towpath offers what is probably the best running surface in town. Runners, cyclists, and hikers love this wide dirt-pack trail that runs for miles between the scenic Potomac River and the canal. The river views are spectacular in places, the placid canal reflects the greenery alongside, and historic lockhouses and locks appear at regular intervals. Mileposts along the towpath keep you informed of your distance. Farther up, in Maryland, the enormous cataract at Great Falls attracts hikers and picnickers.

Another river route is the **Mount Vernon Trail,** a paved path that starts near the Lincoln Memorial, crosses Arlington Memorial Bridge, and goes downriver on the Virginia side of the Potomac for about 16

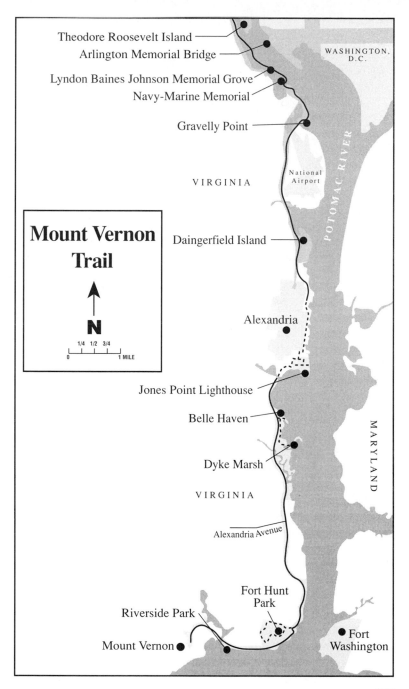

**Mount Vernon
Trail**

N

1/4 1/2 3/4
0   1 MILE

Theodore Roosevelt Island
Arlington Memorial Bridge
Lyndon Baines Johnson Memorial Grove
Navy-Marine Memorial
Gravelly Point

WASHINGTON,
D.C.

VIRGINIA

National
Airport

POTOMAC RIVER

Daingerfield Island

Alexandria

Jones Point Lighthouse

Belle Haven

Dyke Marsh

MARYLAND

VIRGINIA

Alexandria Avenue

Fort Hunt
Park

Riverside Park

Mount Vernon

Fort
Washington

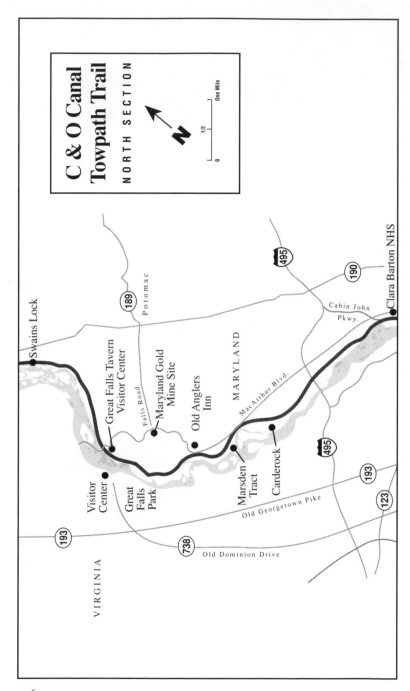

C & O Canal
Towpath Trail

NORTH SECTION

N

0   1/2   One Mile

Swains Lock

Potomac

189

Falls Road

Great Falls Tavern
Visitor Center

Maryland Gold
Mine Site

Old Anglers
Inn

MARYLAND

MacArthur Blvd.

495

190

Cabin John
Pkwy.

Clara Barton NHS

Visitor
Center

Great
Falls
Park

Marsden
Tract

Carderock

495

193

123

Old Georgetown Pike

VIRGINIA

193

738

Old Dominion Drive

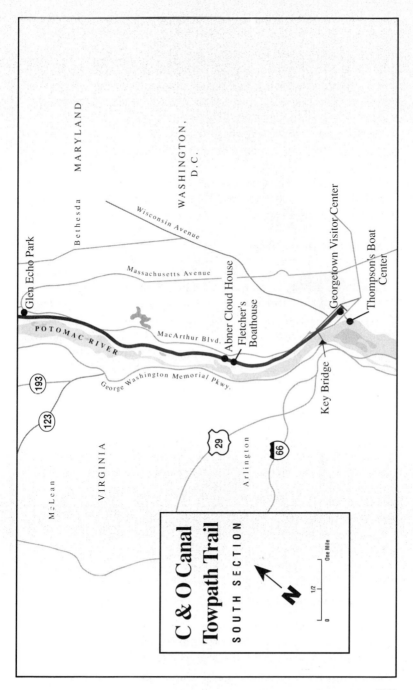

C & O Canal
Towpath Trail
SOUTH SECTION

N

0   1/2   One Mile

miles to Mount Vernon. Unless you're a marathoner, cut this run in half: Run to the airport and back, about seven and a half miles. In blustery fall, winter, and early spring weather, runners and cyclists will find that the better-protected C&O towpath offers more protection from strong winds coming off the river.

West Potomac Park is the best route in the spring, when the Japanese cherry trees are blooming around the Tidal Basin. Start near the Jefferson Memorial, head down Ohio Drive, and make the loop at the end of the park; if you've got any energy left, continue past the Jefferson Memorial and loop around the Tidal Basin. Go early in the morning to beat the crowds.

Getting to the Track

If your hotel is downtown, the Mall is the closest option you have without driving or taking the Metro. If you're staying along the Connecticut Avenue corridor, Rock Creek Park and the C&O Canal towpath are your best bets. In Alexandria or Rosslyn, the Mount Vernon Trail and the Washington and Old Dominion Regional Park are popular paved running paths. In suburban Maryland, Greenbelt Park offers both paved and unpaved surfaces to run on, as well as a one-mile fitness trail outfitted with 20 exercise stations.

—— Swimming

Local waters are polluted to one degree or another, so stick to your hotel swimming pool. The closest saltwater beach is **Sandy Point State Park** in Maryland, about an hour's drive east on US 50 on the shores of the Chesapeake Bay. Atlantic Ocean beaches are a minimum three-hour drive; traffic tie-ups on summer weekends are horrendous as beachgoers funnel into the twin Chesapeake Bay bridges, where multihour backups are routine.

—— Free Weights and Nautilus

Almost all of the major hotels have a spa or fitness room with weight-lifting equipment. For an aerobic workout, most of the fitness rooms offer a Lifecycle, a Stairmaster, or a rowing machine.

Fitness Centers and Aerobics

Many Washington fitness centers are members-only and don't offer daily or short-term memberships. The few exceptions are all coed. **City Fitness,** located on Vermont Avenue, NW, between 14th and 15th streets downtown, features free weights, fixed weights, a full range of aerobic exercise equipment including a Stairmaster, rowing and cycling machines, and a full schedule of aerobics classes. Visitors can take advantage of the facilities for $12 a day. Call (202) 638-3539 for more information.

Washington Sports International, at 1835 Connecticut Avenue, NW (across from the Hilton near Dupont Circle), offers much the same activities and services as City Fitness. The daily rate is $20, a two-week membership is $69, and a month costs $89. For more information, call (202) 332-0100.

On Capitol Hill, the **Washington Office Center Fitness Club** offers a full range of services, including free weights, fixed weights, aerobics classes, and cardiovascular workout equipment. The club, located at 409 3rd Street, SW, charges $5 a day. Call (202) 488-2822.

Tennis

Washington's two public tennis clubs are popular, making it difficult to get a court during peak hours without a reservation. The **Washington Tennis Center,** located at 16th and Kennedy streets in upper Northwest, offers 15 clay courts and 10 hard courts during the warm weather months. In winter, 5 indoor courts are available in addition to the 10 hard courts. The club accepts reservations up to a week in advance. The club is open from 7 A.M. to midnight and rates begin at $15 an hour. Call (202) 722-5949 for more information.

The **East Potomac Tennis Club,** located on Ohio Drive in East Potomac Park, features five indoor and 19 outdoor courts. Reservations for prime-time hours go fast and you need to make reservations a week in advance. Players have a good chance of getting a court without reservations weekdays between 10 A.M. and 3 P.M. Rates range from $15 to $24 an hour. Call (202) 554-5962 for more information.

Recreational Sports
Biking, Hiking, Kayaking, and So On

—— Bicycling

Washington offers both on- and off-road cyclists a wide variety of bicycling, from flat and easy cruises along paved bike paths and the C&O Canal towpath, to challenging terrain in the rolling countryside of nearby Virginia and Maryland.

In early spring and late fall, cyclists should wear riding tights and arm warmers to keep the chill off. From May through October, the temperatures range from comfortable to scorching, especially in the afternoon. Listen to weather forecasts for predictions of afternoon thunderstorms in the late summer; they can be fearsome. Fall is the best season for cycling around Washington, with cool, crisp weather and a riot of color as the leaves turn in mid- to late October. Even in winter, Washington's mild climate offers at least a few days a month that are warm enough to induce cyclists to jump on their bikes.

A variety of bicycles are available for rent at **Thompson Boat Center** (phone: (202) 333-4861), located between the Kennedy Center and Georgetown on the Potomac, and **Fletcher's Boathouse** (phone: (202) 244-0461), above Georgetown on Canal Road. **City Bikes** in Adams-Morgan (phone: (202) 265-1564) rents mountain and hybrid ("city") bikes for $7 an hour and $20 a day. **Proteus Bike & Fitness** rents road, mountain, and hybrid bikes for $30 a day, $45 a weekend, and $65 a week. Proteus has three locations: Adams-Morgan (phone: (202) 332-6666), College Park, Maryland (phone: (301) 441-2929)) and on the C&O Canal at Cabin John (phone: (301) 229-5900).

Road Biking

In downtown Washington, bicycling is better left to couriers. Unrelenting traffic congestion, combined with absent-minded tourists preoccupied with monuments and finding a cheap parking space, makes riding a bike on Washington's streets a brutal experience for all but the most hardened urban cyclists. Luckily, Washington is blessed with a network of bike paths that takes the terror out of riding a skinny-tired bike in — and out of — the city.

In terms of great scenery and enough distance to really get a workout, the **Mount Vernon Trail** is Washington's premier bike path. In addition to pedaling the 16 paved miles to Mount Vernon, cyclists can make side trips to Dyke Marsh wildlife habitat, explore Civil War fortifications at Fort Hunt, and see a 19th-century lighthouse at Jones Point Park.

Another good out-and-back ride is the **Washington and Old Dominion Railroad Regional Park** (W&OD), a 45-mile-long, paved linear bikeway that connects with the Mount Vernon Trail upriver of Arlington Memorial Bridge on the Virginia side of the Potomac. The trail intersects with a series of "bubble" parks in urban Northern Virginia and provides access to the rural Virginia countryside beyond the Capital Beltway. Both the Mount Vernon Trail and the W&OD trail are easily reached from Washington by bicycle by riding across the Arlington Memorial Bridge, at the Lincoln Memorial.

Road riders itching to see beautiful countryside outside the Washington metropolitan area (but within a day's drive) should go to either Middleburg, Virginia, or Frederick, Maryland. **Middleburg,** about 30 miles west of D.C., is in the heart of Virginia's horse country. Beautiful rolling countryside in the foothills of the Blue Ridge Mountains and low-traffic roads bordering thoroughbred horse farms make this area a fantastic place to spin the cranks.

Frederick, Maryland, is about an hour's drive north of Washington. North of town along US 15, covered bridges, narrow back roads, fish hatcheries, and mountain vistas evoke images of Vermont. To the south of Frederick, a 25-mile loop around Sugar Loaf Mountain is a favorite with local road cyclists.

Mountain Biking

Fat-tired cyclists can ride 184 miles one-way on the **Chesapeake and Ohio Canal Towpath,** beginning in Georgetown and following the Potomac River upstream to Cumberland, Maryland. The hardpacked dirt surface gives the illusion of being flat all the way; actually, the trip upriver is slightly uphill.

Hammerheads looking for challenging singletrack and some steep climbing have to do some driving to find it, but it's worth it. The **Fred-**

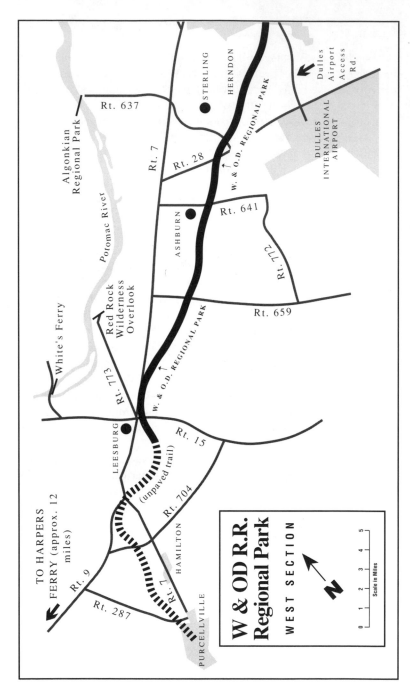

W & OD R.R.
Regional Park

WEST SECTION

Scale in Miles

0 1 2 3 4 5

Dulles Airport Access Rd.

DULLES INTERNATIONAL AIRPORT

STERLING

HERNDON

Rt. 637

Rt. 7

Rt. 28

W. & O.D. REGIONAL PARK

Algonkian Regional Park

Potomac River

ASHBURN

Rt. 641

Rt. 772

Rt. 659

White's Ferry

Red Rock Wilderness Overlook

Rt. 773

W. & O.D. REGIONAL PARK

LEESBURG

Rt. 15

(unpaved trail)

Rt. 704

HAMILTON

Rt. 7

PURCELLVILLE

Rt. 9

Rt. 287

TO HARPERS FERRY (approx. 12 miles)

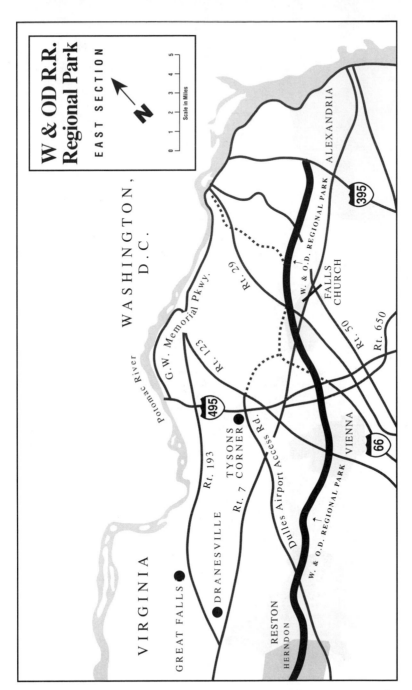

**W & OD R.R.
Regional Park**

EAST SECTION

Scale in Miles

0 1 2 3 4 5

VIRGINIA

WASHINGTON,
D.C.

Potomac River

GREAT FALLS ●

● DRANESVILLE

Rt. 193

G. W. Memorial Pkwy.

Rt. 123

Rt. 193

Rt. 62

TYSONS
CORNER ●

Rt. 7

Dulles Airport Access Rd.

495

W. & O.D. REGIONAL PARK

RESTON

HERNDON

VIENNA

66

W. & O.D. REGIONAL PARK

FALLS
CHURCH

Rt. 50

Rt. 650

ALEXANDRIA

395

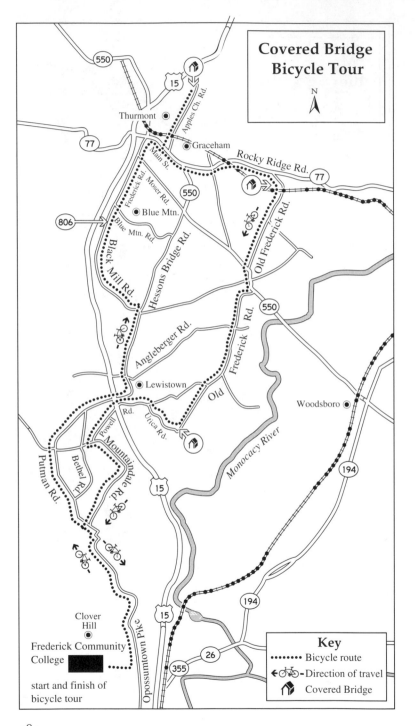

Covered Bridge Bicycle Tour

N

Thurmont

Graceham

Rocky Ridge Rd.

77

Apples Ch. Rd.

550

15

550

Main St.

Frederick Rd.

Moser Rd.

Blue Mtn.

806

Blue Mtn. Rd.

Old Frederick Rd.

Black Mill Rd.

Hessons Bridge Rd.

Angleberger Rd.

Frederick Rd.

550

Lewistown

Old

Woodsboro

Monocacy River

Powell Rd.

Utica Rd.

Mountaindale Rd.

15

194

Putman Rd.

Bethel Rd.

15

194

Clover Hill

Oppossumtown Pike

Frederick Community College

15

26

355

start and finish of bicycle tour

Key

•••••••• Bicycle route

←᚛ᚖ- Direction of travel

🏠 Covered Bridge

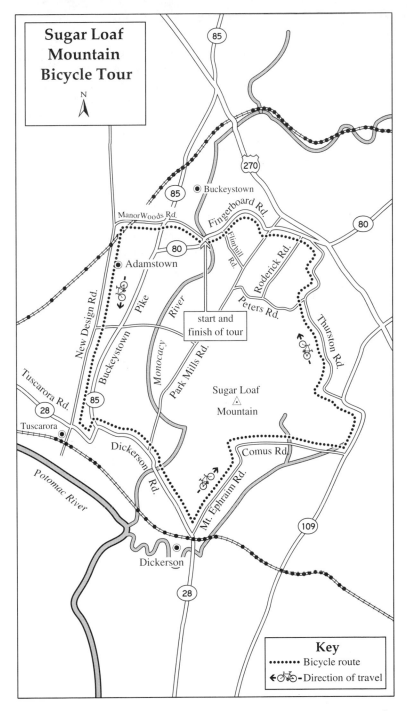

Sugar Loaf
Mountain
Bicycle Tour

N

85

270

85   ● Buckeystown

ManorWoods Rd.   Fingerboard Rd.   80

80   Flinthill Rd.   Roderick Rd.

● Adamstown   Peters Rd.

New Design Rd.   start and finish of tour   Thurston Rd.

Buckeystown Pike   Monocacy River   Park Mills Rd.

Tuscarora Rd.   Sugar Loaf △ Mountain

28   85

● Tuscarora   Comus Rd.

Dickerson Rd.

Potomac River   Mt. Ephraim Rd.   109

28

● Dickerson

Key

•••••• Bicycle route

←🚲– Direction of travel

185

erick Municipal Watershed offers the best technical singletrack this side of West Virginia—and it's a lot closer. Located an hour's drive from Washington near Frederick, Maryland, the 6,000-acre, mountain-top forest is riddled with narrow trails and well-maintained dirt roads. Since there are hardly any signs or trail markers, the Catoctin Furnace Quadrangle topographic map and a compass are a must. Local knowledge helps too; call the Wheel Base, Frederick's pro bike shop, at (301) 663-9288 for maps and advice.

— Hiking

While only about 15 minutes from downtown, **Theodore Roosevelt Island** is a wilderness oasis offering hikers a little over three miles of wide, flat paths through forests, swampy marshes, and rocky beaches. The park is located in the Potomac River across from the Kennedy Center and is only reached by car. Park in the area off the northbound lanes of the George Washington Memorial Parkway on the Virginia side of the river. A footbridge connects the Virginia shore to the island.

The **C&O Canal,** which begins in Georgetown, is a hardpacked dirt path that follows the Potomac River north for 184 miles. Along the way are river views, forest, and wildlife. At **Great Falls Park,** north of Washington on the Virginia side of the river, the Potomac roars over a series of steep, jagged rocks and flows through a narrow gorge. It's a dramatic scene and worth the trip. Hiking trails follow the river and offer views of Mather Gorge. **Rock Creek Park** in Northwest Washington offers 15 miles of hiking trails, plus bridle trails you can hike. Maps are available at the park headquarters, 5200 Glover Road, NW; (202) 426-6829.

— Canoeing and Kayaking

Canoes and rowboats are available for rent on the C&O Canal and the Potomac River at **Thompson Boat Center,** located between the Kennedy Center and Georgetown (phone: (202) 333-4861); **Fletcher's Boat House** at Canal and Reservoir roads above Georgetown (phone: (202) 244-0461); and **Jack's Boats** on K Street in Georgetown (phone: (202) 337-9642). Pedal boats for two can be rented at the Tidal Basin (phone: (202) 484-0206).

Whitewater enthusiasts need go only a few miles north of the Capital

Beltway to find excellent Class I through Class VI rapids year-round on the Potomac. Local boaters boast that it's the best urban whitewater experience in the United States, featuring a very remote, wilderness feel. One of the most popular trips is the Class II Seneca rapids section. The put-in is at Violets Lock, located on River Road (MD 190), north of Potomac, Maryland. Violets Lock is also the take-out, meaning you don't have to run a shuttle: It's a round trip that returns you to your starting point by paddling up the C&O Canal, about one and a half miles below Violets Rock. Below the Seneca rapids, the river is very scenic, featuring many islands and no rapids. But you *must* make the next take-out on the left bank at Maryland's *Great Falls National Park* or become another statistic as the river drops through Great Falls.

Seasoned whitewater boaters may want to try running the Class II–Class III+ rapids that start below Great Falls and end at the Old Angler's Inn. Just like Seneca Rapids, no shuttle is required: Park across the road from the Old Anglers Inn on MacArthur Boulevard on the Maryland side of the Potomac and follow the trail to the put-in. Paddle upstream on the C&O Canal to below Great Falls (at least 100 yards) for the return leg on the river.

— Boat Rides

Ninety-minute excursions on *The Georgetown,* a mule-drawn barge, leave Georgetown on the C&O Canal two to four times daily from April to mid-October. National Park Service guides wear 19th-century costumes, take the boat through a lock, and explain the history of the canal. Board and buy tickets near the Foundry Mall, below M Street at Thomas Jefferson Street, NW. Tickets are $4 for adults, $3 for seniors, and $2.50 for children. Call (202) 472-4376 for schedules and more information.

— Skiing

Moderately good downhill ski slopes are within a couple of hours from Washington and offer dependable, machine-made snow and night skiing from November through March. **Whitetail,** a new $25-million ski area in nearby Pennsylvania, features a vertical drop of almost 1,000 feet, 14 trails, and plenty of lift capacity. Call (717) 328-9400 for information on ski packages, lodging, and lift rates.

Jointly owned **Ski Roundtop** and **Ski Liberty,** also located in south-central Pennsylvania, are about a two- to three-hour drive from Washington. Both offer 600-foot verticals, 13 trails, and 100 percent snow-making. Call Ski Roundtop at (717) 432-9631 and Ski Liberty at (717) 642-8282 for lift rates, hours, and directions.

—— *Horseback Riding*

The Rock Creek Park Horse Center offers guided rides on the equestrian trails located in Rock Creek Park. Rates are $15 an hour and reservations are required. The minimum age is 12. The center, which is open all year, is located at Military and Glover roads in Northwest Washington. Call (202) 362-0118 for more information.

—— *Golf*

Washington has three public golf courses operated on National Park Service land and open from dawn to dusk. Fees are $6 for nine holes and $11 for 18 holes weekdays; weekends, the rates are $7 and $13. Reservations are not accepted. All three courses feature snack bars, pro shops, rental clubs, and gas cars ($9 for nine holes, $15 for 18 holes).

East Potomac Golf Course, located in East Potomac Park across from Washington's waterfront area, offers one 18-hole course, two nine-hole courses, and an 18-hole miniature golf course. It's the busiest of the three courses; plan to arrive at dawn on weekends if you don't want to wait. East Potomac has wide-open fairways, well-kept greens, and great views of surrounding monuments. Call (202) 554-7660 for more information.

Langston Golf Course, at 26th Street and Benning Road, NE (near RFK Stadium), features an 18-hole course and driving range. Langston, the only public course with water holes, is located along the Anacostia River. For more information, call (202) 397-8638.

Rock Creek Golf Course is located at 16th and Rittenhouse streets, NW, four and a half miles north of the White House on 16th Street. It offers duffers a hilly and challenging 18-hole course through rolling hills and wooded terrain. Call (202) 882-7332 for more information.

Spectator Sports

Alas, American's national pastime, **baseball,** is not played professionally in the nation's capital anymore. But Washingtonians have developed a fierce devotion to the Orioles in Baltimore, only an hour away. Visitors to D.C. can make the trek by train and catch the Birds in their new digs, Oriole Park at Camden Yards, near Baltimore's downtown inner harbor. Check the sports section of the *Washington Post* for information on home games and tickets.

For professional **basketball,** the Washington Bullets, former NBA champs, play out of the USAir Arena (formerly the Capital Centre) in suburban Landover, Maryland. Call the USAir Arena box office for ticket information: (301) 350-3400. Take the Beltway to either of two exits, 32 or 33.

The University of Maryland offers topflight college basketball at Cole Field House on its campus in suburban College Park. Call (301) 454-2121 for information. Georgetown University plays its home games at the USAir Arena; call (301) 350-3400 for ticket and schedule information.

Horse racing is available at a number of tracks around Washington; check the *Washington Post* to see which track is in season during your visit. Bus service from the city is usually available.

Harness: Rosecroft Raceway — Oxen Hill, Maryland, (301) 567-4000; Laurel Raceway — Laurel, Maryland, (301) 964-0030.

Thoroughbred: Bowie Race Course — Bowie, Maryland, (301) 262-8111; Laurel Race Course — Laurel, Maryland, (301) 725-0400; Pimlico Race Course — Baltimore, Maryland, (410) 542-9400; Charles Town Raceways — Charlestown, West Virginia, (304) 725-7001.

Lots of luck getting tickets to see **professional football** in Washington: The Redskins have sold out RFK Stadium for years and the team holds the reputation as the hardest ticket to acquire in pro sports. Still interested? Scalpers in front of RFK before game time regularly charge three and four times the correct ticket price — and higher, if the 'Skins are playing Dallas.

College football is another matter. The Maryland Terrapins play in Byrd Stadium at College Park; call (301) 454-2121. The Naval Academy in Annapolis, Maryland, and Howard University in Washington also field teams; check the *Post* for home game information.

Washington's professional **hockey** team, the Capitals, plays at the USAir Arena in Landover, Maryland. Call (301) 350-3400 for information.

PART SEVEN: Visiting Washington on Business

Not All D.C. Visitors Are Headed for the Mall

While most of the 19 million people who come to Washington each year are tourists, not everyone visiting the city has an itinerary centered around the Mall. In fact, almost two million visitors are convention-goers attending shows at the Washington Convention Center, located in downtown Washington. In addition, as the seat of the United States government, the city draws visitors from around the world who fly in to conduct business with federal agencies and a wide array of private organizations headquartered in D.C.

The city is also a center of higher education. The District is home to George Washington University, Georgetown University, American University, Howard University, and the Catholic University of America, among others. As a result, Washington attracts a lot of visiting academics, college administrators, and students and their families.

In many ways, the problems facing business visitors on their first trip to Washington don't differ much from the problems of folks in town intent on seeing Washington's best-known tourist attractions. People visiting on business need to locate a hotel that's convenient, want to avoid the worst of the city's traffic, face the same problems getting around an unfamiliar city, must figure out how to buy a Metro ticket, and want to know the locations of D.C.'s best restaurants. This book can help.

For the most part, though, business visitors aren't nearly as flexible about the timing of their visit as folks who pick Washington as a vacation destination. While we advise that the best times for coming to D.C. are spring and fall, the necessities of business may dictate that January is when you pull into town — or, even worse, early April, when the city is mobbed for the Japanese cherry blossom festivities.

Yet much of the advice and information presented in *The Unofficial Guide* is as valuable to business visitors as it is for tourists. As for our recommendations on seeing the city's many sights . . . who knows?

Maybe you'll be able to squeeze a morning or an afternoon out of your busy schedule, grab this book, and spend a few hours exploring some of the attractions that draw the other 18 million people who visit Washington each year.

The Washington
Convention Center

The Washington Convention Center is an 800,000-square-foot, two-level structure located five blocks from the White House on a 9.7-acre site bounded by New York Avenue, 9th, H, and 11th streets, NW. The center can accommodate 26,000 convention-goers, contains 37 meeting rooms, and features three exhibit halls with 100,000 square feet, 150,000 square feet, and 105,000 square feet of space, respectively. The Center provides all food and beverage services on the premises, including catered meals, 11 permanent concession stands, a 500-seat cafeteria, and a 250-seat cocktail lounge.

For both exhibitors and attendees, the Washington Convention Center is an excellent site for a meeting or trade show. Large and small exhibitors can set up their exhibits with a minimum of effort. Twelve loading docks and huge bay doors make unloading and loading quick and simple for large displays arriving by truck. Smaller displays transported in vans and cars are unloaded in the same area, entering from New York Avenue. Equipment can be carried or wheeled directly to the exhibit area. The exhibit areas and meeting rooms are well-marked and easy to find. For more information call (202) 789-1600.

—— Lodging within Walking Distance of the Convention Center

While participants in city-wide conventions lodge all over town, a few hotels are within easy walking distance of the Convention Center: the Grand Hyatt, Holiday Crowne Plaza, and the Ramada Renaissance. The Grand Hyatt, directly across the street from the Center, features 907 rooms and 60 suites. The Holiday Inn Crowne Plaza, two blocks away at Metro Center, has 454 rooms, each supplied with minibar, and 13 suites. The Ramada Renaissance Hotel Techworld, across the

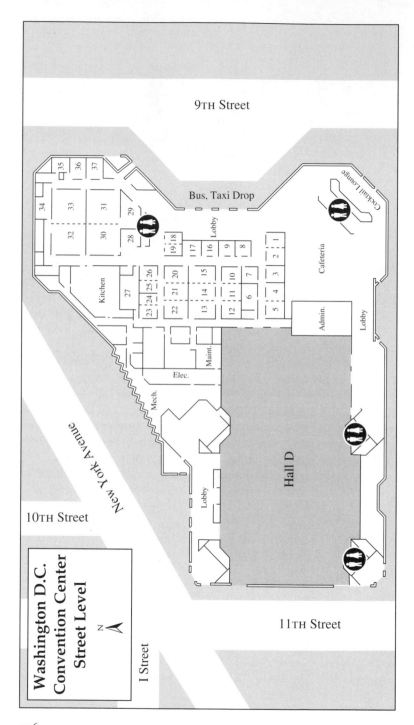

Washington D.C.
Convention Center
Street Level

N

I Street

10TH Street

New York Avenue

9TH Street

Bus, Taxi Drop

Lobby

35 36 37

34 33 31 29

32 30 28

19 18

27

25 26
23 24 21 20

22

Kitchen

Elec.

Maint.

Mech.

117 116 9 8

15 10 7

14 11 6

13 12 5

3 2 1

3

4

Cocktail Lounge

Cafeteria

Lobby

Admin.

Hall D

Lobby

11TH Street

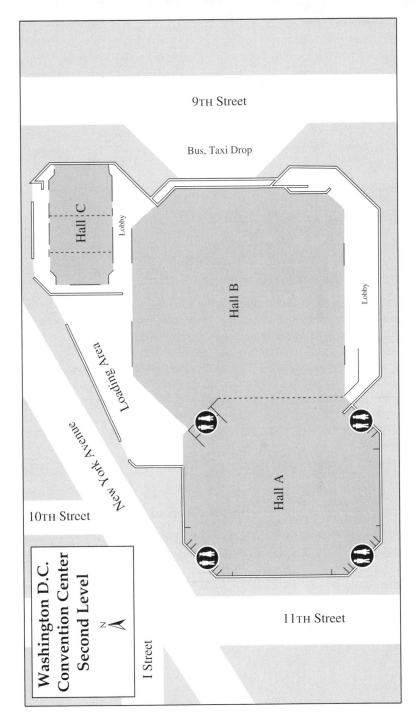

Washington D.C.
Convention Center
Second Level

N

I Street

10TH Street

11TH Street

9TH Street

Bus, Taxi Drop

New York Avenue

Loading Area

Hall C

Lobby

Hall B

Lobby

Hall A

street from the Center, boasts 800 rooms, 80 suites, 25 retail shops, and movie theaters.

Other hotels within a few blocks of the Washington Convention Center are:

Days Inn	220 rooms, 2 suites	2 blocks
Comfort Inn	197 rooms	3 blocks
Henley Park	96 rooms, 15 suites	1½ blocks
Harrington Hotel	300 rooms	3 blocks
J. W. Marriott	773 rooms, 52 suites	4 blocks

See our "Tips for Business Travelers" on pages 82–84 for more information on lodging.

—— *Parking at the Convention Center*

While there's no parking in the Washington Convention Center itself, the surrounding area offers 15 parking lots and garages within a three-block walk. Daily rates run as high as $10 a day, but average around $8.

Metro Center, one of Washington's 70 subway stations, is two blocks away from the Washington Convention Center and offers convention-goers an easy alternative to driving and parking in downtown D.C. On the red line, Metro Center is three stops from Union Station, making it convenient for people who opt to come in by train. Metro Center can be entered from the Grand Hyatt Hotel's lobby, directly across the street from the Convention Center.

—— *Cabs and Shuttles to the Convention Center*

Large, city-wide conventions often provide complimentary bus service from major hotels to the Convention Center. If you are staying at a smaller hotel and wish to use the shuttle bus, walk to the nearest large hotel on the shuttle route. In addition, cabs are relatively cheap and plentiful in Washington. The Metro, D.C.'s subway system, is clean, safe and fast; the nearest station is Metro Center, two blocks from the Convention Center.

— Lunch Alternatives for Convention and Trade Show Attendees

Prices of food from the Convention Center's food service are on the high side, but convention attendees needn't feel trapped: Plenty of good eating establishments are within a few blocks. Directly across the street on 11th Street, NW, is the Capitol City Brewing Company, a pub featuring burgers and like fare. Washington's Chinatown is a block away; the area is packed with good, cheap eateries, including the China Doll at 629 H Street and Go Lo's at 604 H Street.

For a quiet business lunch, the Old Ebbitt Grill at 675 15th Street should fill the bill. For more exotic tastes, try the Moroccan fare at Marrakesh at 617 New York Avenue, or the Burmese cuisine at Burma, 740 6th Street. For fast food, choose from Hardee's, McDonald's, Taco Bell Express, and the Shops at National Place, a three-level mall located at 13th and F streets, NW, that features a food court.

— Convention and Special Events Calendar

The city's considerable convention business (almost two million visitors a year) can make it hard to get a hotel room in and around the city. Use the following list of major 1994 and 1995 convention dates to plan your trip to Washington.

Dates	Convention/Event	Attendees
1994		
Jan. 9–12	National China, Glass and Collectibles	20,000
Jan. 25–27	Communication Networks	22,000
Mar. 7–9	American Society of Association Executives	3,000
Mar. 22–24	Federal Office Systems Expo	60,000
April 7 10	National Electric Sign Association	3,000
April 13–19	Photopro Expo/Photo Lab Expo	20,000
April 29–May 1	Blenheim International Franchise Expo	15,000
May 22–26	American Society of Biochemistry and Molecular Biology	7,000
June 6–9	Armed Forces Communications and Electronics Association	20,000

Dates	Convention/Event	Attendees
June 21–23	A/E/C Systems	30,000
June 27–July 1	Collegium Internationale Neuro-Psychopharmacologicum	8,000
July 27–31	Youth for Christ, USA	18,000
Aug. 10–12	Specialty Advertising Association International	4,500
Aug. 21–25	American Chemical Society	14,000
Aug. 30–Sept. 1	Fed Micro '94, FOSL CD-ROM	17,000
Sept. 13–17	Congressional Black Caucus	10,000
Sept. 21–23	Database World	10,000
Oct. 24–26	American Society of Clinical Pathologists/ College of American Pathologists	4,500
Nov. 9–11	Technology Utilization Foundation	6,000
Nov. 15–17	Super Computing Show '94	3,000
1995		
Jan. 8–11	National China, Glass and Collectibles	20,000
Jan. 24–26	Communication Networks	31,000
Mar. 3–7	Luggage and Leather Goods Manufacturers of America	6,000
Mar. 21–23	Federal Office Systems Expo	60,000
May 22–24	American Society for Microbiology	15,000
June 14–16	The Endocrine Society	5,000
June 26–29	World Confederation for Physical Therapy	6,000
July 5–9	Chiropractic Centennial Foundation	3,000
Aug. 14–16	American Society of Association Executives	5,000
Sept. 20–23	Congressional Black Caucus	10,000
Oct. 8–11	Water Pollution Control Federation	11,000
Dec. 10–13	American Society for Cell Biology	5,000

PART EIGHT: Sight-Seeing Tips and Tours

Plan Before You Leave Home

There are several good reasons why you should take the time to do some planning before coming to Washington to tour its sights. First of all, Washington is a big, sprawling city that covers a lot of real estate. The National Mall, for example, is two miles long — and there's more to Washington beyond that long expanse of green. Spending a poorly planned day traipsing back and forth from monument to museum to federal building to monument can waste a lot of time, energy, and shoe leather.

But it's not only Washington's physical size that makes planning a must: It's the mind-boggling number of tourist attractions that are available. Even if your vacation is a week long, be prepared to make some hard choices about how many sights you can fit into your itinerary. If your visit is shorter, say only two or three days, it's even more imperative that you have a firm idea of what you want to see. Attempting to see too much during your allotted time is exhausting: Your visit becomes a blur of marble monuments and big rooms. As with most large-scale projects, a little research can go a long way in making your trip more pleasurable.

Our recommendation before you leave for Washington is to do some soul-searching and try to reach some decisions about what your interests are. Are you curious about how the government spends all your tax money? Have you always wanted to gaze up at the solemn figure of Lincoln in his marble memorial? Do you love antiques? Are you a military buff? Does technology fascinate you? Do you love exploring art museums? Gardens? Historical houses? Washington offers places to explore for people with all these interests. Yet neither this guide nor any other can tell you what *your* interests are. You gotta do your homework.

Some more advice: To help winnow your choices, get as much written information as you can before you leave — and read it. In addition to this guide, information concerning Washington tourist attractions, hotels, and recreation can be obtained at the public library and travel agencies, or by calling or writing any of the following:

Washington, D.C., Convention and Visitors Association	(202) 789-7000
Washington, D.C., Accommodations	(202) 289-2220
or toll-free	(800) 544-2220
International Visitor Information Center	(202) 939-5566
American Express Travel Service	(202) 457-1300
Smithsonian activities	(202) 357-2020
Congresspersons (U.S. Capitol switchboard)	(202) 224-3121

— Thinking in Categories

Visitors to Washington are often thrown into large groups of tourists as they visit famous and popular edifices such as the U.S. Capitol, the Washington Monument, and the White House. Unless you've made prior arrangements for a VIP tour or Uncle Milt is a congressional staffer, you'll be craning your neck under the Capitol dome with 49 other tourists as you listen to your tour guide's spiel. Our advice: Go with the flow, relax, and enjoy the tour. But not everything you do while in Washington has to turn into a group traipse.

Question: How do you avoid the big crowds that clog the major tourist attractions?

Answer: By organizing your visit around things that interest you.

By charting your own course, you get off the beaten track and visit places that offer higher-quality tours than the canned presentations given in the better-known attractions. Often, you find yourself visiting places with small groups of people who share your interests. In short, you have more fun.

By following your own interests, you can make some intriguing discoveries as you visit Washington:

- a collection of miniature Revolutionary soldiers fighting a mock battle (Anderson House);
- a four-sided, colonial-era mousetrap that guillotines rodents (Daughters of the American Revolution building);
- a tropical rain forest located just off the Mall (Organization of American States building);
- a space capsule you can climb into (Navy Museum);
- Faberge eggs encrusted with diamonds (Hillwood Museum);
- the tomb of the only president buried in Washington (National Cathedral);

- a garden filled with flowers mentioned in the plays of William Shakespeare (the Folger Shakespeare Library);
- a building where scientists and engineers track satellites orbiting the earth (Goddard Space Flight Center); and
- a pub that shows how typical colonial-era Americans lived (Gadsby's Tavern).

As you travel around Washington, you'll discover sights like these and many others that most visitors miss. To help you on your way, we've selected major categories and listed the best destinations for visitors to explore. As you read the list, keep in mind that many attractions overlap. For example, the National Air and Space Museum appeals to both technology and military buffs, while the Woodrow Wilson House is interesting to history fans, lovers of the decorative arts, and folks curious about how the high and mighty conducted their day-to-day lives in the 1920s.

Government

U.S. Capitol
U.S. Supreme Court
White House
Bureau of Engraving and Printing

Federal Bureau of Investigation
Old Executive Office Building
U.S. Department of the Treasury
Voice of America

Monuments and Memorials

Washington Monument
Lincoln and Jefferson memorials
Vietnam Veterans Memorial
Arlington Cemetery
Iwo Jima Memorial
Navy Memorial (7th Street and Pennsylvania Avenue, NW)
Kennedy Center
U.S. Holocaust Memorial Museum
Women in Vietnam Memorial*

National Law Enforcement Officers Memorial (between E and F and 4th and 5th streets, NW)
Franklin Delano Roosevelt Memorial (to be completed in 1995)
Black Revolutionary War Patriots Memorial (targeted for completion in July 1994)

* (to be completed in November 1993 and located near the Vietnam Veterans Memorial on the Mall)

Historic Places

U.S. Capitol
White House

Chesapeake and Ohio Canal
Decatur House

Mount Vernon
Ford's Theatre
Georgetown
Old Town Alexandria
Arlington House

Frederick Douglass House
Octagon House
Old Stone House
Woodrow Wilson House

Art Museums

National Gallery of Art
Hirshhorn Museum and Sculpture
  Garden
Phillips Collection
Corcoran Gallery of Art
National Museum of
  American Art

National Museum of Women in
  the Arts
Sackler Gallery
Dumbarton Oaks
Ansel Adams Collection
Renwick Gallery
National Portrait Gallery

History

National Museum of American
  History
National Portrait Gallery
Folger Shakespeare Library
Lincoln Museum (in Ford's
  Theatre)
National Air and Space Museum
U.S. Holocaust Memorial Museum

Bethune Museum for Black
  Women's History (phone: (202)
  332-1233)
National Archives
Decatur House
Old Town Alexandria
Georgetown
Chesapeake and Ohio Canal

Technology

National Air and Space Museum
National Museum of American
  History
Arts and Industry Building
Goddard Space Flight Center
National Building Museum

National Museum of Health and
  Medicine
Washington Navy Yard
Tech 2000
Intelsat
National Postal Museum

Children

National Zoological Park
Capital Children's Museum
Museum of Natural History
National Air and Space Museum
Washington Monument

National Geographic Society's
  Explorers Hall
Tech 2000
Old Post Office Pavilion
Washington Navy Yard

Bureau of Printing and Engraving
National Museum of American
  History

National Aquarium
National Postal Museum
Federal Bureau of Investigation

Decorative Arts and Antiques

White House
Daughters of the American
  Revolution Museum and
  period rooms
Hillwood Museum
U.S. Department of State
  Diplomatic Reception Rooms
Anderson House
U.S. Department of the Treasury

Christian Heurich Mansion
Decatur House
Octagon House
Dumbarton Oaks
Mount Vernon
Textile Museum
Tudor Place
Old Town Alexandria

Gardens

U.S. Botanical Gardens
Dumbarton Oaks
Tudor Place
Hillwood Museum
Folger Shakespeare Library
Enid A. Haupt Garden (behind
  The Castle on the Mall)

Constitution Gardens
Bishops Garden at Washington
  National Cathedral
Franciscan Monastery
Kenilworth Aquatic Gardens
National Arboretum
Mount Vernon

Military

National Air and Space Museum
Arlington National Cemetery
Vietnam Veterans Memorial
Washington Navy Yard
Anderson House
U.S. Navy Memorial
the Pentagon

Smithsonian's Garber Facility *
Iwo Jima Memorial
Black Revolutionary War Patriots
  Memorial (targeted for
  completion in July 1994)
Women in Vietnam Memorial **

* (a storehouse for the National Air and Space Museum that houses aircraft from both World Wars)
** (to be completed in November 1993 and located near the Vietnam Veterans Memorial on the Mall)

Science

National Museum of Natural
  History
National Museum of American
  History
U.S. Naval Observatory
National Geographic Society's
  Explorers Hall

National Academy of Sciences
National Museum of Health and
  Medicine
National Air and Space Museum
National Aquarium
Arts and Industries Building
Tech 2000

Architecture

U.S. Capitol
Library of Congress (Jefferson
  Building)
Washington Monument
U.S. Supreme Court
Union Station
National Gallery of Art (East
  Building)
Hirshhorn Museum
National Building Museum
Washington National Cathedral
Old Executive Office Building

National Shrine of the Immaculate
  Conception
U.S. Department of the Treasury
the Pentagon
Kennedy Center
Old Post Office Pavilion
House of the Temple
National Postal Museum
National Archives
Daughters of the American
  Revolution Museum
Constitution Hall

Places of Worship

Washington National Cathedral
National Shrine of the Immaculate
  Conception
Islamic Center
Franciscan Monastery

Jewish Historical Society of
  Greater Washington
St. John's Episcopal Church
  (across from the White House)

African-Americans

Frederick Douglass House
  (Cedar Hill)
Anacostia Museum
National Museum of African Art
National Museum of
  American Art

Lincoln Memorial
Bethune Museum for Black
  Women's History
Black Revolutionary War Patriots
  Memorial (targeted for
  completion in July 1994)

Great Views

Washington Monument
Old Post Office Pavilion
Kennedy Center
Washington National Cathedral
Iwo Jima Memorial

Arlington House (Arlington
    National Cemetery)
Mount Vernon
Lincoln and Jefferson memorials

Outdoors

Chesapeake and Ohio Canal
Roosevelt Island
Rock Creek Park

Potomac Park
Mount Vernon Trail
Great Falls Park

Great Places to Walk When You're Sick of Museums

The Mall
Dupont Circle
Embassy Row (Massachusetts
    Avenue northwest of Dupont
    Circle)
anywhere along Connecticut
    Avenue
the bike path along the Potomac
    from the Kennedy Center to
    Georgetown

Georgetown
Fort McNair and the Southwest
    waterfront
National Zoo
Cathedral Avenue between
    Connecticut Avenue and
    Washington National Cathedral
National Arboretum
Kenilworth Aquatic Gardens

— Putting Your Congressperson to Work

A letter to a representative or senator well in advance of your trip (six months is not too early) can bring a cornucopia of free goodies your way: reservations on VIP tours of the White House, the Capitol, the Kennedy Center, the FBI, and the Bureau of Engraving and Printing that can save you hours of time waiting in line, as well as getting you on longer, more informative tours. In addition, your eager-to-please congressperson (he or she wants your vote) can provide timely information about hotels, restaurants, shopping, and special events. It's all free. Just be sure to include the exact dates of your visit.

Here's why you must send off your letter as soon as you know the dates that you'll be in Washington: Senators and House members are limited in the number of spaces on VIP tours that they can provide to constituents. Since all the legislators get the same number of passes, reason dictates that the farther away your state is from Washington, D.C., the better chance you have of getting on a coveted VIP tour. For example, Maryland legislators, some of whose constituents can literally jump on the Metro to reach D.C., are often booked five and six months in advance for the popular White House VIP tours. But if you're from South Dakota, chances are your congressperson will be able to get you reservations during your visit.

There is a downside to the VIP tours: Some of them take place *very* early, usually before the regular, nonreserved tours begin. For example, VIP Capitol tours are scheduled at 8 A.M., 8:15 A.M., and 8:45 A.M.; Bureau of Engraving and Printing VIP tours depart at 8 A.M. Monday through Friday; White House reserved tours take place at 8:15 A.M., 8:30 A.M., and 8:45 A.M. The upside: If you're touring in the spring and summer, you've already resigned yourself to early starts to beat the worst of the crowds anyway. Another myth shattered: The VIP tour of the White House still requires waiting in line. But the tour is longer and, unlike the unreserved version, guided.

How do you reserve a VIP tour? Write a letter to your senator or representative at his or her home office or the one in Washington. For senators, the Washington address is U.S. Senate, Washington, D.C. 20510. For House members, address your letter to the U.S. House of Representatives, Washington, D.C. 20515. Again, don't forget to include the dates you'll be visiting Washington.

A Sample Letter

25 October 1993

The Honorable (your congressperson or senator's name)
U.S. House of Representatives (or U.S. Senate)
Washington, D.C. 20515 (or 20510 for the Senate)

Dear Mr. or Ms. Congressperson,

During the week of [fill in your vacation date] my family and I will be visiting Washington to tour the major attractions on the Mall, Capitol Hill, and downtown. I understand your office can make reservations on VIP tours for constituents.

Specifically, I would like tours for the White House, the Bureau of Engraving and Printing, and the FBI during that week. I'll need four reservations for each tour. If at all possible, please schedule our tours in the middle of our week.

In addition, I'd appreciate any other touring information on Washington you can send me. Thanks in advance for your help.

Yours truly,
[Your name]

Where to Find Tourist Information in D.C.

If you're short on maps or need more information on sight-seeing, restaurants, hotels, shopping, or things to do in Washington, stop by the Washington Visitor Information Center. Located at 1455 Pennsylvania Avenue, NW, the center stocks maps and brochures and is staffed by folks who can offer touring advice. The center is a block east of the White House; phone (202) 789-7038. The center is open Monday through Saturday from 9 A.M. to 5 P.M. and is closed Sundays and major holidays.

Operating Hours

By and large, Washington's major attractions keep liberal operating hours, making it easy for visitors to plan their itineraries without worrying about odd opening and closing times. There are, however, a few exceptions. Of all the major tourist attractions, the Bureau of Engraving and Printing and the White House keep the weirdest hours: both close in the afternoon (the White House at noon) and neither is open seven days a week.

Smithsonian museums are open every day from 10 A.M. to 5:30 P.M. During the summer, hours are often extended into the evening if operating budgets allow. The U.S. Capitol is open from 9 A.M. to 4:30 P.M. daily (with longer evening hours during the summer); the Bureau of Engraving and Printing allows visitors to view its money-printing operation Monday through Friday from 9 A.M. to 2 P.M. (a free time-ticket system is in effect in the spring and summer); and the White House is open from Tuesday through Saturday from 10 A.M. to noon. (During the spring and summer, you need to arrive before 8 A.M. to get a ticket.)

Most monuments, on the other hand, are open 24 hours a day. Our recommendation is to visit the Lincoln and Jefferson memorials after dark. Lit up by floodlights, the marble edifices appear to float in the darkness, and the Reflecting Pool and Tidal Basin dramatically reflect the light. It's much more impressive than by day—and a lot less crowded.

While many sights are open every day, a lot of Washington attractions close on federal holidays: January 1, Martin Luther King Day (the third Monday in January), President's Day, Memorial Day, Independence Day, Labor Day (the first Monday in September), Columbus Day (the second Monday in October), Veterans Day, Thanksgiving, and Christmas (when virtually everything except outdoor monuments and Mount Vernon are closed).

Rhythms of the City

Although it's impossible to be specific, the ebb and flow of crowds follows a pattern throughout the day and the week at major tourist attractions. By being aware of the general patterns, you can sometimes avoid the worst of the crowds, traffic congestion, and long lines.

Mornings are slow, and the quietest time to visit most museums and sights is when they open. As lunchtime approaches, the number of people visiting a popular attraction begins to pick up, peaking around 3 P.M. Then the crowds begin to thin, and after 4 P.M. things start to get quiet again. It follows that the best times to visit a wildly popular place like the National Air and Space Museum is just after it opens and just before it closes. Conversely, when the crowds are jamming the Museum of Natural History during the middle of the day, expand your cultural horizons with a visit to the Sackler and Freer galleries, or the National Museum of African Art. They are rarely, if ever, crowded.

Among days of the week, Monday, Tuesday, and Wednesday see the fewest number of visitors. If you must visit the Washington Monument, the Bureau of Engraving and Printing, the National Air and Space Museum, the National Museum of American History, and the National Museum of Natural History, try to do so early in the week. Attempt to structure your week so that Thursday, Friday, and the weekend are spent visiting sights that are away from the Mall.

If You Visit During Peak Tourist Season

The key to missing the worst of the crowds in spring and summer is to get a hotel close to a Metro station, park the car, and leave it. Then decide what is most important for you to see, and get to those places *early*.

An example: You've miraculously secured a convenient D.C. hotel room in early April. From your in-town window, Washington is laid out before you — and for most of the day, it's a view of gridlocked motor coaches, school buses, families in cars, angry commuters, and jammed sidewalks. Everybody but the commuters is drawn by the Japanese cherry trees in bloom along the Tidal Basin and the Reflecting Pool on the Mall.

But don't rush out the door and join the throngs on their way to see the trees. Because it's early (say, 7 A.M.), your plan is to hit the sights that you want to see before the crowds arrive. So walk to the nearby Metro station and take the train to the Smithsonian station. From there, it's a 10-minute stroll to the Washington Monument — and at 7:30, you're near the front of the line. By 8:30 A.M., you're out of the marble obelisk and on your way to the nearby Bureau of Engraving and Printing. At the ticket office on 15th Street, pick up a time ticket for a tour of the money printing facility that begins at 1:30 P.M. From there, it's a short walk to the Jefferson Memorial and those famous trees.

At 9:30, you stroll toward the Mall for a visit to the National Air and Space Museum as it opens at 10 A.M. At 10:15, you join a free, guided tour. At 11 A.M., you're back on your own again to explore some corners of the museum that interest you.

By noon, the crowds are starting to fill the museum, so you leave Air and Space in search of a bite to eat. Back to the Metro and it's a three-minute ride to L'Enfant Plaza, where you grab lunch in an Italian restaurant that serves great stromboli. Then it's an easy walk to the Bureau of Engraving and Printing to see the stacks of money.

By 2 P.M., you have already visited three of the world's most popular attractions during peak season with almost no waiting in line. Now, you can spend the afternoon exploring a wide range of attractions that never get crowded, even when Washington is besieged by tourists in the spring: the Freer Gallery, the Hirshhorn Museum, the Vietnam Veterans Memorial, the Corcoran Gallery or the DAR Museum, just to name a few.

Intragroup Touring Incompatibility: What It Is and How to Avoid It

The incidence of "Intragroup Touring Incompatibility" (members of the same group having strongly conflicting interests or touring objectives) is high in Washington, thanks to the city's wide variety of touring attractions. An example: Some people would be happy never to leave the National Air and Space Museum; a lot of other folks find that, after an hour or two of staring at old airplanes and spacecraft, it's time to move on.

Children, at the other extreme, haven't the patience or inclination for all the reading required by the exhibits and fizzle out after a couple of hours of touring D.C. museums. In fact, even grown-ups should consider a touring plan that puts reading-intensive attractions such as self-guided museum tours at the beginning of the day, and take guided tours in the afternoon, where you're spoonfed information by a guide and you can put your brain on autopilot.

A touring plan made up before your arrival in Washington can help your group avoid the worst manifestations of intragroup incompatibility. If your group contains, for example, a real "Rocket George," let him linger at the National Air and Space Museum while the rest of you move on to another Mall attraction. Arrange a meeting place later in the day where you can all regroup; both you and Rocket George will be happier.

Washington with Children

Most adult visitors to Washington experience a rush of thrill and pride on viewing the U.S. Capitol, the Washington Monument, and the White House. And, for most of us, those are feelings that hold up well over repeat visits to the nation's capital. In fact, a fascination for the city often begins on a first visit to Washington in grade or high school and can continue through adulthood.

So it follows that Washington is one of the most interesting, beautiful, and stimulating cities in the world for children and young people. Where else can kids visit the president's house, touch a moon rock, feed a tarantula, and view a city from the top of a 555-foot marble obelisk?

Luckily, most popular tourist destinations in Washington offer a lot to hold an adult's attention, too—which means you don't have to worry about parking the kids someplace while you tour a museum. For example, as your kids marvel at the dinosaur skeletons in the Museum of Natural History or feed that giant spider, you can be fantasizing over the Hope Diamond.

Even so, on a Washington vacation with small children, anticipation is the name of the game. Here are some things you need to consider:

Age. Although the big buildings, spaciousness, and excitement of Washington excite children of all ages, and while there are specific sights which delight toddlers and preschoolers, Washington's attractions are generally oriented to older kids and adults. We believe that children should be a fairly mature nine years old to get the most out of popular attractions such as the National Museum of Natural History, the U.S. Capitol, and the White House, and a year or two older to get much out of the art galleries, monuments, and other federal buildings around town.

Time of Year to Visit. If there is any way to swing it, avoid the hot, crowded summer months. Try to go in late September through November or mid-April through mid-June. If you have children of varying ages and your school-age kids are good students, consider taking the older ones out of school so you can visit during the cooler, less-congested off-season. Arrange special study assignments relating to the many educational aspects of Washington. If your school-age children are not great students and cannot afford to miss any school, take your vacation as soon as the school year ends in late May or early June. Nothing, repeat, nothing will enhance your Washington vacation as much as avoiding the early spring and summer months.

Building Naps and Rest into Your Itinerary. Washington is huge and offers more attractions than you can possibly see in a week, so don't try to see everything in one day. Tour in the early morning and return to your hotel midday for a swim (if your hotel has a pool; see below) and a nice nap. Even during the fall and winter, when the crowds are smaller and the temperature more pleasant, the sheer size of D.C. will exhaust most children under eight by lunchtime. Go back and visit more attractions in the late afternoon and early evening.

Where to Stay. The time and hassle involved in commuting to and from downtown Washington and its surrounding neighborhoods will be lessened if you can afford to stay inside the District and near a Metro station. But even if, for financial or other reasons, you lodge outside of Washington, it remains imperative that you get small children off of the Mall for a few hours to rest and recuperate. Neglecting to relax and unwind is the best way we know to get the whole family in a snit and ruin the day (or the entire vacation).

With small children, there is simply no excuse for not planning ahead. Make sure you get a hotel, in or out of Washington, within a few minutes' walk to a Metro station. Naps and relief from the frenetic pace of touring Washington, even in the off-season, are indispensable. While it's true that you can gain some measure of peace by finding a quiet spot near the Tidal Basin to relax, there is no substitute for returning to the familiarity and security of your own hotel. Regardless of what you have heard or read, children too large to sleep in a stroller will not relax and revive unless you get them back to your room.

Another factor in choosing a hotel is whether or not it has a swimming pool. A lot of visitors to D.C. assume that, like most destinations, Washington hotels automatically come with a pool. Alas, it ain't necessarily so. A swimming pool, especially in warmer weather, can be a lifesaver for both you and your kids. So if a refreshing dip is important to your family, be sure to ask before making hotel reservations.

Be in Touch with Your Feelings. While we acknowledge that a Washington vacation can be a capital investment (pardon the pun), remember that having fun is not necessarily the same as seeing everything. When you and your children start getting tired and irritable, call time-out and regroup. Trust your instincts. What would really feel best right now? Another museum, a rest break with some ice cream, going back to the room for a nap? *The way to protect your investment is to stay happy and have a good time, whatever that takes.* You do not have to meet a quota for experiencing every museum on the Mall, seeing every branch of government, or walking through every monument, or anything else. It's your vacation; you can do what you want.

Least Common Denominators. Remember the old saying about a chain being only as strong as its weakest link? The same logic applies to a family touring Washington. Somebody is going to run out of steam first; when they do, the whole family will be affected. Sometimes a cold Coke and a rest break will get the flagging member back into gear. Sometimes, however, as Marshall Dillon would say, "You just need to get out of Dodge." Pushing the tired or discontented beyond their capacity is like driving on a flat tire: It may get you a few more miles down the road but you will further damage your car in the process. Accept that energy levels vary among individuals and be prepared to respond to small children or other members of your group who poop out. Hint: "After we've driven a thousand miles to take you to Washington, you're going to ruin everything!" is not the right thing to say.

Setting Limits and Making Plans. The best way to avoid arguments and disappointments is to develop a game plan before you go. Establish some general guidelines for the day and get everybody committed in advance. Be sure to include:

1. Wake-up time and breakfast plans.
2. What time you need to depart for the part of Washington you plan to explore.
3. What you need to take with you.
4. A policy for splitting the group up or for staying together.
5. A plan for what to do if the group gets separated or someone is lost.
6. How long you intend to tour in the morning and what you want to see, including fall-back plans in the event an attraction is too crowded.

7. A policy on what you can afford for snacks, lunch, and refreshments.
8. A target time for returning to your hotel for a rest.
9. What time you will return to touring D.C. and how late you will stay.
10. Plans for dinner.
11. A policy for shopping and buying souvenirs, including who pays: Mom and Dad or the kids.

Be Flexible. Having a game plan does not mean forgoing spontaneity or sticking rigidly to the itinerary. Once again, listen to your intuition. Alter the plan if the situation warrants. Be prepared to roll with the punches.

Overheating, Sunburn, and Dehydration. In the worst of Washington's hot and humid summers, the most common problems of smaller children are overheating, sunburn, and dehydration. A small bottle of sunscreen carried in a pocket or fanny pack will help you take precautions against overexposure to the sun. Be sure to put some on children in strollers, even if the stroller has a canopy. Some of the worst cases of sunburn we have seen were on the exposed foreheads and feet of toddlers and infants in strollers. To avoid overheating, rest at regular intervals in the shade or in an air-conditioned museum, hotel lobby, or federal building.

Do not count on keeping small children properly hydrated with soft drinks and water fountain stops. Long lines often make buying refreshments problematic and water fountains are not always handy. What's more, excited children may not inform you or even realize that they're thirsty or overheated. We recommend renting a stroller for children six years old and under, and carrying plastic water bottles.

Blisters. Blisters and sore feet are common for visitors of all ages, so wear comfortable, well broken-in shoes and two pairs of thin socks (preferable to one pair of thick socks). If you or your children are unusually susceptible to blisters, carry some precut "Moleskin" bandages; they offer the best possible protection, stick great, and won't sweat off. When you feel a hot spot, stop, air out your foot, and place a Moleskin over the area before a blister forms. Moleskin is available by name at all drugstores. Sometimes small children won't tell their parents about a developing blister until it's too late. We recommend inspecting the feet of preschoolers two or more times a day.

Health and Medical Care. If you have a child who requires medication, pack plenty, and bring it in a carry-on bag if you're flying to Washington. A bottle of liquid Dramamine will come in handy to fight off motion sickness, which can affect kids who are normally fine in a car but may get sick in a plane, train, or boat . . . or vice versa.

A small first aid kit, available at most pharmacies, will handle most minor cuts, scrapes, and splinters, and is easy to pack. Grown-up and children's strength aspirin or Tylenol, a thermometer, cough syrup, baby wipes, a plastic spoon, a night light, and pacifiers will round out a small kit of health-related items for people traveling with children or infants.

Be sure to carry proof of insurance and policy numbers with you. Check with friends or relatives before you leave for Washington to get the name of a pediatrician who practices locally; it could save a lot of time thumbing through the yellow pages if a youngster should fall ill. For emergency treatment, dial 911 or go to the emergency room of the nearest hospital. Here's a list of major hospitals in D.C.:

- Capitol Hill Hospital, 700 Constitution Avenue, NW (phone: (202) 269-8000)
- Children's National Medical Center, 111 Michigan Avenue, NW (phone: (202) 745-5000)
- George Washington University Medical Center, 901 23rd Street, NW (phone: (202) 994-1000)
- Georgetown University Medical Center, 3800 Reservoir Road, NW (phone: (202) 784-2000).

Sunglasses. If you want your smaller children to wear sunglasses, it's a good idea to affix a strap or string to the frames so the glasses won't get lost and can hang from the child's neck while indoors.

If You Become Separated. Before venturing out of your hotel room, sit down with your kids and discuss what they should do if they get separated from you while touring a museum, monument, or federal building. Tell them to find a uniformed guard and ask for help. Point out that the main entrance of most Washington attractions has an information desk where they should go if they temporarily get separated.

We suggest that children under eight be color-coded by dressing them in purple T-shirts or equally distinctive attire. It is also a good idea to sew a label into each child's shirt that states his or her name, your name, and the name of your hotel. The same thing can be accomplished less elegantly by writing the information on a strip of masking tape: hotel security professionals suggest that the information be printed in small letters and that the tape be affixed to the outside of the child's shirt five inches or so below the armpit.

Rainy Days. Rainy days and Mondays can get you down — even while on vacation — and cooped-up children suffer even worse. Museums and galleries are obvious choices during inclement weather (as you can tell from the crowds), but don't rule out some other options to keep children entertained when the sun doesn't shine or if you're museumed-out. Catch a movie at Union Station's nine-screen cinema complex or take the Metro to Alexandria's Torpedo Factory, where 150 craftsmen work and sell their creations Tuesday through Sunday. And don't forget that age-old panacea for boredom — shopping. Union Station, the Old Post Office Pavilion, the Shops at National Place, and Georgetown Park are all indoor shopping centers with interesting specialty stores. If you run out of ideas, check the *Washington Post*'s "Weekend" section for inspiration.

Of course, some attractions can bore active kids to tears — even if it's raining outside. An entire afternoon in the National Gallery of Art can be deadly to eight-year-olds. The best plan is to reward your youngsters for their patience with a trip to someplace really special when the weather clears. The National Zoo should top the list. And you'll enjoy it, too.

A final tip that can help you and your kids weather a storm: Stay in a hotel with a pool; on rainy days, kids love getting wet *indoors*.

The 10 Most Popular Sights for Children

1. The National Air and Space Museum
2. The National Zoo
3. The Capital Children's Museum
4. The National Museum of Natural History
5. The Bureau of Engraving and Printing
6. The Federal Bureau of Investigation
7. The National Museum of American History
8. The National Geographic Society's Explorers Hall
9. Washington Navy Yard
10. The Washington Monument

The 10 Least Popular Sights for Children

1. The National Gallery of Art — West Building
2. The Library of Congress
3. The U.S. Supreme Court
4. The Pentagon
5. The Kennedy Center
6. Dumbarton Oaks museum
7. The National Portrait Gallery
8. The Folger Shakespeare Library
9. The Textile Museum
10. Renwick Gallery

Touring

—— Washington's Top 20 Tours

With only a few exceptions (such as the FBI), it isn't absolutely necessary to join a group tour while visiting Washington's attractions. Simply explore on your own, letting your curiosity and interests be your guide. This strategy works well in a large museum such as the National Museum of Natural History—dinosaur skeletons? an insect zoo? the Hope Diamond? take your pick. At selected locations, though, it can be a nice change of pace to have an expert lead you by the hand and, who knows, enlighten you. What follows is a highly arbitrary list of guided tours that the authors of *The Unofficial Guide* think do a splendid job at introducing visitors to their respective attractions. For more detailed information (i.e. address and phone number) on the following attractions, see Part Nine.

1. U.S. Department of State Diplomatic Reception Rooms. One of the advantages of taking tours that require advance reservations is that the tour guides are top-notch. The guide we encountered on this tour of the $65-million rooms housed on the eighth floor of this otherwise humdrum building really knows her stuff, from the art on the walls to the historical significance of the impressive furniture that fills these spectacular, ornate rooms.

2. U.S. Capitol. While the "introductory" tour offered every 15 minutes to groups of 50 may not be the best way to get a feel for this magnificent building, it's a good start. Stick close to your guide so you can hear his or her comments about the art work on display and the history of the building. Afterwards, you can go back on your own and visit the rooms and chambers you missed on the tour. Warning: This is a confusing building and most people manage to get lost.

3. Washington National Cathedral. While this is an easy place to just wander around in, don't: Take the free tour. The docent (or museum guide) who led my group of out-of-towners showed enthusiasm, a real concern for her charges, and a deep knowledge of the cathedral. She also mentioned the free organ demonstration that followed the tour, which I stayed for. It turned out to be the highlight of my day.

4. *Library of Congress.* This tour starts off with the ubiquitous 20-minute video that explains the internal workings of the world's biggest library. Then you're led by a knowledgeable tour guide to the Jefferson Building and a view of the magnificent Main Reading Room. The Library's mission and collections are mind-boggling.

5. *DAR Museum and Period Rooms.* My tour of the period rooms (there are 33, but no one sees them all on one tour) was led by a poised young woman who really knew her history—and her decorative arts. She also is well informed on the handsome building that serves as DAR headquarters: A special railroad spur was built to bring the massive, solid-marble columns on the front of the building to the site. For antiques lovers, this tour is about two hours of bliss.

6. *The Phillips Collection.* The 45-minute tour highlights the best items in the modern art collection and puts them in the context of the wealthy collector who founded the museum. The guides know their art and manage to tie together different art periods as they talk about the paintings. The comfortable Phillips is a welcome contrast to Mall megamuseums. Guided tours are free and offered on Wednesdays and Saturdays.

7. *Hillwood Museum.* My only complaint about this reservation-only tour was its length—two hours. But it will fascinate anyone interested in the decorative arts, antiques, jewelry, porcelains, paintings, furniture . . . the list goes on. It's a breathtaking collection, and you'll tour in small groups led by knowledgeable guides.

8. *Old Executive Office Building.* Here's another reservation-only tour that gives visitors that "insider" feel. The exterior of this huge, 19th-century palace is considered a monstrosity by many, but its recently renovated interior is magnificent. The elevators still need work, though—nervous types may not enjoy the part where you jump up and down to get the doors to close.

9. *U.S. Department of the Treasury.* This reservation-only, behind-the-scenes tour lets visitors feel like they're really seeing something special. The interior of the building was recently renovated: The tour takes you through sumptuous offices and corridors restored to their mid-19th-century opulence.

10. The Voice of America (VOA).   I liked this small, off-the-beaten-track tour. Most of the visitors who go are from foreign countries and listen to Voice of America broadcasts at home. (Listening to the VOA in the United States requires a shortwave radio.) The docent who led the tour was the widow of a diplomat, witty and conversant about many of the countries that receive VOA broadcasts. And the broadcast studios are really neat.

11. Arlington National Cemetery.   Tourmobile does a good job of transporting visitors around 612-acre Arlington National Cemetery. The thought of trying to see all the sights in the cemetery on foot makes my feet hurt. The bus stops at the Kennedy gravesite, the Tomb of the Unknowns, and Arlington House, where you can linger as long as you like, since you have unlimited boarding privileges to the buses that come about every 15 minutes.

12. The Kennedy Center.   This leisurely tour of the sumptuous performing arts center and JFK memorial gives visitors a behind-the-scenes look at Washington's cultural life, as well as a chance to linger over some of the art work donated to the center from countries from around the world. The 360-degree view of Washington from the center's roof terrace is a knockout.

13. The National Portrait Gallery.   What would have been an aimless ramble through this downtown art museum turned into an informative tour. On a whim, I asked the guard at the information desk when the next guided tour left. The answer: Whenever you're ready. So I got a one-on-one tour from a docent who's the wife of an admiral and really knows her history. The moral: Don't be afraid to ask for a free tour.

14. Decatur House.   A half-hour tour of the Federalist home brings early Washington to life as the tour guide explains what life was like when Stephen Decatur lived here in 1819. Upstairs, visitors get a glimpse of how upper-crust Washington society, including President and Mrs. Kennedy, were entertained by later owners of the house.

15. Woodrow Wilson House.   A video narrated by Walter Cronkite primes you for a detailed tour of the house where President Wilson retired after leaving the White House. He was the only president to live in Washington after leaving office. The house preserves elements of

Wilson's day-to-day life, including an ancient movie projector he used and his meticulously kept basement kitchen.

16. *Christian Heurich Mansion.* This one-hour tour is a bit long, but it gives you an excellent glimpse of how a rich, turn-of-the-century Washington family lived. The craftsmanship that went into this mansion would probably be impossible to duplicate today.

17. *The Franciscan Monastery.* The 45-minute tour includes a beautiful, recently restored church and replicas of shrines in the Holy Land. But the real treat is hair-raising stories of Christian martyrs told by your guide as you wind your way through a replica of Roman catacombs.

18. *The* Washington Post. This is a great tour for anyone who's never seen the insides of a big-city newspaper. On the 45-minute tour, you visit the newsroom, the composition rooms, a small museum showing how it was all done before computers took over, and the big presses.

19. *Gadsby's Tavern.* After seeing nothing but sumptuousness and 20-foot ceilings in Washington's magnificent edifices, it's a relief to make the short trek to Alexandria and see how average Americans lived and worked in the 18th century. The tour of this tavern gives a glimpse of how most people traveled, ate, and slept during the period when Alexandria was a major port — and Washington didn't exist.

20. *FBI Headquarters.* This tour follows a rigid formula, is executed with military precision, features lots of static displays, and is very popular. But is it good? The young women leading the tour recited a series of canned presentations that sounded memorized. Most of the exhibits are inert displays of guns, drug paraphernalia, fingerprinting methods, and old "most wanted" posters. I suspect it's the demonstration of automatic weapons fire at the end of the tour — and the chance to hear a real FBI Special Agent talk and answer questions — that makes this tour so popular.

— *Taking an Orientation Tour*

First-time visitors to Washington can't help but notice the regular procession of open-air, multi-car tour buses — "motorized trolleys" is probably a more accurate term — that prowl the streets along the Mall, the major monuments, Arlington Cemetery, downtown, Georgetown, and upper Northwest Washington. These regularly scheduled shuttle buses drop off and pick up paying customers along a route that includes the town's most popular attractions. Between stops, passengers listen to a tour guide talk about the city's monuments, museums, and famous buildings. The guides also suggest good places to eat and drop tidbits of interesting — and often humorous — Washington trivia.

Our advice: If this is your first trip to Washington, take one of the tours early in your visit.

Here's why: Geographically, Washington is a spread-out city. Attempting to hoof it to Capitol Hill, the Washington Monument, and the Lincoln and Jefferson memorials in one day amounts to cruel and unusual punishment to the body — especially your feet. Throw in a hot and humid Washington afternoon and a few cranky kids, and it's a recipe for vacation meltdown.

Think of the narrated shuttle-bus tours that cruise Washington as a special transportation system that not only gets you to the most popular sights, but also provides a timely education on the city's size and scope. The money you pay for your ticket allows unlimited reboarding privileges for that day, so you can get off at any scheduled stop and reboard a later bus (they run at 30-minute intervals).

Both of the two guided tours that operate on a regular route in the city, Tourmobile and Old Town Trolley, are good values. **Tourmobile** has the National Park franchise and shuttles its open-air, articulated buses to 18 sights around the Mall, Capitol Hill, and Arlington Cemetery from 9 A.M. to 6:30 P.M. between June 15 and Labor Day and from 9:30 A.M. to 4:30 P.M. the rest of the year. For tour information, call (202) 554-7950. Ticket booths are located at Arlington Cemetery, the Lincoln Memorial, and the Washington Monument, but you can board at any red and white Tourmobile stop sign on the route and pay the driver ($10.50 adults, $5 children). The company also runs narrated tours to Mount Vernon (four hours; $25.50 adults, $12.50 for children ages 3 to 11; fee includes admission to the estate) and to the Frederick Douglass Historical Site in Anacostia (two-and-a-half hours; $16 adults, $8 for children ages 3 to 11).

We like the **Old Town Trolley** tours a little better. The route includes the Mall, but also goes to downtown Washington, Dupont Circle, posh Northwest Washington, Embassy Row, and Georgetown. If you're staying at one of the following hotels, you can hop on board and be dropped at your door: Hyatt Regency, Grand Hyatt, J. W. Marriott, Capitol Hilton, Washington Hilton, Omni Shoreham/Sheraton Washington, and the Holiday Inn near the National Air and Space Museum.

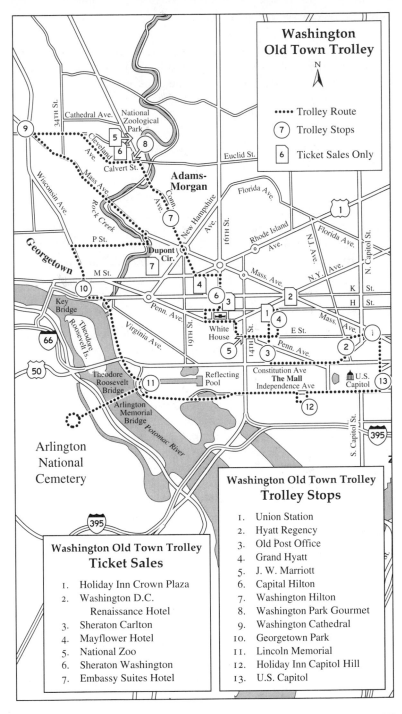

**Washington
Old Town Trolley**

N

····· Trolley Route

(7) Trolley Stops

[6] Ticket Sales Only

**Washington Old Town Trolley
Trolley Stops**

1. Union Station
2. Hyatt Regency
3. Old Post Office
4. Grand Hyatt
5. J. W. Marriott
6. Capital Hilton
7. Washington Hilton
8. Washington Park Gourmet
9. Washington Cathedral
10. Georgetown Park
11. Lincoln Memorial
12. Holiday Inn Capitol Hill
13. U.S. Capitol

**Washington Old Town Trolley
Ticket Sales**

1. Holiday Inn Crown Plaza
2. Washington D.C.
   Renaissance Hotel
3. Sheraton Carlton
4. Mayflower Hotel
5. National Zoo
6. Sheraton Washington
7. Embassy Suites Hotel

Although pulling into all these hotels is a bit tedious (unless one happens to be yours), Old Town Trolley's two-hour tour shows visitors that there's a lot more to Washington than the Mall, museums, and piles of marble.

Old Town Trolley's open-air shuttle buses are somewhat more comfortable than Tourmobile's, and just like with Tourmobile, you get unlimited reboarding privileges from its 14 stops. Hint: If you didn't drive to Washington and don't have a car, make this your chance to visit Washington National Cathedral and Georgetown; neither is close to a Metro station and getting off now can save on cab fare or shoe leather. Tickets ($15 adults; $7 for children ages 5 to 12) can be purchased from the driver or at ticket booths located at most of the stops. The tours begin at 9 A.M. and run on the half-hour till 4 P.M. (5 P.M. Memorial Day through Labor Day). For more information, call (301) 985-3021.

—— *Other Commercial Guided Tours*

While Tourmobile and Old Town Trolley do a good job at shuttling visitors around Washington's major tourist attractions, a number of other local companies offer more specialized tours. Here's a run-down of some tours that are a little different.

Gray Line offers a wide variety of narrated bus tours in and around Washington. Half-day, all-day, and overnight tours take visitors to Washington's most popular sights, including the Mall museums, government buildings, Embassy Row, and Mount Vernon and Alexandria in Virginia. Gray Line also offers a "Washington After Dark" tour to see monuments and federal buildings flooded in lights, a black heritage tour, trips to Harpers Ferry and the Gettysburg battlefield, and tours of Monticello and Williamsburg. Tours depart Union Station; call (202) 289-1995 for more information.

Spirit of Washington Cruises, located at Pier 4, 6th and Water streets, SW, takes visitors on boat tours of the Potomac River spring through fall. The star attraction is the half-day cruise to Mount Vernon, where the boat docks and you can tour the mansion and grounds. Call (202) 554-8000 for information and rates on lunch, dinner, and moonlight dance party cruises aboard an air-conditioned luxury ship.

The Cruise Ship *Dandy* departs Old Town Alexandria for dinner cruises that feature after-dinner dancing. Sights along the way include the floodlit Capitol dome. Call (703) 683-6076 for information and schedules.

Scandal Tours will reinforce every evil thought you ever had about Washington and those who rule. It's a comedy review on wheels — not a sight-seeing tour — and makes stops at, predictably enough, the Watergate complex, the Pentagon, and the Tidal Basin, where a powerful member of Congress once went skinny-dipping with a stripper. Ninety-minute public tours depart Saturdays at 1 P.M., April through Labor Day, from the Washington Hilton, Connecticut Avenue and T Street, NW; call (301) 587-4291 for more information and rates. Private charters are available year-round.

The Guide Service of Washington, the oldest and largest in D.C., offers private, customized VIP tours led by licensed guides. For foreign visitors, guides are available who speak your native tongue. A four-hour tour is a flat rate of $98, plus tax and transportation, regardless of the size of your group. Tours must be paid for in advance. Call (202) 628-2842 for more information.

Liberty Helicopter Tours provide spectacular birds-eye views of the Jefferson and Lincoln memorials as well as other famous Washington sights. Call (202) 863-1313. Flights range in cost from $55 to $119 per person and leave from the Air Pegasus Heliport, 1724 S. Capitol Street, SE, from 9:30 A.M. to 5:30 P.M. daily.

— OPTIMUM ADULT TOURING PLAN

An Optimum Touring Plan in Washington, D.C., requires a good itinerary, a minimum of five days in town (i.e., not including travel time), a surprisingly modest amount of money (most attractions are free), and a comfortable pair of walking shoes. It also requires a fairly prodigious appetite for marble edifices, huge museums, and historical trivia. We will provide an itinerary; the rest is up to you.

With an Optimum Touring Plan, you can see the various attractions in and around Washington without facing huge crowds on the Mall, sitting in restaurants and shops that are jammed to capacity, or trudging through heat and humidity during sweltering afternoons.

Since an Optimum Touring Plan calls for seeing a lot of different parts of D.C., it makes for easier logistics if you stay at a hotel that's in the city and close to a Metro station. But even if your hotel is in the suburbs, you can still use the day-by-day plan as long as you can walk to the Metro. You'll lose some time commuting, but you may save some money on hotel rates. You'll lose even more time if you have to drive to a Metro station and park (see page 240). Once you get in your car and start driving around in D.C., you're defeating the purpose of the Optimum Touring Plan, and you'll know it. We repeat: Don't drive in the city.

If you plan to visit Washington during the busiest months (see pages 26–27), you need to get up early to beat the crowds. Short lines at the Washington Monument and getting into the White House at all are basically incompatible with sleeping in. If you want to sleep late *and* enjoy your touring experience, visit Washington in the fall or winter, when crowds are smaller. The Optimum Touring Plan assumes your visit is during the busy season.

We do not believe there is one ideal itinerary. Tastes, levels of energy, and basic perspectives on what is interesting or edifying vary. This understood, what follows is our personal version of an optimum Washington vacation week.

Before You Go

1. Write your congressperson as far in advance as possible for VIP tour reservations and a packet of free information on visiting Washington.

2. Review our list of other D.C. attractions that require advance reservations, select one or two that interest you, and make them for the afternoon of Day 3 at the same time you write your congressperson.
3. Read through all your information and make an informal list of sights that you and your family want to see during your Washington stay.
4. Break in a pair of thick-soled walking shoes.

On Site

Day 0 — Travel Day

1. Arrive and get settled. Explore the features and amenities of your hotel.
2. If you get checked in by 3 P.M., go to the Mall and visit The Castle, the Smithsonian's visitor center. (If you're not within walking distance, this is an opportunity to get familiar with the Metro. Read our chapter on how it works and take the Red Line to the Smithsonian station.) Since crowds start to thin in the late afternoon, you may have time to duck into the National Air and Space Museum or the Museum of Natural History after viewing the orientation film in The Castle.
3. Take the Metro to Dupont Circle for dinner at the Thai, Japanese, or Greek restaurant of your choice. When you get back to your hotel, check with the desk to find the nearest stop for boarding either the Old Town Trolley or Tourmobile sight-seeing tours. This will save you time in the morning.

Day 1

1. After breakfast at your hotel, board one of the sight-seeing buses for an orientation tour of Washington. The driver sells tickets.
2. Stay on the bus for a complete circuit, which takes about an hour and a half (two hours for Old Town Trolley). You'll gain a good overview of Washington's huge number of attractions that will help you decide what sights you want to see this trip — and what can wait for another visit.
3. For lunch, get off the tour bus at Union Station, an architectural masterpiece, and head for the lower-level food court. Over lunch, decide what stops you want to make from the tour bus this afternoon.

4. Reboard your tour bus at Union Station. In deciding where to get off, consider an attraction that's not convenient to your hotel. On Old Town Trolley, both Georgetown and Washington National Cathedral are good choices. On Tourmobile, consider the Arlington National Cemetery tour. Another hint: Some of the guides on the buses really know their stuff regarding sights, restaurants, and strategies on how to tour D.C. when you're off the bus. Don't be afraid to ask them for suggestions. Tour until dinnertime.

4. Return to your hotel. For dinner, take a cab to Georgetown. After dinner, take in a stroll and some night life.

Day 2

1. An early start: Get to the Mall by 7 A.M. for visits to the White House, the Washington Monument, and the Bureau of Engraving and Printing. (See page 234 for a detailed itinerary.)

2. After lunch, return to your hotel for a nap or a dip in the pool.

3. Around 3 P.M. take the Metro to Dupont Circle, where you can window-shop, stroll down Embassy Row, and stop in Anderson House, a sumptuous mansion and museum. Then have dinner in one of the many restaurants nearby. After dinner, take the Metro to the Mall for a spectacular night view of the city from the top of the Washington Monument.

Day 3

1. Get in line for the FBI tour by 8 A.M. Then hit one of the popular Mall museums right away, before the crowds show up: Air and Space, American History, or Natural History.

2. After lunch, concentrate on some of the best art galleries in the world — the National Gallery of Art and the Hirshhorn Museum and Sculpture Garden. Or take the tour of the U.S. Department of State's Diplomatic Reception Rooms or one of the other reservation-only tours that you set up before the trip. If a few hours off your feet sounds attractive, consider taking in the five-story movie at the Air and Space Museum.

3. Take the Metro to Gallery Place for dinner in Chinatown. Then take the Metro to the Federal Triangle station and go to the Old Post Office Pavilion for dessert and a spectacular night view of Washington from the 315-foot-high clock tower. Afterwards, go to a jazz or blues club.

Day 4

1. Sleep in from your night on the town. In the morning tour Capitol Hill: the U.S. Capitol, the Supreme Court, and the Library of Congress. Eat lunch at a Capitol Hill cafe.
2. If it's a scorching summer day, consider one of these options after lunch: downtown's National Museum of American Art/National Portrait Gallery or the DAR Museum. Around 4 P.M., take the Metro to Woodley Park and walk or take a cab to the National Zoo. For dinner, pick from the many restaurants in Woodley Park. Hit the sack early: You'll be tired.

Day 5

1. Either drive or take the 10 A.M. Tourmobile to Mount Vernon, George Washington's estate on the Potomac River. If you drive, leave before 7:30 A.M. or after 9:30 A.M. to avoid the worst rush-hour traffic.
2. Visit Old Town Alexandria for lunch and more 18th-century Americana. Stop in the Torpedo Factory to shop for unique art and crafts.
3. If you're visiting in the summer, start your evening with a free military band concert held on a rotating basis at 8 P.M. at either the U.S. Navy Memorial (Archives/Navy Memorial Metro), the steps of the U.S. Capitol (Capitol South Metro), or the Sylvan Theatre, located on the grounds of the Washington Monument (Smithsonian Metro). Afterwards take the Metro to the Waterfront station and walk to a Maine Avenue seafood restaurant for dinner.

—— *THE MALL TOURING PLAN*

Adults and children touring Washington on a Tuesday, Wednesday, Thursday, or Friday during spring or summer, who want a peak-season, whirlwind tour of the White House, the Washington Monument, and the Bureau of Printing and Engraving with a minimum of standing in line, will want to follow the following itinerary:

1. Arrive at the White House ticket office on the Ellipse at 7 A.M. This will get you in line early enough that you'll have your tickets for a 10 A.M. tour shortly after the office opens at 8 A.M.

2. Walk to the Mall and up the hill to the base of the Washington Monument. At 8:30 A.M., the line rarely exceeds a 45-minute wait (one wrap around the base). While you're standing in line for the elevator, send someone in your party up 15th Street to the Bureau of Engraving and Printing's ticket booth to get tickets for a tour early in the afternoon (you can specify your time, up to 1:45 P.M.). Pick a time late enough to give you time to tour the White House.

3. After riding to the top of the Washington Monument, you may have time for a quick late breakfast or early lunch at the Commerce Department cafeteria on 15th Street, NW, before the White House opens at 10 A.M. Other nearby options include the Shops at National Place on F Street between 12th and 13th streets, NW, and the Old Ebbitt Grill on 15th Street across from the U.S. Treasury Department.

4. Arrive at the White House at the time specified on your ticket. Don't worry too much if you're late: You can still get in. But don't be *too* late — tours end at noon, although during the busy season hours are sometimes extended to 12:45.

5. After you leave the White House, you may have time for lunch. Consider the options listed above or the Old Post Office Pavilion on New York Avenue.

6. After lunch, walk back to the Bureau of Engraving and Printing on 15th Street for the tour of the money-printing facility.

7. Now you have the rest of the day to explore. Our suggestion is to get off the Mall and visit places off the beaten tourist path: the Postal Museum, the National Museum of American Art and the National Portrait Gallery, or attractions near Dupont Circle.

THE RED LINE TOUR

When things are really hectic down on the Mall — we especially have in mind spring and summer weekends when the crowds are at their worst — consider exploring a wide range of tourist attractions along Metro's red line. You'll avoid the worst of the throngs packing the city, yet still see some of the best sights in Washington. Here's a list of sights you can see, station by station:

1. Union Station: Capital Children's Museum, National Postal Museum, U.S. Supreme Court, U.S. Capitol, Folger Shakespeare Library, Library of Congress

2. Judiciary Square: National Building Museum

3. Gallery Place/Chinatown: National Museum of American Art, National Portrait Gallery, Ford's Theatre

4. Metro Center: National Museum of Women in the Arts

5. Farragut North: National Geographic Society's Explorers Hall

6. Dupont Circle: Phillips Collection, Anderson House, Islamic Center, Woodrow Wilson House, Textile Museum

7. Woodley Park/Zoo: National Zoo, Washington National Cathedral

TOURING STRATEGIES

Attractions Grouped by Metro Station

With the exception of the Red Line Tour (see above), we don't recommend structuring your visit around attractions located near Metro stations. But we do think a list of tourist attractions located within walking distance of Metro stations can help make a last-minute touring selection to fill in part of a morning or afternoon — and maybe save you a buck or two in Metro fares. A warning: Although this list shows what attractions are *closest* to a Metro station, some sights could be as far as 20 minutes away by foot. An example: While the Foggy Bottom/ GWU Metro is the closest to the Lincoln Memorial, it's still about a three-quarter-mile hike.

Red Line

Brookland/CUA. The National Shrine of the Immaculate Conception, the Franciscan Monastery (10-minute and 20-minute walks respectively).

Union Station. Capital Children's Museum, National Postal History Museum, the U.S. Supreme Court, the U.S. Capitol, Senate office buildings, Folger Shakespeare Library

Judiciary Square. National Building Museum, National Law Enforcement Officers Memorial, the Jewish Historical Society of Greater Washington

Gallery Place. National Portrait Gallery, National Museum of American Art, Chinatown, National Building Museum, Washington Convention Center, Ford's Theatre, the FBI

Metro Center. National Museum of Women in the Arts, National Firearms Museum, B'nai B'rith Klutznik Museum, U.S. Department of the Treasury, Tech 2000, the Washington Convention Center, the Shops at National Place

Farragut North. Swank shops on Connecticut Avenue, National Geographic Society's Explorers Hall, the *Washington Post* building

Dupont Circle. Shops and restaurants, Embassy Row, the Phillips Collection, Anderson House, the Islamic Center, Woodrow Wilson House, the Textile Museum, House of the Temple

Woodley Park/National Zoo. National Zoo, Washington National Cathedral, Adams-Morgan (Note: The Zoo is about a 10-minute walk, Adams-Morgan is about 15 minutes and the Cathedral is a half-hour stroll.)

Van Ness/UDC. Intelsat, Hillwood Museum (20-minute walk)

Blue and Orange Lines

Capitol South. Library of Congress, House office buildings, Capitol Hill restaurants, the U.S. Capitol, Folger Shakespeare Library, the U.S. Supreme Court

Federal Center, SW. U.S. Botanical Gardens, the National Air and Space Museum

L'Enfant Plaza. Shops and restaurants, the National Air and Space Museum, the Hirshhorn Museum and Sculpture Garden, the Arts and Industries Building

Smithsonian. The National Mall, the Freer and Sackler galleries, the National Museum of African Art, the Bureau of Engraving and Printing, the National Museum of Natural History, the National Museum of American History, the Washington Monument, the Smithsonian Castle visitor center, the Tidal Basin, the Jefferson Memorial (20 minutes), the U.S. Holocaust Memorial Museum

Federal Triangle. The Old Post Office Pavilion, the National Aquarium, the FBI, Pennsylvania Avenue, National Museum of American History, National Museum of Natural History

McPherson Square. The White House, the *Washington Post* building, Lafayette Park

Farragut West. The Ansel Adams Collection, Decatur House, Renwick Gallery, the Old Executive Office Building, the White House, the Corcoran Gallery of Art, the DAR Museum, the Ellipse

Foggy Bottom/GWU. The Kennedy Center, the U.S. Department of State's Diplomatic Reception Rooms, Vietnam Veterans Memorial, the Reflecting Pool, the Lincoln Memorial, Georgetown (20- to 30-minute walk)

Arlington National Cemetery.   Arlington National Cemetery, the Lincoln Memorial across Memorial Bridge

Pentagon.   The Pentagon

National Airport.   National Airport

King Street.   Old Town Alexandria (15-minute walk), shops and restaurants, the Torpedo Factory (20-minute walk), the George Washington Masonic Memorial

Yellow Line

Gallery Place.   National Portrait Gallery, National Museum of American Art, Chinatown, National Building Museum, Washington Convention Center, Ford's Theatre, the FBI

Archives/Navy Memorial.   The National Archives, the U.S. Navy Memorial, the National Gallery of Art, the National Museum of Natural History

Green Line

Waterfront.   Washington's Potomac River waterfront area (restaurants, marinas, and river cruises), Fort McNair, Arena Stage

—— Seeing Washington on a Tight Schedule

Many visitors do not have five days to devote to visiting Washington. They may be en route to other destinations, or may live within a day's drive, making later visits practical. Either way, efficient, time-effective touring is a must. They cannot afford long waits in line to see attractions or spend hours trying to find a place to park the family car.

Even the most efficient touring plan will not allow the visitor to visit the Mall, Capitol Hill, and Georgetown in one day, so plan on allocating at least an entire day to the Mall (but not just museums), and splitting your remaining days to other parts of Washington that appeal to you.

— *One-Day Touring*

A comprehensive tour of Washington is literally impossible in a day. But day trips to Washington can be a fun, rewarding experience. Pulling it off hinges on following some basic rules.

A. *Determine in Advance What You Really Want to See*

What are the categories that appeal to you most? If it's government, spend your day at Capitol Hill. If it's exploring museums, visit the Mall. If you like trendy shops and a sophisticated ambience, go to Georgetown or Dupont Circle.

B. *Select an Area to Visit*

For example, if visiting the U.S. Capitol is your goal, look at what other nearby attractions on Capitol Hill or the east end of the Mall interest you. That way you won't waste time and steps.

C. *Arrive Early! Arrive Early! Arrive Early!*

This is the single most important key to efficient touring and avoiding big crowds. First thing in the morning, lines are short at the White House ticket office and the Washington Monument. You can visit three famous Washington attractions in one or two hours that would take an entire afternoon if you arrived at noon. Eat breakfast before you arrive so you will not have to waste your prime touring time sitting in a crowded restaurant.

D. *Avoid Bottlenecks*

Helping you avoid bottlenecks and big crowds is what this guide is all about. Bottlenecks occur as a result of crowd concentrations and nonexistent crowd management. Concentrations of hungry people create bottlenecks at restaurants during the lunch and dinner hours; concentrations of visitors heading toward the best-known monuments, memorials, museums, and government buildings create elbow-to-elbow crowds during afternoons. Avoiding bottlenecks involves knowing at what time and where large concentrations of visitors begin to occur. That's why we provide a **Touring Plan** for a lightning-quick visit to the

White House, the Bureau of Engraving and Printing, and the Washington Monument (see page 234).

In addition, daytrippers need to avoid the agony of driving in D.C. traffic if they expect to have any fun and see enough Washington attractions to make the trip worthwhile. There are two ways to do it:

1. Park Your Car in the Suburbs

In suburban Maryland and Virginia, the Metro extends to the Beltway and beyond, eliminating the need for you to battle Washington traffic, as well as saving you time, money, and stomach acid. On weekends, Metro users park for free at any suburban station. During the week, unless you arrive before 7 A.M., your choice of suburban Metro stations is limited to five: Vienna on I-66 in Virginia (which fills by 8 A.M.); New Carrollton (on the Beltway in Maryland); Greenbelt (also on the Beltway in Maryland); Shady Grove (off I-270 in Maryland); and Silver Spring (inside the Beltway in Maryland). We recommend that, unless you can make it to a Virginia station very early, park at a Maryland station. From the outermost suburbs, it's about a 20-minute, stress-free train ride to the Mall.

New Carrollton has plenty of parking, plus a parking garage for overflow. Take Beltway exit 19B and follow the signs to the Metro. Go to the second parking lot, where you can park all day for $1.50. If it's filled, park in the five-level garage for $6 all day. Make sure to pick up a bus transfer in the station on your return trip to qualify for the low rate.

Shady Grove also has plenty of parking for daytrippers. From I-270 near Gaithersburg, take exit 9 (marked "Sam Eig Highway/Metro Station") to I-370 East, which takes you directly to the station. Metro parking is $2.25 for the day; if the Metro lots are filled, park in the nearby garage for $2.50.

Silver Spring is a somewhat less convenient option for daytrippers since it means a short drive inside the Beltway, but it has plenty of commercial parking close by. Take US 29/Colesville Road south from the Beltway and turn left onto Georgia Avenue in downtown Silver Spring; follow the signs to the Metro, loop past it, and park in one of the big parking garages. Parking is around $4 for the day.

2. *Take the Train*

Taking the train to Washington is a snap for day visitors who live along the Eastern Seaboard in from Richmond to Philadelphia. Amtrak and Maryland commuter (MARC) trains arrive at gleaming Union Station, which is located on Metro's red line. You can be on the Mall minutes after getting off your train. On foot from Union Station, visitors are only a few blocks from the U.S. Capitol, the U.S. Supreme Court, the Library of Congress, the Folger Shakespeare Library, and the newest Smithsonian facility, the National Postal Museum.

Excursions Beyond the Beltway

If you've got the time or if your visit to Washington is a repeat trip, consider exploring some places outside the city. From the mountains to the west and the Chesapeake Bay to the east, there's plenty to see. Furthermore, a look at something that's not made of marble or granite can be a welcome relief to eyes wearied by the constant onslaught of Washington edifices and office buildings. Here are a few suggestions for day trips that Washington visitors can make beyond the Beltway.

Annapolis

Maryland's capital for more than 300 years, Annapolis is more than a quaint little town on the Chesapeake Bay — it's one of the biggest yachting centers in the United States. Acres and acres of sailboats fill its marinas. A steady parade of sailboats moves past the *City Dock* during the sailing season, April through late fall. You'll see oyster and crab boats that work the bay, in addition to pleasure boats, cruise ships, and old sailing ships.

Annapolis has been discovered and is now a major bedroom community for well-off Washingtonians. The town boasts fancy shops, fine restaurants, bars, and jazz clubs. On weekends during the summer, Annapolis is packed with visitors. The town is about a one-hour drive from Washington on US 50.

Baltimore

Steamed crabs, H. L. Mencken, the Orioles, and the National Aquarium are just a few of the reasons Washingtonians trek north one hour on a regular basis to this industrial city on the Chesapeake Bay. Washington's visitors have good reason to detour and discover the charms of Baltimore.

Daytrippers can explore the Inner Harbor, dominated by a bilevel shopping mall that's heavy on restaurants and boutiques. Anchored nearby is the U.S. Frigate *Constellation,* the first ship commissioned in the U.S. Navy. The National Aquarium features a tropical rain forest and a sea mammal pavilion—and it's a much larger attraction than the National Aquarium in Washington. Kids will love the Maryland Science Center and nearby Fort McHenry, where Francis Scott Key wrote the national anthem from a boat anchored offshore. If you've got the time, explore some other Baltimore attractions: the B&O Railroad Museum, the Edgar Allan Poe House, and the Babe Ruth House.

Shenandoah National Park

Although it makes for a long day, a drive to Shenandoah National Park in Virginia is a treat for outdoors-lovers, featuring some of the prettiest mountain scenery in the East. A drive along a portion of the 105-mile-long Skyline Drive takes visitors to a nearly endless series of mountain overlooks where you can get out of the car and walk on well-maintained trails. In early June, the mountain laurel blooms in the higher elevations, and in the fall, it's bumper-to-bumper as hordes of Washingtonians rush to see the magnificent fall foliage. It's about a two-hour drive from Washington, one-way.

Harpers Ferry National Historical Park, West Virginia

This restored 19th-century town at the confluence of the Shenandoah and the Potomac rivers offers visitors history and natural beauty in equal doses. At the park's visitor center, you can see a film about radical abolitionist John Brown's 1859 raid on a U.S. armory, an event that was a precursor to the Civil War. Then you can tour a renovated blacksmith's shop, ready-made clothing store, and general store. A short hike to Jefferson Rock is rewarded with a spectacular mountain view of three states (Maryland, Virginia, and West Virginia) and two rivers (the Potomac and the Shenandoah). Thomas Jefferson said the view was "worth a voyage across the Atlantic." Luckily, the trip by car from Washington is only about 90 minutes.

A Tour of Civil War Battlefields

It seems like the entire Civil War was fought in nearby Virginia, Maryland, and Pennsylvania—which is nearly the truth. Visitors with an interest in history and beautiful countryside can tour a number of Civil War sites within a day's drive of Washington.

Gettysburg, where the Union turned the tide against the South, is about two hours north of D.C. While the overdeveloped town is a testament to tourist schlock gone wild, the National Battlefield Park features a museum, a tower that gives sight-seers an aerial view of the battlefield, and many acres of rolling countryside dotted with monuments, memorials, and stone fences. It's a popular tourist destination and worth the drive.

The first battle of the Civil War took place at Bull Run near Manassas, on the fringe of today's Virginia suburbs. The **Manassas National Battlefield Park** features a visitor center, a museum, and miles of trails on the grounds.

The Confederate victory set the stage for the next major battle, at Antietam, across the Potomac River in Maryland. **Antietam National Battlefield,** near Sharpsburg, is the site of the bloodiest day of the Civil War: On September 17, 1862, there were 12,410 Union and 10,700 Confederate casualties in General Robert E. Lee's failed attempt to penetrate the North. The battlefield, about a 90-minute drive from Washington, is 15 miles west of Frederick, Maryland.

A number of later Union campaigns are commemorated at **Fredericksburg and Spotsylvania National Military Park** in Virginia, halfway between Washington and Richmond. Included in the park are the battlefields of Fredericksburg, Chancellorsville, Wilderness, and Spotsylvania. The park is about an hour's drive south of D.C.

Helpful Hints

Designated Meeting Places

Families and groups touring together should designate a meeting spot in case members get separated. On the Mall, good places to link up are in front of The Castle (the Smithsonian visitor center) or in front of the domed National Museum of Natural History. The information desks located in most main museum lobbies are logical meeting places if the group separates. Downtown, it's easy to lose your sense of direction due to a scarcity of landmarks. A good designated meeting place would be a hotel lobby, a department store entrance, or a Metro station.

A Money-Saving Tip

Where *not* to have lunch: The sidewalk food vendors on the Mall, the kiosk in front of the National Museum of Natural History, and the small restaurant down the hill from the Washington Monument charge about a dollar more for a hot dog than the street vendors you see everywhere off the Mall. Unless you're dying of hunger, walk to either Constitution or Independence Avenue, find a street vendor, and save yourself some dough. The hot dogs, by the way, are pretty good.

Another Money-Saving Tip

The Commerce Department, located on 14th Street, NW, across from the Ellipse, has a pleasant basement cafeteria that offers good, cheap fare: a soup and salad bar, pizza and pasta, a grill, deli, and hot entrees. You can get a whole pizza that will feed a family of four for less than $10. It's open Monday through Friday, 9 A.M. to 2 P.M.

Get Off the Mall!

A full day of traipsing from museum to museum along the Mall is exhausting and, for most folks, a one-dimensional experience that's mind-numbing. After a while, it starts to feel like a grade-school field trip—and, later, there's going to be a quiz. Is that a vacation? Snap out of it by breaking up the day and taking the Metro any number of other fascinating destinations, including Dupont Circle, the waterfront, and the National Zoo. Or grab a cab and visit Georgetown, Adams-Morgan, or the Washington National Cathedral.

A Photography Tip

Washington, D.C., with its impressive memorials and federal buildings, is a photographer's mecca. But for a really spectacular shot of downtown Washington, go across the Potomac River to the Iwo Jima Memorial in Arlington. Stand on the hill near the Netherlands Carillon and look toward the Lincoln Memorial. At dawn, the sun rises almost directly behind the U.S. Capitol. At dusk, the panorama of twinkling lights includes the Jefferson and Lincoln memorials, the Washington Monument, and, more than two miles away, the U.S. Capitol.

How to Sneak on a Reservation-Only Tour at the National Archives

For the behind-the-scenes tour of the National Archives, most people call weeks in advance for reservations. If you didn't, however, take a chance and show up at the Pennsylvania Avenue entrance (across from 8th Street) at tour time. If there's a cancellation or a no-show, you're in. The free reserved tours begin at 10:15 A.M. and 1:15 P.M. daily and last about an hour. On the reserved tour, you'll see a working model of the vault that protects the Great Charters and explore the building, including the stacks, microfilm viewing rooms, and exhibits and models that show how researchers preserve documents. The tour ends in the magnificent Rotunda, where the great documents are on display.

Getting a Free Pass to a National Gallery of Art Show

Most people call or stop by weeks in advance to get free "time" tickets that admit them to the wildly popular art exhibits regularly held in the National Gallery of Art's East Wing. What most of them don't know is that 400 tickets per half-hour are reserved for folks like you. Tickets can be picked up any day a show is in progress. Just show up by noon on weekends or 2 P.M. on weekdays at the ticket counter in the main lobby and come back later in the day to see the show.

An Informal Georgetown Tour of JFK Residences

Structure an informal walking tour around Georgetown by viewing — from the outside only, please — a few places where a great American statesman once lived. As a congressman and senator, John F. Kennedy lived in four different houses in Georgetown: 1528 31st Street, NW; 1400 34th Street, NW; 3271 P Street, NW; and 3307 N Street, NW. The last address is where the Kennedys lived just before moving to 1600 Pennsylvania Avenue, NW.

D.C. on the Air

Aside from the usual babble of format rock, talk, easy listening, and country music radio stations, Washington is home to a few radio stations that really stand out for high-quality broadcasting. Tune in to what hip Washingtonians listen to, as listed below:

Format	Frequency	Station
Classical	570/103.5	WGMS-AM/FM
Progressive rock	99.1	WHFS-FM
Classical, NPR	91	WETA-FM
Bluegrass, folk, talk	88.5	WAMU-FM
Jazz	89.3	WPFW-FM
All News	1500	WTOP-AM

How to Tell if the President Is Home

A flag flies over the White House when the President is in Washington. At night, one of the facades on the White House stays lit for the benefit of trench coat–clad TV news reporters who intone to the camera, "Live, from the White House. . . ."

Touring the White House in the Fall and Winter

In the late fall and winter, a line starts forming around 9:15 A.M. for the 10 A.M. White House tour. But by 10:30 A.M., the line is gone; most days, visitors can walk right into the White House without waiting. "People don't believe us when we tell them to come back at 10:30 and there will be no line," shrugged a National Park Service volunteer who helps run the tour. But he's right.

How to Tell if the House or Senate Is in Session

Look for a flag flying over the respective chamber of the U.S. Capitol to determine which, if either, house of Congress is in session. From the Mall, the Senate is to the left of the dome; the House of Representatives is on the right. At night, a light burns on top of the Capitol dome if Congress is in session.

The Best Time to Visit the Washington Monument (Summer)

Do yourself a favor and resist joining a long line wrapping around the base of the Washington Monument — especially if it's summer and both the temperature and humidity are nearing triple digits. You've got some alternatives. First, come back at night to take the 70-second elevator ride to the top. Why? Simple — there's no line and the view is better. If you must get a bird's-eye view of Washington in daylight, try the Old Post Office Pavilion's clock tower: It's not quite as high, but at least you don't have to squint through tiny windows. And there's rarely a line.

Avoiding the Heat on a Sweltering Afternoon

On hot, humid D.C. afternoons, it's imperative to avoid long walks between sights; in fact, you shouldn't leave an air-conditioned building at all, if you can help it. On the Mall, one solution to touring on a hot day is to visit this trio of museums: the National Museum of African Art, the Arthur M. Sackler Gallery, and the Freer Gallery. The first two museums are built underground, so they're probably cool even during a power failure (dark, too). The three museums are connected by tunnels, eliminating the need to venture outside.

More good choices that will reduce the possibility of heat stroke include the Corcoran Gallery of Art, the Phillips Collection, and the National Gallery of Art. Another strategy is to visit museums next to each other (say, the National Museum of Natural History and the National Museum of American History). And don't plan any ambitious treks like a walk to the Jefferson Memorial from the Capitol, or from one end of the Mall to the other, when it's scorchingly hot outside.

D.C. after Dark

Touring Washington's monuments and memorials after dark offers dramatic views of both famous marble edifices and Washington itself.

At night, the Jefferson and Lincoln memorials float in pools of light; from the steps of the Lincoln Memorial, the Eternal Flame at the John F. Kennedy grave site shimmers across the river in Arlington National Cemetery. The scene at the Vietnam Veterans Memorial is a moving experience as people hold flickering matches up to the reflective black marble surface, searching for names.

Capitol Hill: A Family Affair

Rather than just getting in line to tour the U.S. Capitol, give yourself and your kids a real civics lesson you'll all remember: Visit your congressperson or senator.

"Go to your member's office and get a pass to see the House and Senate in session," suggests one of the Capitol guards. "It's a real experience — and the kids will love it. And while you're there, ask for a special tour of the Capitol given by a member's staffperson." House office buildings are across Independence Avenue from the Capitol building; senate office buildings are across Constitution Avenue. Offices are open weekdays during normal business hours and you don't need an appointment. If you don't know the name of your representative, go to either one of your senator's office.

Where the Real Work of Congress Is Done

Most visitors who obtain gallery passes to the House or Senate in session are mildly disappointed: The scene is usually one member giving a speech to a nearly empty chamber, unless you happen to stumble in during a vote. Everyone else is at committee meetings, where the real work is done. Check the Washington Post's "A" section for a list of legislative hearings open to the public, along with their time and location (always in one of the buildings near the Capitol).

Another Photo Tip

Across from the Mall near the Lincoln Memorial is the stately National Academy of Sciences on Constitution Avenue. Outside, Albert Einstein's statue is waiting for you to crawl into its lap so you can have your picture taken; it's a D.C. tradition.

Speeding Through the Ubiquitous Metal Detectors

Virtually every federal building in Washington is equipped with walk-through metal detectors staffed by no-nonsense guards, including the White House, the U.S. Capitol, the Supreme Court, all Senate and House office buildings, and the National Archives. Men: To speed your way through, you should get in the habit of carrying all your change and keys in one place. When your turn comes to pass through the metal detector, dump it all into one of the bowls provided and you'll avoid the tedious drill of passing through the door-sized detector a half-dozen times. (You'll also find out which metal-buckled belt *not* to wear when visiting government buildings.) Women have it easier: Just place your purse on the conveyor that shoots it through an X-ray machine before walking through the detector.

A Worst-Case Touring Scenario

Here's how *not* to visit Washington: On a weekday, load the kids in the family car, and arrive around 8 A.M. — the worst part of rush hour. Then battle your way downtown through bumper-to-bumper traffic, arriving at the Mall about 9:30, your nerves thoroughly frayed. Waste a half-hour looking for a parking space before giving up and shelling out $12 for a space in a parking garage. Next, troop over to the Washington Monument, where the line of waiting people is wrapped around the base twice. Three hours later, exit the monument in a famished state, and overspend by $1 a dog for red hots from a food vendor on the Mall. The total bill for four approaches $20. Then go to the National Air and Space Museum, where it's packed shoulder-to-shoulder around the most popular exhibits.

Later, at the National Museum of Natural History, little Jimmy disappears into the bowels of the paleontological exhibits, and since you didn't agree on a designated meeting place, it takes 45 minutes to track him down. At 5 P.M., you and your family stagger back to the car, just in time to join the afternoon rush hour.

Amazingly, people do this all the time. But it doesn't have to be this way.

Instead of hitting Beltway traffic at 8 A.M., leave a half-hour earlier and go to any suburban Metro station and park. Then it's a 20-minute trip by train downtown. You can be at the Washington Monument by 8 A.M., when the wait in line rarely exceeds 45 minutes. Then pick up tickets for a tour of the Bureau of Engraving and Printing later in the morning at the ticket booth on 15th Street. Next, visit the National Air and Space Museum.

After seeing the money getting printed, eat lunch at the Old Post

Office Pavilion, then take the Metro to Dupont Circle. There, you can visit the Phillips Collection, a really classy art gallery, and tour Anderson House, a sumptuous mansion. Next, go to the National Zoo in the late afternoon or early evening, when the temperature begins to drop and the animals get more active. Eat dinner at a restaurant near the Woodley Park Metro on Connecticut Avenue and then take the Metro back to your car.

The second scenario takes advantage of two things: an early start and no time wasted in traffic or searching for a parking space. It lets you visit at a leisurely pace and gives you the freedom to explore out of the way and unusual sights you normally wouldn't take the time to see. It's the smart way to visit Washington.

—— *Travel Tips for Tourists*

The idea behind visiting any major tourist attraction is to have fun, and you can't do that if you're getting fatigued or crabby. Here are some touring tips you should review before your visit. They're really no more than commonsense rules for any type of outing:

1. Drink plenty of water, especially on hot, humid, sunny Washington afternoons. Dehydration can sneak up and cause physical problems which might ruin your vacation plans. So don't be at all hesitant about drinking more water than you think you'll need.

2. Protect sun-sensitive areas of your body. Shade your head and eyes with a hat. Wear sunglasses. Treat exposed skin with a sunscreen lotion — especially your nose, cheeks, and lips. And if you're wearing sandals, don't forget your feet. You don't have to go to the beach to get a really nasty burn on the tops of your feet!

3. Pace yourself. Washington is filled with good places to sit in the shade and rest, and people-watching is part of the fun.

4. Wear comfortable clothes, especially shoes — shoes that cushion, shoes that are broken in, shoes that won't make your feet too hot. Wear clothing that protects you from the sun and permits the air to circulate around your skin, and doesn't bind or chafe.

5. Keep on good terms with your stomach, but don't let it dictate your trip. Eat a good breakfast before you set out for the day, then snack a lot while touring. Avoid lunch lines, especially those at overpriced museum cafeterias.

6. If you're traveling with teenagers, do yourself and them a favor: Send them off on their own for at least part of a day during your D.C. visit. Arrange to meet them at a specific time and place, and elicit a very firm and definite understanding about this meeting time and place. Give them a watch if they don't have one, a map, and the hotel number for emergencies.

7. Hunger, overheating, tension from fighting the crowds for hours, fatigue — each of these realities of touring and all of them together can combine to produce fussy kids and grumpy adults. You'll notice if someone else in your party is getting unpleasant to be around, but you may not recognize the symptoms in yourself unless you periodically make an effort to run a little self-check and think about your behavior. If you and your party can't salvage things with a rest and a food break, cut your day short and go back to your hotel for a swim, a nap — or a drink in the bar. Visiting Washington is not meant to be a test of your temper and patience, after all. You're here to have fun.

PART NINE:
Washington's Attractions

Where to Go?

Visitors come to Washington from all over the world — and for a lot of different reasons. Some want to see how the U.S. government works (or, as some cynics say, *doesn't* work), others want to see the places where history happened, and many are drawn by the city's magnificent monuments and museums.

It's tough for a guide book to decree to such a diverse group where they should spend their time. Is the National Gallery of Art better than the Air and Space Museum? The answer is yes — if your interests and tastes range more toward Van Gogh than von Braun.

Since we can't read your mind and tell you the top places *you* should visit on your trip to Washington, we'll do the next best thing: give you enough information so that you can quickly choose the places you want to see — with enough detail that you can plan your visit logically — without spending a lot of time (and shoe leather) retracing your steps and standing in line.

Armed with enough information that will allow you to make informed choices about how you spend your valuable time, you can avoid a common mistake a lot of visitors to D.C. make: hitting the Mall for a death march through a blur of Smithsonian museums, federal buildings, and monuments.

Zone 1 — The Mall

Arlington National Cemetery

Type of Attraction: The largest military cemetery in the United States. Guided and self-guided tours.

Location: Across the Potomac from Washington via Arlington Memorial Bridge, which crosses the river near the Lincoln Memorial.

Nearest Metro Station: Arlington Cemetery

Admission: Free

Hours: 8 A.M. to 7 P.M. April through September; closes at 5 P.M. October through March.

Phone: (703) 692-0931

When to Go: Before 9 A.M. in spring and summer

Special Comments: Don't underestimate the ferocity of Washington summer afternoons; in hot weather, get here early.

Overall Appeal by Age Group:

Pre-school	Grade School	Teens	Young Adults	Over 30	Senior Citizens
★	★★	★★★	★★★★	★★★★	★★★★

Author's Rating: Beyond tourism. ★★★★

How Much Time to Allow: Two hours

DESCRIPTION AND COMMENTS   It's not fair to call a visit to Arlington National Cemetery mere sight-seeing; as Americans, our lives are too intimately attached to the 200,000 men and women buried here. They include the famous, the obscure, and the unknown: John F. Kennedy, General George C. Marshall, Joe Louis, Abner Doubleday, and Oliver Wendell Holmes are among them.

Sights located in the cemetery's 612 rolling acres include the Tomb of the Unknown Soldier (guarded 24 hours a day; witness the changing of the guard on the hour from October to March, and on the half-hour the rest of the year), memorials to the crew of the space shuttle Challenger, the Iran Rescue Mission Memorial, and Arlington House, built in 1802. With the ease of touring provided by Tourmobile, Arlington Cemetery should be on every first-time visitor's list of things to see.

TOURING TIPS   To avoid the worst of Washington's brutal summer heat and humidity, plan to arrive as early as possible. Private cars are not allowed inside, but there's plenty of parking near the visitor center at a dollar an hour for the first three hours, then two dollars an hour. Take the Metro instead.

While you can wander around the cemetery on your own, the narrated Tourmobile tour is informative and saves wear and tear on your feet — and at $2.75 for adults and $1.25 for children, it's a good deal. The ticket allows you to get off at all the major sites and reboard at your leisure. The shuttle tours leave the visitor center (where tickets are sold) about every 15 minutes during the spring and summer and at 20- to 25-minute intervals the rest of the year.

If you're touring the Mall by Tourmobile, transferring to the cemetery tour is free for that day only. If you want to tour the cemetery by shuttle bus on a different day, don't pay $10.50 for another full-circuit ticket. Just take the Metro to the Arlington Cemetery station, walk the short distance to the visitor center, buy the cemetery-only ticket, and save a few bucks.

Finally, bathrooms are located in the visitor center. But don't come to Arlington Cemetery when you're hungry: There's no place to eat.

OTHER THINGS TO DO NEARBY   The Pentagon is the next stop on the Metro. The Iwo Jima Memorial and the Netherlands Carillon are about a 20-minute walk from Arlington House (down Custis Walk and through Weitzel Gate). The nearest restaurants via Metro are in Rosslyn and Pentagon City.

Arts and Industries Building

Type of Attraction: A museum highlighting 19th-century American technology. A self-guided tour.

Location: 900 Jefferson Drive, SW, on the Mall.

Nearest Metro Station: Smithsonian

Admission: Free

Hours: 10 A.M. to 5:30 P.M. Depending on budgets, evening hours are extended in the summer.

Phone: (202) 357-2700

When to Go: Anytime

Special Comments: All the exhibits are on one level.

Overall Appeal by Age Group:

Pre-school	Grade School	Teens	Young Adults	Over 30	Senior Citizens
★★	★★★	★★	★★	★★½	★★★

Author's Rating: Fun stuff, but gets tiring fast. ★★

How Much Time to Allow: 30 minutes

DESCRIPTION AND COMMENTS   To celebrate its 100th birthday, America held a fantastic celebration in Philadelphia: the 1876 Centennial Exhibition. Most of it is on display here. Steam engines, printing presses, 19th-century products, old-fashioned elevators and generators—it's a catalog of Victorian and Gilded Age engineering might.

TOURING TIPS   It's a fun museum to visit, full of polished wood and cast iron; a fountain spews water under the dome and the exhibits are close enough to touch. Some people call this a great "warm up" museum that gets you ready for the larger Smithsonian institutions; it's friendly and not overpowering. The 1876 exhibition was organized by states; challenge the kids to find your state's contribution.

OTHER THINGS TO DO NEARBY   The Hirshhorn and the Air and Space Museum are next door. The Museum of Natural History (the one with the dome) is directly across the Mall. Tired of museums yet? Jump on the Metro and get off at Capitol South and explore Capitol Hill. The Metro is also the fastest way to reach two good restaurant locales: L'Enfant Plaza and the Old Post Office Pavilion.

Bureau of Engraving and Printing

Type of Attraction: The presses that print all U.S. currency and stamps. A self-guided tour.

Location: Raoul Wallenberg Place (formerly 15th Street) and C Street, SW (two blocks south of the Mall).

Nearest Metro Station: Smithsonian

Admission: Free

Hours: Monday through Friday, 9 A.M. to 2 P.M. Closed on federal holidays. During Easter and from the last Friday in May through

the last Friday in August, a "time ticket" system is in effect.
The ticket office, located on Raoul Wallenberg Place, opens at
8:30 A.M.

Phone: (202) 447-9709

When to Go: The earlier, the better. During peak season, try to arrive
by 8:30 A.M. and request tickets for a tour later in the morning or
in the early afternoon. In the fall and winter, the line forms at the
long, enclosed entrance on 14th Street.

Special Comments: Small children may have trouble looking over the
ledge and down into the press rooms below.

Overall Appeal by Age Group:

Pre-school	Grade School	Teens	Young Adults	Over 30	Senior Citizens
★★	★★★★	★★★★	★★★★	★★★★	★★★★

Author's Rating: After the novelty of seeing all that cash fades, it's
just a printing plant. ★★

How Much Time to Allow: About 30 minutes when the ticket system
is in effect. In the early fall, when the line snakes out the front
door and up 14th Street, figure on at least two hours.

Average Wait in Line per 100 People Ahead of You: 30 minutes

DESCRIPTION AND COMMENTS   This is a self-guided tour through
rather cramped and shabby glass-lined corridors with a continuous-
loop tape presentation droning in the background. Below are printing
presses and pallets of greenbacks in various stages of completion. The
sign some wag hung on a press, however, says it all: "You have never
been so close yet so far away."

Kids love this place, so it's a sight families should plan on hitting,
even if you're only in town for a short period.

TOURING TIPS   Arrive early — this is one of D.C.'s most popular attractions. During the summer, pick up tickets early so you can do more
creative things than stand around in Washington's heat and humidity.
The ticket office distributes about 180 tickets for every 15-minute tour
between 9 A.M. and 1:45 P.M. (no tour is scheduled at 11:30 A.M.).
Once the tickets for that day are gone, the office closes. On a busy day,
that can be as early as 11:15 A.M. After you pick up your tickets, come
back for your tour and meet near the ticket office on Raoul Wallenberg
Place, where you will be escorted into the building. You have about a
30-minute grace period if you're running late.

For a unique souvenir, check out the bags of shredded money for sale in the visitor center at the end of the tour. For a guided tour, contact your congressperson's office before your trip. The VIP tours are conducted at 8 A.M. Monday through Friday. Bathrooms are located inside the building where the tour begins.

OTHER THINGS TO DO NEARBY   As you exit the building on Raoul Wallenberg Place, the Tidal Basin is a short walk to the left: Benches, tables, a lot of greenery, and the calming effect of water make it a great spot to unwind or eat lunch—or rent a paddleboat. And there's a great view of the Jefferson Memorial. Other sights close at hand are the Holocaust Memorial and the Washington Monument. There aren't a lot of places to eat that are close, however.

Corcoran Gallery of Art

Type of Attraction: A museum that primarily features American art from the colonial period to the present. A self-guided tour.

Location: 17th and E streets, NW, a half-block west of the White House.

Nearest Metro Station: Farragut West

Admission: Suggested donations for adults, $3; students and seniors, $1; family groups of any size, $5; children under 12 free.

Hours: 10 A.M. to 5 P.M. Tuesday through Sunday; till 9 P.M. on Thursday; closed Mondays and major holidays.

When to Go: Anytime

Overall Appeal by Age Group:

Pre-school	Grade School	Teens	Young Adults	Over 30	Senior Citizens
—	★	★★	★★½	★★★	★★★

Author's Rating: Art snobs will feel at home. ★★½

How Much Time to Allow: Two hours

DESCRIPTION AND COMMENTS   Frank Lloyd Wright called this beaux-arts museum "the best designed building in Washington." Inside are works by John Singer Sargent, Mary Cassatt, and Winslow Homer, among others. There's also an abundance of cutting-edge contemporary art. It's a big place with a wide range of periods and styles, so you're bound to see something you like.

TOURING TIPS   Maybe it's because of the art school next door, but this museum has a distinctly serious atmosphere. It's not a place to drag little Johnny and Sally, who would rather be looking at dinosaur bones in the National Museum of Natural History.

OTHER THINGS TO DO NEARBY   Duck into the Organization of American States and enter a rain forest: a courtyard filled with palm trees and the sound of falling water awaits you. Walk up the staircase and peek into the opulent Hall of the Americas. For lunch, stroll up 17th Street toward Pennsylvania Avenue. Le Sorbet, around the corner on G Street, can supply a sandwich and drink for less than $5. Another block north is McDonald's.

Daughters of the American Revolution Museum

Type of Attraction: The 33 period rooms are a cornucopia of decorative arts and antiques. A self-guided museum tour and a guided tour.

Location: 1776 D Street, NW, across from the Ellipse.

Nearest Metro Station: Farragut West

Admission: Free

Hours: 8:30 A.M. to 4 P.M. Monday through Friday; 1 P.M. to 5 P.M. on Sundays. Guided tours of the period rooms are available from 10 A.M. to 3 P.M. Monday through Friday, and from 1 P.M. to 5 P.M. on Sundays. Tours leave every 20 minutes.

Phone: (202) 628-1776

When to Go: Anytime

Special Comments: Expect to do a lot of stair climbing on the tour; you can't enter the rooms, and only two or three visitors at a time can squeeze into doorways to peer inside.

Overall Appeal by Age Group:

Pre-school	Grade School	Teens	Young Adults	Over 30	Senior Citizens
—	★	★½	★★	★★★½	★★★★½

Author's Rating: A "must see" for lovers of antiques and decorative arts. ★★★½

How Much Time to Allow: Two hours

DESCRIPTION AND COMMENTS   This Beaux-Arts building, completed in 1910, is a knockout. The huge columns that grace the front of the building are solid marble; a special railroad spur was built to transport them to the building site. The DAR Museum, predictably enough, emphasizes the role of women throughout American history and includes fine examples of furniture, ceramics, glass, paintings, silver, costumes, and textiles. It's a small museum filled with everyday items out of America's past.

From the interior of a California adobe parlor of 1850, to a replica of a 1775 bed chamber in Lexington, Massachusetts, to the kitchen of a 19th-century Oklahoma farm family, the period rooms place objects in a context of both time and place. Kids will get a kick out of the four-sided mousetrap that guillotines rodents, the foot-controlled toaster, and the sausage stuffer that looks like an early-19th-century version of a Nordic Track machine.

The museum and period rooms are sleepers that a lot of visitors to Washington overlook. But for lovers of antiques and decorative arts, the rooms provide visitors an opportunity to view beautiful objects in authentic period settings. Kids, on the other hand, may prefer the Washington Monument, which isn't far.

TOURING TIPS   Finding the entrance is a bit tough, although the DAR building itself is easy enough to find. At D and 17th (across from the Ellipse), walk about half a block down D Street; the museum and tour entrance is on the side of the building. During the busy spring and summer, the period room tours can get crowded, especially on weekends, so try to arrive before noon.

OTHER THINGS TO DO NEARBY   Walk up the marble steps and into the American Red Cross building to see the Memorial Windows, reputed to be the largest suite of Tiffany windows still in their original location (except for in churches). Their theme is ministry to the sick and wounded. Next door to DAR, the lobby of the Organization of American States building is a bit of a tropical paradise. Head up 17th Street toward Pennsylvania Avenue to find a large selection of restaurants.

Decatur House

Type of Attraction: One of Washington's earliest surviving important residences. A guided tour.

Location: 748 Jackson Place, NW, across from Lafayette Park.

Nearest Metro Stations: Farragut West, Farragut North

Admission: $3

Hours: 10 A.M. to 3 P.M. Tuesday through Friday; noon to 4 P.M. weekends. Closed Mondays, Thanksgiving, Christmas, and New Year's days.

Phone: (202) 842-0920

When to Go: Anytime

Special Comments: The tour involves descending a steep, curving staircase.

Overall Appeal by Age Group:

Pre-school	Grade School	Teens	Young Adults	Over 30	Senior Citizens
★	★	★	★★	★★	★★½

Author's Rating: An interesting yet narrow slice of early Americana. ★★½

How Much Time to Allow: 30 minutes

DESCRIPTION AND COMMENTS   Stephen Decatur was a naval war hero who defeated the Barbary pirates off the shores of Tripoli (ring a bell?) during the War of 1812. If he hadn't been killed in a duel, some say he might have been president. No doubt he built this house in 1819 with presidential aspirations in mind: It's close to the White House. The first floor is decorated in authentic Federalist style and displays Decatur's furnishings and sword. The formal parlors on the second floor reflect a later Victorian restyling. Famous statesmen who resided in the building include Henry Clay, Martin Van Buren, and Edward Livingston.

TOURING TIPS   If you're on a tight schedule, this isn't the place to be blowing your time. But it's an okay rainy-afternoon alternative that gives insight into the early days of Washington.

OTHER THINGS TO DO NEARBY   The Renwick Gallery is around the corner on Pennsylvania Avenue; next to it is Blair House, where foreign dignitaries stay. Decatur House faces Lafayette Park, frequent site of political demonstrations, once home to many homeless, and predictably filled with statues. Across the street is the White House.

Freer Gallery of Art

Type of Attraction: A museum featuring Asian and American art. A self-guided tour.

Location: Jefferson Drive at 12th Street, SW, on the Mall.

Nearest Metro Station: Smithsonian

Admission: Free

Hours: 10 A.M. to 5:30 P.M. daily; closed Christmas Day.

Phone: (202) 357–2700

When to Go: Anytime

Special Comments: This 70-year-old gallery reopened in 1993 after a four-and-a-half year, $26-million renovation.

Overall Appeal by Age Group:

Pre-school	Grade School	Teens	Young Adults	Over 30	Senior Citizens
★	★★	★★½	★★★	★★★½	★★★★

Author's Rating: Gorgeous art on a human scale in a setting that's not overwhelming. ★★★★

How Much Time to Allow: One to two hours

DESCRIPTION AND COMMENTS   Well-proportioned spaces, galleries illuminated by natural light, and quiet serenity are the hallmarks of this newly renovated landmark on the Mall. And the art? It's an unusual blend of American paintings (including the world's most important collection of works by James McNeill Whistler), and Asian paintings, sculpture, porcelains, scrolls, and richly embellished household items. Charles Lang Freer, the wealthy 19th-century industrialist who bequeathed this collection to the Smithsonian, saw similarities of color and surface texture in the diverse assemblage. Surrender to the gallery's tranquility and you may too.

TOURING TIPS   An underground link to the nearby Arthur M. Sackler Gallery creates a public exhibition space, as well as convenient passage between two museums. Don't miss the Peacock Room, designed by James McNeill Whistler; it's widely considered to be the most important 19th-century interior in an American museum. Once the dining room of a Liverpool shipping magnate, it was installed in the Freer Gallery after Freer's death. The ornate room was painted by Whistler to house a collection of blue and white Chinese porcelains. Following a restoration that removed decades of dirt and grime, the room has been restored to its original splendor.

OTHER THINGS TO DO NEARBY   The Sackler Gallery, the National Museum of African Art, and the Enid A. Haupt Garden are within a few steps of the Freer Gallery. Directly across the Mall are the American

History Museum and the Natural History Museum. Walk up the Mall toward the capitol to reach the Arts and Industries Museum, the Hirshhorn Museum of Art, and the National Air and Space Museum. For lunch, take the Metro to either L'Enfant Plaza or the Old Post Office Pavilion.

Hirshhorn Museum and Sculpture Garden

Type of Attraction: A museum of modern art. A self-guided tour.

Location: 7th Street and Independence Avenue, SW, on the Mall.

Nearest Metro Stations: Smithsonian, L'Enfant Plaza

Admission: Free

Hours: 10 A.M. to 5:30 P.M. daily; sculpture garden open 7:30 A.M. to dusk; closed Christmas Day; evening hours may be extended in the summer.

Phone: (202) 357-2700

When to Go: Anytime

Special Comments: The Hirshhorn is a lot of people's favorite art museum on the Mall.

Overall Appeal by Age Group:

Pre-school	Grade School	Teens	Young Adults	Over 30	Senior Citizens
★	★★	★★★	★★★★	★★★★★	★★★★★

Author's Rating: ★★★★★ An outrageous collection of 20th-century art; don't miss it.

How Much Time to Allow: Two hours

DESCRIPTION AND COMMENTS   The art found inside is often as bizarre as the circular building that houses it. Works by modern masters such as Rodin, Winslow Homer, Mary Cassatt, and Henry Moore line the easy-to-walk galleries. The outdoor sculpture garden (set below Mall-level) contains works by Rodin, Giacometti, and Alexander Calder, among many others. The sculpture offers a refreshing contrast to the marble palaces that line the Mall. If you only visit one modern art gallery on your visit, make it the Hirshhorn.

TOURING TIPS   Guided tours of the Hirshhorn are offered at 10:30 A.M., noon, and 1:30 P.M. Monday through Saturday, and at 12:30 P.M. on Sundays. During the summer months, additional docent-led tours are sometimes added.

OTHER THINGS TO DO NEARBY   Two nearby museums, Arts and Industries and Air and Space, offer startling contrasts to the Hirshhorn's treasures. A less jarring experience may be the National Gallery of Art's East Wing, also featuring modern art. The best bets for lunch are L'Enfant Plaza and the Old Post Office Pavilion, both minutes away by Metro. In the summer, the Hirshhorn has an outdoor cafe featuring sandwiches, salads, and great sculpture.

Jefferson Memorial

Type of Attraction: A classical-style monument to the author of the Declaration of Independence and the third U.S. president. A self-guided tour.

Location: Across the Tidal Basin from the Washington Monument.

Nearest Metro Station: L'Enfant Plaza, Smithsonian

Admission: Free

Hours: 24 hours, closed on Christmas Day; staffed from 8 A.M. to midnight.

Phone: (202) 426-6822

When to Go: For the best views, go at night or when the cherry trees along the Tidal Basin are in bloom.

Special Comments: The view from the steps and across the Tidal Basin is one of the best in Washington.

Overall Appeal by Age Group:

Pre-school	Grade School	Teens	Young Adults	Over 30	Senior Citizens
★	★★	★★★	★★★	★★★	★★★

Author's Rating: A favorite at night, but not convenient. ★★½

How Much Time to Allow: 30 minutes

DESCRIPTION AND COMMENTS   The neoclassical, open-air design of this monument reflects Jefferson's taste in architecture. Since it's somewhat off the tourist path, it's less crowded than the monuments on the Mall.

TOURING TIPS   Park interpreters staffing the monument frequently give talks and can answer questions about Jefferson and the monument. Visitors can walk to the memorial along the rim of the Tidal Basin from Independence Avenue or along 14th Street, SW.

OTHER THINGS TO DO NEARBY The Bureau of Engraving and Printing and the Holocaust Memorial are both on 14th Street. The Tidal Basin is great for paddleboating. L'Enfant Plaza has an underground shopping mall with many places to eat.

Lincoln Memorial

Type of Attraction: A classical-style memorial to the 16th American president. A self-guided tour.

Location: At the west end of the Mall.

Nearest Metro Station: Smithsonian, Foggy Bottom/GWU

Admission: Free

Hours: Always open. Rangers on duty from 8 A.M. to midnight, except Christmas Day.

Phone: (202) 426-6895

When to Go: For the best views, visit in the early morning, at sunset, or at night.

Special Comments: At night, facing west across the Potomac River, the eternal flame at John Kennedy's grave is visible.

Overall Appeal by Age Group:

Pre-school	Grade School	Teens	Young Adults	Over 30	Senior Citizens
★★	★★	★★★	★★★	★★★	★★★

Author's Rating: Both solemn and scenic. ★★★

How Much Time to Allow: 30 minutes

DESCRIPTION AND COMMENTS To see what the Lincoln Memorial looks like, just pull out a penny. Yet a visit to this marble monument inspires awe. Historic events took place on the steps: Black soprano Marian Anderson sang here in 1939 after being barred from Constitution Hall; Martin Luther King, Jr., gave his "I Have a Dream" speech here in 1963. The Lincoln Memorial anchors the Mall and should be on anyone's "must see" list.

TOURING TIPS The small Lincoln museum in the basement is no great shakes, but it's worth a peek through a window into the creepy underpinnings of this huge memorial. The Lincoln Memorial's location at the west end of the Mall near the river, however, puts this marble edifice at a distance from any lunch spots except for overpriced Mall hot dog vendors, so eat first. Bathrooms are located on the memorial's ground level.

OTHER THINGS TO DO NEARBY   The Vietnam Veterans Memorial and the Reflecting Pool are directly across from the Lincoln Memorial. The National Academy of Sciences on Constitution Avenue features science exhibits (open Monday through Friday, 9 A.M. to 5 P.M.; free). Outside, tourists can crawl into the lap of an Albert Einstein statue to have their picture taken; it's a D.C. tradition. If you hike a few blocks up 23rd Street or 17th Street, you'll find an alternative to those hot dog vendors.

National Air and Space Museum

Type of Attraction: A museum that chronicles the history of manned flight. A self-guided tour.

Location: On the south side of the Mall near the U.S. Capitol.

Nearest Metro Station: Smithsonian

Admission: Free

Hours: 10 A.M. to 5:30 P.M. Depending on the shape of the federal budget, hours may be extended during Easter and summer.

Phone: (202) 357-2700

When to Go: Before noon or after 4 P.M.

Special Comments: If you want to get tickets for the five-story-high IMAX theater, make the box office on the main floor your first stop. Some special exhibits require passes; check with the information desk in the main lobby.

Overall Appeal by Age Group:

Pre-school	Grade School	Teens	Young Adults	Over 30	Senior Citizens
★★★★	★★★★★	★★★★★	★★★★★	★★★★★	★★★★★

Author's Rating: Absolutely not to be missed. ★★★★★

How Much Time to Allow: Two hours minimum—and you still won't see it all. If possible, try to spread your tour of the museum over two or more visits.

DESCRIPTION AND COMMENTS   This museum is the most visited in the world, drawing about eight million visitors a year. Entering from the Mall, visitors can touch a moon rock, gaze up at the Wright Brothers' plane and the *Spirit of St. Louis,* which Lindbergh flew across the Atlantic in 1927. Everywhere you look is another full-size wonder. The only drawback to this museum is its size — going to every exhibit becomes numbing after a while. If your length of stay allows it, try to split your time here into at least two visits. But it's a must-see for virtually anyone — not just airplane buffs and space cadets.

TOURING TIPS   If you don't have an unlimited amount of time to wander around, try this strategy: After leaving the main lobby, work your way over to Space Hall, where you can tour Skylab and check out the Apollo-Soyuz spacecraft. For more insight into the exhibits, take one of the free, one-hour guided tours starting at 10:15 A.M. and 1 P.M. daily, beginning at the information desk in the main lobby.

While you'll never have to stand in line to get into the National Air and Space Museum, you can avoid a few major bottlenecks by staying away from Skylab, the moon rock, and the cafeteria around lunchtime. Two exhibits featuring interactive video displays are also worth hitting early to avoid lines: "Where Next, Columbus?" (future space travel) and "Beyond the Limits" (computers in aviation and space).

OTHER THINGS TO DO NEARBY   To escape the worst of the crowds, try a stroll through the fragrant U.S. Botanical Gardens, located a block east of the National Air and Space Museum. For lunch, the onsite cafeteria and restaurant feature a great view of the Capitol and expensive, run-of-the-mill dining. Best bet: L'Enfant Plaza, where you can dine elbow-to-elbow with Washington bureaucrats in an underground mall with a wide range of eateries. The entrance is south of the Mall on 10th Street, SW, between D and E streets. In the summer, check out the Hirshhorn's cafe, where you can dine *al fresco* with great art.

National Aquarium

Type of Attraction: The oldest aquarium in the United States. A self-guided tour.

Location: In the basement of the Department of Commerce building on 14th Street, NW.

Nearest Metro Station: Federal Triangle

Admission: Adults $2, children and seniors $.75

Hours: 9 A.M. to 5 P.M. daily, closed Christmas Day

Phone: (202) 482-2925

When to Go: Anytime

Special Comments: A cool, dark oasis on a sweltering summer afternoon.

Overall Appeal by Age Group:

Pre-school	Grade School	Teens	Young Adults	Over 30	Senior Citizens
★★★★	★★★★	★★★	★★	★★	★★

Author's Rating: A basement full of fish tanks. ★½

How Much Time to Allow: One hour

DESCRIPTION AND COMMENTS   Essentially a long room lined with big fish tanks in the basement of an office building, this aquarium is not in the same league with other, newer fish and dolphin emporiums that are springing up all over (such as the one in Baltimore). But children will love it. Small and lacking crowd-pleasing sea mammals, the aquarium figures as a minor exhibit for filling in the odd hour or to escape from a sweltering afternoon. Otherwise, spend your valuable touring time elsewhere.

TOURING TIPS   Sharks get fed at 2 P.M. on Monday, Wednesday, and Saturday; the piranhas get their meals at 2 P.M. on Tuesday, Thursday, and Sunday.

OTHER THINGS TO DO NEARBY   The Washington Monument, the National Museum of American History, and the Old Post Office Pavilion are within a few minutes' walk. The Commerce Department cafeteria, open Monday through Friday from 9 A.M. to 2 P.M., offers good, cheap fare: a soup and salad bar, pizza and pasta, a grill, a deli, and hot entrees. You can get a whole pizza that will feed a family of four for less than $10.

National Archives

Type of Attraction: The magnificent rotunda where the Declaration of Independence and U.S. Constitution are displayed. A self-guided tour.

Location: 7th Street and Constitution Avenue, NW, on the Mall.

Nearest Metro Station: Archives

Admission: Free

Hours: Exhibition Hall open 10 A.M. to 9 P.M. every day, April 1 through Labor Day; 10 A.M. to 5:30 P.M., September through March 31.

Phone: (202) 501-5205

When to Go: Before noon or after 4 P.M. during spring and summer

Special Comments: Small children may need a lift to see the documents; skip it if the line is long.

Overall Appeal by Age Group:

Pre-school	Grade School	Teens	Young Adults	Over 30	Senior Citizens
★	★★	★★½	★★★	★★★	★★★

Author's Rating: A let-down. ★½

How Much Time to Allow: 30 minutes

Average Wait in Line per 100 People Ahead of You: 20 minutes

DESCRIPTION AND COMMENTS   In addition to trying to decipher the faint and flowing script on the sheets of parchment mounted in bronze and glass cases, visitors can stroll through a temporary exhibit of photos and documents covering some aspect of Americana. Most visitors seem as fascinated by the written description of the elaborate security system that lowers the sacred documents into a deep, nuclear-explosion-proof vault each night as they are by seeing the charters themselves — and you can't even see the contraption.

While the rotunda is impressive, most people are surprised at how little there is to see inside this huge building. In fact, there *is* a lot more to see — but you've got to call in advance to arrange a tour. If the line to get in is long, skip it and come back later. It's really not worth the wait.

TOURING TIPS   For a behind-the-scenes view of the workings of the National Archives, arrange to take a reserved tour. During spring and summer, two weeks' notice is recommended. Or take a chance and show up at the Pennsylvania Avenue entrance (across from 8th Street, NW) at tour time. If there's a cancellation or a no-show, you're in. The reserved tours begin at 10:15 A.M. and 1:15 P.M. daily and last about an hour.

On the reserved tour, you'll see a working model of the vault that protects the Great Charters and take a tour of the building, including the stacks, microfilm viewing rooms, and exhibits and models that show how researchers preserve documents. The tour ends at the Rotunda. Oh, and don't miss the gift shop, where the best-selling item is a photograph of President Nixon and Elvis Presley embracing. It's a scream.

OTHER THINGS TO DO NEARBY   Pick a Smithsonian museum you haven't seen yet and dive in. Several good restaurants popular with folks who work in the museums along the Mall are located across Pennsylvania Avenue from the National Archives on Indiana Avenue, NW.

National Gallery of Art—East Building

Type of Attraction: A museum housing modern art and special art exhibitions. A self-guided tour.

Location: 4th Street and Constitution Avenue, NW, on the Mall.

Nearest Metro Station: Archives

Admission: Free

Hours: 10 A.M. to 5 P.M. Monday through Saturday; 11 A.M. to 6 P.M. Sundays; depending on budgets, evening hours are extended in the summer.

Phone: (202) 737-4215

When to Go: Anytime

Special Comments: Usually referred to as the "East Wing" of the National Gallery.

Overall Appeal by Age Group:

Pre-school	Grade School	Teens	Young Adults	Over 30	Senior Citizens
★	★★	★★★	★★★★★	★★★★★	★★★★★

Author's Rating: Even the building is a great work of art. ★★★★★

How Much Time to Allow: Two hours

DESCRIPTION AND COMMENTS Both the interior and exterior of this I. M. Pei–designed building are spectacular, so it's worth a visit even if you hate modern art. Outside, the popular 1978 building consists of unadorned vertical planes. Inside, it's bright, airy, and spacious. Look for art by modern masters such as Picasso, Matisse, Mondrian, Miro, Magritte, Warhol, Lichtenstein, and Rauschenberg. The exhibits change constantly, so there's no telling which of these is on display.

TOURING TIPS Some temporary exhibits (like a recent Gauguin show) are extremely popular and require a free "time ticket" that admits you on a certain day at a specific hour. You may pick up such tickets in advance; tickets are available as much as a month before a show opens. If you don't have a ticket on the day you visit the East Wing, you're not completely out of luck: about 400 tickets per half-hour are set aside every day for distribution that day only. If you want one, arrive at the ticket counter on the main floor by noon (or 2 P.M. during the week). Then come back later to see the exhibit.

When you exit the museum, turn left and check out the high, knife-edge exterior corner wall of the gallery, near the Mall — it's almost worn away from people touching their noses to it.

OTHER THINGS TO DO NEARBY   The West Wing, with its more traditional European art, is connected to the East Building by an underground concourse. The Capitol and the U.S. Botanical Gardens are close by, as is the National Archives.

The cafeteria along the concourse may be the best official Mall eatery, featuring a classy selection of food and an espresso bar. Otherwise, the Old Post Office Pavilion and L'Enfant Plaza offer the best food choices nearby.

National Gallery of Art — West Building

Type of Attraction: Museum featuring European and American art. Self-guided and guided tours.

Location: 6th Street and Constitution Avenue, NW, on the Mall.

Nearest Metro Station: Archives

Admission: Free

Hours: 10 A.M. to 5 P.M. Monday through Saturday; 11 A.M. to 6 P.M. Sundays; depending on budgets, summer hours are extended in the evenings.

Phone: (202) 737-4215

When to Go: Anytime

Special Comments: Usually referred to as the "West Wing" of the National Gallery.

Overall Appeal by Age Group:

Pre-school	Grade School	Teens	Young Adults	Over 30	Senior Citizens
★	★★½	★★★	★★★★	★★★★★	★★★★★

Author's Rating: Art with a capital "A." ★★★★★

How Much Time to Allow: Two hours for a light skimming, but you could spend a week.

DESCRIPTION AND COMMENTS   This is where you find the heavy hitters: Dutch masters such as Rembrandt and Vermeer, plus Raphael, Monet, and Jacques-Louis David, just to name a few. And it's all housed in an elegant neoclassical building designed by John Russell Pope. It's a world-class art museum; first-time visitors should make at least one stop.

TOURING TIPS Most of the museum's paintings are hung in many small rooms, instead of a few big ones, so don't try to speed through the building or you'll miss most of them. When museum fatigue begins to set in, rest your feet in one of the atriums located between the museum's many galleries. If you plan on dragging kids through this massive place, try bribing them with a later trip to the National Zoo.

OTHER THINGS TO DO NEARBY Take the connecting corridor (an underground concourse) to the Gallery's East Building. The Air and Space Museum is directly across the Mall, while the National Archives is in the other direction, across Constitution Avenue.

Probably the best museum cafeteria on the Mall is located along the concourse. Otherwise, L'Enfant Plaza (an underground shopping mall loaded with restaurants and fast food places) and the Old Post Office Pavilion are your best bets for lunch.

National Museum of African Art

Type of Attraction: A museum specializing in the traditional arts of sub-Saharan Africa. A self-guided tour.

Location: 950 Independence Avenue, SW, on the Mall near The Castle (the Smithsonian Institution building).

Nearest Metro Station: Smithsonian

Admission: Free

Hours: 10 A.M. to 5:30 P.M. daily; closed Christmas Day.

Phone: (202) 357-4600

When to Go: Anytime

Special Comments: Provides a quiet respite when other Mall attractions are jammed; an excellent museum shop.

Overall Appeal by Age Group:

Pre-school	Grade School	Teens	Young Adults	Over 30	Senior Citizens
★	★★	★★	★★½	★★½	★★½

Author's Rating: Exquisite sculpture and fascinating household items. ★★

How Much Time to Allow: One hour

DESCRIPTION AND COMMENTS This relatively new subterranean museum, which opened in 1987, is paired with its mate, the Sackler

Gallery, a museum of Oriental art, and separated by an above-ground garden. Inside is an extensive collection of African art in a wide range of media, including sculpture, masks, household and personal items, and religious objects. Intellectually, this museum transports museum-goers far away from the Mall. It's an okay destination for older children, teens, and adults looking for some non-European cultural history and art. This museum is a great alternative on hot and/or crowded days in Washington.

TOURING TIPS   Check at the information desk about guided tours. And don't miss the excellent museum shop, where'll you find textiles, jewelry, scarves and sashes, wood carvings, and a wide selection of African music on tape, CD, and videotape.

OTHER THINGS TO DO NEARBY   This museum is twinned with the Arthur M. Sackler Gallery, and even connects with it below ground — a nice feature on a sweltering Washington afternoon. If the weather's mild, stroll the Enid A. Haupt Garden, which separates the two museums at ground level. Neither museum has a cafeteria; the closest places featuring good selections and reasonable prices are L'Enfant Plaza and the Old Post Office Pavilion. Both are minutes away via the Metro.

National Museum of American History

Type of Attraction: An extensive collection of artifacts reflecting the American experience — historical, social, and technological. A self-guided tour.

Location: 14th Street and Constitution Avenue, NW, on the Mall.

Nearest Metro Stations: Smithsonian, Federal Triangle

Admission: Free

Hours: 10 A.M. to 5:30 P.M. daily; extended summer hours depend on budget restraints. Closed Christmas Day.

Phone: (202) 357-2700

When to Go: To avoid the worst crowds, visit before noon and after 3 P.M.

Special Comments: The immensity of this museum almost demands that visitors try to see it in more than one visit.

Overall Appeal by Age Group:

Pre-school	Grade School	Teens	Young Adults	Over 30	Senior Citizens
★★★	★★★★★	★★★★★	★★★★★	★★★★★	★★★★★

Author's Rating: A collection of national treasures; don't miss it.
★★★★★

How Much Time to Allow: Two hours on a first pass; it would take a week to see it all.

DESCRIPTION AND COMMENTS   Three exhibit-packed floors feature such treasures as the original Star-Spangled Banner, steam locomotives, a Model T Ford, a pendulum four stories high that shows how the earth rotates, a collection of ball gowns worn by First Ladies, Archie Bunker's chair, and an exhibit of typewriters. If you can't find something of interest here, you may need mouth-to-mouth resuscitation. For a lot of people, this ranks as the favorite Mall museum. No wonder: It offers viewers a dizzying array of history, nostalgia, technology, and culture. And kids love it. It's a must-see for virtually all visitors.

TOURING TIPS   At most museums, you look at "stuff," but a lot of the collection at American History is arranged so that viewers can learn about people in the context of their times. To see what we mean—and to help you organize yourself in this bewilderingly large museum— make it a point to see these exhibits: the First Ladies' Exhibition, Field to Factory (about the migration of Southern rural African-Americans to northern cities), and a collection of objects about television that includes Archie Bunker's chair, Fonzie's jacket, one of Mr. Rogers' sweaters, Oscar the Grouch (of "Sesame Street" fame), and, for baby boomers, some items from the "Howdy Doody Show." Check at the information desk for a schedule of tours, demonstrations, concerts, lectures, films, and other activities put on by the museum staff.

One last hint: A lot of people touring the museum on their own overlook the Hall of Transportation in the museum's east wing, which features an excellent collection of cars, trains, and motorcycles. Car aficionados will love it.

OTHER THINGS TO DO NEARBY   Within a short walk are the Washington Monument, the National Aquarium, the Old Post Office Pavilion (lunch!), and the Museum of Natural History. Almost directly across the Mall are the Freer and Sackler galleries, and the National Museum of African Art. And, yes, the American History Museum has a cafeteria and an ice cream parlor.

National Museum of Natural History

Type of Attraction: America's treasure chest of the natural sciences. A self-guided tour.

Location: On the Mall at 10th Street, NW, and Constitution Avenue.

Nearest Metro Stations: Smithsonian, Archives

Admission: Free

Hours: 10 A.M. to 5:30 P.M. Sometimes hours are extended in summer.

Phone: (202) 357-2700

When to Go: Before noon and after 4 P.M.

Special Comments: In the Discovery Room, kids can touch nearly everything. Hours are Monday through Friday, noon to 2:30 P.M. and weekends 10:30 A.M. to 3:30 P.M.

Overall Appeal by Age Group:

Pre-school	Grade School	Teens	Young Adults	Over 30	Senior Citizens
★★★★	★★★★★	★★★★½	★★★★★	★★★★★	★★★★★

Author's Rating: The displays of huge dinosaur fossils and priceless gems alone make this museum a classic. ★★★★½

How Much Time to Allow: Two hours is enough time to see the really cool stuff, but you could easily spend an entire day here.

DESCRIPTION AND COMMENTS Distinguished by its golden dome and the towering bull elephant in the rotunda, the Museum of Natural History is a Washington landmark. It's a bit old-fashioned, with long halls filled with dioramas, display cases, and hanging specimens that reflect the Victorian obsession with collecting things. This museum, along with Air and Space across the Mall, is immensely popular with families, and for a good reason— folks of all ages and tastes will find fascinating things to do here.

TOURING TIPS After entering through the big doors at the Mall entrance, bear right to see the dinosaur skeletons, then go to the second floor to gaze upon cases filled with crystals and gems (the supposedly cursed Hope Diamond is here). If you're not put off by crawling critters, stop by the Insect Zoo, which features a wide array of (live) bugs. Special exhibits are located on the ground level (Constitution Avenue entrance).

OTHER THINGS TO DO NEARBY   While there's a cafeteria on site that's convenient, overpriced, and lousy, a better choice for lunch is the Old Post Office Pavilion, about a block away on 12th Street, NW. The fast-food kiosk in front of the museum is also overpriced: If you crave a hot dog, walk over to Constitution Avenue, find a street vendor, and save a buck.

Old Executive Office Building

Type of Attraction: The ornate building that houses many agencies that are part of the Executive Office of the President. A guided tour.

Location: Next to the White House on Pennsylvania Avenue; use the visitors entrance on 17th Street, NW.

Nearest Metro Station: Farragut West

Admission: Free

Hours: Saturdays from 9 A.M. to 12 noon.

Phone: (202) 395-5895

Special Comments: The recent overhaul of the building skimped on elevators: They're tiny and require visitors to jump up and down to close the doors. Nervous types, beware.

Overall Appeal by Age Group:

Pre-school	Grade School	Teens	Young Adults	Over 30	Senior Citizens
★	★	★½	★★	★★½	★★½

Author's Rating: For those who can't get their fill of ornate buildings. ★★½

How Much Time to Allow: One hour

DESCRIPTION AND COMMENTS   The Old Executive Office Building's baroque, Second Empire exterior falls into the "love it or hate it" category. President Truman, for example, called it "the greatest monstrosity in America." Yet its recently renovated interior is more like a palace than an assembly of government offices — even if they are the offices of the president's minions. The massive building boasts four-and-a-half-foot-thick granite walls, 16-foot ceilings, and nearly two miles of corridors. Grand staircases, bronze stair balusters, four skylight domes, and two stained-glass rotundas grace the interior. Other marvels include the four-story Executive Office of the President Library (constructed of cast iron), the Indian Treaty Room (featuring rich marble wall panelings and gold-leaf ornamentation), and the opulent office of the vice president. This tour offers more than stunning interiors: Pay close attention to the windows and you'll get an overhead view of the White House that's usually reserved for government honchos.

This is another "behind the scenes" tour that lets visitors get a glimpse of a part of Washington that few people ever see. First-time visitors should pass on it, but for those on a second or third trip, it's an interesting Saturday morning diversion.

TOURING TIPS   By guided tour only; advance reservations required. Tours leave between 9 A.M. and 12 noon on Saturdays only. To make a reservation, call (202) 395-5895 Monday through Friday between 9 A.M. and 12 noon. Make reservations at least two weeks before your visit; you'll have to give each visitor's correct name and date of birth. Bring a photo ID when you come; parents can vouch for kids. The one-hour tour is long on walking and short on places to sit. Bathrooms are available once the tour guide gets you out of the waiting area and past the metal detectors.

OTHER THINGS TO DO NEARBY   A lot: The White House, the Renwick Gallery, the Corcoran Gallery of Art, the DAR Museum, the Washington Monument, and the National Aquarium are all within a few blocks.

Old Post Office Tower and Pavilion

Type of Attraction: A multiethnic food court in a spectacular architectural setting; home of the second-best view in Washington; trendy shops. A guided tour.

Location: 12th Street and Pennsylvania Avenue, NW.

Nearest Metro Station: Federal Triangle

Admission: Free

Hours: 8 A.M. to 6 P.M. Monday through Friday; 12 noon to 6 P.M. Saturdays.

Phone: (202) 289-4224

When to Go: Anytime to take the glass elevator up the clock tower; beat the worst of the crowds in the food court after 1 P.M.

Special Comments: This is the place to come when the line at the Washington Monument wraps around the base three times. The food court is a favorite stop for tour buses, making it difficult at times to find a table.

Overall Appeal by Age Group:

Pre-school	Grade School	Teens	Young Adults	Over 30	Senior Citizens
★★★★	★★★★	★★★★	★★★	★★★	★★★

Author's Rating: A great view and a lifesaver for tourists who hate the overpriced, crummy food served in most museums. ★★★½

How Much Time to Allow: One hour for the clock tower.

DESCRIPTION AND COMMENTS   This fine old building, a Pennsylvania Avenue landmark, was slated for demolition, but preservationist groups intervened to save it. Today, the 315-foot clock tower offers a spectacular view of Washington, while the multiethnic food court occupies a stunning, glass-roofed architectural space ten stories high. It offers a complete tourist experience for people of all ages: a view to kill for (and unlike the tiny windows in Big Guy on the Mall, here you see D.C. through large plate glass windows), great food, and a shopping mall. And with its proximity to the Mall and White House, the pavilion is a convenient place to visit for a quick lunch or snack.

TOURING TIPS   It's elbow to elbow in the small elevator to the observation deck. Beware of groups of screaming teenagers in the food court—it's a popular destination for school groups. To reach the glass-enclosed elevators to the observation deck, go to the patio area in the food court. The National Park Service rangers on duty in the tower are a great source of advice about D.C. touring. Ask one to show you the lay of the land from the observation deck.

OTHER THINGS TO DO NEARBY   Make faces at the groupers in the National Aquarium, see an agent rip off some rounds of automatic weapons fire at the FBI, or visit Ford's Theatre. If you can't find anything good to eat in the food court, it's time to go home.

The Pentagon

Type of Attraction: The world's largest office building, and headquarters for the Department of Defense. A guided tour.

Location: Across the Potomac River in Arlington, Virginia.

Nearest Metro Station: Pentagon (the tour office is at the top of the Metro escalator)

Admission: Free

Hours: 9:30 A.M. to 3:30 P.M. Monday through Friday; tours leave every 30 minutes. From October through May, the 10:30 A.M., 1:30 P.M., and 3 P.M. tours are eliminated.

Phone: (703) 695-1776

When to Go: By 9 A.M. during peak season.

Special Comments: Small children and senior citizens may find the brisk pace of this 90-minute tour exhausting.

Overall Appeal by Age Group:

Pre-school	Grade School	Teens	Young Adults	Over 30	Senior Citizens
—	★	★	★½	★½	★★

Author's Rating: Boring. ★

How Much Time to Allow: 90 minutes

DESCRIPTION AND COMMENTS   This tour is a furiously paced run through a sizeable percentage of the Pentagon's 17.5 miles of corridors. Along the way you get to see General MacArthur's West Point uniform, a blur of military paintings, and an exhibit featuring the names of every Medal of Honor winner.

Between flashes of art, keep your eyes peeled for two things: Your guide, who walks backwards the entire time to keep an eye on his charges; and brief glimpses of Pentagon top brass. On my tour I saw Admiral Frank B. Kelso, Chief of Naval Operations. He didn't stop to chat. The tour is best suited for retired military personnel and their dependents—I mean, families.

TOURING TIPS   Eat and go to the bathroom before arriving: Incredibly, the Department of Defense provides neither eating facilities nor rest rooms for visitors to use. For lunch, you must reboard the Metro; the nearest place to eat is Pentagon City. You must have a photo I.D. to get on a tour.

OTHER THINGS TO DO NEARBY   Arlington Cemetery is one Metro station away.

The Renwick Gallery

Type of Attraction: A museum dedicated to American crafts and decorative arts. A self-guided tour.

Location: 17th and Pennsylvania Avenue, NW (diagonally across from the White House).

Nearest Metro Station: Farragut West

Admission: Free

Hours: 10 A.M. to 5:30 P.M. daily.

Phone: (202) 357-2700

When to Go: Anytime

Special Comments: Don't expect an exhibition of hand-woven baskets: The museum features a wide array of mixed-media sculptures, tapestries, and constructions by major contemporary artists.

Overall Appeal by Age Group:

Pre-school	Grade School	Teens	Young Adults	Over 30	Senior Citizens
★	★★	★★	★★	★★½	★★½

Author's Rating: An elegant setting, yet a bit dull. ★★

How Much Time to Allow: One hour

DESCRIPTION AND COMMENTS   Both the art and the Second Empire architecture of the mansion make this Smithsonian museum worth a stop when you're near the White House. Works on display are constructed in glass, ceramics, wood, fiber, and metal. But folks on a first-time visit to Washington or with children should skip it.

TOURING TIPS   Glide up the Grand Staircase to enter the elegant Grand Salon, now an art gallery featuring floor-to-ceiling oil paintings, velvet curtains, and traditional furniture. On the same floor is the Octagon Room, which faces the street and is similarly decorated in the styles of the 1860s and 1870s. The first floor hosts temporary exhibits.

OTHER THINGS TO DO NEARBY   Next door is Blair House, where visiting foreign dignitaries stay; you can't get in, but look for Secret Service agents and diplomatic limos. A plaque on the wrought-iron gates honors a guard who saved President Truman from a would-be assassin. Around the corner on 17th Street is the closest McDonald's to the White House. Arrive early in the morning and maybe you'll catch a glimpse of President Clinton.

The Arthur M. Sackler Gallery

Type of Attraction: A museum dedicated to Asian art. A self-guided tour.

Location: 1050 Independence Avenue, SW, on the Mall near The Castle (the Smithsonian Institution building).

Nearest Metro Station: Smithsonian

Admission: Free

Hours: 9 A.M. to 5:30 P.M. daily; closed Christmas Day.

Phone: (202) 357-4880

When to Go: Anytime

Special Comments: A quiet respite when other Mall attractions are jammed with visitors.

Overall Appeal by Age Group:

Pre-school	Grade School	Teens	Young Adults	Over 30	Senior Citizens
★	★★	★★	★★½	★★½	★★½

Author's Rating: Fabulous but foreign art. ★★½

How Much Time to Allow: One hour

DESCRIPTION AND COMMENTS   Descend through a granite-and-glass pavilion to view a collection of Asian (mostly Chinese) treasures, many of them made of gold and encrusted with jewels. The Sackler is full of exotic stuff that will catch the eye of older children, teens, and adults. Barring a strong interest in the Orient, however, first-time visitors on a tight schedule should visit the Sackler another time.

TOURING TIPS   Stop at the information desk and ask about the guided tours offered throughout the day. The gift shop is an exotic bazaar, featuring paintings, textiles, ancient games, Zen rock garden kits, and plenty of other Asian-influenced items.

OTHER THINGS TO DO NEARBY   The Sackler is connected with its twin, the Museum of African Art, below ground, so that's the logical next stop — especially if the weather is lousy or it's blazingly hot outside. In the spring of 1993, the Freer Gallery reopened after a four-and-a-half-year, $90-million renovation. A new underground corridor connects it to the Sackler.

None of these museums offers a cafeteria, but that's okay: Walk a few steps to the Smithsonian Metro station and in a few moments you're at L'Enfant Plaza or the Old Post Office Pavilion. The only remaining problem is deciding what to eat.

Smithsonian Institution Building (The Castle)

Type of Attraction: Information desks and displays, and a continuously running movie that introduces visitors to the vast number of Smithsonian museums.

Location: 1000 Jefferson Drive, SW, on the Mall.

Nearest Metro Station: Smithsonian

Admission: Free

Hours: 9 A.M. to 5:30 P.M. daily; closed Christmas Day.

Phone: (202) 357-2700

When to Go: Anytime

Author's Rating: Great for first-time Mall visitors. ★★★★

How Much Time to Allow: 30 minutes

DESCRIPTION AND COMMENTS   This red brick building—you can't miss it—contains no exhibits. The Castle serves as an information center that will help you save time and trouble and reduce the frustration that comes from visiting this large and perplexing museum complex.

Step into the theater to see the 20-minute film. It's a bit long, but gives a good idea of what each museum has to offer. Then you can talk to someone at the information desk for specific directions and advice. A nifty map exhibit on the east wall lights up the location of each of the museums on the Mall, as well as other popular D.C. sights, when you press the corresponding button.

U.S. Department of the Treasury

Type of Attraction: Recently restored, this oldest federal office building in Washington houses the offices of the national treasury. A guided tour.

Location: 15th and Pennsylvania Avenue, NW. Visitors enter at the appointment center doors on 15th Street.

Nearest Metro Station: Metro Center

Admission: Free

Hours: Because this is a working office building, guided tours are offered on Saturday mornings only.

Phone: (202) 622-0896

Special Comments: The tour lasts about an hour, and you'll be standing and walking the whole time.

Overall Appeal by Age Group:

Pre-school	Grade School	Teens	Young Adults	Over 30	Senior Citizens
—	★	★½	★★	★★½	★★½

Author's Rating: Austere and cold, like a big bank. ★★

How Much Time to Allow: 90 minutes

DESCRIPTION AND COMMENTS   Recent renovations to the interior of this imposing building next to the White House restored its 1860s atmosphere. For example, the Secretary's Conference and Reception Rooms were reconstructed into the American Renaissance Revival style of the 1860s–1880s period. A recently discovered burglar-proof vault that had been hidden by plasterboard now serves, appropriately enough, as part of the U.S. Treasurer's Office. The tour ends in the marble-walled Cash Room, heralded as the most expensive room in the world when it opened in 1869. This tour is for the person who's been to Washington before and wants to see something unique. First-time visitors, unless they have a strong interest in decorative art or banks, should save it for their next visit.

TOURING TIPS   Advance reservations are required; during spring and summer, call at least two weeks in advance. Kids would be bored silly by this one.

OTHER THINGS TO DO NEARBY   The National Aquarium is in the basement of the Commerce Department; enter on 14th Street, NW. Both F and G streets offer plenty of eating opportunities, including the three-level Shops at National Place. The food court in the Old Post Office Pavilion is about three blocks away on Pennsylvania Avenue.

U.S. Holocaust Memorial Museum

Type of Attraction: A museum and memorial presenting the history of the persecution and murder of six million Jews and others by Nazi Germany during World War II. A self-guided tour.

Location: 100 Raoul Wallenberg Place, SW (formerly 15th Street), near the Mall between the Washington Monument and the Bureau

of Engraving and Printing. Entrances are on Raoul Wallenberg
Place and 14th Street.

Nearest Metro Station: Smithsonian (Independence Avenue exit)

Admission: Free

Hours: 10 A.M. to 5:30 P.M., daily; closed Christmas Day.

Phone: (202) 488-0400

When to Go: After favorable publicity generated large crowds following its opening in the spring of 1993, the Holocaust Museum went
to a "time ticket" system to eliminate long lines during the busy
tourist season. While officials say they have no plans to reinstitute
ticketing in the spring of 1994, more big crowds could mean a
return to time tickets in the spring and summer. Either way, it's
a safe bet that the Holocaust Museum will remain a "must see"
attraction on the Mall; plan on hitting it early in the week and
early in the day.

Special Comments: According to Holocaust Museum officials, the
main exhibit is inappropriate for children under 11 — and we agree.
However, a special exhibit on the museum's first floor, "Daniel's
Story: Remember the Children," is designed for visitors 8 and
older. It gives a child's perspective on the Holocaust, but without
the shocking graphics of the permanent exhibit.

Overall Appeal by Age Group:

Pre-school	Grade School	Teens	Young Adults	Over 30	Senior Citizens
—	★½	★★	★★★	★★★½	★★★★

Author's Rating: As its designers intended, the Holocaust Museum
is ugly, forbidding, and grim — and delivers a stern message about
the evils of racial persecution. It also packs an emotional punch
that may not fit some folks' vacation plans. ★★½

How Much Time to Allow: one and a half to two hours.

DESCRIPTION AND COMMENTS   This new $168 million museum uti-
lizes stunning, high-tech audio-visual displays, advanced computer
technology, and a model of a Nazi death camp, to deliver a message
about one of the darkest periods in human history.

But that's not all. As part of the museum experience, museum-goers
are cast as "victims" of Nazi brutality. The process starts in line to board
the elevators to the fourth floor, where the permanent exhibit begins.

Visitors receive an identity card of a real Holocaust victim matched to their sex and age—a demographic double. You update the card at three printing stations scattered throughout the museum; at the last station, the fate of the victim is revealed. Usually, he or she died in a concentration camp.

The building attacks the emotions of visitors in other, more subtle, ways. The interior of the museum, while spotless, is relentlessly industrial and forbidding—pipes are exposed and rough surfaces of brick and concrete are cold and unwelcoming. Diagonal walls in the exhibition areas create a disorienting effect. Ghostly shapes pass overhead on glass-bottomed walkways, suggesting anonymous prison guards patroling a camp. (Actually, they are visitors walking on footbridges linking the permanent exhibit spaces.) Every moment spent inside the museum is orchestrated to impart the horror of Nazi persecution.

While many exhibits focus on Jewish life prior to the Holocaust and the political and military events surrounding World War II, the most disturbing displays are graphic depictions of Nazi atrocities. Large TV screens scattered throughout the exhibits present still and motion pictures of Nazi leaders, storm troopers rounding up victims, and life inside Jewish ghettoes.

Some of the TV screens are located behind concrete barriers to prevent younger (and, inadvertently, shorter) visitors from seeing them. They show executions, medical experiments on Jewish prisoners, and suicide victims. It's very strong, grim stuff.

TOURING TIPS   Given the unrelenting horror of its subject matter, the Holocaust Museum is at best sobering and, at worst, depressing. There's no bright gloss to put on a museum chronicling the systematic murder of six million people . . . and anyone visiting the Holocaust Museum during a vacation should keep that in mind before placing it on his or her touring agenda, especially if traveling with small children.

OTHER THINGS TO DO NEARBY   The Holocaust Museum occupies some prime real estate near the Mall, Bureau of Engraving and Printing, Washington Monument, Tidal Basin, and Jefferson Memorial, so finding things to do before or after a tour of the museum is easy. The Museum Annex on Raoul Wallenberg Place has a small deli/cafe that's expensive but convenient.

Vietnam Veterans Memorial

Type of Attraction: A memorial to U.S. soldiers who died in Vietnam.

Location: On the west end of the Mall near the Lincoln Memorial.

Nearest Metro Station: Foggy Bottom/GWU

Admission: Free

Hours: This outdoor monument is always open.

When to Go: Anytime

Special Comments: At night this memorial is especially moving as people light matches to search for names inscribed on the wall.

Overall Appeal by Age Group:

Pre-school	Grade School	Teens	Young Adults	Over 30	Senior Citizens
★	★★	★★	★★★	★★★★	★★★★

Author's Rating: Deeply moving. ★★★½

How Much Time to Allow: 30 minutes

DESCRIPTION AND COMMENTS   This long, narrow wall of polished black stone is inscribed with the names of the more than 58,000 Americans who died in Vietnam. Many visitors to the memorial make rubbings of loved ones' names, while others leave flowers, military medals, letters, and gifts along the base of the wall. The wall, a black rift in the earth, packs an emotional wallop.

TOURING TIPS   At both ends of the wall visitors will find books that list the inscribed names and the panel number to help them locate an inscription.

OTHER THINGS TO DO NEARBY   The Lincoln Memorial, the Reflecting Pool, and Constitution Gardens are close by. Across from the Mall, the National Academy of Sciences features science exhibits and a statue of Albert Einstein with a lap that's large enough to sit in for picture-taking. For food, walk up 23rd Street toward Foggy Bottom and an assortment of restaurants and carryouts.

Voice of America

Type of Attraction: The U.S. Government's overseas radio broadcasting studios. A guided tour.

Location: Tours meet at the C Street entrance between 3rd and 4th streets, SW.

Nearest Metro Station: Federal Center SW

Admission: Free

Hours: 45-minute tours begin at 8:40 A.M., 9:40 A.M., 10:40 A.M.,
   1:40 P.M., and 2:40 P.M. Monday through Friday, except holidays.

Phone: (202) 619-3919

Special Comments: A "must" for news junkies.

Overall Appeal by Age Group:

Pre-school	Grade School	Teens	Young Adults	Over 30	Senior Citizens
—	★	★	★★	★★	★★

Author's Rating: Fascinating and informative. ★★½

How Much Time to Allow: 45 minutes

DESCRIPTION AND COMMENTS   After a short video about the VOA,
the knowledgeable tour guide walks you through some of the agency's
34 studios, where you see and hear radio announcers reading newscasts
in languages such as Arabic, Estonian, and Urdu. Worldwide, the VOA
operates more than 100 shortwave radio transmitters and all broadcasts
originate in this building. It's a tour for people interested in media and
world events; it would bore most children silly.

TOURING TIPS   You can call to reserve a place on a tour, but individuals and small groups won't have trouble joining a tour by just showing
up a few minutes before a scheduled departure.

OTHER THINGS TO DO NEARBY   The U.S. Botanical Gardens are around
the corner on Maryland Avenue, SW, and the Mall is two blocks away.
For lunch, try the L'Enfant Plaza underground shopping mall, which is
usually jammed with bureaucrats looking for good, cheap food — and
finding it.

Washington Monument

Type of Attraction: A monument to the first U.S. president.

Location: On the Mall between 15th and 17th streets, NW.

Nearest Metro Station: Smithsonian

Admission: Free

Hours: 8 A.M. to midnight in the summer; 9 A.M. to 5 P.M. September
   through March.

Phone: (202) 426-6841

When to Go: Before 9 A.M. or after 6 P.M.

Special Comments: Waits in line can exceed three hours in daytime during spring and early summer; handicapped people can go directly to the head of the line; skip it in bad weather (the view can be lousy); the stairs are now closed, except for special, guided walk-down-only tours.

Overall Appeal by Age Group:

Pre-school	Grade School	Teens	Young Adults	Over 30	Senior Citizens
★★★★	★★★★★	★★★★★	★★★★★	★★★★★	★★★★★

Author's Rating: Obligatory for first-time visitors. ★★★★★

How Much Time to Allow: 30 minutes on the cramped observation deck can seem like an eternity.

Average Wait in Line per 100 People Ahead of You: 20 minutes.

DESCRIPTION AND COMMENTS   At the top you're 500 feet up, and D.C.'s absence of other tall buildings (it's a law) guarantees a glorious, unobstructed view of Washington — if it's not raining.

For most people, a first-time trip to Washington isn't complete without an ascent of this famous landmark. Yet most of them are surprised when they reach the cramped observation deck: You almost have to elbow your way to the tiny windows to see anything. The view, however, is great. Nobody's ever disappointed once they see it.

TOURING TIPS   The ever-present line of visitors to go up the monument moves at a rate of about 25 (one elevator load) every five minutes. When the line wraps completely around the base of the monument, the wait is between 45 minutes and an hour; during peak visitor periods, it can wrap around three times, making a wait of three hours.

Here's a suggestion from a National Park Service guard whose job is to shepherd visitors up and down the Washington Monument: "Go at night when the line is short. The night view in summer is spectacular. Washington looks like a carnival."

Bathrooms are located behind the outdoor amphitheater on the monument grounds, but use them only in desperate situations: They are usually dirty. A nearby snack bar is overpriced; during the week, try the cafeteria in the basement of the Commerce Department or the food court in the Old Post Office Pavilion.

OTHER THINGS TO DO NEARBY   You're at the heart of tourist Washington: At hand are the Bureau of Engraving and Printing, the Holocaust Museum, the National Museum of American History, and the National

Aquarium. At one end of the Mall is the Lincoln Memorial; the U.S. Capitol is at the other.

The White House

Type of Attraction: The official residence of the President of the United States. A self-guided tour.

Location: 1600 Pennsylvania Avenue, NW.

Nearest Metro Station: McPherson Square, Vermont Avenue exit

Admission: Free

Hours: Tours are 10 A.M. to 12 P.M., Tuesday through Saturday; from March 1 through October 31, first pick up a "time ticket" *for that day only* from the booth on the Ellipse, behind the White House, that allows you to join a tour at a specific time. VIP tours are also available through your congressperson. The busiest period is late May through mid-August.

Phone: (202) 456-7041

When to Go: Get in line at the ticket booth no later than 7:30 A.M. (7 A.M. is better) if you want to be sure of getting a ticket. The booth opens at 8 A.M.

Special Comments: With very little notice and no explanation, public tours are occasionally canceled for the day by the White House. It's a good idea to call the day before you plan to visit. Also, there are no public rest rooms; the closest ones are in the Commerce Department building on 15th Street.

Overall Appeal by Age Group:

Pre-school	Grade School	Teens	Young Adults	Over 30	Senior Citizens
★★	★★★	★★★½	★★★★	★★★★	★★★★

Author's Rating: During high tourist season, the tour requires too much time and effort for this 15-minute experience. ★★

How Much Time to Allow: During spring and summer, block out an entire morning, even though there's time to do something else (like eat breakfast) before your scheduled tour. In the off-season, you can be in and out in less than 30 minutes.

Average Wait in Line per 100 People Ahead of You: 15 minutes—once the line starts moving (off-season only).

DESCRIPTION AND COMMENTS   First things first: You have absolutely zero chance of seeing the president on this tour of the White House.

The all-too-quick tour passes through the ubiquitous metal detectors and into the East Wing lobby; look out the window into the Rose Garden. Then it's up the stairs to the East Room, the Green Room, the Blue Room, the Red Room, and the State Dining Room—and you're done! It's hard to dispute the emotional pull of the presidential residence, but if you're on a first-time visit to Washington on a limited schedule, consider visiting the White House on another trip, preferably in the fall or winter.

TOURING TIPS   The good news: Once you have a ticket, you now are free to do other things until your reserved tour assembles later that morning. The bad news: When you show up for your scheduled tour, it may still be an hour before you actually get in the White House. In the late fall and winter, crowds are lighter and the ticket system is scrapped. Although a line starts forming around 9:15 A.M., by 10:30 it's gone and usually you can walk right into the White House without waiting. So why stand in line?

Aside from the touring strategies outlined above, the only other alternative is to write your congressperson or senator for free tickets to a VIP tour. While you'll still have to get up early (tours are at 8:15, 8:30, and 8:45 A.M.), the VIP tours are longer (between 30 and 45 minutes) and are guided by Secret Service agents who discuss White House history, art, and furnishings; you also may see more rooms than on the regular, unguided tours.

Finally, make trips to the bathroom and eat before your White House visit: There are no rest rooms or public eating facilities.

OTHER THINGS TO DO NEARBY   After picking up your ticket, you'll probably want to get breakfast. Two nearby choices are the Commerce Department cafeteria (the entrance is on 15th Street, NW, across from the Ellipse; weekdays from 9 A.M. to 2 P.M.; cheap) and the Old Ebbitt Grill (675 15th Street, NW; not so cheap).

Across from the White House on Lafayette Square is St. John's Episcopal Church, known as "The Church of the Presidents," because every president since Madison has attended services here. Step inside the small church to view its simple design; on most Wednesdays at noon there's an organ recital.

Behind the White House, check out the line at the Washington Monument. If it doesn't look too long (one wrap around the base or less), this is your chance: Go!

Zone 2 — Capitol Hill

Capital Children's Museum

Type of Attraction: A touchy-feely museum for kids. A self-guided tour.

Location: 800 3rd Street, NE.

Nearest Metro Station: Union Station

Admission: $6 (free for children under two)

Hours: 10 A.M. to 5 P.M. daily. Closed New Year's, Easter, Thanksgiving, and Christmas days.

Phone: (202) 675-4149

When to Go: Anytime

Special Comments: The museum is located in a borderline neighborhood. Either drive or take the Metro to Union Station, where you can grab a cab for the short ride.

Overall Appeal by Age Group:

Pre-school	Grade School	Teens	Young Adults	Over 30	Senior Citizens
★★★★★	★★★★	★★	★½	★	★

Author's Rating: Poor location and a bit shabby. ★½

How Much Time to Allow: To justify the rather steep admission fee, plan on staying at least three or four hours. You'll still have to drag the kids away.

DESCRIPTION AND COMMENTS On the outside it looks like a large school, but the inside is loaded with interactive exhibits that will keep youngsters fascinated for hours. Neato attractions include a cave you can walk through (complete with dripping noises); TV, radio, and animation studios; voice synthesizers; a maze built for ankle biters; and computers that quiz kids.

Alas, although this museum has only been around since 1979, it's already a bit shabby around the edges. On my visit, a lot of the exhibits were closed or not working, and some of the equipment (such

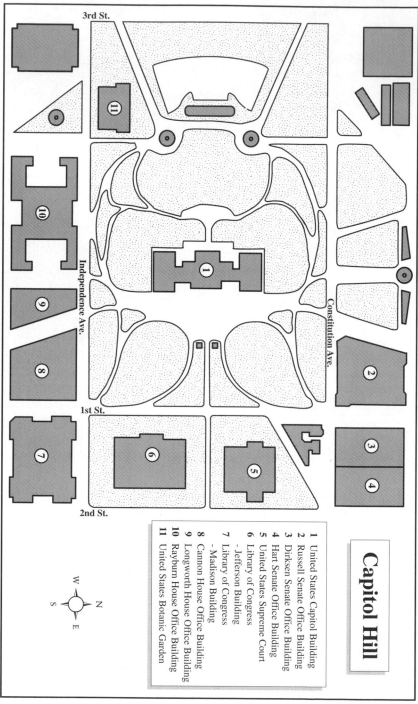

Capitol Hill

1 United States Capitol Building
2 Russell Senate Office Building
3 Dirksen Senate Office Building
4 Hart Senate Office Building
5 United States Supreme Court
6 Library of Congress
   - Jefferson Building
7 Library of Congress
   - Madison Building
8 Cannon House Office Building
9 Longworth House Office Building
10 Rayburn House Office Building
11 United States Botanic Garden

3rd St.

Independence Ave.

Constitution Ave.

1st St.

2nd St.

N
W — E
S

as personal computers) was outdated. But smaller children probably won't notice. A great place to reward tots dragged through boring Mall museums.

TOURING TIPS Plan your visit around lunch at nearby Union Station, since there's nothing else close by. Again, the neighborhood is marginal, so walk in a group, take a cab, or drive. Combine a visit to the Capital Children's Museum with a stop by the National Postal Museum and be a real hero to your kids.

OTHER THINGS TO DO NEARBY Union Station is a combination transportation hub, shopping mall, theater complex, and food emporium. The food court's pricey, but casual, and you're sure to find something you like.

Folger Shakespeare Library

Type of Attraction: A museum and library dedicated to the Bard. A self-guided tour.

Location: 201 East Capitol Street, SE

Nearest Metro Station: Union Station, Capitol South

Admission: Free

Hours: 10 A.M. to 4 P.M. Monday through Saturday; tours at 11 A.M. daily; closed on federal holidays.

Phone: (202) 544-4600

When to Go: Anytime

Special Comments: The library is only available to accredited scholars.

Overall Appeal by Age Group:

Pre-school	Grade School	Teens	Young Adults	Over 30	Senior Citizens
—	★	★½	★★	★★	★★

Author's Rating: Dull. ★★

How Much Time to Allow: One hour

DESCRIPTION AND COMMENTS The Folger houses the world's largest collection of Shakespeare's printed works, as well as a vast array of other rare Renaissance books and manuscripts. But unless you're a scholar doing research, you can't see any of it. Instead, stroll the Great Hall, featuring hand-carved, oak-paneled walls and priceless displays from the museum's collection. You may also visit the three-tiered Elizabethan theater, with walls of timber and plaster, and carved oak columns. The Folger is an incongruous attraction that holds appeal only for people with a love of language, Merrie Olde England, and the theater. But it's worth a peek on a second or third trip to Capitol Hill.

TOURING TIPS   Guided tours of the building, exhibits, and Elizabethan garden are conducted daily at 11 A.M. Special tours of the garden, featuring herbs and flowers grown in Shakespeare's time, are held every third Saturday from April through October at 10 A.M. and 11 A.M. At the west end of the building, a statue of Puck from *A Midsummer Night's Dream* presides over a fountain and pool. The Folger doesn't have much of interest for kids, unless yours have a fondness for gardens or exhibits on Elizabethan England.

OTHER THINGS TO DO NEARBY   The Folger is directly behind the Library of Congress, which sits in front of the U.S. Capitol. The Supreme Court is less than a block away. Walk south on 2nd Street, SE, to find a wide array of restaurants and cafes. The sixth-floor cafeteria in the Library of Congress's Madison Building is a cheap lunch option.

Library of Congress

Type of Attraction: The world's largest library. A guided tour.

Location: 1st Street, SE, on Capitol Hill

Nearest Metro Station: Capitol South

Admission: Free

Hours: 9 A.M. to 5:30 P.M.; closed Christmas and New Year's Day.

Phone: (202) 707-5000

When to Go: Anytime

Special Comments: A trip to the library might not be on most folks' vacation itinerary, but consider making an exception in this case.

Overall Appeal by Age Group:

Pre-school	Grade School	Teens	Young Adults	Over 30	Senior Citizens
—	★	★★	★★★	★★★½	★★★★

Author's Rating: Impressive and informative. ★★★★

How Much Time to Allow: One hour

DESCRIPTION AND COMMENTS   Three huge structures make up the

Library of Congress: the Jefferson, the Madison, and the Adams buildings. For an understanding of what goes on here, take one of the tours offered Monday through Friday at 10 A.M., 1 P.M., and 3 P.M. It starts with a 22-minute video about the varied workings of the library, followed by a walk through a tunnel to the Jefferson Building. The overhead view of the Main Reading Room from the Visitors' Gallery is one of the most impressive sights in D.C. After the tour, which lasts about an hour, you can look at other exhibits in the Madison Library on your own.

The Library of Congress holds strong appeal for folks interested in books, academic research, and antiquities. On the other hand, it won't interest many kids, and most first-time visitors shouldn't waste their valuable touring time here—with one exception, the Main Reading Room; see below.

TOURING TIPS Although the Library consists of three buildings, visitors enter at the Madison Building (the modern one) on Independence Avenue. The tour, with its well-informed guide, is the way to go if you have the time and interest. But if you can't catch a tour—or, like me, would like to see the Main Reading Room from the ground floor— follow the signs for the researchers' entrance to the Jefferson Building (your guide can give you specific directions). If you're at least 18 years old and possess a photo ID, you can stroll in and take a seat at a desk and gaze up at the rotunda. It makes you feel important, and it's a great place to write postcards.

Library materials available here go way beyond books. For instance, the Library of Congress has an extensive collection of recorded music, broadcast material, and films. While ostensibly these research materials are for "serious" researchers only, almost anyone with a strong interest in, say, the recordings of Jimmy Durante can find valuable information and hear rare recordings. For musical material, go to the Recorded Sound Reference Center, located on the first floor of the Madison building, where helpful librarians are ready to assist.

OTHER THINGS TO DO NEARBY The Capitol, Supreme Court, and Folger Library are all within a block or two. Capitol Hill abounds with nearby lunch spots, not the least of which is right here. The sixth-floor cafeteria in the Madison Building is popular with congressional staffers and it's a good deal for visitors.

National Postal History and Philatelic Museum

Type of Attraction: Displays from the largest philatelic collection in the world and exhibits about the social, historical, and technological impact of the U.S. postal system. A self-guided tour.

Location: Washington City Post Office building, 2 Massachusetts Avenue, NE, next to Union Station.

Nearest Metro Station: Union Station

Admission: Free

Hours: 10 A.M. to 5:30 P.M. daily; closed Christmas Day.

Phone: (202) 357-2700

When to Go: Anytime

Special Comments: The Smithsonian's newest museum (opened summer 1993).

Overall Appeal by Age Group:

Pre-school	Grade School	Teens	Young Adults	Over 30	Senior Citizens
★½	★★★	★★	★★	★★½	★★½

Author's Rating: Nifty and new. ★★★

How Much Time to Allow: One to two hours

DESCRIPTION AND COMMENTS   It's more interesting than it sounds — even if you're not one of America's 20 million stamp collectors. Kids will love the real airplanes hanging from the ceiling in the atrium, plus hands-on fun like the chance to sort mail on a train and track a letter from Kansas to Nairobi. Exhibits are arranged so that children and adults are entertained while they're in relative proximity to each other. Themes focus on the history of mail service, how the mail is moved, the social importance of letters, and the beauty and lore of stamps. Serious collectors can call in advance for appointments to see any stamp in the museum's world-class collection or to use the extensive library.

TOURING TIPS   Since this new museum is small by Smithsonian standards, it's easy to whiz through it in a half hour or so. Since it's right across the street from Union Station, many folks will find it convenient to drop in while waiting for a train.

OTHER THINGS TO DO NEARBY   The Capital Children's Museum is only a few blocks away, making a full day of kid-oriented museum-hopping a distinct possibility—without going near the Mall. Union Station's food hall can satisfy any food craving.

The U.S. Supreme Court

Type of Attraction: The nation's highest court. A self-guided tour.

Location: One 1st Street, NE, across from the east front of the U.S. Capitol.

Nearest Metro Station: Union Station, Capitol South

Admission: Free

Hours: 9 A.M. to 4:30 P.M.

Phone: (202) 479-3000

When to Go: Anytime to tour the building. To see the Court in session, the public may attend oral arguments held Mondays, Tuesdays, and Wednesdays, 10 A.M. to 3 P.M., in two-week intervals from October through April; check the "A" section of the *Washington Post*.

Special Comments: Seeing an oral argument here is probably your best chance of witnessing one of the three major branches of the government in operation while in D.C.

Overall Appeal by Age Group:

Pre-school	Grade School	Teens	Young Adults	Over 30	Senior Citizens
—	★	★★	★★★	★★★½	★★★★

Author's Rating: Extremely interesting and enlightening. ★★★★

How Much Time to Allow: One hour to tour the building; plan on at least two hours total to see an oral argument.

DESCRIPTION AND COMMENTS   This magnificent faux-Greek temple is where the nine-member Supreme Court makes final interpretations of the U.S. Constitution and laws passed by Congress. When the court's not in session, visitors may enter the courtroom and hear a short lecture on its workings. An excellent 20-minute film explains the workings of the Supreme Court in more detail. On the ground floor is a small museum, a gift shop, a cafeteria, and a snack bar.

A visit to the Supreme Court is a must for anyone interested in how the federal government works, or how the law works in general. Others should pass it up, although the building itself is impressive.

TOURING TIPS   To see an oral argument, plan on arriving no later than

9 A.M. to get in line. Two lines form: a regular line, for those wishing to hear an entire argument (an hour), and a three-minute line, for folks who just want to slip in for a few moments. Bring quarters: You will have to place personal belongings like backpacks and cameras in coin-operated (quarters only) lockers. Security here is no-nonsense: Visitors pass through *two* X-ray machines before entering the courtroom, where very serious-looking security people walk the aisles. Small children are not allowed in the courtroom during oral arguments.

OTHER THINGS TO DO NEARBY   The U.S. Capitol, the Library of Congress, the National Postal Museum, and the Folger Shakespeare Library are all close by. The comfortable cafeteria on the ground level of the Supreme Court is one of the better government eateries. It's open for lunch from 11:30 A.M. to 3:30 P.M., except for 15-minute periods when only Court employees may enter. Capitol Hill is renowned for its many bars and cafes, many of which are a short walk up 2nd Street, SE.

Union Station

Type of Attraction: A spectacular interior space housing a transportation hub, upscale shops, a theater complex, and a food court.

Location: Massachusetts Avenue and North Capitol Street, NE.

Nearest Metro Station: Union Station

Admission: Free

Hours: Shops open 10 A.M. to 9 P.M. Monday through Saturday; noon to 6 P.M. Sundays.

Phone: (202) 371-9441

When to Go: Anytime

Special Comments: The food court's fare is on the expensive side, but the vast selection justifies the extra cost.

Overall Appeal by Age Group:

Pre-school	Grade School	Teens	Young Adults	Over 30	Senior Citizens
★	★★	★★★	★★★½	★★★½	★★★½

Author's Rating: A beaux arts palace and a great lunch stop. ★★★½

How Much Time to Allow: One hour to wander; longer for shopping or eating.

DESCRIPTION AND COMMENTS   The Main Hall, with a 90-foot barrel-vaulted ceiling, is breathtaking. Shops run the gamut: chic clothing stores, The Great Train Store, bookstores, Brookstone, the Nature Company—more than 100 altogether. In the food court you'll find everything from sushi to ribs, while a nine-screen cinema complex offers solace on a rainy day. First-time visitors to D.C. shouldn't miss this magnificent structure.

TOURING TIPS   Union Station is a great jumping-off point for touring Washington. Capitol Hill is a few blocks away (step out the front and walk toward the big dome), and both Tourmobile and Old Town Trolley tours stop in front. Maryland commuter trains (called MARC) regularly shuttle between D.C. and Baltimore, stopping at points between (round trip to Baltimore is $9.50). To top it off, there's a Metro station in the basement. It's hard to believe that Washington functioned before Union Station's rebirth (at a cost of more than $100 million) in 1988.

OTHER THINGS TO DO NEARBY   The Capital Children's Museum is only a few blocks away. Kids will love it, but either walk in a group or take a cab; the neighborhood is marginal. The Postal Museum is next door, and the U.S. Capitol, the Supreme Court, and the Library of Congress are only blocks away.

U.S. Botanic Garden

Type of Attraction: A permanent collection of tropical, subtropical, and desert plants housed in a stunning, 38,000-square-foot greenhouse. A self-guided tour.

Location: 1st Street and Maryland Avenue, SW, near the U.S. Capitol.

Nearest Metro Station: Federal Center SW

Admission: Free

Hours: 9 A.M. to 5 P.M. daily; till 8 P.M. June through August.

Phone: (202) 226-4082

When to Go: Anytime

Special Comments: Skip it on a sweltering summer afternoon.

Overall Appeal by Age Group:

Pre-school	Grade School	Teens	Young Adults	Over 30	Senior Citizens
★	★½	★★	★★½	★★★½	★★★★

Author's Rating: An excellent and comprehensive collection of plant life. ★★★

How Much Time to Allow: 30 minutes

DESCRIPTION AND COMMENTS   The Conservatory, a building that reflects the grand manner of Victorian architecture (even though it was constructed in the 1930s), houses a living museum on the Mall. The central palm house is complete with a flowing stream, while other sections display orchids, ferns, cacti, and other types of plants in naturalistic settings. While people with green thumbs will want to put these gardens on their first-visit itinerary, most folks will just want to know it's nearby for a quiet break from more hectic sights along the Mall. You can sit down here, relax, read a book—or just do nothing in a magnificent setting.

TOURING TIPS   Before or after strolling through this giant greenhouse, visit Frederic Bartholdi Park, located across Independence Avenue from the Conservatory and named for the designer of the Statue of Liberty. The park features displays of bulbs, annuals, and perennials. The focal point is Bartholdi Fountain, originally exhibited at the 1876 Centennial Exposition in Philadelphia.

OTHER THINGS TO DO NEARBY   The National Air and Space Museum and the Hirshhorn Museum and Sculpture Garden are close, as is the U.S. Capitol. L'Enfant Plaza, about five blocks away, has a shopping mall loaded with restaurants and fast-food outlets.

U.S. Capitol

Type of Attraction: The building where Congress meets. Self-guided and guided tours.

Location: East end of the Mall.

Nearest Metro Stations: Capitol South, Union Station

Admission: Free

Hours: Guided tours begin every 15 minutes in the Rotunda from 9 A.M. to 3:45 P.M. daily, except Thanksgiving, Christmas, and New Year's days. The Rotunda and Statuary Hall are open until 8 P.M. in the summer.

Phone: (202) 225-6827

When to Go: Before 10 A.M. The public entrance is on the east front, the side opposite the Mall. (The Capitol has an east front and a west front, but no "rear.") Walk up the marble stairs toward the dome.

Special Comments: The Capitol hosts about 25,000 visitors a day and most get lost — the building is both large and confusing. Make sure to pick up a map at the tour desk in the Rotunda, and don't be shy about asking one of the many guards on duty for directions.

Overall Appeal by Age Group:

Pre-school	Grade School	Teens	Young Adults	Over 30	Senior Citizens
★	★★½	★★★	★★★★	★★★★½	★★★★★

Author's Rating: Interesting and beautiful. ★★★★½

How Much Time to Allow: One to two hours

Average Wait in Line per 100 People Ahead of You: 30 minutes.

Groups of 50 leave every 15 minutes for the "introductory" tour.

DESCRIPTION AND COMMENTS   The U.S. Capitol manages to be two things at once, an awesome monument to democracy and one of the most important places in the world, as the frequent presence of reporters and film crews outside attests. The rather brief (typically 30 minutes) public tour, however, takes visitors through only a small part of the Capitol: the Rotunda, and a few other rooms, which may include Statuary Hall, the House or Senate chambers (when they're not in session), and the low-ceilinged crypt. Usually, tours get shorter as the crowds get bigger. It's up to the tour guide which rooms you'll visit.

From the soaring Rotunda to the opulent rooms where the House and Senate meet, the Capitol is both physically beautiful and packed with historical significance. For first-time visitors, the tour is both awe-inspiring and relatively quick.

TOURING TIPS   If your plans include viewing a session of Congress, don't make the time-consuming mistake thousands of other visitors make: coming to the Capitol without a pass. Go first to the office of your senator or representative, to pick one up. (Don't forget to ask for maps and other helpful touring goodies while you're there.) Legislative offices are located in six nearby office buildings; basement-level subways and walkways connect the buildings to the Capitol. Call (202) 224-3121 for help locating an office.

The free tour is heavy on the history of the building, but if your group makes it to either the House or Senate chambers, you'll get a good rundown on how Congress operates. (Stick close to the guide if you expect to hear the entire spiel.) As a visitor, however, you're not restricted to the tour: If there's an area you would like to see but didn't on the tour, your guide can give directions on how to find it.

OTHER THINGS TO DO NEARBY   Explore the rest of Capitol Hill: The Supreme Court and Library of Congress face the Capitol's east front. On the other side, the east end of the Mall features the U.S. Botanic Garden and the East Wing of the National Gallery of Art. The Senate Refectory, a sit-down cafeteria, is famous for bean soup. Depending on whether or not the House is in session and the time of day (lunch time is busiest), the House Members Dining Room offers the same food and prices, but a fancier atmosphere. Check with a guard — if the room's not crowded, you can usually get in. Capitol Hill is famous for its bars and restaurants. To find them, walk toward Constitution Avenue and past the Library of Congress's Madison Building located between Independence Avenue and C Street.

Zone 3 — Downtown

B'nai B'rith Klutznick Museum

Type of Attraction: A museum featuring Jewish folk and ceremonial art. A self-guided tour.

Location: 1640 Rhode Island Avenue, NW.

Nearest Metro Stations: Farragut North, Dupont Circle

Admission: Suggested donation $2; seniors and children $1

Hours: 10 A.M. to 5 P.M. Sunday through Friday, except Jewish holidays.

Phone: (202) 857-6583

When to Go: Anytime

Overall Appeal by Age Group:

Pre-school	Grade School	Teens	Young Adults	Over 30	Senior Citizens
★	★½	★½	★★	★★½	★★½

Author's Rating: Small and tasteful, but inconveniently located. ★★½

How Much Time to Allow: One hour

DESCRIPTION AND COMMENTS   Although it's small, the Klutznick Museum features a wide variety of items, from 1,000-year-old coins to modern art. You'll also find the 1790 letter from President George Washington to a Newport, Rhode Island, synagogue. While you don't have to be Jewish to appreciate this attractive museum, for most folks it's not a main attraction.

OTHER THINGS TO DO NEARBY   The National Geographic Society's Explorers Hall, a must-see for kids, is at 17th and M streets, NW. For a limitless selection of eateries, just walk toward Connecticut Avenue.

Federal Bureau of Investigation

Type of Attraction: FBI headquarters. A guided tour.

Location: 10th Street, NW, at Pennsylvania Avenue.

Admission: Free

Hours: Monday through Friday, 8:45 to 4:15 P.M.

Phone: (202) 324-3000

Nearest Metro Stations: Federal Triangle, Archives

When to Go: To beat the crowds, arrive either by 8 A.M. or around lunch hour.

Special Comments: Children should try to stay close to the tour guide, since there's a lot of peering into crime labs through plate glass windows set at adult height.

Overall Appeal by Age Group:

Pre-school	Grade School	Teens	Young Adults	Over 30	Senior Citizens
★★	★★★★★	★★★★½	★★★★	★★★	★★★

Author's Rating: A boring tour and the firearms demo lasts about a minute. ★½

How Much Time to Allow: One hour

Average Wait in Line per 100 People Ahead of You: One hour. Tours of 25 people depart every 15 minutes.

DESCRIPTION AND COMMENTS   After a brief introductory video, the tour guide leads your group through a series of displays highlighting the Bureau's fabled history, with heavy emphasis on gangsters (look for John Dillinger's death mask), spies, and drug smugglers. Then a walk past FBI crime labs, with views through windows of technicians at work in DNA-, document-, and material-identification labs. There's also a collection of valuables confiscated in drug raids that includes expensive jewelry and a ten-and-a-half-foot-tall stuffed brown bear. Next is a short Q & A session with a real Special Agent, who then rips off a few live rounds at paper targets. As the lines attest, this is one of the most popular tours in Washington. Families with school-age children should try to work it into a visit — the kids will love it.

TOURING TIPS   Either get in line well before the first tour starts at 8:45 or, better yet, remember to write your congressperson for a reserved VIP tour that eliminates the waiting. Once you're inside, rest rooms are available before the tour begins.

OTHER THINGS TO DO NEARBY   If the line at the National Archives is short, scoot inside for a peek at the Declaration of Independence. Or go to the Old Post Office Pavilion for lunch in the food court and a trip to the clock tower for the second-best view in Washington.

Ford's Theatre/Petersen House

Type of Attraction: The restored theater where Abraham Lincoln was assassinated, and the house across the street, where he died. A self-guided tour.

Location: 511 10th Street, NW.

Nearest Metro Station: Metro Center, 11th Street exit

Admission: Free

Hours: 9 A.M. to 5 P.M.

Phone: (202) 426-6924

When to Go: Anytime

Special Comments: The theater is closed to visitors on Wednesday and Saturday afternoons, when matinees are in progress. It may also be closed on other afternoons when rehearsals are in progress.

Overall Appeal by Age Group:

Pre-school	Grade School	Teens	Young Adults	Over 30	Senior Citizens
★	★½	★★	★★½	★★½	★★★

Author's Rating: An interesting, but small, museum; the theater is a reconstruction of the original interior. ★★½

How Much Time to Allow: One hour

DESCRIPTION AND COMMENTS   Don't miss the recently updated Lincoln Museum in the basement of the theater, featuring the clothes Lincoln was wearing the night he was shot and the derringer used to kill him. Across the street, Petersen House offers a glimpse of 19th-century Washington. Ford's Theatre, both the museum and where Lincoln was shot, is small. Unless you're a history buff, this is mostly a fill-in stop, at least for first-time visitors.

TOURING TIPS   Start with the theater, then view the museum in the basement before crossing the street to Petersen House.

OTHER THINGS TO DO NEARBY   The FBI, the National Portrait Gallery, and the National Museum of American Art are all close. For lunch, it's four or five blocks to Chinatown or two blocks to the Old Post Office Pavilion or just down the street to Hard Rock Cafe.

National Building Museum

Type of Attraction: A museum dedicated to architecture and the construction arts that's an architectural marvel in its own right. Self-guided and guided tours.

Location: 401 F Street, NW.

Nearest Metro Station: Judiciary Square

Admission: Free

Hours: 10 A.M. to 4 P.M. Monday through Saturday; 12 noon to 4 P.M. Sundays. Closed Thanksgiving, Christmas, and New Year's days.

Phone: (202) 272-2448

When to Go: Anytime

Special Comments: Tours are given at 12:30 P.M. on weekdays and at 12:30 and 1:30 P.M. on weekends.

Overall Appeal by Age Group:

Pre-school	Grade School	Teens	Young Adults	Over 30	Senior Citizens
★★	★★★	★★★	★★★½	★★★½	★★★½

Author's Rating: The Great Hall is eye-popping. ★★★½

How Much Time to Allow: 30 minutes

DESCRIPTION AND COMMENTS   The ideal way to visit this museum would be to walk in blindfolded, then have the blindfold removed. Rather unimposing on the outside, the Pension Building (as this museum is better known to Washingtonians) offers one of the most imposing interiors in Washington, if not the world. The Great Hall measures 316 feet by 116 feet and at its highest point the roof is 159 feet above the floor. Eight marbleized Corinthian columns adorn the interior. It's a must-see, even if all you do is poke your head inside the door.

TOURING TIPS   The exhibits in the museum are on the thin side: The main attraction is the building itself. But if you're interested in architecture and building construction, take the elevator up to see the permanent and temporary exhibits on the second floor.

OTHER THINGS TO DO NEARBY   The three-acre National Law Enforcement Officers Memorial is directly across from the National Building

Museum's entrance on F Street. Engraved on blue-gray marble walls are the names of 12,500 law enforcement officers who died in the line of duty throughout U.S. history. Four groups of striking statues adorning the park each show a lion protecting her cubs.

The Lillian and Albert Small Jewish Museum at 701 3rd Street, NW, offers a glimpse into Washington's historic Jewish presence. The museum features temporary exhibits about the city's Jewish life, while the Adas Israel Synagogue on the second floor is listed in the National Register of Historic Places. Open Sunday through Thursday 11 A.M. to 3 P.M. Closed Saturdays and all major Jewish holidays.

National Firearms Museum *(closed for renovation until November 1994)*

Type of Attraction: A museum exhibiting more than 1,000 firearms. A self-guided tour.

Location: 1600 Rhode Island Avenue, NW.

Nearest Metro Stations: Farragut North, Dupont Circle

Admission: Free

Hours: 10 A.M. to 4 P.M. Monday through Saturday. Closed New Year's, Easter, July 4, Thanksgiving, Christmas Eve, and Christmas Day.

Phone: (202) 828-6253

When to Go: Anytime

Special Comments: The split-level museum requires walking up a short flight of stairs.

Overall Appeal by Age Group:

Pre-school	Grade School	Teens	Young Adults	Over 30	Senior Citizens
★★	★★½	★★	★½	★	★

Author's Rating: Boring unless you're a shooting enthusiast. ★

How Much Time to Allow: 30 minutes

DESCRIPTION AND COMMENTS   This small museum, located in the National Rifle Association building, is crammed with cases filled with guns of every conceivable description. Some are quite odd, like the Mauser antitank rifle. There are also collections of hunting knives, air rifles, and gun-making machinery on display. If you're not a gun enthusiast, give this one a wide berth.

OTHER THINGS TO DO NEARBY   B'nai B'rith Klutznick Museum is a block away. Take the kids to National Geographic's Explorers Hall, at 17th and M streets, NW. You'll find a wide variety of places to eat toward Connecticut Avenue.

National Geographic Society's Explorers Hall

Type of Attraction: A small, high-tech exhibition that delights children. A self-guided tour.

Location: 17th and M streets, NW, four blocks north of the White House.

Nearest Metro Stations: Farragut North, Farragut West

Admission: Free

Hours: 9 A.M. to 5 P.M. Monday through Saturday and holidays; 10 A.M. to 5 P.M. Sundays; closed Christmas Day.

Phone: (202) 857-7588

When to Go: Anytime

Special Comments: The downtown exhibit is handy in an area that's spotty on entertaining things for kids to do.

Overall Appeal by Age Group:

Pre-school	Grade School	Teens	Young Adults	Over 30	Senior Citizens
★★★	★★★★	★★★½	★★★	★★	★★

Author's Rating: Well-done exhibits that aren't overpowering. ★★

How Much Time to Allow: One hour

DESCRIPTION AND COMMENTS   It's like walking through a couple of National Geographic TV specials. Located on the first floor of the National Geographic Society's headquarters, this small collection of exhibits showcases weather, geography, astronomy, biology, exploration, and space science. It's also a bit heavy on quizzes that could prove embarrassing to adults. For example, Earth Station One is a 72-seat amphitheater that simulates orbital flight 23,000 miles above the earth. The interactive program lets kids punch buttons as they answer geography questions posed by the "captain."

TOURING TIPS   Don't miss the extensive sales shop that offers books, videos, maps, and magazines. The courtyard on M Street is a great spot for a brown-bag lunch.

OTHER THINGS TO DO NEARBY   The *Washington Post* building is around the corner on 15th Street; advance reservations are required for the tour there. The Ansel Adams Collection is about three blocks away. The still-imposing Russian embassy is around the corner on 16th Street; you can't go in, but check out the array of antennas on the roof.

National Museum of American Art

Type of Attraction: The largest museum in the world dedicated to American art. A self-guided tour.

Location: 8th and G streets, NW.

Nearest Metro Station: Gallery Place

Admission: Free

Hours: 10 A.M. to 5:30 P.M.; closed on Christmas.

Phone: (202) 357-2700

When to Go: Anytime

Special Comments: The museum is housed in the Old Patent Office Building, sharing quarters with the National Portrait Gallery.

Overall Appeal by Age Group:

Pre-school	Grade School	Teens	Young Adults	Over 30	Senior Citizens
★	★½	★★	★★★	★★★★	★★★★

Author's Rating: An off-the-Mall treasure. ★★★★

How Much Time to Allow: Two hours

DESCRIPTION AND COMMENTS   The collection of paintings (and a few sculptures) spans American history and includes masterworks from the Colonial era, paintings of Indian life, huge 19th-century landscapes, modern and contemporary art, and an in-depth collection of art by African-Americans. Like its neighbor, the National Portrait Gallery, this museum is more intimate than the museums on the Mall. People who don't like art galleries will probably enjoy this one, since there's a good chance of finding something appealing.

TOURING TIPS   While you're here, visit the National Portrait Gallery, also housed inside the Old Patent Office Building.

OTHER THINGS TO DO NEARBY   For lunch, Chinatown is around the corner on 7th Street, and the Patent Pending cafe in the museum is above average. For additional sight-seeing, it's only a short walk to the National Building Museum and Ford's Theatre.

National Museum of Women in the Arts

Type of Attraction: The world's single most important collection of art by women. A self-guided tour.

Location: 1250 New York Avenue, NW.

Nearest Metro Station: Metro Center

Admission: A $3 donation is requested; $2 for children.

Hours: 10 A.M. to 5 P.M. Monday through Saturday; noon to 5 P.M. Sundays. Closed Thanksgiving, Christmas, and New Year's days.

Phone: (202) 783-5000

When to Go: Anytime

Special Comments: Unfortunately, this beautiful museum is in an inconvenient downtown location.

Overall Appeal by Age Group:

Pre-school	Grade School	Teens	Young Adults	Over 30	Senior Citizens
★	★★	★★½	★★★	★★★½	★★★½

Author's Rating: Both the building and the art are superb. ★★★½

How Much Time to Allow: One to two hours

DESCRIPTION AND COMMENTS   This relatively new museum has a permanent collection of paintings and sculpture that includes art by Georgia O'Keeffe, Frida Kahlo, and Helen Frankenthaler, as well as art by women from the 16th century to the present. From the outside, it looks like any other office building along crowded New York Avenue. But inside the former Masonic Grand Lodge are striking architectural features such as a crystal chandelier, a main hall and mezzanine, and the Grand Staircase.

The second-floor balcony hosts temporary exhibits; the third floor is where you'll find the permanent collection. While this beautiful museum is well off the beaten path and deserves to be seen by more people, first-time visitors can wait and enjoy it on a later trip.

TOURING TIPS   Take the elevator to the fourth (top) floor and work your way down. The mezzanine features an attractive cafe offering "light fare," and there's a gift shop on the ground floor.

OTHER THINGS TO DO NEARBY   A block away is the old Greyhound Bus Station, now fully restored into an Art Deco masterpiece; take a peek inside. The Capitol City Brewing Company brews beer on the premises and serves hearty fare like burgers to go with it.

National Portrait Gallery

Type of Attraction: An art museum specializing in portraits of noteworthy Americans. A self-guided tour.

Location: 8th and F streets, NW.

Nearest Metro Station: Gallery Place

Admission: Free

Hours: 10 A.M. to 5:30 P.M. daily

Phone: (202) 357-2700

When to Go: Anytime

Special Comments: A great museum for the Mall-weary.

Overall Appeal by Age Group:

Pre-school	Grade School	Teens	Young Adults	Over 30	Senior Citizens
★	★½	★★	★★½	★★★	★★★½

Author's Rating: Combines art and education. ★★★½

How Much Time to Allow: One hour

DESCRIPTION AND COMMENTS   The Old Patent Office Building, which houses this art museum, is located on the seedy edge of D.C.'s downtown. But don't let the location put you off: If you're interested in U.S. history, you'll enjoy viewing portraits of a panoply of Americans — presidents, statesmen, Native Americans, industrialists, and artists. Unlike most Smithsonian museums, the Portrait Gallery's rooms are on an intimate scale and let you get close to the art. It's not a museum with much appeal to small children, but older kids will enjoy viewing the portraits of U.S. presidents, as will adults. First-time visitors should make the effort.

TOURING TIPS   The museum shares quarters with the National Museum of American Art, so plan on hitting them both. Keep these museums in mind when the crowds are heavy on the Mall; they're easy to get to and never crowded. At the information desk, request a docent-led tour. On the rainy day I toured the museum, I received a delightful, one-on-one tour from a volunteer who's the wife of a Navy admiral—and she really knew her history!

OTHER THINGS TO DO NEARBY   For lunch, Chinatown is right around the corner: Walk through the atrium and leave the building through the Museum of American Art and turn right. Turn left at the next corner (7th Street) and go one block. Also, the museum's Patent Pending cafe offers above-average museum fare. Other sights: Ford's Theatre and the National Building Museum are only a couple of blocks away.

Tech 2000 *(closed as of October 1993)*

Type of Attraction: An exhibition of interactive computer media. A self-guided tour.

Location: Techworld Plaza, 800 K Street, NW.

Nearest Metro Station: Gallery Place (Chinatown exit, 7th and H streets)

Admission: $5 adults, $4 students, $3 senior citizens and children under 12.

Hours: 11 A.M. to 5 P.M., Tuesday through Sunday between Memorial Day and Labor Day; closed Sunday through Tuesday the rest of the year. Also closed on Thanksgiving, Christmas, and New Year's days.

Phone: (202) 842-0500

When to Go: To avoid bus loads of school kids during the week, come after 2 P.M. Weekends are mobbed.

Special Comments: Very close to the Washington Convention Center.

Overall Appeal by Age Group:

Pre-school	Grade School	Teens	Young Adults	Over 30	Senior Citizens
★★	★★★★	★★★★	★★½	★½	★

Author's Rating: Strictly for the computer literate. ★

How Much Time to Allow: Two hours

DESCRIPTION AND COMMENTS   This gallery of computers and video monitors is dedicated to interactive multimedia technology: the integration of broadcast-quality video and audio, computer-generated graphics, and text under the control of a computer program. It's called interactive because it relies on the user to make decisions about what information is going to be shown. Tech 2000 shows about 60 applications of this new computer technology; there are a lot of computer stations where children can explore topics such as chemistry, history, and geography. Art museum tours, a video-disk sampler, and a race car simulator round out the selection. Kids and computer hackers love this stuff. If your idea of fun is *not* sitting in front of a video screen, give this place a wide berth.

TOURING TIPS If Tech 2000 is mobbed with kids, try coming back in the midafternoon or another day. Call the day before to see if any school groups are scheduled.

OTHER THINGS TO DO NEARBY The National Museum of Women in the Arts, the National Firearms Museum, the National Museum of American Art, and the National Portrait Gallery are within a few blocks. For lunch, Chinatown is around the corner.

Washington Post *Building*

Type of Attraction: The offices of America's number two and D.C.'s number one daily newspaper. A guided tour.

Location: 15th and L streets, NW.

Nearest Metro Stations: McPherson Square, Farragut North

Admission: Free; no children under 11.

Hours: One-hour guided tours Mondays and Thursdays at 10 A.M., 11 A.M., 1 P.M., 2 P.M., and 3 P.M.

Phone: (202) 334-7969

Overall Appeal by Age Group:

Pre-school	Grade School	Teens	Young Adults	Over 30	Senior Citizens
—	★	★½	★★½	★★★	★★★

Author's Rating: Great fun for current-events fans. ★★★

How Much Time to Allow: One hour

DESCRIPTION AND COMMENTS Renowned for its president-toppling role 20 years ago in the Watergate scandal, the *Washington Post*'s reputation is second only to that of the *New York Times*. This tour shows how a big newspaper is put together, from the newsroom (where reporters write their stories), to the paste-up department (where articles are laid out on pages), to the press room. The big presses may not be rolling, though: Most of the *Post* is printed at night. While kids will enjoy the presses and a small museum full of old linotype machines, the rest of the tour is quite wordy. This is a tour for people who love newspapers.

TOURING TIPS Advance reservations are required to go on a tour. Most 10 A.M. tours are for school groups. During peak tourist season, tours are limited to 40, which is a lot of people. Expect to climb many stairs. In the late morning and early afternoon, the newsroom is usually quiet. But as you walk through, keep your eyes peeled for

Mr. Woodward's office: Along with Carl Bernstein, rookie reporter Bob Woodward helped break the Watergate story in the early 1970s. Today, he's a *Post* editor.

OTHER THINGS TO DO NEARBY   Directly behind the *Post* building on 16th Street is the embassy of the former Union of Soviet Socialist Republics (USSR). You can't get in, but the roof still bristles with antennas. National Geographic's Explorers Hall is two blocks away at 17th and M streets, NW. Walk a block south to K Street and see well-dressed lobbyists rushing to meetings.

Wilderness Society Ansel Adams Exhibit

Type of Attraction: An exhibit of more than 75 poster-sized prints by the late American landscape photographer.

Location: 900 17th Street, NW.

Nearest Metro Station: Farragut West

Admission: Free

Hours: 10 A.M. to 5 P.M. Monday through Friday.

Phone: (202) 833-2300

When to Go: Anytime

Special Comments: A great fill-in attraction.

Overall Appeal by Age Group:

Pre-school	Grade School	Teens	Young Adults	Over 30	Senior Citizens
—	★	★½	★★	★★½	★★½

Author's Rating: Worth seeing if you're a fan of Western landscapes. ★★½

How Much Time to Allow: 30 minutes

DESCRIPTION AND COMMENTS   This collection, the only one of its kind on the East Coast, includes Adams' famous *Moonrise Hernandez*. It's incongruously located in a big office building (take the elevator to the Wilderness Society's offices on the second floor), but it's easy to get in and out. While this isn't a sight that will make many people's "A" list of places to see in Washington, it's a great little museum to duck into for a quick glimpse of some fabulous photographs, especially for outdoors-lovers. You can also pick up a brochure with information on how to order Ansel Adams prints directly from the gallery in Yosemite National Park, California.

OTHER THINGS TO DO NEARBY   Decatur House and the Renwick Gallery are both about a block away. A block north is K Street, a bustling downtown street famous as the lobbyist center of Washington. Walk a block north to Connecticut Avenue to the heart of Washington's toniest shopping district.

Zone 4 — Foggy Bottom

John F. Kennedy Center for the Performing Arts

Type of Attraction: Both presidential memorial and D.C.'s performing arts headquarters. A guided tour.

Location: New Hampshire Avenue, NW, and Rock Creek Parkway

Nearest Metro Station: Foggy Bottom/GWU

Admission: Free

Hours: 10 A.M. to 11 P.M.

Phone: (202) 467-4600

When to Go: Tours are given from 10 A.M. to 1 P.M.

Special Comments: The leisurely tour lasts about an hour, but is easy on the feet: The Kennedy Center is well carpeted.

Overall Appeal by Age Group:

Pre-school	Grade School	Teens	Young Adults	Over 30	Senior Citizens
★	★	★	★★	★★½	★★★

Author's Rating: So-so art, a huge building, and a great view. ★★

How Much Time to Allow: 1½ hours

DESCRIPTION AND COMMENTS The white rectilinear Kennedy Center facility boasts four major stages and a film theater, and a sumptuous interior shimmering with crystal, mirrors, and deep-red carpets. The Grand Foyer is longer than two football fields. Nations from around the world contributed art and artifacts on display in halls and foyers, such as African art, Beame porcelain, tapestries and sculptures. If rehearsals aren't in progress, the tour includes peeks inside the intimate Eisenhower Theater, the Opera House (featuring a spectacular chandelier), and the Concert Hall, which seats 2,750. Admirers of JFK and culture vultures will love the tour, while kids will probably get bored. But you don't have to take the tour to enjoy the view; take the elevators to the roof terrace.

TOURING TIPS While the guided tour is leisurely and informative, the best way to visit the Kennedy Center is to attend a concert, play, or film. Before or after the event, go up to the seventh floor and stroll the roof terrace—the view at night is terrific.

OTHER THINGS TO DO NEARBY You can lunch or snack at the Kennedy Center's Encore Cafe without securing a second mortgage on your house, but the Roof Terrace Restaurant is expense-account priced.

The infamous Watergate project is across G Street from the Kennedy Center and features expensive shops and restaurants, but you won't find any memorial to a certain burglary that occurred there in 1972. A biking and jogging path along the Potomac River is just below the Kennedy Center; follow it upriver to the Thompson's Boat Center, which rents canoes and bikes. A little farther is Washington Harbour, an upscale collection of shops, restaurants, and condominiums, that also features life-size and lifelike sculptures of tourists, joggers, workers, and artists that add a bit of whimsy to scenic *al fresco* dining along the river.

Hard-core walkers can continue along the path into Georgetown. Walk up Wisconsin Avenue and you enter a world of trendy shops and restaurants and crowded sidewalks. Before you walk too far, remember that Georgetown lacks a Metro station to get you back to where you started.

U.S. Department of the Interior

Type of Attraction: A museum located inside a square-mile chunk of government bureaucracy; a National Park Service office and a retail map outlet. A self-guided tour.

Location: C Street, NW, between 18th and 19th streets.

Nearest Metro Station: Farragut West

Admission: Free

Hours: 8 A.M. to 4 P.M.

Phone: (202) 208-4743

When to Go: Anytime

Special Comments: Go on a rainy day.

Overall Appeal by Age Group:

Pre-school	Grade School	Teens	Young Adults	Over 30	Senior Citizens
★	★★	★	★	★	★

Author's Rating: Boring. ★

How Much Time to Allow: 45 minutes

DESCRIPTION AND COMMENTS   This six-wing, seven-story limestone edifice includes 16 acres of floors, two miles of corridors — and an old-fashioned museum. Dioramas of mines and geothermal power plants, Native American artifacts, and a historical exhibit of the National Park Service crowd the rather dark and quiet exhibit hall. This is definitely a rainy-day kind of a museum, unless you have a strong interest in national parks.

TOURING TIPS   Outdoors-people and map-lovers shouldn't miss the U.S. Geological Survey map store. You can also load up on brochures on any (or all) U.S. national parks at the National Park Service office here. The basement cafeteria can seat 1,500 (open 7 A.M. to 2:45 P.M.).

OTHER THINGS TO DO NEARBY   The DAR Museum and the Corcoran Gallery of Art are around the corner on 17th Street; the Mall is about two blocks south. For places to eat, head north up any numbered street toward Pennsylvania Avenue.

U.S. Department of State Diplomatic Reception Rooms

Type of Attraction: The rooms where visiting foreign dignitaries are officially entertained. A guided tour.

Location: 21st and C streets, NW.

Nearest Metro Station: Foggy Bottom/GWU

Admission: Free

Hours: Tours are given at 9:30 A.M., 10:30 A.M., and 2:45 P.M. Monday through Friday.

Phone: (202) 647-3241

Special Comments: See what $65 million in decorative arts can buy.

Overall Appeal by Age Group:

Pre-school	Grade School	Teens	Young Adults	Over 30	Senior Citizens
★	★★	★★★½	★★★★	★★★★★	★★★★★

Author's Rating: Although most tourists miss this, you shouldn't.
★★★★★

How Much Time to Allow: One hour

DESCRIPTION AND COMMENTS   While the State Department goes about its important work in a building whose architecture is best described as "early airport," the interiors on the eighth floor are something else entirely: A fabulous collection of 18th- and early-19th-century fine and decorative arts fills stunning rooms that are used daily to receive visiting heads of state and foreign dignitaries.

This is a tour for almost anyone: Kids, history buffs, and just casual visitors. It's also a sight that the overwhelming majority of D.C. tourists miss. First-time visitors should make the effort to get reservations well in advance of their trip. Then forget about visiting the White House.

TOURING TIPS   By guided tour only; reservations are required and should be made at least four weeks in advance of your visit. Rest rooms are located near the waiting room and can be visited before and after the tour.

OTHER THINGS TO DO NEARBY   The Lincoln Memorial and Vietnam Veterans Memorial are a short walk away, down 23rd Street to the Mall. The closest places to eat are a few blocks up 23rd Street, away from the Mall.

Zone 5 — Georgetown

Dumbarton Oaks and Gardens

Type of Attraction: A mansion/museum and a beautiful terraced garden. Self-guided tours.

Location: 1703 32nd Street, between R and S streets, NW, in Georgetown.

Admission: Free for the museum; $2 for the garden, which is free on Wednesdays to seniors.

Hours: Museum: Tuesday through Sunday, 2 P.M. to 5 P.M.; garden (weather permitting): November 1 through March 31, 2 P.M. to 5 P.M., and till 6 P.M. the rest of the year.

Phone: (202) 342-3212

When to Go: Anytime

Special Comments: Don't be put off by the hushed surroundings — this is one of the best museums in Washington.

Overall Appeal by Age Group:

Pre-school	Grade School	Teens	Young Adults	Over 30	Senior Citizens
—	★	★★½	★★★½	★★★★	★★★★

Author's Rating: Intimate and gorgeous. ★★★★

How Much Time to Allow: Two hours

DESCRIPTION AND COMMENTS   Most people associate Dumbarton Oaks with the conference held here in 1944 that led to the formation of the United Nations. Today, however, it's a research center for Byzantine and pre-Columbian studies owned by Harvard University. The Byzantine collection is one of the world's finest, featuring bronzes, ivories, and jewelry. The exquisite pre-Columbian art collection is housed in eight interconnected, circular glass pavilions lit by natural light. It's a knockout of a museum.

Dumbarton Oaks Gardens is located around the corner on R Street.

The terraced ten-acre garden is rated one of the top gardens in the United States, featuring an orangery, a rose garden, wisteria-covered arbors, and, in the fall, a blazing backdrop of trees turning orange, yellow, and red. Dumbarton Oaks isn't the kind of museum with much appeal to small children, and some adults may not find much of interest in the collection due to its narrow focus. But combined with the adjacent gardens, it's a worthwhile place to visit when in Georgetown.

TOURING TIPS   Since Dumbarton Oaks doesn't open its massive doors until 2 P.M., combine your visit with a morning trip to Georgetown. If it's raining the day you plan to visit, try to rearrange your schedule so you can come on a nice day; the gardens are terrific.

OTHER THINGS TO DO NEARBY   Take a walking tour of Georgetown and see how lobbyists, politicians, media gurus, and other well-connected and monied denizens of Washington live. If you made advance reservations to see Tudor House, Dumbarton Oaks makes a great side trip. When you get hungry, turn left or right on Wisconsin Avenue and you won't have to go far to find an interesting restaurant or cafe. The Chesapeake and Ohio Canal, which starts in Georgetown, can offer near-wilderness solace to weary tourists.

You may also want to take a stroll through the nearby Montrose and Rock Creek cemeteries, where Clover and Henry Adams are buried beneath the hooded Saint-Gaudens memorial that Mark Twain called "Grief," but Henry Adams referred to as "The Peace of God."

Zone 6 — Dupont Circle / Adams-Morgan

Anderson House

Type of Attraction: A combination mansion and Revolutionary War museum. A self-guided tour.

Location: 2118 Massachusetts Avenue, NW.

Nearest Metro Station: Dupont Circle

Admission: Free

Hours: 1 P.M. to 4 P.M. Tuesday through Saturday; closed national holidays.

Phone: (202) 785-2040

When to Go: Anytime

Special Comments: Children will love the Revolutionary War figurines fighting battles; older folks will marvel at the opulence.

Overall Appeal by Age Group:

Pre-school	Grade School	Teens	Young Adults	Over 30	Senior Citizens
★	★★	★★	★★★	★★★★	★★★★

Author's Rating: Robber-baron decadence. ★★★★

How Much Time to Allow: One hour

DESCRIPTION AND COMMENTS   This mansion along Embassy Row is a real sleeper that few visitors ever see. Built in 1906 by Larz Anderson, a diplomat, it's a reflection of fabulous turn-of-the-century taste and wealth. The two-story ballroom is a stunner, tapestries line the crystal-chandeliered dining room, and paintings by Gilbert Stuart and John Trumbull hang in the billiard room.

Anderson was a member of the Society of the Cincinnati, whose members are descendants of French and American officers who served in the Revolutionary Army. After his death, his widow donated the mansion to the society. Today the building serves the society as both headquarters and museum. Even first-time visitors to D.C. should make the effort to see this spectacular mansion, which is located a block or so from Dupont Circle.

TOURING TIPS   The first floor contains displays of Revolutionary War artifacts. On the second floor, the mansion remains as it was originally furnished, with 18th-century paintings, 17th-century tapestries from Brussels, and huge chandeliers.

OTHER THINGS TO DO NEARBY   Take a walk along Embassy Row or browse the shops around Dupont Circle. Other sights within walking distance include the Phillips Collection (modern art), the Christian Heurich Mansion, the Textile Museum, and the Woodrow Wilson House.

The Christian Heurich Mansion

Type of Attraction: The lavish home of a wealthy turn-of-the-century Washington businessman. A guided tour.

Location: 1307 New Hampshire Avenue, NW (two blocks south of Dupont Circle).

Nearest Metro Station: Dupont Circle

Admission: $3

Hours: Guided tours Wednesday through Saturday, noon to 3:15 P.M. Closed on federal holidays.

Special Comments: Don't be put off by the grimy exterior.

Overall Appeal by Age Group:

Pre-school	Grade School	Teens	Young Adults	Over 30	Senior Citizens
—	★	★½	★★½	★★★	★★★

Author's Rating: An outrageous Gilded Age interior. ★★★

How Much Time to Allow: One hour

DESCRIPTION AND COMMENTS   It's doubtful that any amount of money could re-create what wealthy brewer Christian Heurich built in the early 1890s: a regal, 31-room mansion full of richly detailed mahogany and oak woodwork, elaborate plaster moldings, and a musician's balcony that lets live music be heard throughout the first floor. It may be the most opulent home open to the public in Washington. The building also serves as headquarters for the Historical Society of Washington and houses its library. While most first-time visitors to Washington shouldn't feel obliged to spend time here, it's worth a look on a later trip. People who love decorative arts should put it on their "A" list.

TOURING TIPS   Unless you're a real antiques fanatic, the tour is a bit too long. Tell the guide you've got to catch a train, and if there's no one else on the tour you can see it all in about a half hour. The small garden behind the museum is a popular spot for a brown-bag lunch.

OTHER THINGS TO DO NEARBY   Walk to Dupont Circle for a whiff of Washington's bohemian side: Trendy cafes, shops, bookstores, and restaurants crowd Connecticut Avenue. Expect to be panhandled about every 50 feet in fair weather; the street merchants crowding around the Metro entrances suggest a Middle East bazaar. Note: Good deals can be had.

House of the Temple

Type of Attraction: A Masonic temple modeled after one of the Seven Wonders of the World. A guided tour.

Location: 1733 16th Street, NW.

Nearest Metro Station: Dupont Circle

Admission: Free

Hours: Guided tours 8 A.M. to 2 P.M. Monday through Friday.

Phone: (202) 232-3579

When to Go: Anytime

Special Comments: Unless you have an abiding interest in Freemasonry, the tour is way too long.

Overall Appeal by Age Group:

Pre-school	Grade School	Teens	Young Adults	Over 30	Senior Citizens
—	★	★	★	★	★

Author's Rating: Spectacular but cold. ★

How Much Time to Allow: Two hours (less if you're willing to lie to the tour guide; see below).

DESCRIPTION AND COMMENTS   The walls are 8 feet thick, the exterior is surrounded by 33 massive columns that support a magnificent pyramidal roof and, inside, the Temple Room features a soaring 100-foot ceiling and 1,000-pipe organ. Unfortunately, with the exception of the exterior, you have to take an excruciatingly boring guided tour to see these goodies. You're guaranteed to be bored silly by displays of bric-a-brac and memorabilia belonging to long-dead Masonic leaders. There is one, slightly bizarre, treat: The J. Edgar Hoover Law Enforcement Room, a shrine to the Mason and lifelong FBI chief. But unless you're a rabid fan of J. Edgar, after about two minutes you'll be . . . bored.

TOURING TIPS   Arrive around 1 P.M. on a quiet afternoon and tell the tour guide you've got to catch a train at 2:30. Then plead for an abbreviated tour, which he may grudgingly provide if there aren't any other tourists on hand for a tour. But even reduced to an hour, the tour is too long.

OTHER THINGS TO DO NEARBY   The House of the Temple is on the edge of a marginally safe neighborhood, so make a beeline toward Dupont Circle, where you'll find plenty to do. Six blocks west on S Street are the Textile Museum and the Woodrow Wilson House.

Islamic Center

Type of Attraction: A mosque. A self-guided tour.

Location: 2551 Massachusetts Avenue, NW

Nearest Metro Station: Dupont Circle

Admission: Free

Hours: 10 A.M. to 5 P.M.; closed Fridays to non-Muslims.

Phone: (202) 332-8343

When to Go: Anytime

Special Comments: You must take off your shoes to go inside, and no shorts or short dresses are allowed; women must cover their heads and wear long-sleeved clothing.

Overall Appeal by Age Group:

Pre-school	Grade School	Teens	Young Adults	Over 30	Senior Citizens
★	★½	★½	★★	★★	★★

Author's Rating: Exotic and surprisingly small. ★½

How Much Time to Allow: 15 minutes

DESCRIPTION AND COMMENTS   A brilliant white building and slender minaret mark this unusual sight on Embassy Row. Visitors must remove their shoes before stepping inside to see the Persian carpets, elegantly embellished columns, decorated arches, and huge chandelier.

Alas, with America's focus on the Middle East and things Islamic, I was disappointed on my visit to the Islamic Center: It fell a little short on giving any useful insight into that troubled part of the world. The small bookstore next to the mosque was filled with Arabic texts and translations of the Koran, but no one was behind the counter to answer my questions. Though close to other tourist sights, the mosque seems to have missed an opportunity to educate D.C. visitors about Islam. Those with a strong interest in the Middle East should call a week in advance for the one-hour guided tour.

TOURING TIPS Make this small, exotic building a part of a walk down Embassy Row. But unless you have an interest in Islam, it's not worth going out of the way to see.

OTHER THINGS TO DO NEARBY Take a short walk and tour the Textile Museum and the Woodrow Wilson House. On Tuesday through Saturday afternoons, the opulent Anderson House is open. The Phillips Collection is an intimate modern art museum that's a refreshing change of pace from huge Mall museums.

Phillips Collection

Type of Attraction: The first museum dedicated to modern art in the United States. A self-guided tour.

Location: 1600 21st Street, NW.

Nearest Metro Station: Dupont Circle

Admission: Weekends: $5 for adults, $2.50 for seniors over 62 and full-time students. No charge for visitors under 18. During the week, the museum requests contributions at the same level.

Hours: Mondays through Saturdays 10 A.M. to 5 P.M.; Sundays noon to 7 P.M. Closed New Year's Day, Fourth of July, Thanksgiving, and Christmas.

Phone: (202) 387-2151; or (202) 387-0961 for a visitor information recording.

When to Go: Anytime

Special Comments: With lots of carpeting and places to sit, the Phillips Collection is a very comfortable museum to tour.

Overall Appeal by Age Group:

Pre-school	Grade School	Teens	Young Adults	Over 30	Senior Citizens
—	★	★★	★★★½	★★★★	★★★★

Author's Rating: One of the best art museums in Washington. ★★★★

How Much Time to Allow: Two hours

DESCRIPTION AND COMMENTS   Founded by Duncan Phillips, grandson of the founder of the Jones and Laughlin Steel Company, the Phillips Collection is set in the family's former mansion, which helps explain its intimate and comfortable feeling. The collection is too large for everything to be on display at once, so the art is constantly rotated. Expect to see works by Monet, Picasso, Miro, Renoir, and Van Gogh, among other modern masters. The large and ornate Music Room is as spectacular as the art hanging on its walls. If you've seen the Hirshhorn and the National Gallery of Art's East Wing, this should be on your agenda. It's a classy museum on a very human scale.

TOURING TIPS   The kids would probably prefer a trip to the zoo. Take advantage of the free, 45-minute guided tours given at 2 P.M. on Wednesdays and Saturdays. The well-informed guides do a good job of giving a context for the paintings and sculptures, the building, and its founder's taste in modern art.

OTHER THINGS TO DO NEARBY   Cross Massachusetts Avenue and see another eye-popping mansion, the Anderson House (open Tuesday through Saturday from 1 P.M. to 4 P.M.). Dupont Circle hosts a myriad of cafes, restaurants, and fast-food joints to satisfy hunger pangs.

Textile Museum

Type of Attraction: A museum dedicated to textile arts. A self-guided tour.

Location: 2320 S Street, NW.

Nearest Metro Station: Dupont Circle

Admission: Free; $5 donation suggested.

Hours: 10 A.M. to 5 P.M. Monday through Saturday; 1 P.M. to 5 P.M. Sundays. Closed federal holidays and December 24.

Phone: (202) 667-0441

When to Go: Anytime

Special Comments: The museum is wheelchair accessible but not barrier-free. Call ahead if you have special needs.

Overall Appeal by Age Group:

Pre-school	Grade School	Teens	Young Adults	Over 30	Senior Citizens
—	★	★★	★★½	★★½	★★★

Author's Rating: Interesting, but small and esoteric. ★★

How Much Time to Allow: One hour

DESCRIPTION AND COMMENTS   Cloth, a mass-produced commodity in the West, no longer enjoys much prestige as an art form. But it's a different story in the rest of the world. The museum's collection ranges from countries as diverse as India, Indonesia, China, Mexico, Guatemala, and Peru. Intricate designs and rich colors grace more than 14,000 textiles and 1,400 carpets dating from ancient times to the present day.

Because the items can't be exposed to light for long periods of time, the exhibits are constantly rotated. This museum is much more interesting than it sounds — the rich colors derived from natural dye processes and elaborate details in the fabrics are subtly beautiful. Definitely for distinct tastes, but not to be missed if it appeals to you.

TOURING TIPS   Don't miss the pleasant garden behind the museum. The gift shop is chock-full of books and items related to textiles and rugs.

OTHER THINGS TO DO NEARBY   The Woodrow Wilson House is next door, and the Islamic Center is around the corner on Massachusetts Avenue. In the other direction, S Street crosses Connecticut Avenue, where you can shop and dine to your heart's content.

Woodrow Wilson House

Type of Attraction: The final home of the 28th U.S. president. A guided tour.

Location: 2340 S Street, NW.

Nearest Metro Station: Dupont Circle

Admission: $4

Hours: 10 A.M. to 4 P.M. Tuesday through Sunday. Closed Thanksgiving, Christmas, and New Year's days.

Phone: (202) 387-4062

When to Go: To avoid a crowded tour during spring and summer, arrive before noon.

Special Comments: Lots of stairs, including a steep, narrow descent down a back staircase.

Overall Appeal by Age Group:

Pre-school	Grade School	Teens	Young Adults	Over 30	Senior Citizens
★	★★	★★★	★★★	★★★½	★★★½

Author's Rating: Interesting and informative. ★★★½

How Much Time to Allow: 90 minutes

DESCRIPTION AND COMMENTS   After Woodrow Wilson left office in 1921, he became the only former president to retire in Washington, D.C.—and he did so in this house. The tour starts with a 25-minute video narrated by Walter Cronkite that puts this underrated president in perspective and fires you up for the tour. Ninety-six percent of the items in this handsome Georgian Revival town house are original, so visitors get an accurate picture of aristocratic life in the 1920s. On the tour you'll see Wilson's extensive library, his bedroom, his old movie projector, and beautiful furnishings.

TOURING TIPS   The basement kitchen is virtually unchanged from Wilson's day, with original items such as an ornate wooden icebox and a coal- and gas-fired stove. Peek inside the pantry, still stocked with items from the '20s such as Kellogg's Corn Flakes ("wonderfully flavored with malt, sugar and salt"). This is another tour that gives visitors the feeling they've been somewhere special and off the beaten tourist track.

OTHER THINGS TO DO NEARBY   The Textile Museum is next door. Embassy Row is around the corner on Massachusetts Avenue, and in the other direction, Connecticut Avenue bustles with shops and restaurants.

Zone 7—Upper Northwest

Washington National Cathedral

Type of Attraction: The sixth-largest cathedral in the world. Guided and self-guided tours.

Location: Massachusetts and Wisconsin avenues, NW.

Nearest Metro Station: The Woodley Park/National Zoo station is about a half-hour walk; drive or take a cab.

Admission: Free

Hours: 10 A.M. to 4:30 P.M. daily, September through April; till 9 P.M. May through August.

Phone: (202) 537-6207

When to Go: Anytime

Special Comments: Take the 30-minute, docent-led tour.

Overall Appeal by Age Group:

Pre-school	Grade School	Teens	Young Adults	Over 30	Senior Citizens
★	★★	★★★½	★★★★★	★★★★★	★★★★★

Author's Rating: A Gothic masterpiece. ★★★★★

How Much Time to Allow: One hour

DESCRIPTION AND COMMENTS If you've been to Europe, you'll experience déjà vu when you visit this massive Gothic cathedral. It's a tenth of a mile from the nave to the high altar; the ceiling is 100 feet high. Don't miss the Bishop's Garden, modeled on a medieval walled garden, or the Pilgrim Observation Gallery and a view of Washington from the highest vantage point in the city. Small children may not enjoy being dragged around this huge cathedral, but just about anyone else will enjoy its magnificent architecture and stone carvings.

TOURING TIPS During the school year, try to catch the free organ demonstration given Wednesdays at 12:15 P.M. Carillon recitals are on Saturdays at 12:30 P.M. The Cathedral isn't well served by public transportation, but walking there takes you through safe, pleasant neighborhoods that are home to Washington's elite: It's about a half-hour stroll up Cathedral Avenue from the Woodley Park/National Zoo Metro.

OTHER THINGS TO DO NEARBY   The National Zoo is about a half-hour walk from National Cathedral, or take a cab. For lunch, walk two blocks north on Wisconsin Avenue to Cleveland Park and choose between Thai, Chinese, Mexican, and pizza restaurants. The best deals are at G. C. Murphy's, which features gyros, pita sandwiches, minipizzas, subs, pastry, and Italian coffee. Most items on the menu are under $4.

National Zoological Park

Type of Attraction: The Smithsonian's world-class zoo. A self-guided tour.

Location: 3001 Connecticut Avenue, NW.

Nearest Metro Stations: Woodley Park/National Zoo, Cleveland Park

Admission: Free

Hours: Grounds: 8 A.M. to 8 P.M. May through mid-September; 8 A.M. to 6 P.M. mid-September through April. Buildings are open from 9 A.M. to 4:30 P.M.

Phone: (202) 673-4800

When to Go: Anytime. In the summer, avoid going during Washington's sweltering afternoons.

Special Comments: Many sections of the paths winding through the Zoo's 163 acres are steep.

Overall Appeal by Age Group:

Pre-school	Grade School	Teens	Young Adults	Over 30	Senior Citizens
★★★★★	★★★★★	★★★★	★★★½	★★★½	★★★½

Author's Rating: A first-rate operation in a beautiful setting. ★★★★½

How Much Time to Allow: Two hours just to see the most popular attractions; a whole day to see it all. Better yet, see the Zoo over several visits.

DESCRIPTION AND COMMENTS   The National Zoo emphasizes natural environment, with many animals roaming large enclosures instead of pacing in cages. And it's all found in a lush woodland setting in a section of Rock Creek Park. Two main paths link the many buildings and exhibits: Olmstead Walk, which passes all the animal houses, and the steeper Valley Trail, which includes all the aquatic exhibits. They add up to about two miles of trail. The Zoo's nonlinear layout and lack of sight lines make a map invaluable; pick one up at the Education Building near the entrance. The most popular exhibits include the famous giant panda (formerly a pair, now down to one), the great apes, the white tiger, and the cheetahs. But for diversity and a good chance of seeing some animal activity, check out the Small Mammal House, the Invertebrate House (kids can look through microscopes), and the huge outside bird cages (the condors look the size of Volkswagens).

If your visit to Washington is long enough to include forays away from the Mall, make this beautiful park part of your itinerary. Aside from a wide variety of wildlife on view, the wooded setting is a welcome relief from viewing too much marble downtown.

TOURING TIPS   Plan to visit either early or late in the day. Animals are more active, temperatures are cooler — and crowds are thinner. During busy periods, some exhibits are subject to "controlled access" to prevent crowding; in other words, you may have to wait in line to get in. Panda feeding is at 11 A.M. and 3 P.M. (while it's usually a mob scene, it's also the only time to glimpse some activity from this docile creature.) Other feedings and demonstrations occur throughout the day at the cheetah, elephant, seal, and sea lion exhibits; check at the Education Building for times.

OTHER THINGS TO DO NEARBY   If you've done the Zoo justice, your feet will hurt and your energy level will be too depleted for much else: Go back to your room. Lunch spots abound three blocks north on Connecticut Avenue; from there it's a short walk to the Cleveland Park Metro. But if you've got feet of steel, take the half-hour hike to the National Cathedral.

Hillwood Museum

Type of Attraction: A mansion housing fabulous art treasures
(a guided tour) and formal gardens on a 25-acre estate (a self-guided tour).

Location: 4155 Linnean Avenue, NW.

Nearest Metro Station: Van Ness/UDC. For a pleasant 20-minute walk, go south on Connecticut Avenue past the Star Trek-y Intelsat complex on the right, then turn left on Upton Street. Follow Upton to Linnean, turn right, and walk about a block to the estate entrance. Or grab a cab.

Admission: $10 for the house tour and gardens; $2 to visit the formal gardens and auxiliary buildings alone.

Hours: House tours begin at 9 A.M., 10:30 A.M., 12 noon, and 1:30 P.M. Tuesday through Saturday; the gardens are open 11 A.M. to 3 P.M. Hillwood is closed during February.

Phone: (202) 686-8500

When to Go: Spring is the most beautiful season to tour the house and gardens, but these are popular destinations for garden clubs, so you must secure reservations well in advance.

Special Comments: The tour involves a lot of walking and standing. No children under 12.

Overall Appeal by Age Group:

Pre-school	Grade School	Teens	Young Adults	Over 30	Senior Citizens
—	—	★★	★★★	★★★★½	★★★★½

Author's Rating: Stunning. ★★★★½

How Much Time to Allow: Three hours. The tour itself is almost two hours, but doesn't include the formal gardens and auxiliary buildings.

DESCRIPTION AND COMMENTS   She was a girl from Michigan who inherited two things from her father: good taste and General Foods. That, in a nutshell, is the story of Marjorie Merriweather Post, who bought this Rock Creek Park estate in 1955, remodeled the mansion, and filled it with exquisite 18th- and 19th-century French and Russian decorative art.

"Fabulous" is not too strong a word to use in describing the collection of Imperial Russian objects on display. Mrs. Post was married to the U.S. ambassador to Russia in the 1930s—a time when the communists were unloading "decadent," pre-Revolution art at bargain prices. Mrs. Post literally bought warehouse-loads of stuff: jewels, dinner plates commissioned by Catherine the Great, Easter eggs by Carl Fabergé, and chalices and icons. She then had the loot loaded onto her yacht, *Sea Cloud* (the largest private ship in the world), for shipment home. The very best of the booty is on display here. The tour provides a glimpse into Mrs. Post's lavish lifestyle.

TOURING TIPS   Advance reservations are required to tour the mansion. Call at least two weeks in advance in the spring, although you may luck into a cancellation by calling a day or two before your planned visit. Children under 12 are not admitted on the tour. Plan your visit so that you have enough time to stroll the gardens. The estate also has a cafe that serves breakfast, lunch, and tea; a gift shop; and a greenhouse offering plants for sale.

OTHER THINGS TO DO NEARBY   Intelsat, near the Van Ness/UDC Metro, looks like a building out of the 21st century. That's no surprise, since the firm is an international conglomeration that produces satellites. The lobby features models and prototypes of its products hanging from the ceiling. For lunch, there are plenty of restaurants to choose from near the Metro station on Connecticut Avenue.

National Museum of Health and Medicine

Type of Attraction: A medical museum. A self-guided tour.

Location: On the grounds of Walter Reed Army Medical Center, located between 16th Street and Georgia Avenue, NW, near Takoma Park, Maryland.

Nearest Metro Station: Takoma Park. If you have a car, drive.

Admission: Free

Hours: 9:30 to 4:30 weekdays; 11:30 to 4:30 weekends and holidays. Closed Thanksgiving, Christmas Eve and Christmas Day, New Year's Eve and New Year's Day.

Phone: (202) 576-2348

When to Go: Anytime

Special Comments: A must-see for adolescent boys.

Overall Appeal by Age Group:

Pre-school	Grade School	Teens	Young Adults	Over 30	Senior Citizens
—	★★★★	★★½	★½	★	★
	(specifically, 12-year-old boys)				

Author's Rating: Unsettling and bizarre. ★

How Much Time to Allow: One hour

DESCRIPTION AND COMMENTS   The perfect museum for family fun — if you happen to be the Addams Family. The unsqueamish will thrill to skeletons, Siamese twins in formaldehyde, gruesome medical instruments, bottled human organs, a huge display of antique microscopes, interactive videos, a condom display (!), and an exhibit on AIDS. A lot of exhibits were out of order or removed on my visit. The bathrooms, oddly enough, were dirty too. This museum will appeal to a narrow range of people: doctors, nurses, and folks working in the public health field.

TOURING TIPS   It's a brisk, 15-minute walk to the museum from the Takoma Park Metro station. As you exit the station, turn right and walk under the railroad tracks, then turn right at Blair Road. Walk one block to Dahlia Street and turn left. Walter Reed is about six blocks straight ahead. The museum is directly behind the large white building; you can walk around it on the left.

Years ago, when this museum was on the Mall, it was a favorite place for local kids to take their out-of-town friends and gross them out. Alas, those days are over, now that the museum is hidden in this vast hospital complex near the Maryland border. Yet, it remains the ultimate tourist destination for those seeking something . . . different.

OTHER THINGS TO DO NEARBY   Nothing recommended.

Zone 8—Northeast

Basilica of the National Shrine of the Immaculate Conception

Type of Attraction: The largest Catholic church in the U.S. and the seventh-largest religious structure in the world. Guided and self-guided tours.

Location: 4th Street and Michigan Avenue, NE, on the campus of the Catholic University of America.

Nearest Metro Station: Brookland/Catholic University

Admission: Free

Hours: 7 A.M. to 6 P.M. daily, November 1 through March 31; till 7 P.M. the rest of the year. Guided tours are conducted Monday through Saturday from 9 A.M. to 11 A.M. and from 1 P.M. to 3 P.M., and on Sundays from 1:30 P.M. to 4 P.M.

Phone: (202) 526-8300

When to Go: Anytime

Special Comments: It's a huge cathedral and it requires a lot of walking.

Overall Appeal by Age Group:

Pre-school	Grade School	Teens	Young Adults	Over 30	Senior Citizens
★	★	★	★	★	★½

Author's Rating: Sterile and cold. ★

How Much Time to Allow: One hour

DESCRIPTION AND COMMENTS   A huge, blue-and-gold onion dome lends Byzantine overtones to this massive cathedral, as does the wealth of colorful mosaics throughout its interior. Yet the architecture is lean and stark, and many of the figures in the mosaics and stained-glass windows look cartoonish. It's not in the same league with the awe-inspiring National Cathedral across town. Sure is big, though.

TOURING TIPS   Skip the guided tour, which stops in every one of the dozens of chapels. Instead, grab a map at the information desk on the ground (crypt) level and enter Memorial Hall, which is lined with chapels. Then go up the stairs (or elevator) to the Upper Church.

OTHER THINGS TO DO NEARBY   The Franciscan Monastery is a brisk, 20-minute walk away: Continue past the Metro station on Michigan Avenue to Quincy Street, turn right, and walk about four blocks. The Basilica has a small cafeteria on the ground level; a better bet is the Pizza Hut on Michigan Avenue.

Franciscan Monastery and Gardens

Type of Attraction: A working monastery. A guided tour.

Location: 1400 Quincy Street, NE.

Nearest Metro Station: Brookland/Catholic University. From the station exit, turn left, walk up to Michigan Avenue, turn left, and walk over the bridge. Continue on Michigan Avenue to Quincy Street, turn right, and walk four blocks.

Admission: Free

Hours: Guided tours on the hour from 9 A.M. to 4 P.M. Monday through Saturday; 1 P.M. through 4 P.M. Sundays.

When to Go: Anytime

Phone: (202) 526-6800

Special Comments: The tour involves negotiating many narrow, steep stairs and low, dark passageways.

Overall Appeal by Age Group:

Pre-school	Grade School	Teens	Young Adults	Over 30	Senior Citizens
—	★★½	★★	★★	★★	★★

Author's Rating: Beautiful architecture, peaceful grounds — and kind of spooky. ★★

How Much Time to Allow: One hour

DESCRIPTION AND COMMENTS   Built around 1900 and recently restored, this monastery has everything you'd expect: quiet, contemplative formal gardens, a beautiful church modeled after Hagia Sophia in Istanbul, and grounds dotted with replicas of shrines and chapels found in the Holy Land. What's really unusual is the sanitized crypt beneath the church, which is more Hollywood than Holy Land. (You almost expect to run into Victor Mature wearing a toga.) It's a replica of the catacombs under Rome and is positively — if inauthentically — ghoulish. As you pass open (but phony) grave sites in the walls, the guide narrates hair-raising stories of Christian martyrs eaten by lions, speared, stoned to death, beheaded, and burned at the stake. Shudder.

TOURING TIPS   The Franciscan Center, located across the street from the monastery, has rest rooms and a snack bar. Two parking lots are located across 14th Street.

OTHER THINGS TO DO NEARBY   The Basilica of the National Shrine of the Immaculate Conception — let me catch my breath — is just past the Metro station on Michigan Avenue. For lunch, a Pizza Hut is conveniently located near the Metro.

U.S. National Arboretum

Type of Attraction: A 444-acre collection of trees, flowers, and herbs. A self-guided tour.

Location: Off New York Avenue in Northeast Washington.

How to Get There: Drive. Take New York Avenue from downtown and enter on the service road on the right just past Bladensburg Road.

Admission: Free

Hours: 8 A.M. to 5 P.M. Monday through Friday; 10 A.M. to 5 P.M. weekends and holidays. The information center is open 8 A.M. to 4:30 P.M. weekdays; the gift shop is open 10 A.M. to 3 P.M. weekdays. The National Bonsai Collection is open from 10 A.M. to 3:30 P.M. Closed on Christmas Day.

When to Go: In the spring, fields of azaleas are in bloom. The world-class bonsai collection is a treat all year.

Special Comments: The arboretum is mobbed in the spring; the rest of the year is usually tranquil.

Overall Appeal by Age Group:

Pre-school	Grade School	Teens	Young Adults	Over 30	Senior Citizens
★	★½	★½	★★	★★½	★★★

Author's Rating: Interesting and beautiful; hard to get to. ★★½

How Much Time to Allow: One hour to half a day.

DESCRIPTION AND COMMENTS   With nine miles of roads and more than three miles of walking paths, the U.S. National Arboretum offers visitors an oasis of quiet and beauty for a drive or a stroll. Even people without green thumbs will marvel at the bonsai collection, dwarf trees that are more like sculptures than plants. One specimen, a Japanese white pine, is 350 years old. Folks with limited time who aren't gardening enthusiasts, however, shouldn't spend their valuable touring hours on a visit.

TOURING TIPS   Flowering dogwood and mountain laurel bloom well into May. The rest of the year, it's a fine place to go for a long walk. The surrounding neighborhoods aren't safe, so either drive or take a cab.

Kenilworth Aquatic Gardens

Type of Attraction: A national park devoted to water plants. A self-guided tour.

Location: 1900 Anacostia Drive, SE, across the Anacostia River from the National Arboretum.

How to Get There: Drive. Go south on Kenilworth Avenue from its intersection with New York Avenue. Exit at Eastern Avenue and follow signs to the parking lot off Anacostia Avenue.

Admission: Free

Hours: 7 A.M. to 4:15 P.M. daily.

When to Go: June and July to see hardy water plants; July and August to see tropical plants and lotus.

Special Comments: The gardens are located in a dangerous neighborhood. Don't take public transportation.

Overall Appeal by Age Group:

Pre-school	Grade School	Teens	Young Adults	Over 30	Senior Citizens
★	★★	★★	★★★	★★★	★★★

Author's Rating: Unique. ★★★

How Much Time to Allow: One hour

DESCRIPTION AND COMMENTS   In addition to pools filled with water lilies, water hyacinth, lotus and bamboo, the gardens teem with wildlife such as opossum, raccoon, waterfowl, and muskrats. It's an amazing place to visit on a clear summer morning.

TOURING TIPS   Come in the morning, before the heat closes up the flowers. Don't take public transportation; the surrounding neighborhood is unsafe. Drive or go by cab.

Zone 9 — Southeast

Frederick Douglass National Historic Site

Type of Attraction: Cedar Hill, the preserved Victorian home of abolitionist, statesman, and orator Frederick Douglass. A guided tour.

Location: 1411 W Street, SE, in Anacostia.

How to Get There: Drive; Anacostia is unsafe for pedestrians day or night. From the Mall, take Independence Avenue east past the Capitol to 2nd Street, SE, where it is intersected by Pennsylvania Avenue. Bear right onto Pennsylvania Avenue and go to 11th Street, SE, and turn right. Cross the 11th Street Bridge and go south on Martin Luther King, Jr., Avenue to W Street, SE. Turn left and go four blocks to the visitor center parking lot on the right.

Another option during the summer is Tourmobile, which offers a two-and-a-half–hour guided tour to Cedar Hill. Call (202) 554-7950 or stop at a Tourmobile ticket booth at Arlington Cemetery, the Lincoln Memorial, or the Washington Monument for more information. Rates are $16 for adults and $8 for children.

Admission: Free

Hours: 8:30 A.M. to 4:30 P.M. daily October through April; 9 A.M. to 5 P.M. May through September. Closed New Year's, Thanksgiving, and Christmas days.

Phone: (202) 426-5960

When to Go: Anytime

Special Comments: Do *not* take the Metro to Anacostia. The entire area is unsafe; Cedar Hill, administered by the National Park Service, is safe.

Overall Appeal by Age Group:

Pre-school	Grade School	Teens	Young Adults	Over 30	Senior Citizens
★	★★	★★★	★★★	★★★½	★★★½

Author's Rating: Informative and interesting. ★★★½
How Much Time to Allow: 90 minutes

DESCRIPTION AND COMMENTS This lovely Victorian home on a hill overlooking Washington remains much as it was in Douglass' time. The former slave, who among other achievements became U.S. ambassador to Haiti, spent the final 18 years of his life in this house. Douglass lived here when he wrote the third volume of his autobiography, *Life and Times of Frederick Douglass.*

For people interested in the history of the civil rights movement and genteel life in the late 1800s, Cedar Hill is a find. Our well-informed guide provided a detailed commentary on Douglass' life and times. Look for Douglass' bar bells on the floor next to his bed. Most children, however, may find it dull.

TOURING TIPS A late afternoon visit is almost like stepping back into the 19th century, since the house is preserved as it was when Douglass died in 1895: There's no electricity and the gathering shadows in the house evoke the past. Be sure to see "The Growlery," a small, one-room structure behind the main house Douglass declared off-limits to the household so that he could work alone.

OTHER THINGS TO DO NEARBY The Anacostia Museum is a short drive. However, Anacostia, Washington's first suburb and an area rich in black history, sits in the middle of a war zone. It's okay to drive during daylight, but it's not an area to visit on foot or at night.

Anacostia Museum

Type of Attraction: A Smithsonian museum focusing on African-American history and culture. A self-guided tour.

Location: 1901 Fort Place, SE, in Anacostia.

How to Get There: Budgets permitting, the Smithsonian operates free shuttle buses from the Mall to the Anacostia Museum (and back) during the spring and summer. The shuttles run on the hour, Monday through Friday. For specific information on where to board the buses and the schedule, stop at any museum information desk on the Mall.

To drive: From the Mall, take Independence Avenue east past the Capitol to 2nd Street, SE, where it is intersected by Pennsylvania Avenue. Bear right onto Pennsylvania Avenue and go to 11th Street, SE, and turn right. Cross the 11th Street Bridge and follow signs to Martin Luther King, Jr., Avenue (left lanes). Follow MLK Avenue to Morris Road (third traffic signal) and turn left. Go up the hill to 17th Street, SE, where Morris Road becomes Erie Street. In about five blocks, Erie Street becomes Fort Place; the museum is on the right. Because this part of Southeast Washington is unsafe for pedestrians, we don't recommend taking public transportation.

Admission: Free

Hours: 10 A.M. to 5 P.M. daily; closed Christmas Day.

Phone: (202) 357-2700

When to Go: Anytime. But either call first or pick up a brochure at The Castle on the Mall to find out what's on view before making the trip.

Special Comments: This "neighborhood" museum features temporary, special exhibits; between shows, there is often very little to see, so call first.

Overall Appeal by Age Group: Since the museum features special exhibitions that change throughout the year, it's not really possible to rate this Smithsonian facility's appeal by age group.

Author's Rating: Again, the temporary exhibitions make it impossible to rate this museum.

How Much Time to Allow: Based on its size, allow one hour.

DESCRIPTION AND COMMENTS   Located on the high ground of old Fort Stanton, the Anacostia Museum features changing exhibits on black culture and history, and the achievements of African-Americans. Unfortunately for out-of-town visitors, it's in a location that's difficult to reach.

TOURING TIPS   To save yourself the frustration of arriving between major shows, either call the museum first or pick up a flyer at The Castle on the Mall.

OTHER THINGS TO DO NEARBY   Frederick Douglass National Historic Site is a short drive. However, Anacostia sits in the middle of a war zone. It's okay to drive through during daylight, but it's not an area we advise visitors to visit on foot or at night.

Washington Navy Yard

Type of Attraction: Three military museums and a U.S. Navy destroyer. Self-guided tours.

Location: 9th and M streets, SE, on the waterfront.

Nearest Metro Station: Eastern Market. Because this is an unsafe neighborhood any time of day, we recommend visitors either drive (parking is available inside the gate) or take a cab.

Admission: Free

Hours: 9 A.M. to 4 P.M. Monday through Friday; 10 A.M. to 5 P.M. Memorial Day through Labor Day, weekends and holidays.

Phone: Navy Museum: (202) 433-4882; Marine Corps Historical Museum: (202) 433-3534; Navy Art Gallery: (202) 433-3815.

When to Go: Anytime

Special Comments: A nice contrast to the look-but-don't-touch Mall museums.

Overall Appeal by Age Group:

Pre-school	Grade School	Teens	Young Adults	Over 30	Senior Citizens
★★	★★★½	★★★	★★	★★	★★★

Author's Rating: Hands-on fun for kids; informative for adults. ★★½

How Much Time to Allow: Two hours

DESCRIPTION AND COMMENTS   Exhibits in the Navy Museum include 14-foot-long model ships, undersea vehicles *Alvin* and *Trieste,* working sub periscopes, a space capsule that kids (and wiry adults) can climb in, and, tied up at the dock, a decommissioned destroyer to tour. The Marine Corps Historical Museum is less hands-on, featuring exhibit cases and Marine Corps mementos. The Navy Art Gallery is a small museum with paintings of naval actions painted by combat artists.

A strong interest in the military is a prerequisite for making the trek to the Washington Navy Yard, and it's not a side-trip that many first-time visitors make. But kids will love it.

TOURING TIPS   Don't make my mistake — jumping off at the Metro's Navy Yard station and walking 10 scary blocks to the Navy Yard entrance; drive or take a cab. It's too bad these museums are so far off the beaten path, because there's a lot here to see and do.

OTHER THINGS TO DO NEARBY   Nothing recommended.

Zone 10—Maryland Suburbs

NASA/Goddard Space Flight Visitor Center

Type of Attraction: NASA's 1,100-acre, campuslike facility in suburban Maryland, including a small museum and other buildings. Self-guided and guided tours.

Location: Greenbelt, Maryland.

How to Get There: Drive. From downtown Washington, go out New York Avenue, which becomes the Baltimore-Washington Parkway (I-295). Take the MD 193 East exit, just past the Capital Beltway. Drive about two miles past the Goddard Space Flight Center's main entrance to Soil Conservation Road and turn left. Follow signs to the visitor center. Note: Metro is scheduled to reach Greenbelt in late 1993. Call the Goddard Visitor Center to see if shuttles are being offered.

Admission: Free

Hours: 10 A.M. to 4 P.M. daily; closed Thanksgiving, Christmas, and New Year's days.

Phone: (301) 286-8981

When to Go: Anytime

Overall Appeal by Age Group:

Pre-school	Grade School	Teens	Young Adults	Over 30	Senior Citizens
★	★★★	★★★	★★★	★★★	★★★

Author's Rating: Informative but far away. ★★½

How Much Time to Allow: One hour for the daily tours; two hours for the Sunday tours.

DESCRIPTION AND COMMENTS   The small museum inside the visitor center is loaded with space hardware; think of it as a mini–Air and Space Museum. While most folks will get their fill and then some of space craft at the museum on the Mall, a visit to NASA's Greenbelt facility is the icing on the cake for hard-core space cadets.

TOURING TIPS   One-hour tours are given at 11:30 A.M. and 2:30 P.M. Monday through Saturday. On first and third Sundays of the month, you can take longer walking tours; and on second and fourth Sundays you can take bus tours. The Sunday tours of the center are offered on a first-come, first-served basis and take visitors to special working areas that show satellite control and tracking operations, test and evaluation facilities, and communication operations. Try to catch the two-hour bus tours that take visitors to a number of different buildings around Goddard. In the spring and fall, an all-day Open House features an even wider array of tours, plus entertainment. Call the center for a schedule.

OTHER THINGS TO DO NEARBY   Drive through the adjacent Agricultural Research Center, a collection of farms where the U.S. Department of Agriculture studies farm animals and plants. The roads are narrow and quiet — it's a rural oasis in the heart of Maryland's suburban sprawl.

Zone 11 — Virginia Suburbs

Mount Vernon

Type of Attraction: George Washington's 18th-century Virginia plantation on the Potomac River. A self-guided tour.

Location: 16 miles south of Washington.

How to Get There: To drive from Washington, cross the 14th Street Bridge into Virginia, bear right, and get on the George Washington Memorial Parkway south. Continue past National Airport into Alexandria, where the Parkway becomes Washington Street. Continue straight; Washington Street becomes the Mount Vernon Memorial Parkway, which ends at Mount Vernon.

Tourmobile offers four-hour, narrated bus tours to Mount Vernon daily, April through October. Departures are at 10 A.M., 12 P.M., and 2 P.M. Tickets are $16.50 for adults and $8 for children 3 to 11 years old. The price includes admission to Mount Vernon. Call Tourmobile at (202) 554-7950 for more information.

Admission: $7 for adults, $6 for senior citizens 62 and over, and $3 for children ages six through eleven.

Hours: 8 A.M. to 5 P.M. March through October; 9 A.M. to 4 P.M. November through February. Open every day, including Christmas.

Phone: (703) 780-2000

When to Go: Generally, before 10 A.M., especially in hot weather. But sometimes tour and school buses arrive before the gates open, creating a line to buy tickets and tour the mansion. Come around 3 P.M. and you're sure to avoid the buses — and the lines. When longer hours are in effect, you must clear the grounds by 5:30.

Special Comments: During Christmas, the decorated mansion's seldom-seen third floor is open to the public.

Overall Appeal by Age Group:

Pre-school	Grade School	Teens	Young Adults	Over 30	Senior Citizens
★★	★★★★	★★★	★★★★½	★★★★★	★★★★★

Author's Rating: Not to be missed. ★★★★★
How Much Time to Allow: Two hours

DESCRIPTION AND COMMENTS   Folks on a quick trip to Washington won't have time to visit Mount Vernon, but everyone else should. The stunning view from the mansion across the Potomac River is pretty much the same as it was in Washington's day. Unlike most historic sites in D.C., Mount Vernon gives visitors a real sense of how 18th-century rural life worked, from the first president's foot-operated fan chair (for keeping flies at bay while he read) to the rustic kitchen and outbuildings.

TOURING TIPS   Mount Vernon is *very* popular and tourists pull up by the bus load in the spring and summer months — sometimes before the grounds open. During the high tourist season, Monday, Friday, and Sunday mornings before 11 A.M. are the least busy periods. If you want to avoid big crowds, go around 3 P.M., but you must leave the grounds by 5:30 P.M. When crowds are small in the winter, visitors are frequently given guided tours of the mansion.

OTHER THINGS TO DO NEARBY   Mount Vernon offers a snack bar, two gift shops, a post office, and a sit-down restaurant. Rest rooms can be found near the museum on the grounds or between the gift shop and snack bar near the entrance. Visit Old Town Alexandria on your way to or from Mount Vernon. A stop at Gadsby's Tavern is appropriate, since that's what George Washington used to do.

Old Town Alexandria

Type of Attraction: A restored colonial port town on the Potomac River, featuring 18th-century buildings on cobblestone streets, trendy shops, bars and restaurants, parks, and a huge art center.

Location: In suburban Virginia, eight miles south of Washington.

Nearest Metro Station: King Street

Admission: Some historic houses charge $3 for admission. Admission to the Torpedo Factory Art Center, the Lyceum, the Lloyd House, and the George Washington Masonic National Memorial is free.

Hours: Historic houses, shops, and the Torpedo Factory Art Center open by 10 A.M. and remain open through the afternoon.

When to Go: Anytime

Special Comments: The most scenic spot for a brown-bag lunch is the picnic tables located at the foot of 1st Street, on the Potomac River.

Overall Appeal by Age Group:

Pre-school	Grade School	Teens	Young Adults	Over 30	Senior Citizens
★★	★★★	★★★	★★★★½	★★★★½	★★★★½

Author's Rating: A satisfying contrast to awesome D.C. ★★★★

How Much Time to Allow: Half a day. If it's the second half, stay for dinner; Old Town Alexandria has a great selection of restaurants.

DESCRIPTION AND COMMENTS   Alexandria claims both George Washington and Robert E. Lee as native sons, so history buffs have a lot to see. Topping the list are period revival houses that rival those in Georgetown, another old port up the river; Gadsby's Tavern (open Tuesday through Saturday, 10 A.M. to 5 P.M., and Sunday from 1 P.M. to 5 P.M.; guided tours at quarter of and quarter past the hour); Christ Church; and the Lee-Fendall House.

This revitalized city on the Potomac is crammed with exotic restaurants (Thai, Indian, Lebanese, Greek) and shops (art, jewelry, children's books, antiques, Persian carpets). And, unlike those in Georgetown, the eating and drinking establishments in Old Town aren't overrun by suburban teenagers on weekends.

TOURING TIPS   As you exit the King Street Metro, either board a DASH bus for a quick trip down King Street to Old Town ($.75), or walk to your left and turn right onto King Street for a pleasant 15-minute stroll toward the river. The closest visitor center is at The Lyceum, where two art galleries and a museum of the area's history are featured; from King Street, turn right onto Washington Street and walk a block. There's also a small museum featuring prints, documents, photographs, silver, furniture, and Civil War memorabilia.

Farther down King Street on the left is *Ramsay House,* built in 1724 and now Alexandria's official visitor center, open daily from 9 A.M. to 5 P.M., except Thanksgiving, Christmas, and New Year's days. Ramsay House makes a good starting point for a walking tour of Old Town Alexandria.

The *Torpedo Factory Arts Center* at the foot of King Street features more than 150 painters, printmakers, sculptors, and other artists and craftspeople. Visitors can watch artists at work in their studios housed in the former munitions factory.

If you drive to Alexandria, park your car in a metered space and go to a visitor center to pick up a pass that lets you park free for 72 hours in any metered zone inside Alexandria city limits. But parking is scarce and the King Street Metro is conveniently located.

OTHER THINGS TO DO NEARBY   About a mile west of the center of Alexandria is the George Washington Masonic National Memorial. A free tour features a view from the 333-foot tower, Washington memorabilia, a 370-year-old Persian rug valued at $1 million, and more information about Masonry than you probably want. The 70-minute tours are given Monday through Saturday. Open daily 9 A.M. to 5 P.M. Mount Vernon, George Washington's plantation on the Potomac, is eight miles downriver.

PART TEN: Shopping in Washington

Mall Shopping

It should come as no surprise that Washington—where residents earn the highest median household income in the nation—has a lot of shopping. You might say it's been malled to death. On Saturday afternoons, roads leading to the malls are as congested as commuter routes during rush hour.

Suburban Malls

Most of the suburban malls are cookie-cutter versions of what you probably have back home. One exception is **The Fashion Centre** at Pentagon City in Arlington, Virginia, a beautiful building filled with less-commonplace shops, including Crate and Barrel, the Museum Company, the Nature Company, Macy's, and Nordstrom, the Seattle-based clothing retailer renowned for its service and selection. The Pentagon City Metro stop, on the blue line, deposits shoppers right into the mall.

Malls in D.C.

There are fewer malls within city limits. **Georgetown Park,** near the intersection of M Street and Wisconsin Avenue, is the most extravagant, featuring a lush Victorian design and some even fancier retailers. Two Washington landmarks have lately been reborn as shopping centers: the **Old Post Office Pavilion** and **Union Station.** The Pavilion, on Pennsylvania Avenue just north of the Smithsonian, is the place for stocking up on souvenirs. Union Station, the city's restored train station on Massachusetts Avenue, is a grand beaux arts building whose glory is undiminished by its collection of shops. Be sure to wander into the East Hall, which has kiosks selling one-of-a-kind jewelry, crafts, and other merchandise.

Great Neighborhoods
for Window-Shopping

If malls make you crazy, Washington has a number of neighborhoods made for window-shopping.

—— *In Georgetown*

In Georgetown, the city's largest walk-and-shop district, most of the stores are right along M Street and Wisconsin Avenue. Georgetown has more than a few shops specializing in one-of-a-kind crafts — including ceramics at *American Hand* (2906 M Street, NW; (202) 965-3273), jewelry and wooden crafts at *Appalachian Spring* (1415 Wisconsin Avenue, NW; (202) 337-5780) and Southwestern imports from *Santa Fe Style* (1413 Wisconsin Avenue, NW; (202) 333-3747). For beautiful but more traditional gifts, old-line Georgetowners prefer *Little Caledonia* (1419 Wisconsin Avenue, NW; (202) 333-4700) and *Martin's* (1304 Wisconsin Avenue, NW; (202) 338-6144). Shops for antiques, artwork, books, and shoes are plentiful here, too, and you'll find a preponderance of stores selling teen fashions — notably, *Commander Salamander* (1420 Wisconsin Avenue, NW; (202) 337-2265), *Betsey Johnson* (1319 Wisconsin Avenue, NW; (202) 338-4090) and *Urban Outfitters* (3111 M Street, NW; (202) 342-1012).

—— *In Adams-Morgan*

In Adams-Morgan, along 18th Street and Columbia Road, amid all the ethnic eateries, you'll find wacky gifts at shops with equally wacky names. Try *Maybe Baby* (1840 18th Street, NW; (202) 986-0995) and *Wake Up Little Suzie* (2316 18th Street, NW; (202) 328-7577). Funky home furnishings are big here, too — the weirder the better — you'll find them at *Retrospective* (2324 18th Street, NW; (202) 483-8112), *Home-*

works (2405 18th Street, NW; (202) 483-5857), and *Skynear and Company* (2122 18th Street, NW; (202) 797-7160). If you're visiting around Christmastime, don't miss the displays of ornaments at *Noteworthy* (2420 18th Street, NW; (202) 232-4468). And this is the neighborhood to look for ethnic clothing and crafts (see Ethnic Goods, below).

— In Dupont Circle

Dupont Circle is for shoppers looking to enrich the mind — it's full of art galleries and bookstores. South of the circle, on Connecticut Avenue, NW, between N and K streets, are high-end retailers such as *Polo Ralph Lauren, T. Anthony* luggage, *Burberrys,* and *Cartier.*

— In Chevy Chase

At the northwest edge of D.C., where it blends into Montgomery County, well-heeled shoppers love the stretch of Wisconsin Avenue from about Jenifer Street to Park Avenue. With two malls — **Mazza Gallerie** and **Chevy Chase Pavilion** — and lots of freestanding boutiques, there is much browsing and spending to do. Among the shops: *Neiman-Marcus, Jackie Chalkley,* and *Gazelle,* which is a great spot for wearable art; *Joan and David, Pottery Barn, Lord & Taylor, Saks Fifth Avenue, Gucci,* and other couture clothiers (see Designer Clothing, below).

— On Capitol Hill

On Capitol Hill, most shops are in the vicinity of Eastern Market — an actual market where vendors set up tables selling produce, baked goods, and flea market bric-a-brac located on 7th Street between Pennsylvania and Independence avenues. There, amid the restaurants and bars, are secondhand clothing shops and first-rate crafts stores — particularly *Mazi* for jewelry (311 7th Street, SE; (202) 547-2555) and *Moon, Blossoms and Snow* for unusual gifts such as glass salt-and-pepper shakers shaped like cacti or handpainted dog dishes (225 Pennsylvania Avenue, SE; (202) 543-8181).

In Old Town Alexandria

Alexandria, Virginia, is a walker's delight, too, with shops clustered up, down, and around King Street, most of them selling antiques, crafts, and home furnishings.

Specialty Shops

Antiques. Serious antique-seekers get out of town — driving an hour or more to the countryside of Maryland, Virginia, West Virginia, or Pennsylvania for the bargains. But you will find treasures — though few bargains — in and around the city. The largest concentration of such shops is on **"Antique Row"** in Kensington, Maryland, about four miles from the D.C. line. There are more than 50 antique dealers on **Howard Avenue,** with smaller shops east of Connecticut Avenue and larger warehouses west of Connecticut.

In Georgetown and Alexandria, you'll find a variety of shops selling 18th-, 19th-, and 20th-century collectibles. One Georgetown favorite is *Christ Child Opportunity Shop* (1427 Wisconsin Avenue, NW; (202) 333-6635), where, on the second floor, you'll find silver, china, paintings, and other cherishables on consignment from the best Georgetown homes.

Art. The city's best selection of art for sale — traditional, modern, and ethnic — can be found around **Dupont Circle.** Your best bet, besides looking along Connecticut Avenue, is to head west off Connecticut onto R Street, where there are a dozen galleries within two blocks. Up Connecticut Avenue, *The Farrell Collection* (2633 Connecticut Avenue, NW; (202) 483-8334) represents the work of more than 600 artists, who craft jewelry, ceramics, glass, wood, and fiber.

Another popular source for art is the *Torpedo Factory Art Center* in Old Town Alexandria (105 N. Union Street; (703) 838-4565), where 150 artists in a range of media — painting, sculpture, jewelry, and more — have set up studios. You can buy their work, or simply watch them create.

Bargains. Washington may have its million-dollar houses, expense-account restaurants, and pricey private schools, but it also has a surprising number of discount outlets. Savvy shoppers never pay full price for their Coach bags, their Lancôme cosmetics, or their Polo dress shirts.

Some of the best buys are in warehouses buried in industrial parks —

not worth a drive unless you know where you're going and you know what you're after. What is worth a trip is **Potomac Mills Mall** in Dale City, Virginia — one of the world's largest outlet malls. Just 45 minutes south of D.C., off I-95, this 250-store mall (phone: (800) VA-MILLS) gets more visitors each year than any other Virginia tourist attraction — more than Colonial Williamsburg. It's nearly impossible to hit all of the stores, which include Swedish furniture designer *IKEA,* and outlets for *Nordstrom, Eddie Bauer, Nike, Laura Ashley, Fitz and Floyd, Benetton,* and *Georgetown Leather Design.*

If you can't make it to Potomac Mills, Washington now has its first inside-the-Beltway off-price mall, **City Place** in Silver Spring, Maryland (Phone: (301) 589-1091). At the intersection of Colesville Road (Route 29) and Fenton Street, three blocks north of the Silver Spring Metro (red line), City Place's best assets are *Nordstrom Rack, Marshalls,* and its shoe outlets.

Bookstores. There's little wonder why Washingtonians are well-read: Almost everywhere you look, there is a bookstore. There are general-interest chains like *B. Dalton* and *Borders,* but the majority are small independents, many with narrow specialties such as art, travel, Russian literature, or mystery.

If you're in a book-browsing mood, you might take the red line to Dupont Circle or the orange line to Farragut West. Between these two Metro stops, along and just off Connecticut Avenue between S and I streets, are some of the city's best bookstores.

Walking south from S Street, NW, toward Dupont Circle, you'll hit the *Newsroom,* with an exhaustive stock of foreign-language periodicals (1753 Connecticut Avenue, NW; (202) 332-1489); *Mystery Books* (1715 Connecticut Avenue, NW; (202) 483-1600); *Lambda Rising,* a gay/lesbian book shop (1625 Connecticut Avenue, NW; (202) 462-6969); *Kramerbooks,* a bookstore and cafe that's quite the scene on weekends, when it's open 24 hours (1517 Connecticut Avenue, NW; (202) 387-1400). Right off the circle on P Street you'll find *Second Story Books,* a terrific source for used books where, for $3, they'll search for any out-of-print edition (2000 P Street, NW; (202) 659-8884); and *Backstage,* which sells scripts and performing arts books (2101 P Street, NW; (202) 775-1488). Down side streets you can seek out *Lammas,* devoted to feminist concerns (1426 21st Street, NW; (202) 775-8218); and *Olsson's Books and Records,* the city's most beloved general-interest booksource, with a selective but broad inventory (1307 19th Street, NW; (202) 785-1133).

Over by Farragut West, you'll find political and business books in *Sidney Kramer* (1825 I Street, NW; (202) 293-2685); volumes on the visual arts at *Franz Bader* (1911 I Street, NW; (202) 337-5440); travel guides at *The Map Store* (1636 I Street, NW; (202) 628-2608); and literary criticism, biography, poetry, and a good general stock, as well as frequent Saturday-afternoon readings at *Chapters* (1512 K Street, NW; (202) 347-5495).

Two other special bookstores are farther north on Connecticut Avenue, in the neighborhood known as Tenleytown. *Politics & Prose* specializes in psychology, politics, and the works of local authors—and hosts many of their book-signing parties (5015 Connecticut Avenue, NW; (202) 364-1919). The store recently opened a basement coffee bar on-site. A few blocks away is *Cheshire Cat Children's Bookstore*, a treasure trove for kids and parents, complete with a play area (5512 Connecticut Avenue, NW; (202) 244-3956).

Designer Clothing.

Maryland Border. In the free-spending '80s, couture clothiers couldn't open shops fast enough in Washington. While the '80s may be gone, most of the boutiques remain. And most are in **"Gucci Gulch"**—a row of chic shops extending from the 5200 to 5500 blocks of Wisconsin Avenue, from the upper edge of the District of Columbia right into Montgomery County, Maryland. Among the boutiques: *Saks Jandel, Gucci, Hugo Boss, Jaeger, Georgette Klinger, Elizabeth Arden, Cartier, Saks Fifth Avenue, Joan and David,* and *Gianfranco Ferre.*

Virginia. Here, the gold-card crowd heads to **Fairfax Square,** a mall on Leesburg Pike in Tysons Corner that is home to *Tiffany & Company, Gucci, Fendi, Hermes,* and *Louis Vuitton.*

Washington, D.C. In the District, the grand old Willard Hotel on Pennsylvania Avenue houses a set of shops that includes *Chanel* and *Jackie Chalkley,* good for crafty clothing.

Ethnic goods. Whether it's a dashiki or a Rasta hat you're after, you'll find it in Adams-Morgan. Along 18th Street and Columbia Road, NW, are a number of shops selling clothing and gifts from Africa, South America, Asia, and other foreign lands. One of the best is *Nomad,* owned by an anthropologist (2407 18th Street, NW, second floor; (202) 332-2998). *Sun Gallery Goldsmiths* features African-inspired jewelry, including dazzling pieces in amber (2322 18th Street, NW; (202) 265-

9341). Also in Adams-Morgan are numerous mom-and-pops selling the foods of Africa and Latin America.

Insider Shops. Although the White House, the House of Representatives, and even Camp David have monogrammed and souvenir merchandise, it's available only to special staff. Outsiders who want to look like Washington insiders do have a few options, however.

The *Tobacco Shop* in the Dirksen Senate office building (1st and C streets, NE; (202) 224-4416) is open to the public, and sells souvenirs emblazoned with the Senate seal. You can buy G-man gear in the *FBI Gift Shop* (9th at Pennsylvania Avenue, NW, Room 8704; (202) 324-3414). The *Foreign Affairs Recreation Association* shop (21st and C streets, NW; (202) 647-0482) sells State Department stuff—from luggage tags to T-shirts. The *NASA Exchange* gift shop (300 E Street, SW; (202) 358-0162) is for astronaut wannabes.

And although the neighbors won't notice anything special about your American flag—unless of course you tell them—you can buy a flag that has flown over the U.S. Capitol. You can even request that your flag be raised on a particular date. Contact your representative for details. Delivery takes about three weeks, and prices are as follows: $7.50 for a three-by-five-foot nylon flag, $8.25 for a three-by-five in cotton; $17.50 for a five-by-eight-foot nylon flag, $18.25 for one in cotton.

Museum Shops. Some of Washington's greatest finds are in its museum gift shops. A museum's orientation is a good guide to its shop's merchandise—prints and art books fill the *National Gallery of Art* shop, model airplanes and other toys of flight are on sale at *Air and Space.*

Some good museum shops are often overlooked by tourists: *The National Building Museum* shop, which sells design-related books, jewelry, and gadgets; the *Arts and Industries* shop, a pretty, Victorian setting stocked with Smithsonian reproductions; the *Department of the Interior Museum's Indian Craft Shop,* which sells one-of-a-kind creations at the museum and in Georgetown Park Mall; the *National Museum of African Art* shop, a bazaar filled with colorful cloth and wooden ceremonial instruments such as hand drums and tambourines; the *Arthur M. Sackler Gallery* shop, with cases full of brass Buddhas, Chinese lacquerware, and porcelain; and the newly expanded shop at the *John F. Kennedy Center for the Performing Arts,* stocked with videos, opera glasses, and other gifts for performing arts lovers.

Political Memorabilia. If you're a serious collector, no doubt you already know about stores selling political buttons and ribbons, auto-graphed letters and photos, commemorative plates and pens. If you're not a collector, these shops can be as fun to browse through as museums, except that you can touch and you can take it home. Two such shops, within walking distance of one another, are *Capitol Coin and Stamp* (1701 L Street, NW; (202) 296-0400) and *Political Americana* (685 15th Street, NW; (202) 638-5107), which also has a branch inside Union Station.

Oriental Rugs. Washington, D.C., offers the broadest selection of handmade oriental rugs available in the United States. In fact, there is so much competition here that prices are forced below what you would expect to pay for comparable quality in other American cities. Though shops are sprinkled all around the greater Washington area, the greatest concentration of stores is located on Wisconsin Avenue from north of Georgetown to Bethesda.

Wine and Gourmet Foods. *Mayflower Wines* joined forces with the *Sutton Place Gourmet* shops in 1992 to provide four one-stop fine food shops in the greater Washington area. Each shop offers an excellent selection of wines and an impressive variety of gourmet and ethnic foods. The wine buyers travel abroad each year to select the stores' wine inventory, and are particularly tuned in to Italian reds. Visitors to the stores from outside of the District, Virginia, and Maryland can buy wine and have it shipped home without paying local sales tax. If you buy a case, you will more than cover your shipping on what you save on tax. If you do not have time to shop in person, the *Mayflower at Sutton Place Gourmet* publishes a newsletter describing highly touted (and reasonably priced) wines. The newsletter also includes recipes. To receive the free newsletter call (202) 363-5800.

Writing Implements. *Fahrney's* (1430 G Street, NW; (202) 628-9525) has all the write stuff: For more than 70 years Fahrney's has sold nothing but beautiful pens, including Watermans and Montblancs.

Cookery. *La Cuisine* (323 Cameron Street, Alexandria, Virginia; (703) 836-4435) has tools for the serious chef: very serious cookware and books.

Swimwear. *Signature Swimwear* (211 S. Strand Street, Alexandria, Virginia; (703) 548-1166) is an Old Town shop that custom-makes swimsuits in the pattern and material you choose.

Salon Products. *Skin Fitness,* in the Capitol Hilton (16th and K streets, NW; (202) 638-3888), is a small salon that not only delivers expert facials for problem skin, but sells products specially made for acne-prone and troubled skin.

PART ELEVEN: Dining and Restaurants

A Comment on
Washington Cuisine

⸺ The New Washington Cookery

The great calorie inflation is over in Washington. Dollar for dollar (and pound for pound), dining in Washington has never been better: more varied, healthier, more affordable—and, in those other cases, more apt to be worth the expense.

Ethnic Influence

This onetime cholesterol capital of the world has discovered not only its natural resources—its regional specialties and farm produce—but also its imported ones, the rainbow of immigrant chefs and cuisines and the even more intriguing pidgin cuisines that are constantly being created here. Consider the possibilities in a restaurant called "Cajun Bangkok" or "Thai Roma," or one that advertises Chinese-Mexican or Italian-Creole.

One of the most enjoyable aspects of visiting Washington, therefore, is dining out, especially when you explore more exotic cuisines and new trends—even, for the newly watchful, haute health restaurants, where additives and chemicals are banned. So this is more than a list of the 80 "best" kitchens in the Washington area; it's a compendium of the best and the broadest, with an eye toward the unusual and even the mercurial.

New Restaurant Districts

Our list is also broad in the geographical sense, because along with the awakening of the Washington palate has come a rearrangement of the dining map. While Georgetown remains a busy shopping and night-life area, it is no longer the dominant restaurant strip. The revitalized downtown area, the ethnically mixed Adams-Morgan neighborhood, and the northwest suburbs—particularly the Asian polyglot of Wheaton and Bethesda with their "golden triangles" of restaurants — have all emerged as livelier locations. (Certain neighborhoods have such concentrations of particular restaurants, whether because of the ethnic communities in the area or commercial trend-hopping, that they have joking nicknames: "Little Saigon" for Arlington, Virginia; "Ethiopia" for Adams-Morgan, which is also a Latin American hub; and "Santa Fe East" for Bethesda, Maryland.)

Scoping Out the Lunch Crowd

Although in the old days the price of a meal proved its importance, and by implication, the diners', it's more important now to be able to speak of a kitchen's imagination, its beer selection, its service, even its bottled water. And, in a city where time really is money, one can also categorize the area's restaurants by their midday clientele: power lunchers, hour lunchers (very often at ethnic restaurants, which are rather quicker on the uptake than traditional white-linen establishments), flower lunchers (the remnants of the leisure class), and shower lunchers, those roving bands of office workers who seem always to be celebrating someone's great occasion but who want individual checks.

If you're not sure which kind of restaurant you've just walked into, glance around at the beverage glasses. Power lunchers are more likely to order a cocktail, hour lunchers a beer, flower lunchers wine, and shower lunchers soft drinks or pitchers with paper fans.

Industry Trends

The passing of the kind of inflation that padded prices has had a rather more serious impact on the restaurant industry in Washington. Several of the finer establishments, caught between the pincers of exorbitant rent and declining expense-account business, have closed. A few have downscaled, and some of the most influential chefs in the area are opening what might be called "off-the-rack" restaurants (cafes and pizzerias) in addition to their designer rooms. More intriguingly, some rival chefs are becoming partners: Galileo godfather Roberto Donna, who started the off-price trend with his Adams-Morgan kitchen I Matti, and Jean-Louis Palladin of the Watergate, arguably the two finest chefs in the city, have opened a seafood market and minitrattoria together near Dupont Circle called Pesce.

The restaurant profiles that follow (we say 80, although several cover more than one location) are intended to give you a sense of the atmosphere and advantages of a particular establishment as well as its particular cuisine. None should be taken as gospel, because one drawback of Washington's new appetite for adventure is that restaurants open and close—and promising chefs play musical kitchens—with breathtaking speed.

And, blame it on yuppie consciousness, gourmet magazine proliferation, or real curiosity, the increased interest in the techniques of cooking has also produced a demand for variety, for constantly challenging presentations and guaranteed freshness. Consequently, many of the fancier restaurants change their menus or a portion thereof every day, and more change seasonally, so the specific dishes recommended at particular places may not be available on a given night. Use these critiques as a guide, an indication of the chef's interests and strengths — and weaknesses, too. These are not puff-piece profiles; we'll tell you what's not worth trying.

The New Hotel Dining

If you have little time to ponder the choices, you can fairly safely go with the pros. When it comes to hotel dining rooms, Washington contradicts the rule of thumb; many of the better chefs, including a dozen or so not profiled in depth here, are working in hotels. This is a mutually beneficial arrangement, allowing the chefs to concentrate on managing a kitchen, not a business; and providing an extra attraction to potential clients. Since Washington's hotels expect to attract a largely expense-account business, they generally offer menus on the expensive side. In addition to the restaurants listed, we recommend those at the *Morrison-Clark Inn,* the *Embassy Row Hotel* (Lucie), the *Henley Park* (Coeur de Lion), the *Mayflower* (Nicholas), the *ANA* (the Colonnade), the *Ritz-Carlton–Pentagon City,* the *Willard,* the *Phoenix Park* (Powerscourt), the *Wyndham-Bristol* (Bristol Grill), the *Radisson Mark Terrace* (Chardonnay), and the *J. W. Marriott* (Celadon), to name a few.

Diners' Special Needs

These profiles also attempt to address the special requirements of diners who use wheelchairs or braces. Because so many of Washington's restaurants occupy older buildings and row houses, options for wheelchair users are unfortunately limited. In most cases, wheelchair access is prevented right at the street; but many restaurants offering easy entrance to the dining room keep their rest rooms up or down a flight of stairs. Both are listed here as having "no" disabled access. "Fair" access suggests that there is an initial step or small barrier to broach, or that passage may be a bit tight; but that once inside the establishment, dining is comfortable for the wheelchair user. Again, hotel dining rooms are good bets, because lobby access is needed for baggage and deliveries. Newer office buildings and mixed shopping and entertainment complexes have ramps and elevators that make them wheelchair accessible; the ones above subway stations even have their own elevators.

We have not specially categorized restaurants as offering "vegetarian" or other "restricted" diets, because almost all Washington restaurants now offer either vegetarian entrees on the menu or will make low-salt or low-fat dishes on request. Use common sense: A big-ticket steakhouse is unlikely to have many nonmeat options, but since few countries in the world eat as much meat as Americans, most ethnic cuisines are good bets for vegetarians.

Getting to a Restaurant of Your Choice

All but a few of the restaurants here are accessible either by public transportation or a short drive. If you are planning a lengthier vacation and renting a car, or staying with friends who can make advance preparations, there are a couple of four- and five-star establishments 60 to 90 minutes from downtown, the *Inn at Little Washington* in Washington, Virginia (phone: (703) 675-3800) and *L'Auberge Chez Francois* in Great Falls, Virginia (phone: (703) 759-3800). L'Auberge requires that reservations be made two to four weeks in advance, but sometimes it has last-minute cancellations, particularly on weeknights.

Eating on the Go

Sight-seers and shoppers in the Washington area don't have to stop to eat. Aside from the cafeteria-style food courts in most shopping malls, full-service restaurants of many varieties (particularly those "hour lunch" types) tend to cluster around shops and sights. Several of the Smithsonian's museums, including the *National Gallery,* the *Fine Arts Collection,* and the *Air and Space Museum* have cafes or cafeterias, not to mention that all the vendors your kids can stand are parked in and around the Mall. And, although we tend to avoid national franchise restaurants in our list, there is one local chain worth mentioning for its versatility and convenience: *The American Cafe* has a dozen locations around the area, all in subway developments or tourist/shopping areas, and a broad selection of carefully prepared food: hearty salads, sandwiches, and pastas.

—— Places to See Faces

Washington may not really be Hollywood on the Potomac (although so many movie stars come to town to lobby for their pet causes, it's getting close), but there are celebrity faces aplenty. And since being seen is part of the scene — and getting star treatment is one of the perks of being famous — celebrities tend to be visible in dependable places, particularly at lunch.

The venerable steak-and-lobster *Palm,* with its wall-to-wall caricatures of famous customers and its bullying waiters, is still a popular media and legal-eagle hangout. And at lunch, it's far more affordable than at night, when entrees are priced by the pound (1225 19th Street, NW; (202) 293-9091). *Duke Zeibert's* matzo-ball soup and megasandwich haven, where the Redskins' Super Bowl trophies share the spotlight with the Baltimore Orioles' World Series prize, is Gossip Central, home to radio personalities such as Larry King and Sonny Jurgenson (1050 Connecticut Avenue, NW; (202) 466-3730).

Pol-watchers, check out the *Monocle* for congressmen (107 D Street, NE; (202) 546-4488); *Two Quail* for congresswomen (320 Massachusetts Avenue, NE; (202) 543-8030); or *La Colline* for committee staffers (400 North Capitol Street, NE; (202) 737-0400). *Bullfeathers* is full of national committee staffers, both parties (410 1st Street, NW; (202) 543-5005), *Le Mistral* has lobbyists (223 Pennsylvania Avenue, SE; (202) 543-7477). The *Hay-Adams* is where the power breakfast was born, starring White House staff and federal bureaucrats (1 Lafayette Square, NW; (202) 638-6600), and the *Powerscourt* (520 North Capitol Street, NW; (202) 737-3776) is the branch office of Bostonian politicians. Behind-the-scenes power-wielders, "spouses of," and social arbiters congregate at the Ritz-Carlton's *Jockey Club* (2100 Massachusetts Avenue, NW; (202) 659-8000) and *Maison Blanche* (1725 F Street, NW; (202) 842-0070).

World Bank and OAS suits lunch at *Taberna del Alabardero* (1776 I Street, NW; (202) 429-2200); corporate write-offs go to the *Prime Rib* (2020 K Street, NW; (202) 466-8811) and *Tiberio's* (1915 K Street, NW; (202) 452-1915), which is also where Art Buchwald is imperially ensconced. Treasury and White House staff crowd the neighboring *Old Ebbitt Grill* (675 15th Street, NW; (202) 347-4801) and the *Occidental Grill* (14th Street and Pennsylvania Avenue, NW; (202) 783-1475); they get together to critique the high-horsed low-country Carolina cuisine at *Georgia Brown* (915 15th Street, NW; (202) 393-4499). And, among the low-profile politicians and working press who frequent the *Market Inn*, especially in shad roe season, are rumored to be CIA and other professionals who are incognito (200 E Street, SW; (202) 554-2100).

The Restaurants

—— *Our Favorite Washington Restaurants*

We have developed detailed profiles for the best restaurants (in our opinion) in town. Each profile features an easily scanned heading which allows you, in just a second, to check out the restaurant's name, cuisine, Star Rating, cost, Quality Rating, and Value Rating.

Star Rating. The star rating is an overall rating which encompasses the entire dining experience, including style, service, and ambience in addition to the taste, presentation, and quality of the food. Five stars is the highest rating possible and connotes the best of everything. Four-star restaurants are exceptional and three-star restaurants are well above average. Two-star restaurants are good. One star is used to connote an average restaurant that demonstrates an unusual capability in some area of specialization, for example, an otherwise unmemorable place which has great barbecued chicken.

Cost. To the right of the star rating is an expense description which provides a comparative sense of how much a complete meal will cost. A complete meal for our purposes consists of an entree with vegetable or side dish, and choice of soup or salad. Appetizers, desserts, drinks, and tips are excluded.

Inexpensive	$14 and less per person
Moderate	$15–30 per person
Expensive	Over $30 per person

Quality Rating. On the far right of each heading appears a number and a letter. The number is a quality rating based on a scale of 0–100, with 100 being the highest (best) rating attainable. The quality rating is based expressly on the taste, freshness of ingredients, preparation, presentation, and creativity of food served. There is no consideration of price. If you are a person who wants the best food available, and cost is not an issue, you need look no further than the quality ratings.

Value Rating. If on the other hand you are looking for both quality

373

and value, then you should check the value rating, expressed in letters. The value ratings are defined as follows:

A   Exceptional value, a real bargain
B   Good value
C   Fair value, you get exactly what you pay for
D   Somewhat overpriced
F   Significantly overpriced

Location. Just below the heading is a small locator map. This map will give you a general idea of where the restaurant described is located. For ease of use, we divide Washington into 11 geographic zones.

Zone 1.   The Mall
Zone 2.   Capitol Hill
Zone 3.   Downtown
Zone 4.   Foggy Bottom
Zone 5.   Georgetown
Zone 6.   Dupont Circle/Adams-Morgan
Zone 7.   Upper Northwest
Zone 8.   Northeast
Zone 9.   Southeast
Zone 10. Maryland Suburbs
Zone 11. Virginia Suburbs

If you are staying downtown and intend to walk or take a cab to dinner, you may want to choose a restaurant from among those located in Zone 3. If you have a car, you might include restaurants from contiguous zones in your consideration. (See pages 12–22 for detailed zone maps.)

Because restaurants are opening and closing all the time in Washington, we have tried to confine our list to establishments with a proven track record over a fairly long period of time. Newer restaurants (and older restaurants under new management) are listed but not profiled. Those newer or changed establishments which demonstrate staying power and consistency will be profiled in subsequent editions. Also, the list is highly selective. Non-inclusion of a particular place does not necessarily indicate that the restaurant is not good, but only that it was not ranked among the best in its genre. Detailed profiles of each restaurant follow in alphabetical order at the end of this chapter. (Also, we've listed the type of payment accepted at each restaurant using the following code: AMEX = American Express (Optima), CB = Carte Blanche, D = Discover, DC = Diners Club, MC = MasterCard, and VISA is self-explanatory.)

The Best Restaurants in the Washington Area

Type of Restaurant	Overall Rating	Price	Quality Rating	Value Rating
Afghani				
Panjshir	★★½	Inexpensive	79	A
Barbecue				
Old Glory	★★★	Moderate	83	B
Red Hot & Blue	★★½	Moderate	79	B
Brazilian				
Grill from Ipanema	★★½	Moderate	78	C
Cajun				
Louisiana Express	★★★	Inexpensive	80	A
Caribbean				
Fish, Wings & Tings	★★½	Inexpensive	79	B
Cafe Atlantico	★★½	Moderate	77	C
Chinese				
Seven Seas	★★★	Moderate	84	B
Tony Cheng's Mongolian	★★★	Inexpensive	83	A
Good Fortune	★★½	Inexpensive	79	B
Ethiopian				
Meskerem	★★★½	Inexpensive	89	B
Adulis	★★★½	Inexpensive	87	B
Zed's	★★½	Inexpensive	79	B
French/International				
Jean-Louis	★★★★★	Very expensive	98	B
Le Lion d'Or	★★★★	Expensive	92	C
Gerard's Place	★★★½	Expensive	89	C
Palladin	★★★	Moderate	84	C
Le Caprice	★★★	Expensive	83	C
La Colline	★★★	Moderate	82	A
German				
Wurzburg Haus	★★½	Moderate	79	B
Greek				
Mykonos	★★★½	Moderate	85	B
Indian				
Bombay Club	★★★½	Expensive	89	C
Aditi	★★★	Inexpensive	84	B
Bombay Bistro	★★½	Inexpensive	75	A

The Best Restaurants in the Washington Area (continued)

Type of Restaurant	Overall Rating	Price	Quality Rating	Value Rating
Indonesian				
Sabang	★★½	Inexpensive	75	B
Italian				
Galileo	★★★★★	Very expensive	98	C
i Ricchi	★★★★	Expensive	94	B
Obelisk	★★★½	Expensive	88	B
I Matti	★★★½	Moderate	88	B
Vincenzo	★★★	Expensive	84	C
Donna Adele	★★★	Expensive	83	C
Notte Luna	★★★	Moderate	81	C
Bice	★★½	Moderate	79	C
Japanese				
Tako Grill	★★★½	Moderate	89	B
Unkai	★★★½	Expensive	89	C
Tachibana	★★★	Moderate	84	B
Sushi Kappo Kawasaki	★★★	Expensive	82	D
Korean				
Sam Woo	★★★½	Moderate	85	B
Yokohama	★★★	Moderate	84	A
Woo Lae Oak	★★★	Moderate	82	A
Lebanese				
Lebanese Taverna	★★½	Moderate	79	B
Bacchus	★★	Moderate	73	B
New American				
Citronelle	★★★½	Expensive	88	C
Vidalia	★★★½	Moderate	87	B
Jefferson Hotel	★★★½	Expensive	86	B
Old Angler's Inn	★★★	Expensive	84	C
John Hay Room	★★★	Expensive	84	C
Nora	★★★	Moderate	82	C
1789	★★★	Expensive	82	C
Occidental Grill	★★★	Moderate	80	B
Market Street Grill	★★½	Moderate	79	C
Tabard Inn	★★½	Moderate	77	B
Cities	★★½	Moderate	77	C
701	★★½	Expensive	77	C
Capitol City Brewing Co.	★½	Moderate	67	B

The Best Restaurants in the Washington Area *(continued)*

Type of Restaurant	Overall Rating	Price	Quality Rating	Value Rating
New Southwest				
Red Sage	★★★★	Expensive	94	B
Santa Fe East	★★★	Moderate	84	B
Cottonwood Cafe	★★★	Expensive	82	B
Armadilla Grill	★★	Moderate	72	C
Pizza				
Pizzaria Paradiso	★★★	Inexpensive	83	A
Seafood				
Sea Catch	★★★	Moderate	84	B
Southern				
Georgia Brown	★★★½	Moderate	86	B
Dixie Grill	★½	Inexpensive	68	C
Spanish/South American				
Taberna del Alabardero	★★★½	Expensive	87	C
Terramar	★★★	Moderate	84	B
Jaleo	★★½	Moderate	79	C
Andalucia	★★½	Moderate	77	B
Las Pampas	★★½	Moderate	75	C
Steak				
Morton's of Chicago	★★★½	Very expensive	89	C
Prime Rib	★★★½	Expensive	88	B
Sam & Harry's	★★★½	Expensive	88	C
Tex-Mex/Central American				
El Patio	★★★	Moderate	84	C
Austin Grill	★★★	Inexpensive	82	A
Rio Grande	★★½	Moderate	78	C
Thai				
Busara	★★★½	Moderate	85	B
Duangrat	★★½	Moderate	79	C
Star of Siam	★★½	Inexpensive	75	A
Dusit	★★	Inexpensive	70	A
Turkish				
Nizam	★★	Moderate	72	B

The Best Restaurants in the Washington Area (continued)

Type of Restaurant	Overall Rating	Price	Quality Rating	Value Rating
Vietnamese				
Little Viet Garden	★★★	Inexpensive	84	A
Pho Cali/Quality Seafood	★★★	Inexpensive	82	A
Taste of Saigon	★★½	Moderate	79	A
Saigon Gourmet	★★½	Inexpensive	77	B

— More Recommendations

Here are a few quick recommendations for special interest groups:

The Best Bagels

Chesapeake Bagel Bakery   many area locations

Bagel City   12119 Rockville Pike, Rockville, Maryland (301) 231-8080

Bethesda Bagel   4819 Bethesda Avenue, Bethesda, Maryland (301) 652-8990

The Best Burgers

Clyde's   3236 M Street, NW (202) 333-9180; 8332 Leesburg Pike, Tysons Corner, Virginia (703) 734-1901; and Reston Town Center, Reston, Virginia (703) 787-6601

The Brickskeller   1523 22nd Street, NW (202) 293-1885

Old Ebbitt Grill   675 15th Street, NW (202) 347-4801

T-Bone's   7016 Wisconsin Avenue, Bethesda, Maryland (301) 652-8837

Brewbaker's   6931 Arlington Road, Bethesda, Maryland (301) 907-2602

Union Street Public House   121 South Union Street, Alexandria, Virginia (703) 548-1785

The Best Beer

The Brickskeller   1523 22nd Street, NW; (202) 293-1885

The Crow Bar   1006 20th Street, NW (202) 223-2972

The Big Hunt   1345 Connecticut Avenue, NW (202) 785-2333

Bardo   2000 Wilson Boulevard, Arlington, Virginia (703) 527-9399

Strangeways   2830 Wilson Boulevard, Arlington, Virginia (703) 243-5272

Galaxy Hut   2711 Wilson Boulevard, Arlington, Virginia (703) 525-8646

The Union Jack Pub   1733 N Street, NW (202) 393-3000

Royal Mile Pub   2407 Price Avenue, Wheaton, Maryland (301) 946-4511

Kangaroo Katie's   7511 Greenbelt Road, Greenbelt, Maryland (301) 474-9011

Hard Times Cafe   3028 Wilson Boulevard, Arlington, Virginia (703) 528-2233; 1404 King Street, Alexandria, Virginia (703) 683-5340; and Woodley Gardens Shopping Center, 1117 Nelson Street, Rockville, Maryland (301) 294-9720

Capitol City Brewing Co.   1100 New York Avenue, NW (11th and H streets) (202) 628-2222

The Best Single-Malt Scotch Collection

Washington Grill   New Hampshire Avenue and M Street, NW (202) 775-0800

Bullfeathers   410 1st Street, NW (202) 543-5005

Metro Centre Grill   775 12th Street, NW (202) 737-2200

The Best Afternoon Teas

Jefferson Hotel   1200 16th Street, NW (202) 347-2200

Henley Park Hotel   926 Massachusetts Avenue, NW (202) 638-5200

Four Seasons Hotel   2800 M Street, NW (202) 342-0444; and 1250 South Hayes Street, Arlington, Virginia (703) 415-5000

Hay-Adams Hotel   16th and H streets, NW (202) 638-6600

Ritz-Carlton Hotel   2100 Massachusetts Avenue, NW (202) 293-2100

The Best Sunday Brunches

The Kennedy Center Roof Terrace   Virginia and New Hampshire avenues, NW; (202) 416-8555

The Four Seasons Hotel Garden Terrace   2800 Pennsylvania Avenue, NW (202) 342-0840

Ploy   2218 Wisconsin Avenue, NW (202) 337-2324

Old Ebbitt Grill   675 15th Street, NW (202) 347-4801

ANA Hotel Colonnade   24th and M streets, NW (202) 457-5000

Normandie Farm Inn   10710 Falls Road, Potomac, Maryland (301) 983-8838

Clyde's   3236 M Street, NW (202) 333-9180; 8332 Leesburg Pike, Tysons Corner, Virginia (703) 734-1901

The Best Pizza

Pizzaria Paradiso   2029 P Street, NW (202) 223-1245

Soul Brothers Pizza   14th and U streets, NW (202) 387-7685

Zio's   9083 Gaither Road, Gaithersburg, Maryland (301) 977-6300

Faccia Luna   2400 Wisconsin Avenue, NW (202) 337-3132; and 2909 Wilson Boulevard, Arlington, Virginia (703) 276-3099

Primi Piatti   2013 I Street, NW (202) 223-3600; and 8045 Leesburg Pike, Tysons Corner, Virginia (703) 893-0300)

Pizza de Resistance   2300 Clarendon Boulevard, Arlington, Virginia (703) 351-5680

The Best Lunch Buffets

Sam Woo   1054 Rockville Pike, Rockville, Maryland (301) 424-0495

Bombay Bistro   98 West Montgomery Avenue, Rockville, Maryland (301) 762-8798

Allegro   Sheraton Carlton, 923 K Street, NW (202) 879-6900

Good Fortune 2646 University Boulevard West, Wheaton, Maryland (301) 929-8818

Fortune 5900 Leesburg Pike, Falls Church, Virginia (703) 998-8888

The Best Views

Sequoia 3000 K Street, NW (202) 944-4200

Hotel Washington Roof 515 15th Street, NW (202) 638-5000

Tony & Joe's 3000 K Street, NW (202) 944-4545

The Gangplank 600 Water Street, SW (202) 554-5000

The View Key Bridge Marriott, 1401 Lee Highway, Arlington, Virginia (703) 243-1740

New Heights 2317 Calvert Street, NW (202) 234-4110

The Chart House 1 Cameron Street, Alexandria, Virginia (703) 684-5080

The Best Bar Food or Appetizers

Citronelle Latham Hotel, 3000 M Street, NW (202) 625-2150

Red Sage 615 14th Street, NW (202) 638-4444

Cottonwood Cafe 4844 Cordell Avenue, Bethesda, Maryland (301) 656-4844

The Best Restaurant Rest Rooms

The Hay-Adams 1 Lafayette Square, NW (202) 638-6600

The Mayflower 1127 Connecticut Avenue, NW (202) 347-3000

Notte Luna 809 15th Street, NW (202) 408-9500

Red Sage 615 14th Street, NW (202) 638-9444

The Most Entertaining Decor

Filomena's 1063 Wisconsin Avenue, NW (202) 337-2782

Red Sage 615 14th Street, NW (202) 638-4444

Pizzaria Paradiso 2029 P Street, NW (202) 223-1245

Sfuzzi Union Station, Massachusetts Avenue and North Capitol Street (202) 842-4141

Notte Luna 809 15th Street, NW (202) 408-9500

The Best Wee-Hours Service

Au Pied du Cuchon 1329 Wisconsin Avenue, NW (202) 333-2333

Kramerbooks & Afterwords Cafe 1517 Connecticut Avenue, NW (202) 387-1462

Bistro Français 3128 M Street, NW (202) 338-3830

Soul Brothers Pizza 14th and U streets, NW (202) 387-7685

Zig-Zag Cafe 1524 U Street, NW (202) 986-5949

American City Diner 5532 Connecticut Avenue, NW (202) 244-1949

Tastee Diner 7731 Woodmont Avenue, Bethesda, Maryland (301) 652-3970; 8516 Georgia Avenue, Silver Spring, Maryland (301) 589-8171; and 10536 Lee Highway, Fairfax, Virginia (703) 591-6720

Amphora 377 Maple Avenue West, Vienna, Virginia (703) 938-7877

Sang Rok Su 2500 Columbia Pike, Arlington, Virginia (703) 920-2661

The Best Coffee

Zig-Zag Cafe 1524 U Street, NW (202) 986-5949

Puccini's 1620 L Street, NW (202) 223-1975

Dean & DeLuca 3276 M Street, NW (202) 342-2500

The Best Raw Bars

The Plutocrat 201 Massachusetts Avenue, NE (202) 547-9275

The Sea Catch 1054 31st Street, NW, rear (202) 337-8855

Georgetown Seafood Grill 3063 M Street, NW (202) 333-7038

The Best Sushi Bars

Tako Grill   7756 Wisconsin Avenue, Bethesda, Maryland (301) 652-7030

Unkai   1520 24th Street, NW (202) 466-2299

Ginza   1009 21st Street, NW (202) 833-1244

Tachibana   4050 Lee Highway, Arlington, Virginia (703) 528-1122

Atami   3155 Wilson Boulevard, Arlington, Virginia (703) 522-4787

Sakana   2026 P Street, NW (202) 887-0900

Matuba   2915 Columbia Pike, Arlington, Virginia (703) 521-2811; and 4918 Cordell Avenue, Bethesda, Maryland (301) 652-7449

Sushi-Ko   2309 Wisconsin Avenue, NW (202) 333-4187

Aditi

Quality	Value
84	B

Indian   ★★★   **Inexpensive**

3299 M Street, NW
(202) 625-6825

Georgetown   Zone 5

Reservations: Suggested
When to go: Anytime
Entree range: $4.95–13.95
Payment: VISA, MC, AMEX, DC, D
Service rating: ★★★
Friendliness rating: ★★★
Parking: Street
Bar: Full service
Wine selection: Fair
Dress: Business, casual, informal
Disabled access: No
Customers: Local, tourist, ethnic

Lunch: Tuesday–Saturday, 11:30 A.M.–2:30 P.M.; Sunday, noon–2:30 P.M.
Dinner: Sunday–Thursday, 5:30–10 P.M.; Friday and Saturday,
5:30–10:30 P.M.

Setting & atmosphere: To stretched nerves, Aditi offers the Arabian Nights hidden-courtyard effect: From the busy street, one enters through a white-washed brick exterior — sometimes with the flourish of a turbaned doorman — into a soothing, two-story burgundy and celadon den.

House specialties: Twice-cooked chicken Makhanwala, tandoori-roasted and then sauteed with tomatoes; spicy lamb vindaloo; vegetarian "meatballs."

Other recommendations: Pilaf; stir-fried lamb; okra curry; the $4.95 bread sampler.

Summary & comments: Since Aditi makes a point of substituting olive oil for the usual clarified butter, it can be said to serve the healthiest of samosas; since the kitchen knows about keeping the oil hot, it also serves some of the best and least greasy ones imaginable. The tandoori oven does fine service here as well.

Adulis

			Quality	Value
Ethiopian	★★★½	Inexpensive	87	B

2325 South Eads Street, Crystal City
(703) 920-3188

Virginia suburbs   Zone 11

Reservations: Accepted
When to go: Anytime
Entree range: $4–7.50
Payment: VISA, MC, AMEX, DC
Service rating: ★★★
Friendliness rating: ★★★
Parking: Small lot, street
Bar: Full service
Wine selection: House
Dress: Informal, casual
Disabled access: Good
Customers: Local, ethnic

Lunch & dinner: Sunday–Thursday, 11 A.M.–11 P.M.; Friday and Saturday, 11 A.M.–midnight

Setting & atmosphere: Simple but hospitable, with weavings and cooking utensils as decoration.

House specialties: Kitfo (beef tartare); cabbage and carrots aleicha; vegetarian samplers; red lentils.

Summary & comments: In too many Ethiopian kitchens (like old soul-food kitchens), pots of vegetables are left to stew too long and get mushy. Here, lentils, carrots, potatoes, and peas are all fully cooked but with texture and flavor undiminished. The kitfo is not only the best in town, meticulously chopped to a silky smoothness and slicked with a chili-spiked oil, it must be a loss leader — a huge mound for $4.50. And, for the faint of heart, it can be ordered cooked. For a further explanation of Ethiopian cuisine, see the listing for Meskerem.

Andalucia

Quality	Value
77	B

Spanish   ★★½   **Moderate**

12300 Wilkins Avenue, Rockville
(301) 770-1880

Maryland suburbs   Zone 10

Reservations: Recommended
When to go: Anytime
Entree range: $11.50–17
Payment: VISA, MC, AMEX, D
Service rating: ★★★
Friendliness rating: ★★★½
Parking: Lot, street
Bar: Full service
Wine selection: Fair
Dress: Informal, casual
Disabled access: Good
Customers: Local, ethnic

Lunch: Tuesday–Friday, 11 A.M.–2:30 P.M.
Dinner: Tuesday–Friday, 5:30–10 P.M.; Saturday, 5:30–10:30 P.M.;
Sunday, 4–9:30 P.M. Closed Monday.

Setting & atmosphere: This unassuming storefront in a semi-industrial ware-house/office park has only travel poster art and sentiment to dress it; it's Spanish family style.

House specialties: Paella and zarzuela, a Spanish bouillabaisse; whole red snapper on rock salt.

Other recommendations: Listen to the daily specials, often as many as 8 or 10, often featuring veal sirloin with dry sherry and fresh seafood such as grouper with lobster sauce and smoky grilled squid on roasted sweet peppers.

Entertainment & amenities: A classical/flamenco guitarist provides background music weeknights.

Summary & comments: This southern Spanish restaurant is more Mediterranean than "Latin," more tomato and onion sauce than salsa, and it has a modern penchant for lightly cooked seafood. This is family style cooking, but Sunday dinner quality; the many bilingual family groups prove it. A second branch has just opened in Bethesda.

Armadilla Grill

Southwestern/Native American ★★ Moderate

Quality	Value
72	C

8011 Woodmont Avenue, Bethesda
(301) 907-9637

Maryland suburbs   Zone 10

14201 Sullyfield Circle, Chantilly
(703) 631-9332

Virginia suburbs   Zone 11

Reservations: Recommended
on weekends
When to go: Anytime
Entree range: $6.95–18.95
Payment: VISA, MC, AMEX
Service rating: ★★★
Friendliness rating: ★★★★
Parking: Meters, street (Bethesda);
free lot (Chantilly)
Bar: Full service
Wine selection: House
Dress: Informal, casual
Disabled access: No
Customers: Local

Dinner: Sunday, Tuesday–Thursday, 5–10 P.M.; Friday and Saturday,
5–11 P.M. Monday, closed (Bethesda). Sunday, closed (Chantilly).

Setting & atmosphere: Pueblo-influenced, with stepped terracotta walls,
Navajo blanket–patterned tablecloths, and a rough-mantel fireplace in the
lounge. Native American artifacts and animal skulls on the walls.

House specialties: "Navajo nachos," an Indian fry bread pizza topped with
smoky grilled chicken and guacamole; chicken and green chili stew; and daily
Native American specials such as red bean and lamb stew.

Other recommendations: The smell of mesquite smoke is its own advertisement: the fajitas are excellent. For beer drinkers, Armadilla has some unusual
microbrews and its own locally produced ale and lager on tap. The Bethesda
bartender, "Bear," makes the best margaritas north of Mexico, one at a time.

Entertainment & amenities: The lightest, crispest tortilla chips and the
freshest, chunkiest salsa around are complimentary appetizers.

Summary & comments: This is a back-to-authentics cantina rather than a
hoity-toity Southwest "experience." The attempt to update indigenous dishes is
intriguing, even if unlikely to spark a host of imitators. The food is certainly
hearty, and the adjustable chili level suits everyone's taste.

Austin Grill

Tex-Mex ★★★ **Inexpensive**

Quality	Value
82	A

2404 Wisconsin Avenue, NW
(202) 337-8080

Georgetown   Zone 5

801 King Street, Alexandria
(703) 684-8969

Virginia suburbs   Zone 11

Reservations: Not accepted
When to go: Late afternoon, late night
Entree range: $4.25–11.95
Payment: VISA, MC, AMEX, D, DC
Service rating: ★★★
Friendliness rating: ★★★
Parking: Street
Bar: Full service
Wine selection: Fair
Dress: Casual
Disabled access: Alexandria only
Customers: Local, student

Lunch & dinner: Tuesday–Thursday, 11:30 A.M.–11 P.M.; Friday and Saturday, 11:30 A.M.–midnight; Sunday and Monday, 11:30 A.M.–10 P.M.
Dinner: Monday, 5:30–10:30 P.M. (Washington only)

Setting & atmosphere: Hot adobe pastels, angular art-joke graphics, and Tex-Mex pun art and T-shirts in a funky vinyl-booth roadhouse setting. Great Texas music on the PA.

House specialties: Quesadillas with chorizo or crabmeat; green and red salsas; "Austin special enchilada" with three sauces; chopped all-meat chili (beef or chicken); grilled chili-rubbed shrimp and scallops; grilled fish; pork loin enchilada with mole sauce.

Other recommendations: Margaritas; fajitas; huevos rancheros.

Summary & comments: The perfect antidote for designer chili cuisine. The original Georgetown branch made its first friends just from the smell of the smoker out back. Some runners swear by the hot-hot sauce—it gets their endorphins going.

Bacchus

					Quality	Value
Lebanese		★★		**Moderate**	**73**	**B**

1827 Jefferson Street, NW
(202) 785-0734 Dupont Circle/Adams-Morgan Zone 6

7945 Norfolk Avenue, Bethesda
(301) 657-1722 Maryland suburbs Zone 10

Reservations: Suggested
When to go: Anytime
Entree range: $11.25–14.75
Payment: VISA, MC, AMEX
Service rating: ★★½
Friendliness rating: ★★
Parking: Street; valet (Bethesda)
Bar: Full service
Wine selection: Brief
Dress: Informal, casual
Disabled access: Jefferson Street,
no; Norfolk Avenue, good
Customers: Local, business

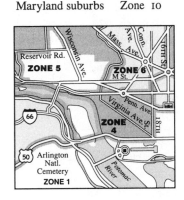

Lunch: Monday–Friday, noon–2:30 P.M.
Dinner: Monday–Thursday, 5–10 P.M.; Friday and Saturday, 6–10:30 P.M.;
Sunday, 6–10 P.M. (Bethesda only; downtown closed)

Setting & atmosphere: The D.C. location is a simple, pleasantly crowded English basement downtown; in Bethesda, it's a villa with carved screens, whitewashed walls, and more leisurely atmosphere.

House specialties: Mezza, a platter of two-bite appetizers served simultaneously, including stuffed phyllo turnovers of spinach or cheese; kibbeh, a steak tartare with cracked wheat; zucchini pancakes; grilled sausages; stuffed eggplant; stuffed grape leaves, etc.

Other recommendations: Fried smelts; fatayer bel sbanegh, a spinach and coriander pastry; stuffed cabbage with pomegranate sauce; kebabs; hummus topped with ground lamb.

Summary & comments: For whatever reason, the Bethesda location is more consistent, and the food just a little sprightlier; but appetizers in particular are always good at both sites. The Washington location has no separate nonsmoking section.

Bice

Italian   ★★½   **Moderate**

Quality	Value
79	C

601 Pennsylvania Avenue, NW (entrance on Indiana Avenue)
(202) 638-2423   Downtown   Zone 3

Reservations: Recommended
When to go: Anytime
Entree range: $10–21
Payment: VISA, MC, AMEX, DC
Service rating: ★★½
Friendliness rating: ★★
Parking: Valet
Bar: Full service
Wine selection: Good
Dress: Dressy, business
Disabled access: Good
Customers: Local, business

Lunch: Monday–Friday, 11:30 A.M.–3 P.M.
Dinner: Sunday–Thursday, 5:30–10 P.M.; Friday and Saturday,
5:30–11:30 P.M.

Setting & atmosphere: Pleasantly restrained, with a woody, clubby bar and a bright, airy dining room hung with what looks like cleverly framed wallpaper samples.

House specialties: Smoked duck; steamed bass; seafood risotto; roast duck with duck confit; beef and fish carpaccio; ravioli stuffed with duck, beets and turnips, or mushrooms.

Other recommendations: Grilled salmon; sausage with cannelini; veal ragout; pappardelle with duck and lentils.

Summary & comments: Although this Italian restaurant can be one of the town's best, it has grown sloppy and, worse, occasionally surly. Risottos are creamy and transporting one day, cobby the next. A tagliolini with shrimp, asparagus, and fresh tomatoes arrives with nary an asparagus tip in sight. The basket of foccacia is wonderful—if you get it. And the question of ordering mineral water vs. tap gets an extra and unpleasant twist here: Choosing mineral water means getting the whole bottle, and for $5. (There is a note on the menu, but the question of water is usually posed before you've had a chance to see it.) Still, on a day when the fish is tender and the pasta sleek, Bice is hard not to like.

Bombay Bistro

			Quality	Value
Indian	★★½	Inexpensive	**75**	**A**

98 West Montgomery Avenue, Rockville
(301) 762-8798   Maryland suburbs   Zone 10

Reservations: Not accepted
When to go: Anytime
Entree range: $4.95–9.95
Payment: VISA, MC
Service rating: ★★★
Friendliness rating: ★★★
Parking: Free lot
Bar: Beer and wine
Wine selection: House
Dress: Casual
Disabled access: Limited
Customers: Local, ethnic, business

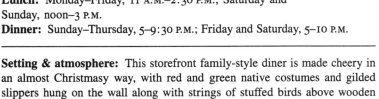

Lunch: Monday–Friday, 11 A.M.–2:30 P.M.; Saturday and Sunday, noon–3 P.M.
Dinner: Sunday–Thursday, 5–9:30 P.M.; Friday and Saturday, 5–10 P.M.

Setting & atmosphere: This storefront family-style diner is made cheery in an almost Christmasy way, with red and green native costumes and gilded slippers hung on the wall along with strings of stuffed birds above wooden booths. The kitchen and staff are visible down the length of one wall.

House specialties: Tandoori chicken; el maru, a bowlful of rice and crispy noodles with a texture between granola and trail mix; mulligatawny soup; baingan bhartha (tandoori eggplant); roasted vegetables; mild chicken tikka or spicy chicken madras; oothapam, a South India "crepe" of lentil and rice dough stuffed with onions, tomatoes, and green peppers.

Other recommendations: Lamb rogan josh or shish kebab; chicken or vegetable biriyani; beef badam pasanda, an almond-spiked stew; a sampler platter with chicken tikka, rogan josh, cucumber raita, puri, lentils, and spinach or eggplant.

Summary & comments: Located among the lawyers' warrens of historic Rockville, this squeeze-'em-in eatery started out as an Indians' Indian lunch-spot, but the word leaked out. Nowdays, you may have to wait for a table at dinner, which is the second good reason to go for the all-you-can-eat lunch-time buffet. The first good reason is the price: $5.95 on weekdays and $7.95 on weekends.

Bombay Club

Indian ★★★½ **Expensive**

Quality	Value
89	C

815 Connecticut Avenue, NW
(202) 659-3727   Downtown   Zone 3

Reservations: Recommended
When to go: Anytime
Entree range: $6.95–18.50
Payment: VISA, MC, AMEX, DC
Service rating: ★★★½
Friendliness rating: ★★★★
Parking: Valet
Bar: Full service
Wine selection: Very good
Dress: Jacket and tie suggested
Disabled access: Good
Customers: Local, business, ethnic

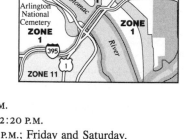

Brunch: Sunday, 11:30 A.M.–2:30 P.M.
Lunch: Monday–Friday, 11:30 A.M.–2:20 P.M.
Dinner: Monday–Thursday, 6–10:30 P.M.; Friday and Saturday,
6–11 P.M.; Sunday, 5:30–9 P.M.

Setting & atmosphere: British officers' club decor, with pale salmon and aquamarine walls, giant palms, ceiling fans, and shutters; a dark wood lounge to one side; and a conservatory-style piano bar in the front.

House specialties: Tandoori-marinated and roasted salmon; grilled scallops; honey-marinated chicken; mustard greens; lamb curried with dried apricots; lobster.

Other recommendations: Lamb curry; okra curry; fried fish with poppy seeds; grilled eggplant. Vegetarian dishes are available in full or appetizer portions. A sampler of dishes called a "thali" is a good introduction.

Entertainment & amenities: Piano-bar entertainment at happy hour.

Summary & comments: The nice distinction this kitchen brings to its myriad breads, vegetable dishes, and particularly its seafood sets it apart from typical curry houses; the flavors are unusually clean and engrossing. The chili-fired chicken is as hot as advertised but salt-free, for a pleasant change.

Busara

Thai ★★★½ **Moderate**

Quality	Value
85	B

2340 Wisconsin Avenue, NW
(202) 337-2340

Georgetown   Zone 5

Reservations: Recommended
When to go: Before 7:30 or after 9:30
Entree range: $6.95–15.95
Payment: VISA, MC, AMEX, DC, CB
Service rating: ★★★½
Friendliness rating: ★★★
Parking: Valet
Bar: Full service
Wine selection: Fair
Dress: Informal
Disabled access: No
Customers: Local, ethnic

Lunch: Monday–Friday, 11 A.M.–3 P.M.; Saturday and Sunday, 11:30 A.M.–4 P.M.
Dinner: Sunday–Thursday, 5–11 P.M.; Friday and Saturday, 5 P.M.–midnight

Setting & atmosphere: This Thai spot is aggressively and cheekily modern. The decor of molded hard black rubber, brushed steel, slate and heavily lacquered flame-streaked tabletops looks as if it was created by a former hot rod customizer—not to mention the ice blue neon overhead (the word "busara" means "blue topaz"), and post-pop art. Outside a partially covered patio curves around a miniature, but elegant, Japanese garden with fountain.

House specialties: Rice-fattened eesan sausage with pork and cabbage; roasted quail with asparagus and oyster sauce; cellophane noodles with three kinds of mushrooms; filet of sea trout with salmon mousse served on a banana leaf; marinated pork sate with both a tomato-peanut sauce and a chili-spiked vinegar dip; duck in red curry; Thai bouillabaise in coconut milk.

Other recommendations: Tiger shrimp grilled over watercress; vegetarian pad thai; soft-shell crabs and whole flounder; lobster tail in white pepper.

Entertainment & amenities: Live jazz in the new upstairs bar suite, Wednesday through Saturday.

Summary & comments: This is a Siamese grin of a joint with the emphasis on presentation as much as preparation and a lightened-up attitude toward greens and veggies that makes them crisp and filling. A wide variety of spicing is represented (the chili-pod symbols next to menu items are fairly reliable for gauging heat) and extra sauces or peppers are easy to obtain.

Cafe Atlantico

			Quality	Value
Caribbean	★★½	Moderate	77	C

1819 Columbia Road, NW
(202) 328-5844   Dupont Circle/Adams-Morgan   Zone 6

Reservations: Not accepted
When to go: Early or late
Entree range: $9.25–12.95
Payment: VISA, MC, AMEX, DC
Service rating: ★★★
Friendliness rating: ★★★½
Parking: Valet
Bar: Full service
Wine selection: Minimal
Dress: Casual
Disabled access: Fair
Customers: Local, embassy

Dinner: Sunday–Thursday, 5:30–10 P.M.; Friday and Saturday, 5:30 P.M.–midnight

Setting & atmosphere: Crowded but friendly new-age black-and-glass cafe that suggests a curio cabinet—or an international supper club, especially on weekend nights, when the tables pull back for Latin dancing.

House specialties: "Jerk" red snapper, rubbed with the Caribbean pepper paste; a rum-spiked lamb curry with tomato and coconut; codfish fritters with chili dip; seared marinated flank steak.

Other recommendations: Grilled mixed seafood; sausage and pickled greens; pork glazed with rum and brown sugar; escabeche (marinated fish, like a Caribbean seviche).

Entertainment & amenities: Complimentary biscuits called "bakes," redolent of pepper and served with a black bean spread.

Summary & comments: This is a cheery, uncomplicated little kitchen that starts well—with the caipirinhas and appetizers—and keeps up the fun.

Capitol City Brewing Co.

Quality	Value
67	B

New American ★½ **Moderate**

1100 New York Avenue, NW (enter at 11th and H streets)
(202) 628-2222   Downtown   Zone 3

Reservations: Not accepted
When to go: Anytime
Entree range: $5.25–22.95
Payment: VISA, MC, AMEX
Service rating: ★★★
Friendliness rating: ★★★½
Parking: Pay lots, meters
Bar: Full service
Wine selection: Limited
Dress: Business, informal, casual
Disabled access: Good
Customers: Local, tourist, business

Open: Monday–Saturday, 11–2 A.M.; Sunday, 11 A.M.–midnight

Setting & atmosphere: Half renovated warehouse, half fantasy diner, with booths, red vinyl revolving stools, painted murals of imaginary beerworks, and sacks of hops and malt lying about; good CD jukebox.

House specialties: Sausages of the day, available in a three-pack; pork chops in a red wine sauce with pineapple chutney; grilled salmon and chicken; miniribs.

Other recommendations: Hamburger; mildly spicy shrimp.

Entertainment & amenities: Baskets of freshly baked hard and soft pretzels.

Summary & comments: This is as much singles bar and convention-center hangout as brewpub, as suggested by the remarkably comprehensive liquor bar in the center of the room. The kitchen features heartily conceived but not always carefully executed food; except perhaps for the sausages, the more straightforward the choice the better. Both the on-site brews—generally a couple of ales, a porter, a stout, and a lager—and the available microbrews from elsewhere are of increasingly reliable quality.

Le Caprice

		Quality	Value
French	★★★ Expensive	**83**	**C**

2348 Wisconsin Avenue, NW
(202) 337-3394   Georgetown   Zone 5

Reservations: Recommended
When to go: Anytime
Entree range: $13.50–22
Payment: VISA, MC, AMEX, DC
Service rating: ★★★
Friendliness rating: ★★★
Parking: Valet
Bar: Full service
Wine selection: Good
Dress: Dressy or informal
Disabled access: No
Customers: Local

Lunch: Tuesday–Friday, 11:45 A.M.–2 P.M.
Dinner: Tuesday–Thursday, 6–10 P.M.; Friday and Saturday, 6–10:30 P.M.;
Sunday, 6–9:30 P.M. Closed Monday.

Setting & atmosphere: A tiny, two-story town house whose rooms suggest the parlors of a small comfy pension; in good weather tables are set on the front terrace.

House specialties: Alsatian-influenced French farm classics, notably the choucroute of sausages, smoked pork, and duck confit with fermented turnips in place of the usual sauerkraut; elegant pastry crusts over chicken dishes; puff pastry toques over crab-stuffed artichoke bottoms; smoked fish thinly sliced into salads; country-estate versions of game such as rolled leg and saddle of rabbit stuffed with rabbit mousse and served over braised cabbage; a bacon-stuffed venison roll braised in red wine.

Other recommendations: Puff pastry again, in a salmon tartare and mousse "napoleon"; daily fish specials; beef tenderloin poached in bouillion.

Summary & comments: This is one place where simplicity is not always a virtue, since the "ordinary" dishes seem to be handled by the kitchen staff while chef-owner Edmond Foltzenlogel is caught up in the more demanding entrees; thus, plain, fresh asparagus can be overcooked and salads sometimes over-dressed. Foltzenlogel's talents prevail, however, with silken quiche-custard tarts the size of butter pats served as complimentary appetizers; and again, the more unusual the creation, the more attention it receives. Le Caprice offers two fixed-price dinners each evening: a set, almost homey, three-course menu for $18.50 and a fancier four-course presentation, with some choices, for $29.50.

			Quality	Value
New American	★★½	Moderate	**77**	**C**

2424 18th Street, NW
(202) 328-7194   Dupont Circle/Adams-Morgan   Zone 6

Reservations: Recommended
When to go: Anytime
Entree range: $12.95–21.95
Payment: VISA, MC, AMEX, DC
Service rating: ★★½
Friendliness rating: ★★★
Parking: Street; valet, weekends
Bar: Full service
Wine selection: Fair
Dress: Informal, casual
Disabled access: Good
Customers: Local

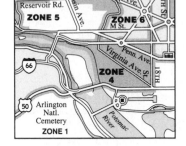

Brunch: Sunday, 11 A.M.–3:30 P.M.
Lunch & dinner: Saturday, 2–11:30 P.M.; Sunday, 11 A.M.–10 P.M.
Dinner: Monday–Thursday, 6–11 P.M.; Friday and Saturday, 6–11:30 P.M.; Sunday, 6–10 P.M.

Setting & atmosphere: The decor changes in the main dining room according to the cuisine of the times; the front room, a casual dining room/bar, is a re-creation of an auto service garage, with rising glass portals, a concrete slab bar, hubcaps suspended in air, and a wood grill in the rear like a pig iron melter.

House specialties: Pizzas, usually a half-dozen choices from $10 to $12; grilled rabbit sausage with cabbage confit; smoked duck ravioli with artichokes; sauteed rapini and feta over crostini; veal pappardelle; free-range chicken with mushroom-stuffed skin.

Other recommendations: Risotto (a little heavy on the parmesan); grilled meats or seafoods; seafood-stuffed poblanos.

Summary & comments: Chef Mary Richter may be the second most restless mind (after Jean-Louis Palladin) in a Washington kitchen; she changes the entire theme, decor and cuisine, of her restaurant every several months, saluting various capitals of the world. Cities has been Russian, Sicilian, French, Mexican, Thai, and Turkish; most recently she repatriated temporarily for a go at Los Angeles cuisine.

Citronelle

New American   ★★★½   **Expensive**

Quality	Value
88	C

3000 M Street, NW (Latham Hotel)
(202) 625-2150   Georgetown   Zone 5

Reservations: Recommended
When to go: Lunch, before 9
Entree range: $19–26
Payment: VISA, MC, AMEX
Service rating: ★★★★
Friendliness rating: ★★★½
Parking: Valet
Bar: Full service
Wine selection: Good
Dress: Business, dressy, informal
Disabled access: Excellent
Customers: Local, tourist, business

Lunch: Sunday–Saturday, 11:30 A.M.–2 P.M.
Dinner: Sunday–Thursday, 6–10 P.M.; Friday and Saturday, 5:30–10:30 P.M.

Setting & atmosphere: Using a series of small level shifts and cutaway ceilings, the designers of this pretty but not showy establishment have made the space seem both intimate and expansive. The upstairs lounge is classic flannel gray and green; the downstairs rooms have a conservatory touch, with dark green wicker armchairs, glass accent doors, and blessedly simple greenery. The star attraction is the kitchen — glass-fronted and almost fully visible — as are the six chefs, two preppers, and salad chef.

House specialties: Appetizers: White tuna carpaccio (actually yellowtail) with ginger vinaigrette; luxuriant sauteed fois gras with chanterelles; creamy crab coleslaw wrapped in savoy cabbage; crab cannelloni. Entrees: Roasted lobster; veal chop with mini–goat cheese ravioli; grilled swordfish; ribeye; rare tuna chateaubriand; rack of lamb.

Other recommendations: Wild mushroom napoleon; shrimp with red slaw.

Summary & comments: It's tempting to pass up the entrees and load up on appetizers, which, at between $8 and $14 (for the fois gras, a truly generous portion), make more of a meal for the money. "Cannelloni" is actually a crabmeat terrine rolled in a broad noodle canopy-striped with saffron and squid ink. Simple grilled swordfish is made memorable by a wreath of angelhair-fine potato crisps and a bed of lentils; the peony of transparently sliced yellowtail lies on a painted bed of sauce and under a garnish of seaweed and baby endive.

La Colline

	Quality	Value
French ★★★ **Moderate**	**82**	**A**

400 North Capitol Street
(202) 737-0400   Capitol Hill   Zone 2

Reservations: Recommended
When to go: Anytime
Entree range: $16.50–21.95
Payment: VISA, MC, AMEX,
CB, DC
Service rating: ★★★★
Friendliness rating: ★★★★
Parking: Street, validation after 5
Bar: Full service
Wine selection: Good
Dress: Business, dressy, casual
Disabled access: Good
Customers: Business, local, tourist

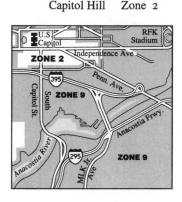

Breakfast: Monday–Friday, 7–10 A.M.
Lunch: Monday–Friday, 11:30 A.M.–3 P.M.
Dinner: Monday–Saturday, 6–10 P.M. Closed Sunday and holidays.

Setting & atmosphere: An unfussy, conference-style reception room at one side is the only concession to the office-building shoebox exterior; the main dining room is large, two-tiered, and made less "executive" with nostalgic paintings and French country-kitchen cupboards.

House specialties: Foie gras and homemade pâté; shellfish risottos; cassoulet; sweetbreads and tripe; cool lobster salad; lamb shanks; seafood stews.

Other recommendations: Homemade sausages, usually lamb or seafood; calves' liver; herb-dressed swordfish; simple trout or sole meunière.

Summary & comments: La Colline manages to serve old-homey French food in such quantity (and with such hospitable style) that you'd expect the quality to fall off, but somehow it never does. The quantity of business this Senate-side favorite does also keeps the prices steady; the greatest bargain around is the nightly three-course dinner for $17.50. Presentation is simple and untrendy, but exact; salmon or swordfish steaks on beds of vermouth-flavored sauce, sweetbreads bull's-eyed over concentric circles of bordelaise and herb wine deglazings. Game dishes and rowdy, hearty stews, along with the organ meats most Americans are still only discovering, are always good bets.

Cottonwood Cafe

New Southwestern   ★★★   Expensive

Quality	Value
82	B

4844 Cordell Avenue, Bethesda
(301) 656-4844   Maryland suburbs   Zone 10

Reservations: Recommended
When to go: Anytime
Entree range: $12.65–19.25
Payment: VISA, MC, AMEX
Service rating: ★★★
Friendliness rating: ★★★
Parking: Valet
Bar: Full service
Wine selection: Fair
Dress: Informal, business
Disabled access: Good
Customers: Local, business

Lunch & dinner: Monday–Thursday, 11 A.M.–10 P.M.; Friday and Saturday, 11 A.M.–11 P.M.; Sunday, 5:30–10 P.M.

Setting & atmosphere: A very pretty, jewel-toned bow to the American Southwest, with terracotta walls, murals of pueblos, wall sconces like mood rings, a few artifacts, and wrought-iron salamander door pulls, and a staff uniformed in turquoise and amethyst shirts with bolos and boots.

House specialties: "Rattlesnake bites," jalapenos stuffed with baked shrimp and cheese; blue cornmeal–crusted calamari with tomato chili glaze; a Southwest-style paella with sun-dried Indian corn and black beans amongst the shellfish; smoked pork loin stuffed with shiitakes, spinach, and asiago cheese.

Other recommendations: Chili sausage and shrimp tossed with black pepper pasta, sun-dried tomatoes and shiitakes; shrimp, sweet potato, and spinach folded into a tortilla and quick-fried.

Entertainment & amenities: Cottonwood has built-in entertainment—owner J. J. Fletcher's stories of rodeo life (he's a former champ), Navy SEAL adventures (he's one of those, too), and life in general.

Summary & comments: Under its new chef, Cottonwood has pared away its few flaws—a little too much salt, a little too much cream—and developed a sharper, cleaner style. Spice is enticing, though the staff can guide you through the various degrees. The wine list is all-American.

Dixie Grill

Quality	Value
68	**C**

Southern   ★½   **Inexpensive**

518 10th Street, NW
(202) 628-4800

Downtown   Zone 3

Reservations: Accepted for six
or more
When to go: Anytime
Entree range: $7–10.75
Payment: VISA, MC, AMEX, DC
Service rating: ★★★
Friendliness rating: ★★★
Parking: Pay garage
Bar: Full service
Wine selection: House
Dress: Business, informal
Disabled access: Good
Customers: Local, tourist

Lunch & dinner: Monday–Friday, 11 A.M.–1:30 A.M.; Saturday, noon–
1:30 A.M.; Sunday, noon–10 P.M.

Setting & atmosphere: Both Washington and Southern insiders' joke on Southern culture on the cute edge: part pool hall, part family diner, and at least when it comes to cold drinks, a real dust-quenching bit of nostalgia: It stocks about 20 Southern soft drinks, from NuGrape and RC (say "ar-uh-sea") cola to HOKO and Barq's Root Beer.

House specialties: Catfish fingers in cornmeal; red beans & rice (known as "the poor man's dinner"); chicken-fried steak.

Other recommendations: Fried okra (in little scrambled-up bites, not whole as in Jamaican kitchens); milk-fried chicken; corn pudding.

Summary & comments: This is truly Washington as Hollywood-on-the-Potomac: One owner is a former Touchstone Pictures veep, the other is a partner in the city's most successful chain of semi-disposable beer bars, and the original chef grew up in Mississippi, trained in France, and was a personal chef in L.A. The decor is even Hollywood's version of an Arkansas power joint—with hillbilly music posters, transplated barn siding, half a chassis from one of Rusty Miller's stock cars going head-to-head with a T. Rex. And the minipool hall upstairs has just the right musical touch: an all-southern CD jukebox. Now if they could just find a Confederate soldier monument and a single traffic light.

Donna Adele

	Quality	Value
Italian ★★★ **Expensive**	**83**	**C**

2100 P Street, NW
(202) 296-1142   Dupont Circle/Adams-Morgan   Zone 6

Reservations: Recommended
When to go: Anytime
Entree range: $13.95–28.95
Payment: VISA, MC, AMEX, DC
Service rating: ★★★½
Friendliness rating: ★★★½
Parking: Validated
Bar: Full service
Wine selection: Good
Dress: Business, dressy
Disabled access: No
Customers: Local, business

Lunch & dinner: Monday–Thursday, 11:30 A.M.–10:30 P.M.; Friday, 11:30–11 P.M.; Saturday, 5:30–11 P.M.; Sunday, 5:30–9:30 P.M.

Setting & atmosphere: The outer room of this pretty little restaurant is a glass-enclosed brick terrace with a view of the busy Dupont Circle sidewalk; inside, a modestly elegant gray room offers only its stores of wine and copper-bottomed saucepans as distractions from the food.

House specialties: Grilled rib of veal with wild mushrooms; sweetbreads with spinach and pancetta; a mole-style grilled pork loin with a balsamic vinegar and chocolate sauce; linguini with strips of swordfish, green olives, and capers; pasta stuffed with eggplant and basil; and basil pasta with scallops or smoked trout.

Other recommendations: Grilled fish (usually six to eight choices); saffron fettucini with veal sauce; appetizers of fresh marinated anchovies or grilled eggplant; rabbit whenever offered.

Summary & comments: Chef Enzo Fargione worked for several years for Roberto Donna, and it shows; his light but not reticent saucing of pastas and his grilling of fresh fish are first rate, although his combinations are a little less arresting.

Duangrat

Thai ★★½ **Moderate**

Quality	Value
79	C

5878 Leesburg Pike, Falls Church
(703) 820-5775   Virginia suburbs   Zone 11

Reservations: Helpful
When to go: Anytime
Entree range: $6.95–19.95
Payment: VISA, MC, AMEX, CB
Service rating: ★★★½
Friendliness rating: ★★★
Parking: Free lot
Bar: Full service
Wine selection: Limited
Dress: Informal, casual
Disabled access: Fair
Customers: Locals

Lunch: Monday–Friday, 11:30 A.M.–2:30 P.M.; Saturday and Sunday, 11:30 A.M.–4 P.M.
Dinner: Monday–Thursday, 5–10:30 P.M.; Friday, 5–11 P.M.; Saturday, 4–11 P.M.; Sunday, 4–10:30 P.M.

Setting & atmosphere: A delicate European, almost deco-style restaurant, especially in the upstairs dining room with its pink linens, curio cabinets, and black and gray sconces. Waitresses in their bright silk costumes seem to match the floral arrangements.

House specialties: Whole fish with basil and chilis; charbroiled fish wrapped in banana leaves; chili-marinated squid and shrimp salads; ground peanut curries with coconut milk.

Other recommendations: Seafood dishes, particularly the mixed seafood over rice noodles, which includes soft-shell crabs in season; pork dishes; quail in white rather than the usual black pepper.

Entertainment & amenities: On Friday and Saturday evenings, dancers perform traditional Thai dances in full costume; it's free, but make reservations specifically for upstairs.

Summary & comments: This kitchen bows to the French influence, further restrained by suburban tastes — even its spicy dishes lack some of the bite and variety some of the newer Thai establishments offer — and it isn't as generous with portions as some; but it has a consistently reliable quality and often exquisite presentation. Exploring its hybrid style even further, the management has opened an assertively French-Thai spot, Le Chef d'Oeuvre, next door.

Dusit

Quality	Value
70	A

Thai ★★ **Inexpensive**

2404 University Boulevard West, Wheaton
(301) 949-4140   Maryland suburbs   Zone 10

Reservations: Accepted
When to go: Anytime
Entree range: $5.95–10.95
Payment: VISA, MC, AMEX
Service rating: ★★★
Friendliness rating: ★★½
Parking: Small lot, street
Bar: Full service
Wine selection: House
Dress: Casual
Disabled access: Limited
Customers: Local, ethnic

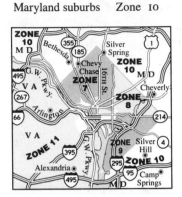

Lunch & dinner: Sunday–Thursday, 11:30 A.M.–10 P.M.; Friday and Saturday, 11:30 A.M.–11 P.M.

Setting & atmosphere: This otherwise plain mauve-and-lilac room is enlivened by a few splashes of neon; a small shrine hoisted on the rear wall gazes benignly out over the customers.

House specialties: Marinated shrimp, butterflied raw and topped with peppers and garlic; crab and potato "puffs" (more like empanadas); squid with white pepper; twice-cooked duck; crispy whole flounder with pork and black bean sauce.

Other recommendations: Squid with basil; red (sweet) curried pork; diced duck roll; stir-fried crabs in black bean sauce.

Summary & comments: This is a deceptively modest restaurant, with 20 appetizers and more than 80 entrees that run from mild to spanky, though none is blistering. Dishes are simple, too, almost purist, without so much of the onion and vegetable stretchers common to many Asian kitchens. There are four types of curries here, all good: green, red, Panang-style, and country-style, without coconut milk.

Fish, Wings & Tings

			Quality	Value
Caribbean	★★½	Inexpensive	**79**	**B**

3400 K Street, NW
(202) 338-0408   Georgetown   Zone 5

2418 18th Street, NW
(202) 234-0322   Dupont Circle/Adams-Morgan   Zone 6

Reservations: Not accepted
When to go: Anytime
Entree range: $4.50–8.50
Payment: VISA, MC, AMEX
Service rating: ★★★
Friendliness rating: ★★★
Parking: Street
Bar: Beer and wine
Wine selection: None
Dress: Casual
Disabled access: Fair
Customers: Locals, international

Lunch & dinner: Tuesday–Thursday, noon–10 P.M.; Friday and Saturday, noon–11 P.M. Closed Sunday and Monday.

Setting & atmosphere: As cheerfully funky as a real Jamaican roadside cafe, all primary colors and indoor-outdoor plastic chairs; but hipped up with glass bricks.

House specialties: Jerk chicken thighs; oxtail stew; goat curry. Extra hot sauce available for calloused palates.

Other recommendations: Grilled fish, especially mackerel or snapper; vinegar-dipped fried fish; sometimes creoles; homemade ginger beer.

Summary & comments: The menu changes a bit every day, mostly depending on the choices of fish and curry meat available; the jerk chicken here is a legend, but many people prefer the sweeter pineapple wings. There is a mixed-veggie curry as well that is popular among PC neighbors. The Georgetown branch, also known as the Hibiscus Cafe, has a broader menu and even funkier design.

Galileo

Quality	Value
98	**A**

Italian ★★★★★ **Very expensive**

1110 19th Street, NW
(202) 293-7191   Dupont Circle/Adams-Morgan   Zone 6

Reservations: A must
When to go: Anytime
Entree range: $16.95–32.95
Payment: VISA, MC, AMEX, CB, DC, D
Service rating: ★★★★
Friendliness rating: ★★★½
Parking: Valet (except Sunday)
Bar: Full service
Wine selection: Excellent
Dress: Dressy, business
Disabled access: Good
Customers: Local, tourist, business, gourmet mag groupies

Lunch: Monday–Friday, 11:30 A.M.–2 P.M.
Dinner: Monday–Thursday, 5:30–10 P.M.; Friday and Saturday, 5:30–10:30 P.M.; Sunday, 5–9:30 P.M.

Setting & atmosphere: A gracious stone and plaster palazzo with vaulted recessed booths and a trompe l'oeil mural leading into a Renaissance eternity.

House specialties: Four- and five-course menus de gustacione, and a three-course pasta sampler, each dictated by the day's market. Among the frequent offerings are game birds—squab, woodcock, guinea hen—and red game such as venison and rabbit. Sea urchin appears fairly often, usually caressing a delicate pasta, as do wild mushrooms or truffles.

Other recommendations: Rack of veal; sweetbreads however prepared; grilled or roasted seafood; gnocchi.

Summary & comments: Among the city's finest restaurants by any account. Chef Roberto Donna's creations, such as the duck sausage–stuffed ravioli and pappardelle with venison, quickly appear on menus elsewhere in town. He also offers the longest, best, and probably priciest Italian wine list in Washington—but with style: Where else can you order Dom Perignon by the glass? (It's $25, but still. . . .) Even the bread sticks and loaves, which come in a half-dozen flavors, are to be savored. Sauces and presentations are rarely showy, and purees often stand in for cream. Regular customers get white-glove treatment; tourists (and obvious food trend victims) may find the staff a trifle condescending, but spit-and-polish precise.

Georgia Brown

Southern   ★★★½   **Moderate**

Quality	Value
86	B

950 15th Street, NW
(202) 393-4499   Downtown   Zone 3

Reservations: Helpful
When to go: Anytime
Entree range: $8.95–16.95
Payment: VISA, MC, AMEX,
DC, CB
Service rating: ★★★½
Friendliness rating: ★★★½
Parking: Valet
Bar: Full service
Wine selection: Very good
Dress: Business, informal
Disabled access: Good
Customers: Business, local, tourist

Lunch & dinner: Monday–Thursday, 11 A.M.–11 P.M.; Friday, 11 A.M.–
midnight; Saturday, 5:30 P.M.–midnight; Sunday, 5:30–11 P.M.

Setting & atmosphere: An almost too-sophisticated take on Southern garden district graciousness, with vinelike wrought iron overhead and sleek wood
curves and conversation nooks; the spanking black-and-white kitchen, visible
from the main dining room, is almost the only bit of decor remaining from its
previous incarnation as the smart and adventuresome McPherson Grill.

House specialties: Beautiful white shrimp, heads still on, with spicy sausage
over grits; the same extravagant shrimp in an untypical coconut milk–green
onion gravy; grilled black grouper with peach-mint chutney; spicy duck
sausage gumbo; pan-crisped sweetbreads (an appetizer, but rich enough for a
meal); grilled duck breast over mesclun with a pureed blackberry dressing.

Other recommendations: Braised rabbit with wild mushrooms; medallions
of beef with bourbon-pecan sauce; grilled salmon with asparagus.

Entertainment & amenities: Live jazz Saturday nights.

Summary & comments: This is not low-country cuisine (except perhaps for
the high-octane planter's punch), it's haute Southern: beautifully updated versions of dishes you might have found in Charleston or Savannah or even New
Orleans in the pre-Prudhomme era. Presentation is distinctive without being
showy and portions are generous. And actually, there is one other hangover
from the old McPherson Grill — the farm-biscuit-like scones.

Gerard's Place

				Quality	Value
French	★★★½		Expensive	**89**	**C**

915 15th Street, NW
(202) 737-4445

Downtown   Zone 3

Reservations: Recommended
When to go: Monday
Entree range: $17.50–26.50
Payment: VISA, MC, AMEX
Service rating: ★★★
Friendliness rating: ★★½
Parking: Street
Bar: Beer and wine
Wine selection: Good
Dress: Business, dressy
Disabled access: Very good
Customers: Business, local, tourist

Lunch: Monday–Friday, 11:30 A.M.–2 P.M.
Dinner: Monday–Thursday, 5:30–10 P.M.; Friday and Saturday, 6–10:30 P.M.; Closed Sunday.

Setting & atmosphere: A quietly powerful room, painted simply in charcoal and terracotta and studded with a series of stark pencil lithographs.

House specialties: Perfectly poached (and invisibly fork-sliced) lobster topped with a tricolor confetti of mango, avocado, and red bell pepper in lime-sauterne sauce; "foie gras of the sea," known to sushi connoisseurs as ankimo or monk-fish liver, only here served lightly crusted and grilled rare, as rich as real foie gras but a fraction of the calories and guilt; terrine of quail bound by quail liver; boned rabbit rolled and wrapped in Japanese seaweed.

Other recommendations: Pot au feu of cured duck; crusty broiled sweetbreads; an iced-lime custard napoleon dessert.

Entertainment & amenities: On Monday, Gerard's Place waives not only the corkage fee but the mark-up on wines as well.

Summary & comments: Gerard Pangaud prepares classic food unobtrusively lightened to modern nutritional standards, but the bourgeois-style service — plain clunky plates, mass-market wine glasses used for both red and white — seems too clumsy to match. He offers a tasting menu for $50 a head, but everyone at the table has to order it. A more satisfying alternative to the tasting menu is to order several different dishes for your party to share.

Honors & awards: Pangaud's restaurant in Paris had two Michelin stars.

Good Fortune

Quality	Value
79	B

Chinese ★★½ **Inexpensive**

2646 University Boulevard West, Wheaton
(301) 929-8818   Maryland suburbs   Zone 10

Reservations: Suggested
When to go: Lunch
Entree range: $8.95–12.95
Payment: VISA, MC, AMEX
Service rating: ★★★
Friendliness rating: ★★★
Parking: Street
Bar: Full service
Wine selection: House
Dress: Informal, casual
Disabled access: Good
Customers: Local, ethnic

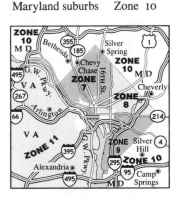

Lunch & dinner: Monday–Thursday, 11:30–1 A.M.; Friday and
Saturday, 11:30–2 A.M.; Sunday, 11–1 A.M.

Setting & atmosphere: An odd cinderblock sort of pagoda outside, a large,
pink banquet room inside, with carved lions and an ancestor altar at one end.

House specialties: Unusual dishes featuring conch, sea anemone, squid, and
frog legs; sauteed squid with tangy sweet and sour cabbage; shrimp and scallops in black bean sauce; oyster stew with ginger and scallons; dim sum at
lunch every day.

Other recommendations: Whole fried fish or, more healthfully, steamed with
julienned ginger; appetizers of bouncy shrimp mousse mounded and fried
around snow-crab claws like seafood lollipops; scallop and shrimp mousse
with black bean sauce.

Summary & comments: Cantonese cooking is the Rodney Dangerfield of
Chinese cuisine, but this wide-ranging kitchen deserves plenty of respect.
Larger groups may want to order the 8- or 10-course banquets ($17–20 a per-
son). Good Fortune is especially popular at lunch, and rightfully, for its dim
sum from carts. The seafood is more consistent than the beef and pork dishes,
which are sometimes chewy.

Grill from Ipanema

			Quality	Value
Brazilian	★★½	Moderate	78	C

1858 Columbia Road, NW
(202) 986-0757   Dupont Circle/Adams-Morgan   Zone 6

Reservations: Accepted weekdays
before 7:30 only
When to go: Early, especially
Wednesday and Saturday; or after 10.
Entree range: $12.95–19.95
Payment: VISA, MC, AMEX, DC
Service rating: ★★½
Friendliness rating: ★★★½
Parking: Valet
Bar: Full service
Wine selection: Limited
Dress: Informal, casual
Disabled access: Good
Customers: Local, ethnic, embassy

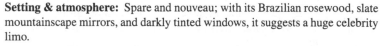

Brunch: Saturday and Sunday, noon–4 P.M.
Dinner: Monday–Thursday, 5–11 P.M.; Friday, 5 P.M.–midnight; Saturday,
4 P.M.–midnight; Sunday, 4–11 P.M.

Setting & atmosphere: Spare and nouveau; with its Brazilian rosewood, slate mountainscape mirrors, and darkly tinted windows, it suggests a huge celebrity limo.

House specialties: Feijoada, a black bean/smoked pork/collard greens stew served Wednesdays and Sundays only (hence the crush); shellfish stews in either cilantro and pepper or palm oil and coconut sauces; carne de sol, a salt-cured, milk-resuscitated beef roast grilled and thinly sliced.

Other recommendations: Grouper and leeks in phyllo dough; marinated grilled shrimp; a mug of smooth black bean soup spiked with cachaca (Brazilian rum).

Summary & comments: A young and lively atmosphere, especially after 10 when the bar gets busy and the music turns up. The caipirinha, a cachaca and lime cocktail, is particularly popular and potent. Because of the limited reservations policy, and a certain tendency of the Portuguese-speaking staff to prefer regular customers, the wait can be annoying—which also adds to the caipirinhas' popularity. Skip the Brazilian wines, incidentally; though inoffensive, they are basically table wines, and confusingly labeled: The merlot tastes like a thin zin, the chablis like a sauvignon.

I Matti

Italian ★★★½ **Moderate**

Quality	Value
88	B

2436 18th Street, NW
(202) 462-8844   Dupont Circle/Adams-Morgan   Zone 6

Reservations: Suggested
When to go: Anytime
Entree range: $8.75–18.95
Payment: VISA, MC, AMEX, CB
Service rating: ★★★
Friendliness rating: ★★★½
Parking: Valet
Bar: Full service
Wine selection: Very good
Dress: Informal
Disabled access: Good
Customers: Locals, business lunchers

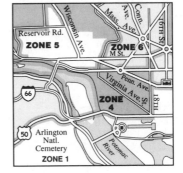

Lunch & dinner: Monday–Thursday, noon–11 P.M.; Friday and Saturday, noon–11:30 P.M.; Sunday, 11:30 A.M.–10 P.M.

Setting & atmosphere: A bright, welcoming wood-and-plaster trattoria with a cutaway balcony upstairs, a smaller dining area near the partially exposed kitchen, and a friendly, crowded stone bar.

House specialties: Osso bucco; a mixed skewer of chicken, rabbit, sausages, pancetta, and vegetables; a rabbit cutlet topped with prosciutto and fontina; crepes filled with braised duck and topped with a mustard "jam."

Other recommendations: Game specials such as quail roasted with slivers of garlic tucked under the skin and served over mesclun; cappellini dressed with fresh crabmeat and bits of fresh tomato; a benevolent rather than salty caponata made tangy by rings of calamari; grape leaves stuffed with cheese, wrapped in pancetta, and grilled.

Summary & comments: This is the less formal sibling of Roberto Donna's Galileo restaurant, where the food is often as good and only slightly less ornate. The only thing keeping it from its fourth full star is lingering inconsistency—infrequent in the food, a little more frequent in the service. Pastas include farfalle in a red beet and basil sauce and, as an alternative to the familiar alfredo, a sinfully smooth maccheroncini with gorgonzola, mascarpone, and pistachios. Only a Donna trattoria would offer three versions of carpaccio and four flavors of bruschetta. One side of the wine list gives red and white wines by price—$15, $20, and $25 a bottle—while another page shows more impressive vintages ranging up to about $80.

---

i Ricchi

			Quality	Value
Italian	★★★★	Expensive	**94**	**B**

1220 19th Street, NW
(202) 835-0459   Dupont Circle/Adams-Morgan   Zone 6

Reservations: Suggested
When to go: Lunch (almost the
same menu but a few dollars less)
or early dinner
Entree range: $14.95–21.95
Payment: VISA, MC, AMEX,
CB, DC
Service rating: ★★★★
Friendliness rating: ★★★★
Parking: Valet
Bar: Full service
Wine selection: Fine
Dress: Dressy, business
Disabled access: Good
Customers: Business, local, tourist

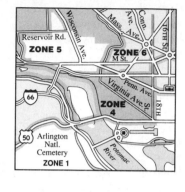

Lunch: Monday–Friday, 11:30 A.M.–2 P.M.
Dinner: Monday–Thursday, 5:30–10 P.M.; Friday and Saturday,
5:30–10 P.M. Closed Sunday.

Setting & atmosphere: This stone and terracotta-tile room evokes a villa courtyard with *H&G* detailing — gilded magnolia branches draped in muslin, floral tiles. The wood-burning stove makes the whole restaurant smell like fresh bread.

House specialties: Brick-pressed grilled half chicken; rolled florentine of pork and rabbit; pasta with hare; a miraculously light fritto misto; a mixed grill of sausage, quail, and veal; scottiaglia, a mixed platter of braised meats.

Other recommendations: The risotto of the day; grilled fresh fish; the warm salad of shrimp, cannelini, and green beans; the punning "ricchi e poveni," roasted goat chops; thick winter soups; Tuscan toast slathered with chicken livers.

Summary & comments: The oak-fired grill is the other fiery attraction, and the grilled meats and seafoods taste, with pure Tuscan assurance, only of smoke and rosemary. (Like many of the finer restaurants in town, i Ricchi changes its menu seasonally, but the grill is always featured.) Despite its prime law-and-lobby location, i Ricchi is arguably the most affordable fancy Italian restaurant in town, though the competition is quickening.

Jaleo

				Quality	Value
Spanish		★★½	**Moderate**	**79**	**C**

480 7th Street, NW
(202) 628-7949

Downtown   Zone 3

Reservations: Limited
When to go: Early evening
Entree range: $9.75–19.75
Payment: VISA, MC, AMEX
Service rating: ★★★
Friendliness rating: ★★★
Parking: Valet
Bar: Full service
Wine selection: Good
Dress: Business, informal
Disabled access: Good
Customers: Local, tourist

Lunch & dinner: Monday, 11:30 A.M.–10 P.M.; Tuesday–Thursday, 11:30 A.M.–11:30 P.M.; Friday, 11:30 A.M.–midnight.
Dinner: Saturday, 5:30–midnight; Sunday, 5:30–10 P.M.

Setting & atmosphere: A combination tapas bar, chic competition, and piazza, with bits of wrought iron, a lush suedelike gray decor, and a partial copy of the John Singer Sargent painting from which it takes its name.

House specialties: Tapas, bite-sized appetizers (four to a plate) meant to help wash down glasses of sangria and sherry and pass hours of conversation. Among the best: tuna carpaccio; grilled quail; spinach with apples; pine nuts and raisins; eggplant flan with roasted peppers; serrano ham and tomatoes on foccacia.

Other recommendations: Sausage with white beans; grilled portobello mushrooms (getting to be a local staple); lightly fried calamari; paella.

Summary & comments: Jaleo has taken tapas, a late-blooming bar fad, and built an entire menu around them—there are five times as many tapas as whole entrees. And if you're with three or four people, you can just about taste everything in sight. (In fact, the first time, you may want to go extra slow: The plates look so small, and the palo cortada goes down so smoothly, that you can overstuff yourself without realizing it.) The bar does a heavy business, too, especially pre- and post-theater. It's already so trendy that if you really want to celeb-spot, go off rush hour; they're already ducking the crowds.

Jean-Louis

French ★★★★★ **Very expensive**

Quality	Value
98	B

2650 Virginia Avenue, NW (Watergate Hotel)
(202) 298-4488   Foggy Bottom   Zone 4

Reservations: Required
When to go: Early
Entree range: Fixed price only
Payment: VISA, MC, AMEX,
CB, DC
Service rating: ★★★★
Friendliness rating: ★★★
Parking: Valet
Bar: Full service
Wine selection: Excellent
Dress: Jacket and tie required
Disabled access: Good
Customers: Local, tourist, gourmet mag groupies

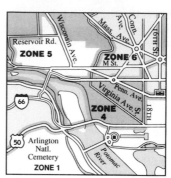

Dinner: Monday–Saturday, 5:30–10 P.M. Closed Sunday.

Setting & atmosphere: This lower-level dining room in the battleship Watergate is old "continental" style with immaculately white linen and mirrors—just a frame for the food.

House specialties: There is no recipe, only style: tiny baby vegetables and young tender game; seafoods as quenelles or airy cakes; pureed vegetable "creams."

Other recommendations: Anything involving sea urchin, lobster, seafood quenelles, truffles, rabbit, lamb, salmon, or tuna.

Summary & comments: Jean-Louis Palladin probably made possible Washington's entrance into restaurant greatness. He creates whole new menus every day, prix fixe only ($85 for five courses and the bargain version, a $43 four-course pretheater version available from 5:30–6:30 only) that are legendary displays of culinary daring. This is the most expensive restaurant in town, especially once wine is included; but that is fair payment both for Palladin's restless creativity and his insistence on the freshest, rarest ingredients. Presentations are typically "layered," beginning with a reduction or emulsion bed and topped off with an audacious garnish—miniature vegetables or perhaps shavings of truffle or ginger. The most delicate and least familiar of shellfish, such as monkfish liver or lobster coral, are usually paired with pasta.

Palladin is one of only two area chefs, the other being Gerard Pangaud, to have been awarded two stars by the *Guide Michelin*.

Jefferson Hotel

New American ★★★½ **Expensive**

Quality	Value
86	B

1200 16th Street, NW
(202) 833-6206

Downtown   Zone 3

Reservations: Recommended
When to go: Anytime
Entree range: $18.25–23.50
Payment: VISA, MC, AMEX
Service rating: ★★★
Friendliness rating: ★★★½
Parking: Valet
Bar: Full service
Wine selection: Good
Dress: Dressy, business
Disabled access: Good
Customers: Local, business, tourist

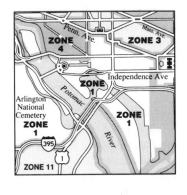

Brunch: Sunday, 11 A.M.–3 P.M.
Lunch: Monday–Saturday, noon–2:30 P.M.
Dinner: Daily, 6–10:30 P.M.

Setting & atmosphere: A clubby, Federal-era suite with claret walls and golden oak wainscoting; satirical etchings and Founding Fathers memorabilia on the walls.

House specialties: "Cornmeal flapjacks" (really more like crepes) layered with country ham, asparagus, and scallops with a cheddary cream sauce; black-eyed pea cake with preserved pheasant; venison marinated in crushed juniper and served over cabbage; rabbit sausage with red cabbage.

Other recommendations: Salmon, wrapped in cabbage in red wine sauce or sauteed over caramelized squash; roasted veal in Jack Daniel's and ham sauce with hominy; smoked scallops.

Entertainment & amenities: Free appetizer morsels such as airy smoked salmon mousse on cucumber slices or barbecued rail.

Summary & comments: Chef Will Greenwood calls this seasonal "New Virginia cuisine," emphasizing Shenandoah Valley and Chesapeake Bay ingredients played off against each other in unusual ways. The food can be rich — cream sauces are full-bodied and game reductions assertive — but seafood is tenderly handled: whole brook trout stuffed with crab and crawfish is served skinned, its head removed at the table, over a just-tangy watercress puree. Home-smoked scallops are so smooth they're almost spreadable. Greenwood also offers a five-course tasting menu each night for $45 a person. Frequent Cabinet and media sightings.

John Hay Room

	Quality	Value
New American ★★★ **Expensive**	**84**	**C**

1 Lafayette Square, NW (16th and H, Hay-Adams Hotel)
(202) 638-6600   Downtown   Zone 3

Reservations: Recommended
When to go: Anytime
Entree range: $22–24
Payment: VISA, MC, AMEX
Service rating: ★★★
Friendliness rating: ★★★
Parking: Valet
Bar: Full service
Wine selection: Good
Dress: Jacket and tie required
Disabled access: No
Customers: Business, local, tourist

Breakfast: Monday–Friday, 6–11:30 A.M.
Brunch: Saturday and Sunday, 10 A.M.–2:30 P.M.
Lunch: Monday–Friday, 11:30 A.M.–2 P.M.
Dinner: Daily, 6–10 P.M.

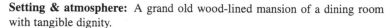

Setting & atmosphere: A grand old wood-lined mansion of a dining room with tangible dignity.

House specialties: Roasted fresh fish, such as grouper, monkfish, or cod; lobster ravioli; grilled sea bass on a raft of asparagus and grilled plum tomato coulis; spit-roasted rack of veal; a mixed grill of squab, quail, and duck with Japanese eggplant.

Other recommendations: Rock lobster and wild mushroom strudel; roasted prawns; a warm salad of black sea bass, savoy cabbage, and sesame vinaigrette.

Summary & comments: The recently hired executive chef Patrick Clark has upended this once fusty and overformal power dining room. Using primarily American ingredients, but with an eclectic sense of condiments, he lets his fish and fowl take their own bows. Even in a town where lobster ravioli is a standard, his is remarkable: silken, rich, and airy. The menu changes daily, but these dishes are typical of Clark's style (and his consideration: his three sous-chefs are given credit on the menus as well).

Lebanese Taverna

Quality	Value
79	B

Lebanese   ★★½   Moderate

2621 Connecticut Avenue, NW
(202) 265-8681   Dupont Circle/Adams-Morgan   Zone 6

5900 Washington Boulevard, Arlington
(703) 241-8681   Virginia   Zone 11

Reservations: Parties of 10 or more
(D.C.); parties of 7 or more (Arlington)
When to go: Anytime
Entree range: $8.75–14.50
Payment: VISA, MC, AMEX
(CB, DC, D downtown only)
Service rating: ★★★★
Friendliness rating: ★★★★
Parking: Street
Bar: Full service
Wine selection: Brief
Dress: Informal, casual
Disabled access: Good
Customers: Local, ethnic, embassy

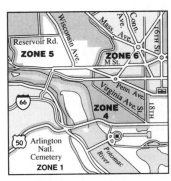

Lunch: Monday–Friday, 11:30 A.M.–2:30 P.M.
Dinner: Monday–Thursday, 5:30–10:30 P.M.; Friday and Saturday,
5:30–11 P.M.; Sunday, 5–10 P.M. (D.C. only). Monday–Friday, 5–10 P.M.;
Saturday, 11:30 A.M.–10 P.M.; Closed Sunday (Arlington).

Setting & atmosphere: A modestly fronted space made gracious and exotic
by exposed-beam planters trailing ivy; carved wooden screens, palms, and
country tile.

House specialties: Marinated beef and lamb, rotisserie-grilled; whole rotisserie chicken thinly swaddled in Lebanese dough and served with garlic; lamb
over crushed wheat bulgar and chickpeas; a mixed-grill kebab; spiced leg of
lamb grilled and thinly sliced.

Other recommendations: Fattoush, the Lebanese salad of day-old bread,
tomatoes, cucumbers, mint, lemon, and parsley; "Lebanese pizza" from the
wood-burning stove, particularly the vegetarian version with roasted sesame
seeds and thyme; pilafs topped with grilled meat.

Summary & comments: This is the best place in town to try mezza, the assortment of appetizers served in small portions for sharing and lingering over.
Among the choices: sauteed endive with coriander and caramelized onions;
tangy baba ganouj; cheese- or spinach-stuffed pastries; and the vegetarian
mixes of fresh string beans and tomatoes or fava beans and garlic.

Le Lion d'Or

French ★★★★ **Expensive**

Quality	Value
92	C

1150 Connecticut Avenue, NW
(202) 296-7972   Dupont Circle/Adams-Morgan   Zone 6

Reservations: Required
When to go: Anytime
Entree range: $21–33
Payment: VISA, MC, AMEX, CB, DC
Service rating: ★★★★
Friendliness rating: ★★★
Parking: Validation for lot
Bar: Full service
Wine selection: Very good
Dress: Jacket and tie required
Disabled access: No
Customers: Local, business, tourist

Lunch: Monday–Friday, noon–2 P.M.
Dinner: Monday–Saturday, 6–10 P.M. Closed Sunday.

Setting & atmosphere: Old continental-style room with leather banquettes, tableside service carts, and faience platters around the walls.

House specialties: Whole lobster presented with pasta; lobster soufflé; rack of lamb.

Other recommendations: Game; rolled crepes with oysters and caviar; squab; red snapper baked in a papiotte of thinly sliced potatoes.

Summary & comments: Chef/owner Jean-Pierre Goyenvalle is a Washington institution, a purveyor of the best in classic French cuisine who does not believe nouvelle is necessarily better. Whole fresh fish is broiled in salt and skinned at the table; pâté is wrapped in pastry; squab and filet of lamb are pan-sauteed and simply deglazed. But classic need not be hidebound: an almost guilt-free morsel of foie gras is served in ravioli or melted over pasta. Seafood is always a fine bet.

Little Viet Garden

Quality	Value
84	A

Vietnamese ★★★ **Inexpensive**

3012 Wilson Boulevard, Clarendon
(703) 522-9686   Virginia suburbs   Zone 11

Reservations: Accepted
When to go: Anytime
Entree range: $4.95–9.95
Payment: VISA, MC, AMEX, DC, D
Service rating: ★★★½
Friendliness rating: ★★★
Parking: Free lot
Bar: Full service
Wine selection: Limited
Dress: Casual, informal
Disabled access: Good
Customers: Local, ethnic, business

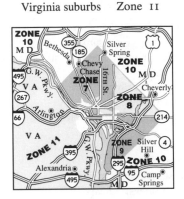

Lunch & dinner: Daily, 11 A.M.–10 P.M.

Setting & atmosphere: A gay jungle of a garden room with plastic plants and twinkling holiday lights; in good weather, a terrace offers outdoor dining.

House specialties: Viet Garden steak, almost a bourgignon with charbroiled flavor; roast quail with a black pepper vinaigrette dipping sauce; mixed seafood and vegetables with a tangy sauce in a crispy noodle basket (when available).

Other recommendations: Golden pancake, a crisp-fried crepe stuffed with shrimp, chicken, and vegetables; marinated beef grilled in grape leaves; caramel chicken with ginger.

Entertainment & amenities: Live jazz nightly.

Summary & comments: This fairly young dining room in the heart of Clarendon's "Little Saigon" neighborhood labors valiantly in the shadow of better-known spots, notably the yuppie-crowded Queen Bee across the street; but it has much brighter sauces and much crisper frying than most, except for a problematical shrimp toast.

Louisiana Express

Quality	Value
80	A

Cajun   ★★★   Inexpensive

4921 Bethesda Avenue, Bethesda
(301) 652-6945   Maryland suburbs   Zone 10

Reservations: Not accepted
When to go: Anytime
Entree range: $2.75–13.50
Payment: VISA, MC
Service rating: ★★★
Friendliness rating: ★★★½
Parking: Small lot, street
Bar: Beer and wine
Wine selection: House
Dress: Casual
Disabled access: No
Customers: Local

Breakfast: Monday–Saturday, 7:30–11 A.M.
Brunch: Sunday, 9 A.M.–2:30 P.M.
Lunch & dinner: Sunday–Thursday, 11 A.M.–10 P.M.; Friday and Saturday, 11 A.M.–11 P.M.

Setting & atmosphere: This is a real New Orleans po'boy bar—just tables, chairs, a suggestion of trellises—and an order-at-the-window format. There are a few outside tables in summer.

House specialties: Fried catfish po'boy sandwich; dirty rice with chicken livers and andouille sausage; seafood creole.

Other recommendations: Catfish or redfish beignets fried in cornmeal; andouille eggrolls; cajun-spiced steak and cheese; eggs Benedict or sardou on Sunday; pralines.

Summary & comments: The menu is sort of Chinese style: Most of the dishes here—gumbos, stir-frys, étouffés and jambalayas—can be ordered with chicken, shrimp, sausage, seafood, or "the works," and are priced accordingly. Blackened redfish is homey, not in any way fancy-shmantzy. In fact, nothing here is particularly haute, it's just good-hearted. Rotisserie chicken can be had cajun-rubbed, but it's not the best version around. For those who like a sugar rush in the mornings, the classic powdered-sugar beignets, three for a buck, with cafe au lait is the best breakfast this side of Jackson Square. The catfish beignets are the best fried bite of anything around.

Market Street Bar & Grill

New American   ★★½   Moderate

Quality	Value
79	C

1800 Presidents Street (Hyatt Regency), Reston
(703) 709-6262   Virginia suburbs   Zone 11

Reservations: Recommended
When to go: Anytime
Entree range: $12.50–21.50
Payment: VISA, MC, AMEX, CB, DC, D
Service rating: ★★★★
Friendliness rating: ★★★
Parking: Free lot
Bar: Full service
Wine selection: Good; all domestic
Dress: Business, informal
Disabled access: Good
Customers: Local, tourist, business

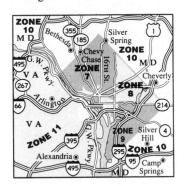

Lunch: Monday–Friday, 11:30 A.M.–2:30 P.M. Brunch: Sunday, 10:30 A.M.–2 P.M.
Dinner: Monday–Thursday, 5:30–10 P.M.; Friday and Saturday, 5:30–11 P.M.; Sunday, 5–9 P.M.

Setting & atmosphere: Bright and chic, with black-and-white checks the theme (even on the staff's trousers) and green marble bars and brass trim.

House specialties: Polenta served three ways, with slices of roquefort, wild mushroom, or tomatoes; tender poached calamari rings with sweet peppers and tangy greens; shrimp and scallops in sun-dried tomato risotto; grilled salmon in pastry; braised lamb shank.

Other recommendations: Grilled salmon fettucini with artichoke hearts; a creamy seafood casserole; roasted red snapper fillet over lentils.

Entertainment & amenities: Live jazz Friday through Sunday.

Summary & comments: This formerly conservative kitchen has begun to find its mission with a welcome vengeance. There are still a few saggy moments — cream sauces are a little overrich, roast duck is crispy enough on the outside but with too much fat underneath, and gumbos (which change daily) lack as simple a flavor boost as a squeeze of lemon — but most of the shellfish dishes in particular are delightful. The house bread, a sort of cornbread-scone hybrid topped with melted butter, sprinkled with coarse salt, and presented with a sage butter, is direly addictive. There is also a separate menu of daily specials — three or four each day — and a commendable list as well of a dozen wines, all available by the glass.

Meskerem

Ethiopian   ★★★½   **Inexpensive**

Quality	Value
89	**B**

2434 18th Street, NW
(202) 462-4100   Dupont Circle/Adams-Morgan   Zone 6

Reservations: Suggested
When to go: Anytime
Entree range: $7.95–10.95
Payment: VISA, MC, AMEX, DC
Service rating: ★★★
Friendliness rating: ★★★
Parking: Street
Bar: Full service
Wine selection: Minimal
Dress: Casual
Disabled access: Good
Customers: Locals, tourists

Lunch & dinner: Daily, noon–midnight.

Setting & atmosphere: Simple but cheerful, with "skylight" rays painted blue and white and Ethiopian-style seating for the limber on leather cushions at basket-weave tables on the balcony.

House specialties: Kitfo (tartare); lamb tibbs (breast and leg meat sauteed with onions and green chilis); shrimp watt; beef or lentil and green chili sambussa (fried pastries); cabbage and carrots in a gentle sauce.

Other recommendations: Chicken alicha for the spice-intimidated; zilbo (lamb and collard greens).

Summary & comments: There are three things novices need to know about Ethiopian food; first, it's eaten with the hands, using a spongy pancake called injera as plate, spoon, and napkin all in one. Second, "alicha" is the name of the milder stew or curry preparation, and third, "watt" is the spicier one. Most main ingredients, vegetables as well as meat and chicken, can be ordered either way. Washington's many Ethiopian restaurants (there may be a dozen in Adams-Morgan alone) offer similar menus, in some cases without much distinction between stews; but Meskerem is one of the best. If you want a sampler—a tray-sized injera palette—order the "mesob." "Meskerem," incidentally, is the first month of the 13-month Ethiopian calendar, the one which corresponds to September, which is the end of the rainy season and thus akin to springtime.

Morton's of Chicago

		Quality	Value
Steak	★★★½ Very expensive	89	C

3251 Prospect Street, NW
(202) 342-6258 Georgetown Zone 5

8075 Leesburg Pike (Fairfax Square Shopping Center), Tysons Corner
(703) 883-0800 Virginia suburbs Zone 11

Reservations: Recommended
When to go: Early for prime rib
Entree range: $14.95–50.00
Payment: VISA, MC, AMEX, CB, DC
Service rating: ★★★
Friendliness rating: ★★★
Parking: Valet
Bar: Full service
Wine selection: Good
Dress: Business, dressy
Disabled access: Prospect Street, fair; Leesburg Pike, good
Customers: Business, local, tourist

Lunch: Monday–Friday, 11:30 A.M.–2:30 P.M. (Virginia only)
Dinner: Monday–Saturday, 5:30–11 P.M.; Sunday, 5–10 P.M.

Setting & atmosphere: This loud, brash men's club chophouse with LeRoy Neiman sports art and carts of raw meat rolling around is almost as much a competition as a dining experience, and with the vigor of the bartending, waiting for a table, likely even with a reservation, is a test of endurance.

House specialties: Porterhouse; smoked salmon; lobsters by the pound; the broiled veal chop that is becoming a steakhouse standard.

Other recommendations: Swordfish; lamb chops.

Summary & comments: This is the original cholesterol test, steak as straight as it comes, and as prime as it comes. Prime rib is one of the signature dishes here, but some people never make it in time, as it sells out early in the evening. Another special is the three-pound "double porterhouse" for couples, family groups, or *Guinness Book* aspirants. All the classics are here—New York strip, filet mignon so large it belies the name, Delmonico—and the vegetables are just as predictable: mountainous baked potatoes, spinach, tomatoes (problematical), asparagus.

Disabled patrons: At the Tysons Corner location, tell the valet to notify the dining staff that you will be using the elevator.

Mykonos

			Quality	Value
Greek	★★★½	Moderate	**85**	**B**

1910 K Street, NW
(202) 331-0370 Foggy Bottom Zone 4

Reservations: Helpful (dinner only)
When to go: After 1:30 or for dinner;
it's a lunch hour express
Entree range: $9.95–16.95
Payment: VISA, MC, AMEX, DC, D
Service rating: ★★★½
Friendliness rating: ★★★★
Parking: Validated
Bar: Full service
Wine selection: Limited
Dress: Business, informal
Disabled access: No
Customers: Ethnic, business

Lunch: Monday–Friday, 11:30 A.M.–3:30 P.M.
Dinner: Monday–Thursday, 5:30–10:30 P.M.; Friday, 5:30–11 P.M.;
Sunday, 5–10 P.M.

Setting & atmosphere: The brightest Greek decor since the heyday of Taverna Creketou in Alexandria: lots of whitewashed "plaster" walls with marine blue accents, slate flooring, archways, and sun-drenched paintings and travel posters.

House specialties: A fine vegetarian platter featuring stuffed eggplant, spanikopita, lemon and parsley-drenched white beans, and Greek salad, among other things; grilled salmon (a real slab, crusty and moist); spinach and feta-stuffed flounder and a similar chicken breast; roasted lamb or broiled chops.

Other recommendations: An appetizer of eggplant roasted to caramelizing and topped with tomatoes and pine nuts; lamb du jour at lunch, particularly the shanks; veal with mabrodaphne wine and mushrooms.

Summary & comments: There's not a faster way to lose those old prejudices against Greek cooking than to sample Mykonos' versions of fried squid or even stuffed grape leaves; the spanikopita, served as a complementary appetizer, is far and away the best in town with greens that seem too tangy and fresh to be just spinach. There are various combination platters, but for two or more the "deluxe dinner," 15 dishes served in three presentations for $19.95 a head, is the banquet of your dreams. Mykonos uses a fair amount of oil, but first-class olive oil it is; and the feta is delicate instead of rank.

Nizam

Quality	Value
72	B

Turkish ★★ **Moderate**

523 Maple Avenue West, Vienna
(703) 938-8948

Virginia suburbs   Zone 11

Reservations: Recommended
When to go: Weekends
Entree range: $11.95–22.50
Payment: VISA, MC, AMEX
Service rating: ★★★
Friendliness rating: ★★★
Parking: Free lot
Bar: Full service
Wine selection: Limited
Dress: Informal, casual
Disabled access: No
Customers: Local, ethnic

Lunch: Tuesday–Thursday, 11 A.M.–3 P.M.; Friday, 11 A.M.–2:30 P.M.
Dinner: Tuesday–Thursday, 5–10 P.M.; Friday and Saturday, 5–11 P.M.;
Sunday, 4–10 P.M. Closed Monday.

Setting & atmosphere: A modest, pretty room filled with hanging plants and brassware tucked inside its shopping center exterior.

House specialties: Donner kebab, sliced marinated lamb rolled, rotisserie grilled, then pinwheel sliced and served with tomato and yogurt sauce (available Tuesdays and weekends); lamb shank with eggplant; ground lamb with sauteed pita and smoked eggplant; baba ganouj.

Other recommendations: Manti, a sort of Turkish ravioli related to the Afghani aushak; char-grilled chicken.

Entertainment & amenities: "Kebab" is the most prominent word on Nizam's menu, and so the grilling (and marinating) is given great care. But unlike some Turkish kitchens, this one doesn't forget the little things, like seasoning the stuffed grape leaves (these are studded with pine nuts and raisins) or draining the oil from the moussaka. Some critics sniff that the donner kebab isn't as authentic as home-style, which has layers of many meats, but its admirers are louder.

Nora

			Quality	Value
New American	★★★	Moderate	**82**	**C**

2132 Florida Avenue, NW

(202) 462-5143   Dupont Circle/Adams-Morgan   Zone 6

Reservations: Recommended
When to go: Anytime
Entree range: $16.95–21.95
Payment: VISA, MC
Service rating: ★★★½
Friendliness rating: ★★★★
Parking: Street
Bar: Full service
Wine selection: Good
Dress: Business, casual
Disabled access: No
Customers: Local

Dinner: Monday–Thursday, 6–10 P.M.; Friday and Saturday, 6–10:30 P.M. Closed Sunday.

Setting & atmosphere: A pretty corner town house with exposed brick walls and a gallery of handcrafts, quilt pieces, and faux naif art in the dining rooms; an enclosed greenhouse balcony in the rear is the prettiest area.

House specialties: Shellfish; organ meats from additive-free animals; salads of baby heads of lettuce; home-cured gravlax or trout; veal or lamb stews and ragouts.

Other recommendations: Duck-filled ravioli; roasted salmon; vegetarian platters.

Summary & comments: Nora, the neighborhood hangout of the Dupont Circle A and B lists, was haute organic before organic was chic. The back of the menu, which changes daily, lists the specific farms where the meat, produce, dairy products, and eggs — naturally low in cholesterol, according to the supplier — are raised. Nora's own all-edible flower and herb garden alongside the restaurant is indicative. The cost of acquiring such specialized ingredients is passed on, but reasonably. Nora was also ahead of the crowd on introducing alternative grains and pastas, and it was the first restaurant to make lentils that didn't taste like a Zen penance. It was also among the first to take presentation seriously. Now that the Clintons have dined here, it may become more of a tourist attraction.

Notte Luna

California Italian   ★★★   **Moderate**

Quality	Value
81	C

809 15th Street, NW
(202) 408-9500

Downtown   Zone 3

Reservations: Recommended
When to go: Anytime
Entree range: $8.25–16.95
Payment: VISA, MC, AMEX
Service rating: ★★★
Friendliness rating: ★★★
Parking: Valet
Bar: Full service
Wine selection: Good
Dress: Informal, business, casual
Disabled access: Good
Customers: Local, business, tourist

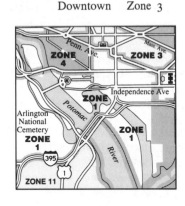

Lunch & dinner: Monday–Thursday, 11 A.M.–11 P.M.; Friday, 11 A.M.–midnight.
Dinner: Saturday, 5 P.M.–midnight; Sunday, 5–11 P.M.

Setting & atmosphere: A cross between a designer boutique, a disco, and a cathedral: sconces, neon, trompe l'oeil Romantic murals, and a ceiling full of flying buttresses. Italian language tapes play over the PA in the rest rooms; the exposed kitchen makes a pleasant clatter, and a tented sidewalk cafe is in use year-round.

House specialties: Mussels in grainy mustard and grappa broth; grilled swordfish with black olive pesto; crabmeat ravioli; 12 pizzas with anything-goes toppings, notably the gravlax, dill mascarpone, red onion, and caviar mix called the "bagel pizza"; a BLT of pancetta, tomato, and bitter greens; and a bacon, spinach, and mozzarella blend.

Other recommendations: Osso bucco; saffron fettucini with grilled salmon and fennel.

Entertainment & amenities: Live jazz on Sunday evenings.

Summary & comments: This is a very energetic, hip take on California neopolitan. The pizza dough is unusual and definitely a matter of taste—a dry, crackery dough sprinkled with coarse salt—but the toppings are great fun. The complimentary caponata and parmesan toast appetizers are delicious but dangerously thirst-inspiring.

Obelisk

Quality	Value
88	B

Italian ★★★½ **Expensive**

2029 P Street, NW
(202) 872-1180   Dupont Circle/Adams-Morgan   Zone 6

Reservations: Recommended
When to go: Anytime
Entree range: Prix fixe only
Payment: VISA, MC
Service rating: ★★★
Friendliness rating: ★★★½
Parking: Street
Bar: Full service
Wine selection: Good
Dress: Business, informal
Disabled access: No
Customers: Local, business

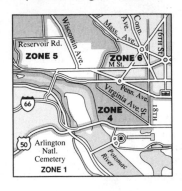

Dinner: Monday–Saturday, 6–10 P.M. Closed Sunday.

Setting & atmosphere: A tiny room that's elegant and good-humored; the customers, staff, and accoutrements—not only the room's floral centerpiece and silver chest but the astonishingly light breadsticks and bottles of grappa—work intimately elbow to elbow.

House specialties: Chef Peter Pastan has figured out the cure for overlong, overrich menus—he offers a fixed-price menu with only two, maybe three, choices per course. Among typical openers: artichokes with goat cheese; caramel-soft onion and cheese tart; crostini; a thick soup; and free appetite-rousers, including crispy fried cheese and potato or rice balls. The second course is apt to be seafood or pasta; the third, veal, fish, and perhaps game bird; and then cheese and/or dessert. The four-course meal, at $33, is a quality bargain in this town.

Other recommendations: For dessert, the dish of biscotti with sherry dipping sauce.

Summary & comments: Pastan's hand is so deft he doesn't need to over-dress anything; sauces are more like glazes, and pungent ingredients—olives, pine nuts, garlic, and greens—are perfectly proportioned to their dish. Oddly, considering the quality of the herb-infused olive oil in use at Pastan's Pizzaria Paradiso annex next door, the oil here seems unremarkable.

Occidental Grill

	Quality	Value
New American ★★★ Moderate	80	B

1475 Pennsylvania Avenue, NW
(202) 783-1475   Downtown   Zone 3

Reservations: Recommended
When to go: Anytime
Entree range: $13.95–19.95
Payment: VISA, MC, AMEX, DC
Service rating: ★★★★
Friendliness rating: ★★★★
Parking: Pay lot
Bar: Full service
Wine selection: Good
Dress: Informal, business
Disabled access: Good
Customers: Local, business, tourist

Lunch & dinner: Monday–Saturday, 11:30 A.M.–11:30 P.M.;
Sunday, noon–9 P.M.

Setting & atmosphere: The best of old-club style, with a red-plush dining room upstairs and an informal corporate mess hall in white linen downstairs. Every square inch of wall space is taken up by photos of government and media vets.

House specialties: Hearty appetizers that can easily serve as light entrees (and are often a better bargain proportionately), including a signature charred rare tuna with orange and ancho chili vinaigrette; catfish strips fried in pecan flour on roasted pepper coulis; smoked trout with fennel, snow peas, and daikon sprouts in soy-anise dressing. Seafood is especially good here: marlin with banana, green peppercorns, and Myers rum topped with mango relish; marinated fillet of salmon with napa cabbage and ginger/coriander vinaigrette; braised rockfish with smoked garlic.

Other recommendations: Tuna au poivre; veal loin chop with shiitake mushrooms and spiced pear; cornish hen with a spanky green olive and ginger sauce.

Summary & comments: This is a courtly and comfy restaurant that treats tourists (it's within view of the White House) and hotel guests as well as its regular customers. Dishes are new-cuisine mainstream, but cleverly combined.

Old Angler's Inn

New American   ★★★   **Expensive**

Quality	Value
84	C

10801 MacArthur Boulevard, Potomac
(301) 299-9097   Maryland suburbs   Zone 10

Reservations: Recommended
When to go: Anytime
Entree range: $18–30
Payment: VISA, MC, AMEX, DC
Service rating: ★★½
Friendliness rating: ★★½
Parking: Free lot
Bar: Full service
Wine selection: Brief
Dress: Dressy, business
Disabled access: No
Customers: Local

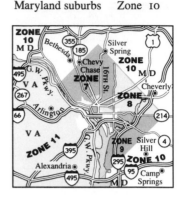

Brunch: Sunday, noon–2:30 P.M.
Lunch: Tuesday–Saturday, noon–2:30 P.M.
Dinner: Tuesday–Sunday, 6–10:30 P.M. Closed Monday.

Setting & atmosphere: A beautiful old-fashioned inn above the river, with a blazing fireplace in the parlor bar downstairs and a huddle of small dining rooms up a narrow spiral iron staircase (and bathrooms out of the servants' quarters). The stone terrace is open in good weather.

House specialties: Lobster; buttery (but butterless) pumpkin soup; stuffed grilled quail or cornish hen; rabbit sausage with couscous; shrimp with a fresh coarse salsa.

Other recommendations: Fillets of fresh fish such as sea bass; rack of lamb.

Summary & comments: This has always been a beautiful site, but years of haphazard service and pretentious, overpriced food nearly ruined Old Angler's reputation. (The wine list is still underconsidered and overpriced.) The hiring of chef Jeffrey Tomchek has helped tremendously, and the service has improved as well, although two nights' dinners will still veer from excellent to only fair. The regular menu sometimes seems staid, but daily specials are obviously closer to Tomchek's heart. Upon request, the kitchen will provide a much more intriguing five-course tasting dinner for $55 a head, which you may request with all or no seafood, no red meat, etc. A recent all-vegetarian version included a butternut squash ravioli, potato-cheese soup, and beautifully orchestrated mixed salad with truffles.

Old Glory

Barbecue   ★★★   **Moderate**

Quality	Value
83	**B**

3139 M Street, NW
(202) 337-3406   Georgetown   Zone 5

Reservations: Parties of 8 or more
only, for lunch or weekday dinner
When to go: Afternoon
Entree range: $6.25–14.95
Payment: VISA, MC, AMEX
Service rating: ★★½
Friendliness rating: ★★★
Parking: Pay lots
Bar: Full service
Wine selection: Minimal
Dress: Casual, informal
Disabled access: Good
Customers: Local, tourist

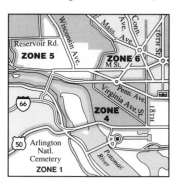

Lunch & dinner: Monday–Thursday, 11:30 A.M.–11:30 P.M.; Friday
and Saturday, 11:30–12:30 A.M.; Sunday, 11 A.M.–11 P.M. (Brunch
served 11 A.M.–3 P.M.)

Setting & atmosphere: A chic and cheeky take on roadhouse diner decor
with a sort of Six Flags theme: The state colors of Tennessee, Texas, Georgia, Arkansas, and the Carolinas hang overhead, while each table is armed
with bottles of six different barbecue sauces — mild, sweet, vinegary, tomato-y,
etc. — named for the same six states. A mix of old and new country and honky-
tonk music on the PA.

House specialties: Pork ribs or beef short ribs; "pulled" (shredded rather than
chopped) pork shoulder; smoked chicken; smoked ham.

Other recommendations: Pit-grilled burgers with cheddar and smoked bacon;
marinated and grilled skewered vegetables.

Summary & comments: This trendy finger-lickers' stop is surprisingly good,
particularly when it comes to the sort of Southern side dishes that rarely travel
well. The biscuits are fine (the cornbread isn't) and the hoppin' john — black-
eyed peas and rice — is better than authentic; it's neither mushy nor greasy.
The potato salad is made of tiny red potatoes still jacketed. The creamy mustard slaw is crisp and the corn on the cob (in season) is splendid. Besides
a custom-brewed ale and lager, Old Glory has a refreshing custom root beer
on tap.

Palladin

Quality	Value
84	C

French   ★★★   **Moderate**

2650 Virginia Avenue, NW (Watergate Hotel)
(202) 298-4455   Foggy Bottom   Zone 4

Reservations: Recommended
When to go: Anytime
Entree range: $13.50–19.95
Payment: VISA, MC, AMEX,
CB, DC
Service rating: ★★★
Friendliness rating: ★★★
Parking: Valet
Bar: Full
Wine selection: Good
Dress: Dressy, business
Disabled access: Good
Customers: Business, tourist, feds

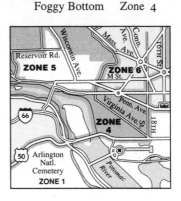

Breakfast: Daily, 7–10:30 A.M.
Lunch: Daily, 11:30 A.M.–2:30 P.M.
Dinner: Daily, 5:30–10:30 P.M.

Setting & atmosphere: This round-shouldered prow of the USS Watergate has one of the great romantic views of the Potomac in town, made private-condo luxurious with snowy linen.

House specialties: Roasted (not broiled) trout or perch; rosemary-rubbed veal chop; sauteed salmon; sweetbreads pursed in cabbage; snails fricassee with crispy duck skin; striped bass en croute (foil, really) with tapenade.

Other recommendations: For closet stew lovers, a meat-heavy pot au feu; veal "cheeks" in a walnut-stain red wine reduction; sturgeon sauteed with "essence of caviar"; blanquette of veal.

Summary & comments: Only Jean-Louis Palladin could think of this as relaxed or bistro cuisine, but compared to his intricate jewel-box presentations down the hall at Jean-Louis (see separate listing), Palladin is only semi-extravagant. It's also "classic" bourgeois, meaning such homey dishes as pig's head sausage are revived and made elegant in a terrine; veal cheeks are substituted for pork cheeks; and while the confit of duck is properly silken, the consommé the carcasses leave behind is nearly grease-free and studded with immaculate french cuffs of ravioli.

Las Pampas

				Quality	Value
Argentine/Tex-Mex		★★½	Moderate	75	C

3291 M Street, NW
(202) 333-5151   Georgetown   Zone 5

Reservations: Helpful
When to go: Anytime
Entree range: $9.95–19.95
Payment: VISA, MC, AMEX, CB, DC
Service rating: ★★★
Friendliness rating: ★★★
Parking: Street
Bar: Full service
Wine selection: Good
Dress: Informal, business
Disabled access: No
Customers: Local, tourist, diplomatic

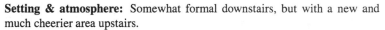

Lunch & dinner: Sunday–Thursday, noon–11 P.M.; Friday and Saturday, noon–3 A.M.

Setting & atmosphere: Somewhat formal downstairs, but with a new and much cheerier area upstairs.

House specialties: The mixed grill for one or two, including short ribs, kidneys, sweetbreads, chorizo, and black sausage; churrasco, the national beef cut (naturally muscular, not overtenderized); whole boneless chicken, marinated and grilled.

Other recommendations: Grilled seafood; a combination grill of churrasco, chicken, and chorizo; New York strip.

Entertainment & amenities: Live music upstairs on weekends.

Summary & comments: For a long time, Las Pampas might as well have been called Las Pompous, taking its steaks and its prices much too seriously; service bordered on the contemptuous, and the quality of cooking depended on the presence of the owner. In recent years, however, it's added the lighter dishes (fajitas are among the better bets — skip the nachos), allowing for a more energetic mix of customers. It's also trimmed back the prices and provided a more hospitable atmosphere to go with its admirable beef, which is, after all, its claim to fame. Note the showy char-grill in the front window and the assortment of South American wines.

Panjshir

			Quality	Value
Afghani	★★½	**Inexpensive**	**79**	**A**

924 West Broad Street, Falls Church
(703) 536-4566 — Virginia suburbs — Zone 11

224 Maple Avenue West, Vienna
(703) 281-4183 — Virginia suburbs — Zone 11

Reservations: Accepted
(Vienna only)
When to go: Anytime
Entree range: $9.95–13.95
Payment: VISA, MC, AMEX
Service rating: ★★★
Friendliness rating: ★★★
Parking: Small lot
Bar: Full service
Wine selection: House
Dress: Informal, casual
Disabled access: Vienna only
Customers: Local, business, ethnic

Lunch: Monday–Friday, 11:30 A.M.–2:30 P.M. (Falls Church); Monday–Saturday, 11:30 A.M.–2 P.M. (Vienna)
Dinner: Daily, 5–11 P.M. (Falls Church); daily, 5–10 P.M. (Vienna)

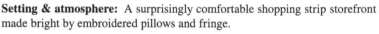

Setting & atmosphere: A surprisingly comfortable shopping strip storefront made bright by embroidered pillows and fringe.

House specialties: Zardack palow, sliced carrots, prunes, chickpeas, and walnuts tossed with lamb and rice (available without meat); quorma-e-seib, apples baked with tomato sauce, prunes, walnuts, split peas, and lamb; shalgram, turnips with brown sugar, ginger, and onion served as a vegetarian dish or with lamb.

Other recommendations: Aushak, the Afghan ravioli in which the scallions are on the inside and the ground meat is on the outside; a combination kebab of beef, lamb chops, chicken, and lamb; beef and chickpea–stuffed sambosays.

Summary & comments: Panjshir uses only soybean oil, and unusually little of that; the use of mint and coriander are generous, and rice is pasta-smooth.

El Patio

Salvadoran   ★★★   Moderate

Quality	Value
84	C

1120 20th Street, NW
(202) 466-7876   Dupont Circle/Adams-Morgan   Zone 6

Reservations: Accepted
When to go: Anytime
Entree range: $9.95–12.95
Payment: VISA, MC, AMEX
Service rating: ★★★
Friendliness rating: ★★★
Parking: Garage
Bar: Full service
Wine selection: Good
Dress: Business, informal
Disabled access: Good
Customers: Business, locals

Lunch: Monday–Friday, 11:30 A.M.–2:30 P.M.
Dinner: Monday–Thursday, 5:30–10 P.M.; Friday and Saturday, 5:30–10:30 P.M. Closed Sunday.

Setting & atmosphere: As its name suggests, El Patio is a bright enclosed veranda of brick and glass with iron terrace furniture and a real outdoor terrace in good weather.

House specialties: Squid stuffed with sausage; grilled fresh fish; grilled sausage-stuffed quail; vinegar-dressed pork with yucca.

Other recommendations: Winter stews of beef or veal; grilled and glazed shrimp; fajitas.

Summary & comments: Owner/chef Hector Guerra trained with two of Washington's premier chefs, the nouvelle/nouveau Yannick Cam and new Italian Roberto Donna, and he himself is Salvadoran; so what is developing here is another pigdin cuisine: new Central American. His kitchen understands modern tastes in service, presentation, and portion as well as preparation. Chili rellenos are roasted and peeled, not fried; what is fried—yucca, empanadas, onions—is light and crisp. Fresh fish is grilled (trout or salmon), lamb and veal are grilled or stewed. Heat-seekers look elsewhere; there are more herbs than spices here, even in the salsas.

Pho Cali/The Quality
Seafood Place

			Quality	Value
Vietnamese	★★★	Inexpensive	82	A

1621 S. Walter Reed Drive (at Glebe Road), Arlington
(703) 920-3800   Virginia suburbs   Zone 11

Reservations: Accepted
When to go: Anytime
Entree range: $7.95–15.95
Payment: VISA, MC, AMEX
Service rating: ★★★★
Friendliness rating: ★★★★
Parking: Small lot, street
Bar: Full service
Wine selection: Minimal
Dress: Casual, informal
Disabled access: Fair
Customers: Local, international

Lunch & dinner: Sunday–Thursday, 9 A.M.–10 P.M.; Friday and
Saturday, 9 A.M.–11 P.M.

Setting & atmosphere: A smallish room made cheery with the plastic plants
and miniature lights that appear to be a Viet-decor cliché; a much nicer wooden
patio outside offers seating in good weather.

House specialties: Whole steamed fish (usually red snapper or flounder, sometimes rockfish) with either scallions or black bean sauce; buttered sweet roast
quail with lemon–black pepper dipping sauce; weirdly dignified whole fried
fish.

Other recommendations: Fried soft-shell crabs in season; pho, the Vietnamese noodle soup with an assortment of beef cuts or tripe as topping;
seafood fondue (sea anemone, shrimp, clams, jellyfish, scallops, etc.) for two.

Summary & comments: This is not just a friendly place, it's almost overwhelming; the staff is so helpful it's nigh on to garrulous. And it can be very
generous: As in several other Vietnamese restaurants, the appetizer-sized roast
quail is as big as the entree, but here that's three whole birds; and extra rice
is included free with leftovers packages. The kitchen believes a little tang is
good for the soul, and the blandest of the dishes—mixed seafood hot pots or
a starchy rice-noodle bird's nest—are the least impressive. Seafood is tenderly
handled, with the exception of squid, which can be disappointingly chewy.
Fresh crabs are especially good. There are also several multicourse dinners
offered for two, four, or six people—the last, at $59.95, a real bargain. Not
quite as great as the $4.95 large pho pot, though.

Pizzaria Paradiso

Pizza   ★★★   Inexpensive

Quality	Value
83	A

2029 P Street, NW
(202) 223-1245   Dupont Circle/Adams-Morgan   Zone 6

Reservations: Not accepted
When to go: Anytime except
about 8–10 P.M.
Entree range: $4.95–15.75
Payment: VISA, MC
Service rating: ★★★
Friendliness rating: ★★★
Parking: Street
Bar: Beer and wine
Wine selection: Limited
Dress: Casual
Disabled access: No
Customers: Local, tourist, student

Lunch & dinner: Monday–Thursday, 11 A.M.–11 P.M.; Friday and
Saturday, 11 A.M.–midnight; Sunday, noon–10 P.M.

Setting & atmosphere: As tiny as this upper room is, it's hilariously decorated, with trompe l'oeil stone walls opening at the "ruined roof" to a blue sky; columns with capitals of papier-mâché veggies; a wood-burning stove painted like a smokestack; and semi-impressionistic painted cardboard pizzas like Amish hexes around the walls (a sly comment on the mass-market competition, perhaps?).

House specialties: Pizzas with four cheeses or "the atomica," with salami, black olives, and hot peppers; zucchini, eggplant, peppers, and fresh buffalo mozzarella; mussels (yes!); and potato with pesto sauce and parmesan.

Other recommendations: Thick sandwiches made with foccacia, including roast lamb and roasted veggies, as well as multimeat Italian subs and pork with hot peppers.

Summary & comments: It may seem extravagant to give such high marks to a pizzeria, but pizza this good—shoveled in and out of the deep oven, with a splash of extra-virgin olive oil and a handful of cheese tossed on at the last moment—makes most American takeout blush. It's almost a redefinition of pizza. This restaurant also has real attitude—not commercial camp, just an irresistible new wave nonchalance. No larger than its next-door sibling, Obelisk, Pizzaria Paradiso shoehorns them in and rolls them out at an astonishing but validating rate.

Prime Rib

			Quality	Value
Steak	★★★½	**Expensive**	**88**	**B**

2020 K Street, NW
(202) 466-8811

Foggy Bottom   Zone 4

Reservations: Recommended
When to go: Lunch
Entree range: $16–24
Payment: VISA, MC, AMEX, CB, DC
Service rating: ★★★★
Friendliness rating: ★★★½
Parking: Valet
Bar: Full service
Wine selection: Good
Dress: Jacket and tie required
Disabled access: Good
Customers: Business, local

Lunch: Monday–Friday, 11:30 A.M.–3 P.M.
Dinner: Monday–Thursday, 5–11 P.M.; Friday and Saturday, 5–11:30 P.M. Closed Sunday.

Setting & atmosphere: The presence up front of the Lucite grand piano makes a strange, slightly disco, first impression, but this black and gold room is veddy veddy civilized.

House specialties: Prime rib; lobster; crab imperial.

Other recommendations: Calves' liver; grilled fish.

Summary & comments: If Morton's is a red meat marathon, and Sam & Harry's a pinstripe convention, the Prime Rib is a strategy session—a little more reasonable in price and without the brand-your-own-beef attitude. It's a power-lunchers' paradise, and worth every penny of it; at night the bar does a surprisingly busy singles business—but again, very civilized.

Red Hot & Blue

Quality	Value
79	B

Barbecue   ★★½   **Inexpensive**

1600 Wilson Boulevard, Clarendon
(703) 276-7427   Virginia suburbs   Zone 11

16811 Crabbs Branch Way (Grove Shopping Center), Gaithersburg
(301) 948-7333   Maryland suburbs   Zone 10

Reservations: Not accepted
When to go: Weekdays
Entree range: $4.75–16.45
Payment: VISA, MC (CB, DC
Clarendon only)
Service rating: ★★★
Friendliness rating: ★★★
Parking: Street (freelot,
Gaithersburg)
Bar: Full service
Wine selection: Limited
Dress: Casual
Disabled access: Good (at both locations)
Customers: Local, tourist

Lunch & dinner: Monday–Thursday, 11 A.M.–10 P.M.; Friday, 11 A.M.–
11 P.M.; Saturday, noon–11 P.M.; Sunday, noon–10 P.M.

Setting & atmosphere: This is a get-down-to-it diner with crowds to spare but, fortunately, with a rowdy-friendly bar to wait in.

House specialties: Wet (rubbed and sauced) or Memphis-style dry (smoked and rubbed) pork ribs in half or full "slabs"; pulled pork shoulder sandwich; pulled chicken sandwich.

Other recommendations: The Tennessee Triple, your choice of three meats with slaw, beans, and bread; smoked beef brisket chili; smoked chicken nachos.

Summary & comments: Although there are burgers, ham and home-smoked turkey sandwiches, and salads on the menu, the ribs are this Memphis transplant's raison d'être. Barbecue is, of course, a source of constant bickering among adherents; these ribs can be overdone and the meat chewy, but they remain stand-in-line popular — which is one reason there is also a carryout with a handful of tables a few blocks away (3014 Wilson Boulevard; (703) 243-1510).

Red Sage

New Southwestern   ★★★★   **Expensive**

Quality	Value
94	A

605 14th Street, NW
(202) 638-4444   Downtown   Zone 3

Reservations: Essential for dining room; not accepted in chili bar
When to go: Anytime
Entree range: $13.50–27.50
Payment: VISA, MC, AMEX, DC
Service rating: ★★★★
Friendliness rating: ★★★
Parking: Pay lots with validation
Bar: Full service
Wine selection: Good
Dress: Dressy, informal
Disabled access: Excellent
Customers: Local, tourist, gourmet mag groupies

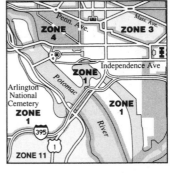

Lunch: Monday–Friday, 11:30 A.M.–2:15 P.M.
Dinner: Daily, 5:30–10:30 P.M. Chili bar open daily till midnight.

Setting & atmosphere: A fun and funny $5-million-plus new wave slant on Santa Fe chic, with cast-iron lizard door handles, plaster clouds with "lightning" in the chili bar, $100,000 worth of glass etched with campfires and broncos and, uh, "dude" and "dudette" rest rooms.

House specialties: Wild mushroom/swiss chard ravioli; cinnamon-smoked quail with wild rice; tuna carpaccio with habanero pesto; Jamaican-barbecued chicken with jerk-chicken sausage; a vegetarian plate with poblano tamales and wood-roasted mushrooms; sausage of the day (venison, duck, rabbit, even wild boar); venison chili in the chili bar.

Other recommendations: The Cubana Torta, griddled pork loin with ham and cheese; Indian flatbread veggie pizza with chili pesto.

Entertainment & amenities: There is a combination souvenir/cook's store next door, where you can buy Red Sage's jalapeno-spiked corn-and-molasses bread mix alongside T-shirts and posters.

Summary & comments: After the biggest preopening ballyhoo of the decade, and the inevitable deflation, Red Sage has found its feat, and its heat, gloriously. The roasted-chilis cuisine made famous by owner Mark Miller is a pungent panoply rather than a painful blur; each dish is seasoned with just the right flavor of pepper and to just the right degree, so that you are constantly astonished by the nuances. The smoking is exceptional here, too; the cinnamon quail is silken. All meats and game are steroid-free.

Rio Grande Cafe

			Quality	Value
Tex-Mex	★★½	Moderate	**78**	**C**

4919 Fairmont Avenue, Bethesda
(301) 656-2981   Maryland suburbs   Zone 10

4301 North Fairfax Drive, Ballston
(703) 528-3131   Virginia suburbs   Zone 11

1827 Library Street (Reston Town Center), Reston
(703) 904-0703   Virginia suburbs   Zone 11

Reservations: Not accepted
When to go: Thursday; early or
late dinner
Entree range: $7.25–12.95
Payment: VISA, MC, AMEX,
CB, DC, D
Service rating: ★★½
Friendliness rating: ★★★½
Parking: Street
Bar: Full service
Wine selection: House
Dress: Casual
Disabled access: Good
Customers: Local, tourist

Lunch & dinner: Monday–Thursday, 11 A.M.–10:30 P.M.; Friday and
Saturday, 11:30 A.M.–11:30 P.M.; Sunday, 11:30 A.M.–10:30 P.M.

Setting & atmosphere: Cheeky tortilla warehouse, with crates of Southwestern beer on the floor, jokey "native" art, and an improbably torturous tortilla machine grinding out the pancakes.

House specialties: Cabrito, baby barbecued goat and goat ribs, available only on Thursdays; grilled quail; chili rellenos.

Other recommendations: Frog legs; grilled shrimp; enchiladas.

Entertainment & amenities: Complimentary tortilla chips and an erratic but generally feisty salsa.

Summary & comments: Rio Grande may not have invented the frozen-margarita-in-a-machine technique, but they perfected it, and got a pretty good recipe going, too. You almost never have to wait for a refill — which is a good thing, since you may be waiting for a table. On the other hand, it may make you feel as if you're drinking on an assembly line. Chat up the bartenders; you'll feel better.

Sabang

			Quality	Value
Indonesian	★★½	Inexpensive	75	B

2504 Ennalls Avenue, Wheaton
(301) 942-7859

Maryland suburbs   Zone 10

Reservations: Helpful
When to go: Anytime
Entree range: $6.50–21
Payment: VISA, MC, AMEX
Service rating: ★★★
Friendliness rating: ★★★
Parking: Street
Bar: Full service
Wine selection: Minimal
Dress: Informal, casual
Disabled access: Good
Customers: Local, ethnic

Lunch & dinner: Monday–Thursday, 11 A.M.–10 P.M.; Friday and Saturday, 11 A.M.–11 P.M.; Sunday, noon–10 P.M.

Setting & atmosphere: An elaborately distracting room, with splendidly carved animals, huge peacock fans, statuary, and the ornate, oversized umbrella-shades of Indonesia stuck around the room.

House specialties: Various fish—red snapper and grouper among them—offered in sauces ranging from a light curry to a tangy but not really challenging chili-tomato sauce; anything (beef, fish, pork) in kalio sauce, a delicious coconut/coriander potion.

Other recommendations: Vegetarian dishes; pork or beef satay with either sweet or hot peanut dipping sauces.

Entertainment & amenities: Thickly cushioned seats and the intriguing offer to sell 10 of the carved wooden napkin holders, which are fish or frogs or shrimp turned on themselves, for $6.

Summary & comments: A fun way to sample Sabang's kitchen is to order a *rijsttafel,* the Dutch-style "rice table" of numerous small portions. There are four types here, ranging from the vegetarian to the "super" seafood version, priced at from $27 to $55 for two and involving 15 to 17 dishes. Some dishes admittedly get repetitious, particularly in the vegetarian version; but the fish dishes are remarkable.

Saigon Gourmet

Quality	Value
77	B

Vietnamese   ★★½   **Inexpensive**

2635 Connecticut Avenue, NW
(202) 265-1360   Dupont Circle/Adams-Morgan   Zone 6

Reservations: Helpful
When to go: Anytime
Entree range: $7.50–11.95
Payment: VISA, MC, AMEX, DC
Service rating: ★★★
Friendliness rating: ★★★
Parking: Street
Bar: Full service
Wine selection: Fair
Dress: Informal, casual
Disabled access: Good
Customers: Local

Lunch: Daily, 11:30 A.M.–3 P.M.
Dinner: Daily, 5–10:30 P.M.

Setting & atmosphere: Restrained, discreet, with a crane theme in the art and quiet background music.

House specialties: Cinnamon beef; flank steak rolled around aromatic, braised carrots; marinated pork skewer-grilled and wrapped in rice crepes; marinated quail roasted in coconut juice; baby squid stuffed with shrimp; crab and pork in pineapple and red wine.

Other recommendations: Crispy noodles topped with shrimp, beef, chicken, scallops, and vegetables in black bean sauce; honey-marinated beef rolled around onions and grilled.

Summary & comments: Vietnamese cooking is delicate, and can be bland; but Saigon Gourmet has a refreshing clarity and subtle snap to its sauces, and uses naturally sweet-sour citrus juices, especially pineapple, to refresh seafood. Still, many experienced Asian diners will find it a bit conservative.

Sam & Harry's

Steak ★★★½ **Expensive**

Quality	Value
88	C

1200 19th Street, NW
(202) 296-4333 Dupont Circle/Adams-Morgan Zone 6

Reservations: Recommended
When to go: Anytime
Entree range: $16–30
Payment: VISA, MC, AMEX, CB, DC
Service rating: ★★★★
Friendliness rating: ★★★★
Parking: Valet
Bar: Full service
Wine selection: Very good
Dress: Business, dressy
Disabled access: Good
Customers: Business, local

Lunch: Monday–Friday, 11:30 A.M.–2:30 P.M.
Dinner: Monday–Saturday, 5:30–11 P.M. Closed Sunday.

Setting & atmosphere: Dark columns and woodwork pun on (or provide protective camouflage for, depending on your point of view) the silk-stocking law and lobby firms that surround this expense-account parlor; lots of glass and French doors make seating flexible and intimate without being crowded.

House specialties: The signature steak is a two-inch-thick New York strip; also, prime rib, lobsters in the three- to four-pound range, crab cakes.

Other recommendations: Veal T-bones; fried calamari; shrimp and scallop salad (lunch only).

Entertainment & amenities: The adjoining Evening Star Jazz Bar offers live music and light entrees every evening.

Summary & comments: This is a state-of-the art—or in cholesterol terms, state-of-the-heart—challenge to older, established steakhouses. Modeled on Morton's of Chicago, where one of the owners once worked, Sam & Harry's serves everything in giant portions, including triple-sized salads and baked potatoes the size of small pets. The staff is so used to splitting meals, even those potatoes, that they sometimes bring extra plates without waiting—and you'll still need a doggie bag. Steaks are nicely seasoned without being oversalted; rare here means rare. Potatoes are offered in six or seven versions. Salads offer a little variety, too; one features goat cheese, apples, pecans, and endive.

Sam Woo

Quality	Value
85	B

Korean   ★★★½   **Moderate**

1054 Rockville Pike, Rockville
(301) 424-0495

Maryland suburbs   Zone 10

Reservations: Accepted
When to go: Anytime
Entree range: $7.95–27
Payment: VISA, MC, AMEX
Service rating: ★★★
Friendliness rating: ★★★
Parking: Free lot
Bar: Full service
Wine selection: House
Dress: Casual
Disabled access: Good
Customers: Local, ethnic, business

Lunch & dinner: Monday–Friday, 11:30 A.M.–10:30 P.M.; Saturday and Sunday, noon–10:30 P.M.

Setting & atmosphere: Rather simple, with varnished wood; sushi bar and Japanese banners to one side.

House specialties: Monkfish stew, spicy shredded beef, and rice soup; yook hwe bibimbag (raw beef with vegetables and rice); a sort of sashimi version of raw fish and vegetables with noodles; bulgoki (sweet-soy marinated Korean barbecue); tripe stew (for two).

Other recommendations: Sushi; spicy squid or octopus in a skillet; flounder with chili sauce; tempura.

Summary & comments: This is the best example of two long-related cultures meeting American tastes—food that is classically Japanese, jazzed up with Korean flair and even a touch of trendy Thai spice. Grill-topped tables offer Korean-style barbecuing applied to homey dishes, such as beef tongue, as well as chicken or pork. The all-you-can-eat lunch buffet for $6.95 draws big crowds and offers both Korean- and Japanese-style dishes.

Santa Fe East

Quality	Value
84	B

New Southwest ★★★ **Moderate**

110 South Pitt Street
(703) 548-6900   Virginia suburbs   Zone 11

Reservations: Recommended
When to go: Weekdays before 7:30
Entree range: $9.95–17.95
Payment: VISA, MC, AMEX
Service rating: ★★
Friendliness rating: ★★★
Parking: Street
Bar: Full service
Wine selection: Limited but good
Dress: Informal, casual
Disabled access: Good
Customers: Local, tourist

Lunch & dinner: Sunday–Thursday, 11:30 A.M.–10 P.M.; Friday and Saturday, 11:30 A.M.–11 P.M.

Setting & atmosphere: Unquestionably one of the prettiest restaurants in this area, with exposed brick and wood planking, trompe l'oeil windows, cigar store Indian carvings, artifacts both old and new, bright pueblo details, and a lovely enclosed courtyard (two, in fact; one off the dining room and the other off the bar).

House specialties: Smoked trout mousse; goat cheese–stuffed poblano peppers fried in blue corn meal and topped with shredded-meat chili (appetizer); poached salmon relleno; crab empenadas; cheese raviolini with shrimp and artichokes; tuna with red chili pesto, salsa and coconut, and a coconut duck enchilada on a bed of braised cabbage.

Other recommendations: Scallops wrapped in bacon; smoked lamb.

Summary & comments: Both menu and wine items are listed as bold, moderate, or subtle; maybe they should also be marked "live" or "Memorex," because this is two different kitchens depending on whether Alison Swope is at home. One of the area's first really innovative new Southwest chefs, Swope has a fine touch, but it doesn't seem to be contagious, which has led some original fans to look elsewhere. The other thing to keep in mind about Santa Fe East is that sometimes even customers with reservations have to wait in the bar. However, the slump in attendance has been a useful lesson: Service seems to be improving and the food remains fine.

Sea Catch

				Quality	Value
Seafood		★★★	**Moderate**	**84**	**B**

1054 31st Street, NW
(202) 337-8855   Georgetown   Zone 5

Reservations: Recommended
When to go: Happy hour for raw
bar specials
Entree range: $15.75–23
Payment: VISA, MC, AMEX, DC, D
Service rating: ★★★
Friendliness rating: ★★½
Parking: Validated
Bar: Full service
Wine selection: Good
Dress: Casual, business
Disabled access: Good
Customers: Local, business

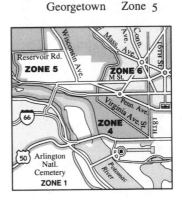

Lunch: Monday–Saturday, noon–3 P.M.
Dinner: Monday–Saturday, 5:30–10 P.M. (raw bar 5–10 P.M.). Closed Sunday.

Setting & atmosphere: Sleekly elegant, with a white marble raw bar, polished-wood dining room with fireplace, and, in good weather, a balcony overlooking the Chesapeake and Ohio Canal.

House specialties: House-smoked salmon and big-eye tuna; black bean blini with American caviar and lime sour cream; crab cakes; a papiotte of oysters and lobster with wild mushrooms and leeks; steamed whole red snapper with oysters and braised red cabbage.

Other recommendations: Jumbo scallops pan-seared with arugula; grilled shrimp with chorizo and ancho chilis; oysters steamed with scallions and black beans (lunch only); chicken breast with lemon grass and coconut milk.

Summary & comments: This is an underrated seafood establishment for people who suffer from fear of frying. The key here is balance: The kitchen likes to play with its presentations, but not to the point where the quality or texture of the shellfish is obscured. A baked halibut has the body to bear up under a green peppercorn crusting, and its meatiness is matched by a fennel and oyster sauce; trout, on the other hand, is just prodded by a bit of sun-dried tomato (for salt) and watercress (for pepper). Daily specials are a good bet. Those who prefer the straighter stuff may order lobster steamed, grilled, broiled, baked, or poached; a variety of fresh fish (there is no freezer in the kitchen, proof of the chef's dedication to freshness) brushed with oil and grilled; or an updated surf-and-turf of tenderloin and crab-stuffed mushrooms.

Quality	Value
77	C

New American   ★★½   **Moderate**

701 Pennsylvania Avenue, NW
(202) 393-0701   Downtown   Zone 3

Reservations: Recommended
When to go: Anytime
Entree range: $11.50–16.95
Payment: VISA, MC, AMEX, DC
Service rating: ★★★★
Friendliness rating: ★★★
Parking: Valet
Bar: Full service
Wine selection: Very good
Dress: Dressy, business, informal
Disabled access: Excellent
Customers: Business, local, tourist

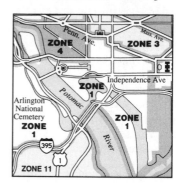

Lunch: Monday–Friday, 11:30 A.M.–3 P.M.
Dinner: Monday–Thursday, 5:30–11 P.M.; Friday and Saturday, 5:30 P.M.–midnight; Sunday, 5:30–9:30 P.M.

Setting & atmosphere: Elegant, sweeping, deco curves with striking modern art and bright window expanses.

House specialties: Caviar and vodka from the caviar bar, and tapas, served at lunch and all evening, including mussels in chervil, squid in beer, marinated eggplant and quail; charred giant rib steak in cracked white pepper; "alternative cuisine" vegetarian dishes.

Other recommendations: Oysters on the half shell with shrimp salsa; shrimp-ricotta ravioli; ginger and soy-flavored spaghetti squash; polenta with wilted greens.

Entertainment & amenities: Live jazz every evening.

Summary & comments: 701 offers a broad range of fun-fancy dining, from a whole night of caviar or tapas to cassoulets and pastas. If anything, such versatility may be its only weakness; sometimes a few of the entrees, which change frequently, seem not quite finished (or, alternatively, overdone). But this ambitious restaurant improves every month. 701 also offers a generous, three-course pretheater meal, available 5:30 to 7 P.M., for $19.95.

New American   ★★★   **Expensive**

Quality	Value
82	C

1226 36th Street, NW
(202) 965-1789   Georgetown   Zone 5

Reservations: Recommended
When to go: Anytime
Entree range: $16–29
Payment: VISA, MC, AMEX, DC
Service rating: ★★★
Friendliness rating: ★★★
Parking: Valet
Bar: Full service
Wine selection: Good
Dress: Jacket required
Disabled access: No
Customers: Local, business, tourist

Dinner: Monday–Thursday, 6–10 P.M.; Friday, 6–11 P.M.; Saturday, 5–11 P.M.; Sunday, 5–10 P.M.

Setting & atmosphere: A meticulously maintained Federal town house with blazing fireplaces and historic poise.

House specialties: The "Chesapeake Bay hot pot," a spicy, broth-based nouvelle bouillabaise; baked Gorgonzola polenta with lobster and wild mushrooms; venison medallions with fennel; grilled veal chops.

Other recommendations: Rack of lamb painted with honey; peanut-molasses–crusted quail; swordfish with glazed fennel.

Summary & comments: This menu, inspired by seasonal availability, showcases regional game and seafoods with care and respect. The kitchen aims to re-create and reclaim classic dishes—duck breast accompanied by duck confit, or roasted oysters—rather than inventing novel treatments. In other words, it's a culinary tender of the flame, rather than an innovator. Sometimes that's good, as when foie gras is seared and made smart by the peppery accompaniment of watercress and chicory. Sometimes it seems too much, as when a char-grilled strip steak is dressed with molasses and Smithfield ham sauce. In general, however, sauces are poised but not pretentious; one is well satisfied without becoming sated.

Seven Seas

				Quality	Value
Chinese	★★★	Moderate		84	B

1776 East Jefferson Street (1776 Plaza Shopping Center), Rockville
(301) 770-5020   Maryland suburbs   Zone 10

Reservations: Only for 5 or more
When to go: Early on weekends
Entree range: $6.95–14.95
Payment: VISA, MC, AMEX
Service rating: ★★★
Friendliness rating: ★★½
Parking: Free lot
Bar: Full service
Wine selection: House
Dress: Informal, casual
Disabled access: No
Customers: Ethnic, local

Lunch & dinner: Daily, 11:30 A.M.–1 A.M.

Setting & atmosphere: A large, bustling series of rooms divided by oriental archways and a few paintings; sushi bar and bar to one side.

House specialties: Fresh seafood and fish, particularly blue and Dungeness crabs available in spicy black bean, ginger, or mild Cantonese sauces; tiny Manila or giant razorback clams; live Pacific scallops looking (and tasting) more like mild oysters and topped with julienned scallion and ginger; steamed whole fish, particularly the slightly fatty black cod (it stays moist and the fatty layer drops away), simmered at the table in light ginger and soy broth.

Other recommendations: Jumbo shrimp in ginger sauce; squid in black bean sauce; wrap-it-yourself lettuce rolls with minced seafood and water chestnut filling.

Summary & comments: The first thing you see in this Shanghai palace is the tanks of live lobsters, crabs, and shellfish and the menu board of seafood specials: pink scallops, green-shelled mussels, Manila clams, Ice Island cod, and red, blue, and Dungeness crabs among them. Although this is a full-range Chinese restaurant, seafood is what they do best. There are also Japanese items on the menu, but though the fish itself is fine, the cold, pasty, and poorly seasoned version of sushi rice doesn't pass muster.

Star of Siam

		Quality	Value
Thai	★★½ **Inexpensive**	**75**	**A**

1136 19th Street, NW
(202) 785-2838 — Dupont Circle/Adams-Morgan — Zone 6

2446 18th Street, NW
(202) 986-4133 — Dupont Circle/Adams-Morgan — Zone 6

Reservations: Accepted
When to go: Anytime
Entree range: $8.25–12.50
Payment: VISA, MC, AMEX, DC, D
Service rating: ★★★
Friendliness rating: ★★★
Parking: Street
Bar: Full service
Wine selection: House
Dress: Casual
Disabled access: No
Customers: Local

Lunch & dinner: Monday–Saturday, 11:30 A.M.–11 P.M.
Dinner: Sunday, 4–11 P.M.

Setting & atmosphere: Both are in bright town houses (the 19th Street one predominantly lavender and horticulture, the Adams-Morgan site with a traditional seating area of multicolored cushion-chairs in a vast loft). Both eschew kitschy oriental idols or paintings.

House specialties: Fried whole fish with chili; shrimp and scallops with basil and chilis; red curry with duck, pineapple, and coconut; green curry of chicken with eggplant.

Other recommendations: Spicy rice noodles with beef and basil; Thai-style sweet and sour pork; shrimp, scallops, and squid with onions, chilis, and basil.

Summary & comments: Flavors come in colors here: green, red, yellow, and even a pale pink, tinted by basils and chilis and coconut milk. Beef can be stringy though, not fully seared, and noodle dishes are nondescript, though generous. However, the classic basil/chili treatments here are fresh and pungent, and the seafood salad–style appetizers are flavored but not overpowered by onion.

Sushi Kappo Kawasaki

Japanese   ★★★   **Expensive**

Quality	Value
82	D

1140 19th Street, NW
(202) 466-3798   Dupont Circle/Adams-Morgan   Zone 6

Reservations: Recommended
When to go: Anytime
Entree range: $12–30
Payment: VISA, MC, AMEX, DC
Service rating: ★★★
Friendliness rating: ★★★
Parking: Street
Bar: Limited liquor
Wine selection: House
Dress: Business, informal
Disabled access: No
Customers: Ethnic, local, business

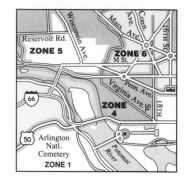

Lunch: Monday–Friday, noon–2:30 P.M.
Dinner: Monday–Saturday, 5:30–10 P.M. Closed Sunday.

Setting & atmosphere: A natty, samurai-print and varnished wood hideaway in the English basement of a modern charcoal gray office building, divided into a corridor of small dining areas, with three private tatami rooms in the rear.

House specialties: Sushi; tempura.

Other recommendations: Broiled eel; nabeyaki udon, a chicken-based soup with fat noodles, seafood, and shrimp.

Summary & comments: This is an offshoot of an earlier sushi bar that catered primarily to Japanese businessmen with expense accounts. The clientele is much the same and so are the prices: at least 25% higher and in some cases as much as twice as expensive as most other sushi bars in town, although the quality is very high and the pieces, particularly of the fatty tuna delicacy known as toro, quite large. To preserve its freshness, however, Sushi Kappo keeps the temperature of its sushi bar rather low, and the fish occasionally loses a bit of its flavor, so it's a toss-up. The tempura here is the best in town — light, greaseless, and crisp. Service depends to some degree on customers' familiarity with the staff and food (or language). Sushi Kappo also offers a kaiseki dinner (see the listing for Unkai for an explanation) for $60 and up.

Tabard Inn

Quality	Value
77	B

New American   ★★½   Moderate

1739 N Street, NW
(202) 833-2668   Dupont Circle/Adams-Morgan   Zone 6

Reservations: Recommended
When to go: Anytime
Entree range: $15–22
Payment: VISA, MC
Service rating: ★★½
Friendliness rating: ★★★
Parking: Street
Bar: Full service
Wine selection: Limited
Dress: Informal
Disabled access: No
Customers: Locals, power women

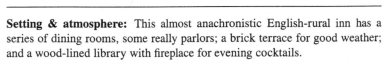

Breakfast: Daily, 7–10 A.M.
Brunch: Saturday and Sunday, 11 A.M.–2:30 P.M.
Lunch: Monday–Friday, 11:30 A.M.–2:30 P.M.
Dinner: Sunday–Tuesday, 6–10:30 P.M.; Wednesday–Saturday, 6–11 P.M.

Setting & atmosphere: This almost anachronistic English-rural inn has a series of dining rooms, some really parlors; a brick terrace for good weather; and a wood-lined library with fireplace for evening cocktails.

House specialties: Vegetarian platters; home-smoked bluefish or trout; seafood salads and pastas; blini of buckwheat waffles and salmon; chicken with ever-shifting seasonings; grilled game birds.

Other recommendations: Vegetable salads; daily specials; Asian-spiced calamari or eggplant; smoked salmon and cheese napoleons; house-peppered vodka.

Summary & comments: The Tabard likes to use its own additive-free farm produce whenever possible, so spring and summer veggies and herbs are particularly good. The menu hopes to cover most of the bases every day, so there's usually at least one chicken, one pasta, one veggie special, etc.; the menu always commands interest, though the success of each dish may vary. Chef Carole Wagner Greenwood also understands the use as well as the value of novelty grains.

Taberna del Alabardero

Quality	Value
87	C

Spanish   ★★★½   **Expensive**

1776 I Street, NW (entrance on 18th Street)
(202) 429-2200   Downtown   Zone 3

Reservations: Recommended
When to go: Anytime
Entree range: $17.50–27.50
Payment: VISA, MC, AMEX, DC
Service rating: ★★★★
Friendliness rating: ★★★
Parking: Free next door
Bar: Full service
Wine selection: Very good
Dress: Jacket and tie required
Disabled access: Good
Customers: Local, embassy, ethnic

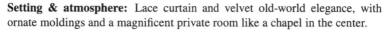

Lunch: Monday–Friday, 11:30 A.M.–3 P.M.
Dinner: Monday–Thursday, 5:30–10 P.M.; Friday and Saturday,
5:30–11 P.M. Closed Sunday.

Setting & atmosphere: Lace curtain and velvet old-world elegance, with ornate moldings and a magnificent private room like a chapel in the center.

House specialties: Lobster paella at night, less rarified versions at lunch; boneless rabbit and lobster medallions dealt alternately on the plate; duck confit; sweetbreads.

Other recommendations: Daily specials, particularly game; quail; rabbit hunter's stew.

Summary & comments: The food here can seem as weighty as its dignity. The best way to experience Taberna's richness is via the tapas menu, a selection of a dozen smaller-sized dishes, including a serving of the paella, for $3.50 to $6.50 apiece (and you can linger as long as you like). Choices include artichoke bottoms baked with ham; empanadas; grilled chorizo; poached calamari in a salad of sweet peppers. There is also a list of a dozen sherries by the glass and red or white sangria.

Tachibana

Quality	Value
84	B

Japanese   ★★★   Moderate

4050 Lee Highway, Arlington
(703) 528-1122

Virginia suburbs   Zone 11

Reservations: Accepted
When to go: Anytime
Entree range: $4.50–12
Payment: VISA, MC, AMEX, DC
Service rating: ★★★
Friendliness rating: ★★★
Parking: Small lot
Bar: Full service
Wine selection: House
Dress: Informal, casual
Disabled access: No
Customers: Local, ethnic

Lunch: Monday–Friday, 11:30 A.M.–2 P.M.
Dinner: Monday–Thursday, 5–10 P.M.; Friday and Saturday, 5–10:30 P.M.

Setting & atmosphere: An oddly pretty, keyhole-shaped, wood-trimmed room with a minirotunda and a second floor over the sushi bar.

House specialties: Teriyaki jaw of yellowtail; squid tempura; shabu-shabu (requires 24 hours' notice); soft-shell crabs in season.

Other recommendations: One-pot meals such as nabeyaki or sukiyaki, available in vegetarian versions; traditional grilled salmon over rice with green tea poured over it.

Summary & comments: This may not be one of the grandest sushi bars in the area, but it's one of the best. Although some of the high-quality sushi here has American names, it tends to be authentic under the seaweed skin: "Washington roll," for example, is broiled eel with scallions and shiso, the basil-like Japanese herb. Tachibana's seafood is fresh and generously sliced, and the teriyaki jaw of yellowtail enormous. The homier soups and stews, not available in more trend-minded shops, are not only fine bargains but real comfort food; after all, Japanese mothers have been making nabemono as long as Jewish mothers have been making chicken soup.

Tako Grill

			Quality	Value
Japanese	★★★½	**Moderate**	**89**	**B**

7756 Wisconsin Avenue, Bethesda
(301) 652-7030   Maryland suburbs   Zone 10

Reservations: Not accepted
When to go: Before 7
Entree range: $7.50–12
Payment: VISA, MC, AMEX
Service rating: ★★★★
Friendliness rating: ★★★
Parking: Street
Bar: Wine and beer
Wine selection: House
Dress: Casual, informal
Disabled access: Good
Customers: Local, business

Lunch: Monday–Friday, 11:30 A.M.–2 P.M.
Dinner: Monday–Thursday, 5:30–9:45 P.M.; Friday and Saturday,
5:30–10:15 P.M. Closed Sunday.

Setting & atmosphere: A clean, white and wood-rafter suggestion of a traditional Japanese home; the lacquered tables are by the head itamae (sushi chef),
and the staff takes turns painting murals.

House specialties: Grilled jaw of yellowtail; ankimo, a monkfish liver pâté;
soft-shell crabs tempura-fried and chopped into hand rolls. What the chef feels
are the best choices each night are highlighted on the menu.

Other recommendations: Grilled whole red snapper or rainbow trout; glazed
grilled eel; tiny candied whole octopus.

Summary & comments: In addition to some of the best and freshest sushi
and sashimi in the area, Tako has a hot-stone grill called a robotai, on which
whole fish, large shrimp, and a variety of fresh vegetables are cooked. The line
of customers waiting to get in is the surest evidence of Tako's quality, and the
one drawback of its no-reservations policy; however, the owners are negotiating to expand, which should ease the problem. Tako is also unusually free
with the rarer accompaniments: sea cucumber, mountain potato, tiny radish
sprouts, etc. Weekday lunches are a business special: soup, salad, rice, and a
daily entree (orange roughy, chicken teriyaki, pork cutlet), plus six pieces of
rolled sushi for $5.95.

Taste of Saigon

Vietnamese ★★½ **Moderate**

Quality	Value
79	A

410 Hungerford Drive, Rockville
(301) 424-7222   Maryland suburbs   Zone 10

Reservations: Accepted
When to go: Anytime
Entree range: $4.50–17
Payment: VISA, MC, AMEX,
CB, DC, D
Service rating: ★★★
Friendliness rating: ★★★★
Parking: Free lot
Bar: Full service
Wine selection: Limited
Dress: Informal
Disabled access: Good
Customers: Local, business, ethnic

Lunch & dinner: Monday–Thursday, 11 A.M.–10 P.M.; Friday and
Saturday, 11 A.M.–11 P.M.; Sunday, 11 A.M.–9:30 P.M.

Setting & atmosphere: An intriguingly angular, sleek gray-and-black lacquer
room slyly tucked into the back of a plain office building.

House specialties: Venison (in season) with curry and cellophane noodles;
stuffed baby squid; steamed whole rockfish; caramelized soft-shell crabs (in
season) with black beans; choice of seafoods—lobster, soft shells, scallops, or
shrimp—in a house special black pepper sauce.

Other recommendations: Cornish hen stuffed with pork; boneless roast
quail; grilled pork with mushrooms, peanuts and cellophane noodles.

Summary & comments: The specials here are interesting dishes; it's as if the
kitchen were as intrigued as the diners. The beef dishes are average, but the
seafood and game bird entrees are particularly good.

Terramar

Spanish/South American ★★★ **Moderate**

Quality	Value
84	B

7800 Wisconsin Avenue, Bethesda
(301) 654-0888

Maryland suburbs   Zone 10

Reservations: Recommended
When to go: Anytime
Entree range: $10.95–22.95
Payment: VISA, MC, AMEX, D, DC
Service rating: ★★★
Friendliness rating: ★★★★
Parking: Valet (weekends)
Bar: Full service
Wine selection: Moderate
Dress: Dressy, casual
Disabled access: Good
Customers: Local, embassy, ethnic

Lunch: Tuesday–Friday, 11:30 A.M.–2:30 P.M.
Dinner: Tuesday–Friday, 5–10 P.M.; Saturday, 5–11 P.M.; Sunday
5–9 P.M. Closed Monday.

Setting & atmosphere: A lovely little enclosed, Spanish-style courtyard, with red tiles, a central fountain, a canopy bar, and stucco room dividers.

House specialties: Churrasco, the muscular skirt steak of South America marinated, grilled, and served with three sauces; pan-fried red snapper; pan-seared, pepper-rubbed bluefish; roast pork with lime; caballo bayo, a shredded-beef tortilla.

Other recommendations: Mixed grill of tuna, salmon, and shrimp in the shell. Tapas, particularly Tabasco-dipped chicken wings; white bean salad; salmon croquettes; meat and raisin empanadas; a corn, black bean, and roasted onion salad; and vigaron, a pork and cabbage salad.

Summary & comments: Chef/owner Bernardo Sevilla comes from two of Nicaragua's most prominent families; both the old-world hospitality of this establishment and its clientele reflect that. Although at first more heavily "terra" than "mar," Terramar now handles seafood with intimate ease. Of particular interest are the sherries. A meal of tapas—there are two dozen to choose from—and sherry (or tequila, for the initiate) is a pleasant and leisurely way to explore the menu. Entrees are accompanied by rice, beans, and two kinds of plantains, green and ripe.

Tony Cheng's
Mongolian Restaurant

Chinese ★★★ **Inexpensive**

Quality	Value
83	**A**

619 H Street, NW
(202) 842-8669

Downtown   Zone 3

Reservations: Accepted
When to go: Anytime
Entree range: $5–13.95
Payment: VISA, MC, AMEX
Service rating: ★★½
Friendliness rating: ★★★
Parking: Street
Bar: Full service
Wine selection: House
Dress: Informal, casual
Disabled access: Fair
Customers: Local, tourist, ethnic

Lunch & dinner: Sunday–Thursday, 11 A.M.–11 P.M.; Friday and Saturday, 11 A.M.–midnight

---

Setting & atmosphere: A big, bright, open room with woven chairs and a giant iron grill in the center surrounded by coolers.

House specialties: Mongolian hot pot, a stockpot of broth with vegetables and noodles to which one adds more ingredients—clams, squid, oysters, chicken, even tripe—for from $1.95 to $3.95 per ingredient; Mongolian barbecue, a sort of similar pick-your-flavor arrangement, but all you can eat is cooked on the grill.

Other recommendations: None—it's a two-item menu, in effect.

Summary & comments: The barbecue is the more fun choice: Customers fill a serving bowl with meats, seafood, or vegetables from the cooler trays then hand it over to the chef, who dumps the whole plateful onto the grill and stir-fries it—the Mongolian version of teppanyaki. The cooked dish is flavored with soy sauce, ginger, rice wine, garlic, or chili oil and eaten at the table by stuffing it into little sesame rolls. Tony Cheng's has become a secret indulgence for dieters, incidentally, especially the hot pot.

Unkai

				Quality	Value
Japanese	★★★½	Expensive		**89**	**C**

1250 24th Street, NW
(202) 466-2299

Georgetown   Zone 5

Reservations: Recommended
When to go: Anytime
Entree range: $11.50–24.50
Payment: VISA, MC, AMEX, CB, DC, D
Service rating: ★★★★
Friendliness rating: ★★★
Parking: Garage, street
Bar: Full service
Wine selection: Fair
Dress: Business, dressy
Disabled access: Good
Customers: Ethnic, local, business

Lunch: Monday–Friday, 11:30 A.M.–2 P.M.
Dinner: Monday–Friday, 5:30–10 P.M.; Saturday, 5–9:30 P.M. Closed Sunday.

Setting & atmosphere: A sleek, modern, slate-gray and black layout with polished stones and a hint of flowing water in the Japanese style; there are several traditional tatami rooms for small parties.

House specialties: Kaiseki, an aristocratic style of cuisine that is the rarified evolution of the once ostensibly simple (but also elaborately coded) tea ceremony, is rarely offered to the public. As much a philosophy as a cuisine, kaiseki is a series of courses in which various artistically presented dishes suggest the four seasons: Here it's offered in four versions, emphasizing tempura, sushi, sumibiyaki (char-grilled dishes), and the chef's special kaiseki, an exquisite and suitably expensive ($80 and up per person) rendition of food as art. This special kaiseki is recommended for the knowledgeable, or at least the imaginative, or for platinum-card expense accounts.

Other recommendations: Unkai, which belongs to the ANA corporation, not remarkably has a fine, high-quality sushi bar; it also has tappanyaki cuisine, made famous and, by Japanese standards, vulgarly flashy, by the Benihana chain; instead of twirling knives, Unkai offers sausage, salmon, and tuna from the grill, as well as lobster from the tank.

Summary & comments: A beautiful and prestigious restaurant, but one whose finest dishes may seem fussy and overexpensive to any who are not serious adherents of classic Japanese cuisine. There is an elevator around the back of the restaurant for disabled patrons.

Vidalia

		Quality	Value
New American	★★★½ Moderate	**87**	**B**

1990 M Street, NW
(202) 659-1990   Dupont Circle/Adams-Morgan   Zone 6

Reservations: Recommended
When to go: Anytime
Entree range: $13.50–19
Payment: VISA, MC, AMEX, DC
Service rating: ★★★★
Friendliness rating: ★★★
Parking: Valet
Bar: Full service
Wine selection: Very good
Dress: Business, dressy, informal
Disabled access: Good
Customers: Business, local, tourist

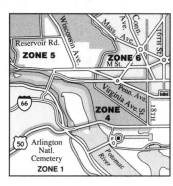

Lunch: Monday–Friday, 11:30 A.M.–2:30 P.M.
Dinner: Monday–Saturday, 5:30–10:30 P.M. Closed Sunday.

Setting & atmosphere: Although this is actually a below-stairs establishment (disabled access is through the office lobby elevators), it's remarkably bright for a basement, and as new-Southern revival as a Martha Stewart magazine: sponged buttercup walls (the chef's wife's handiwork), dried flower wreaths, stripped-wood bannisters and dowels.

House specialties: Roasted sweetbreads with morels and a tang of bacon and mustard greens; wild mushroom ragout flavored with ham; an appetizer (light meal sized) of arugula topped with asparagus, seared raw salmon, fennel, and shiitakes; scallops with roasted eggplant; double pork chop with a sweet-sour apple vinegar and honey sauce; roasted tomato soup with lump crab.

Other recommendations: Monkfish with a roasted onion and cabbage chutney; tuna steak "au poivre" with beef marrow; seared salmon with roasted onion puree and cracked mustard seed. For light fare, go into the Onion Bar and check out the $4 tapas.

Summary & comments: Jeff Buber is another of those chefs who delights in native American ingredients based on sheer flavor rather than tradition. His luxuriant sauces aren't low cal but he serves them with a light touch. Buber also offers a modern sort of blue plate special—the daily vegetarian special. Particularly if you dally over the big first-course salads and the scones, Vidalia can be a bargain. One caveat for cornbread purists: Buber's is sugared.

Vincenzo

	Quality	Value
Italian ★★★ **Expensive**	84	C

1606 20th Street, NW

(202) 667-0047 Dupont Circle/Adams-Morgan Zone 6

Reservations: Recommended
When to go: Anytime
Entree range: $14–25
Payment: VISA, MC, AMEX, DC
Service rating: ★★★
Friendliness rating: ★★½
Parking: Valet
Bar: Full service
Wine selection: Good but limited
Dress: Dressy, business
Disabled access: Good
Customers: Local, business, tourist

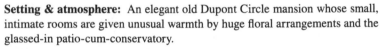

Lunch: Tuesday–Friday, noon–2 p.m.
Dinner: Monday–Friday, 6–9:30 P.M.; Saturday, 6–10 P.M. Closed Sunday.

Setting & atmosphere: An elegant old Dupont Circle mansion whose small, intimate rooms are given unusual warmth by huge floral arrangements and the glassed-in patio-cum-conservatory.

House specialties: Sea bass and mixed shellfish poached in parchment; four or five fresh fish grilled with matched sauces each day; spicy squid and spinach saute.

Other recommendations: A daily three-course $25 dinner, usually with three choices per course; veal and wild mushroom stew; pastas dressed with shellfish, olives and anchovies or simple tomato and basil; lamb and artichokes sauteed with a light egg and lemon sauce.

Summary & comments: Once D.C.'s best Italian seafood specialist, Vincenzo had slipped from its longtime prominence, what with the influx of showier Italian restaurants; but it has shaken off its torpor and risen to the challenge — a little less "grand" in recipe creation, but with a quiet pride in quality in its stead. Disabled access is through the rear.

Woo Lae Oak

			Quality	Value
Korean	★★½	Moderate	**79**	**A**

1500 South Joyce Street, Arlington
(703) 521-3706

Virginia suburbs   Zone 11

Reservations: Accepted
When to go: Anytime
Entree range: $8.50–16
Payment: VISA, MC, AMEX
Service rating: ★★★★
Friendliness rating: ★★★
Parking: Free lot
Bar: Full service
Wine selection: Fair
Dress: Casual, informal
Disabled access: No
Customers: Ethnic, local

Lunch & dinner: Daily, 11:30 A.M.–10:30 P.M.

Setting & atmosphere: California Asian, this freestanding section of an apartment complex is a big curving slice of a room on stilts, with modernized versions of traditional woodslat and rice-paper decor. All tables have barbecue grills built in.

House specialties: Shin sun ro, a fancy hot pot (Korean shabu-shabu) that requires 24-hour notice; saeng sun jun, battered and grilled fish; bulgoki, the familiar sweet-soy beef barbecue; spicy fish stew in a pot; yookhwe bibim bap, marinated raw sirloin strips with spinach, bean sprouts, zucchini, etc., in sesame oil; boneless short rib cubes.

Other recommendations: Beef liver, heart, tongue, and tripe for the more intrepid barbecuers; broiled salmon; sliced raw fish, cut in generous, steak-fry-sized pieces, not the thin Japanese layers. Modum yori, a combination grill platter, including a whole fish, shrimp, chicken, and beef, is a huge family meal, but requires a day's advance notice.

Summary & comments: This is not food to eat alone. The fun is barbecuing (or in the case of the many hot-pot dishes, dipping) with friends. Besides, many of the dishes are made for two; and the sashimi appetizer is so big—about 24 pieces—that it's either a meal or a first course for several. Many dishes are cut-price at lunch.

Wurzburg Haus

Quality	Value
79	B

German   ★★½   **Moderate**

7236 Muncaster Mill Road (Red Mill Shopping Center), Rockville
(301) 330-0402   Maryland suburbs   Zone 10

Reservations: Not accepted
When to go: Anytime
Entree range: $6.75–13.50
Payment: VISA, MC, AMEX, D
Service rating: ★★★
Friendliness rating: ★★★
Parking: Free lot
Bar: Beer and wine
Wine selection: Limited
Dress: Casual
Disabled access: Good
Customers: Local

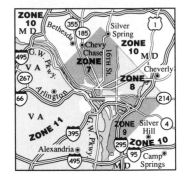

Lunch & dinner: Monday–Thursday, 11:30 A.M.–9 P.M.; Friday, 11:30 A.M.–
10 P.M.; Saturday, noon–10 P.M. Closed Sunday.

Setting & atmosphere: Just a strip mall storefront, but tangibly hospitable and beer-hall chummy with lots of chalet-pointed wood accents and travel posters.

House specialties: Four kinds of veal schnitzel, two predictably breaded, but all, particularly the unbreaded version in paprika sauce, surprisingly moist; the smoked pork brauerwurst and the veal weisswurst; herring in sour cream; a fine sauerbraten with red cabbage and potato pancakes; occasional game specials.

Other recommendations: Black Forest chicken with bing cherries; boneless trout; for sausage fans, a sampler platter of four.

Entertainment & amenities: A strolling accordianist performs polka music Friday and Saturday evenings.

Summary & comments: There are a couple of real German beers on tap here that are usually hard to find and a dozen others in bottles. This is a good place to remember why German food is such comfort food, though maybe not such a good place to pursue a diet. "Hearty" is almost a pun here for "straight to your heart." You could hold the line for dessert by ordering the trout broiled and the pork chop baked—but why bother? Wurzburg Haus also operates a carryout market a few doors down.

Yokohama

				Quality	Value
Korean/Japanese	★★★	Moderate		**84**	**A**

11300-B Georgia Avenue, Wheaton
(301) 949-7403   Maryland suburbs   Zone 10

Reservations: Accepted
When to go: Anytime
Entree range: $8.95–30
Payment: VISA, MC, AMEX
Service rating: ★★★
Friendliness rating: ★★★★
Parking: Small lot, street
Bar: Beer and wine
Wine selection: House
Dress: Informal
Disabled access: Fair
Customers: Ethnic, local

Lunch & dinner: Tuesday through Thursday, 11:30 A.M.–10:30 P.M.; Friday and Saturday, 11:30 A.M.–11 P.M.; Sunday, noon–10:30 P.M. Closed Monday.

Setting & atmosphere: An island of surprising quiet in the heart of Wheaton's flourishing restaurant max-mall, Yokohama is traditional in its plain wood and screen decor, with partitions that confer surprising privacy for smaller groups; larger groups use the central tables. Only a few stools are at the sushi bar itself.

House specialties: From the Korean menu, a spectacular (and jumbo-sized) version of spicy julienned squid marinated and sauteed with sweet and hot peppers and onions; beef dumpling soup; pajyun, the Korean-style pancake with beef, oysters, and shrimp; hwaidupbap, a typically Korean take on chirashi sushi with the raw fish and rice topped with chili sauce; and the classic marinated and grilled beef or chicken (and here, pork as well). From the Japanese menu, salmon teriyaki, various combinations of sushi and sashimi, and broiled sweet-water eel.

Other recommendations: Tripe-noodle casserole, here offered for one instead of only two (but for $20); vegetarian offerings of tempura or cold buckwheat noodles; noodles in "black sauce" and diced pork.

Summary & comments: A fairly new but striking contender in a booming field, Yokohama is generous both in the size of its portions and in its complimentary tastes of sushi. And it has faith in Americans' penchant for chili sauces. Like most contemporary sushi bars, this one has invented a couple of signature rolls (the Yokohama, for example, is a hand roll of tuna, salmon, and flounder).

Zed's

			Quality	Value
Ethiopian	★★½	**Inexpensive**	**79**	**B**

3318 M Street, NW
(202) 333-4710   Georgetown   Zone 5

Reservations: Accepted for parties
of 5 or more
When to go: Anytime
Entree range: $6.95–8.95
Payment: VISA, MC, AMEX
Service rating: ★★★
Friendliness rating: ★★★
Parking: Street
Bar: Full service
Wine selection: House
Dress: Informal
Disabled access: No
Customers: Local, tourist, ethnic

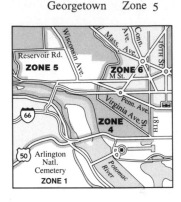

Lunch & dinner: Sunday–Thursday, 11 A.M.–11 P.M.; Friday
and Saturday, 11–1 A.M.

Setting & atmosphere: Rent is high in Georgetown, and Zed's doesn't try to compete on decor, which, considering its two narrow shoebox levels, would be tough anyway. The atmosphere sort of depends on the "kindness of strangers" effect, and the decor consists of a few framed travel posters advertising Ethiopia's "13 Months of Sunshine" and a handful of handicrafts.

House specialties: Bozena shuro, a spicy stew of yellow split peas with beef; cauliflower, bean, and carrot stew; chicken strips in red pepper sauce; broiled beef short ribs.

Other recommendations: Red lentil watt; mild lamb alicha.

Summary & comments: Although prices are slightly higher at Zed's than at most Ethiopian restaurants, the quality of the injera, made here with a lighter millet dough, and the few unusual dishes make Zed's notable. And accustomed as they are to student and tourist traffic, the staff is very tolerant. For explanations on eating Ethiopian (i.e., with your hands), see listing for Meskerem.

APPENDIX

Hotel	Room Star Rating	Zone	Street Address
Adams Inn	★★	7	1744 Lanier Place, NW Washington, DC 20009
American Inn of Bethesda	★★	10	8130 Wisconsin Avenue Bethesda, MD 20814
Arlington Renaissance Hotel	★★★¹/₂	11	950 N. Stafford Street Arlington, VA 22203
Bellevue Hotel	★★★	2	15 E Street, NW Washington, DC 20001
Best Western Arlington Inn	★★	11	2480 S. Glebe Road Arlington, VA 22206
Best Western New Hampshire Suites	★★★	6	1121 New Hampshire Avenue, NW Washington, DC 20037
Best Western Old Colony Inn	★★★	11	625 First Street Alexandria, VA 22314
Best Western Rosslyn Westpark	★★¹/₂	11	1900 N. Fort Myer Drive Arlington, VA 22209
Best Western Skyline Inn	★★★	9	10 "I" Street, SW Washington, DC 20024
Best Western Tyson's Westpark	★★¹/₂	11	8401 Westpark Drive McLean, VA 22102
Canterbury Hotel	★★★★	6	1733 N Street, NW Washington, DC 20036
Capitol Hilton	★★★★¹/₂	3	16th and K Streets, NW Washington, DC 20036
Carlton Hotel	★★★★¹/₂	3	923 16th Street & K Street, NW Washington, DC 20006
Carlyle Suites Hotel	★★★	6	1731 New Hampshire Avenue, NW Washington, DC 20009
Center City Hotel	★★¹/₂	7	1201 13th Street, NW Washington, DC 20005
Channel Inn Hotel	★★★¹/₂	1	650 Water Street, SW Washington, DC 20024
Comfort Inn Ballston	★★¹/₂	11	1211 N. Glebe Road Arlington, VA 22201
Comfort Inn Downtown	★★★	3	500 H Street, NW Washington, DC 20001
Comfort Inn Landmark	★★¹/₂	11	6254 Duke Street Alexandria, VA 22314
Comfort Inn Van Dorn	★★★¹/₂	11	5716 S. Van Dorn Street Alexandria, VA 22310

Local Phone	Fax	800 Reservations	Rack Rate	No. of Rooms	On-site Dining	Pool
(202) 745-3600	None	(800) 578-6807	$$+	25	No	No
(301) 656-9300	(301) 656-2907	(800) 323-7081	$$$–	76	Yes	Yes
(703) 528-6000	(703) 528-4386	(800) 228-9898	$$$+	209	Yes	Yes
(202) 638-0900	(202) 638-5132	(800) 327-6667	$$$	140	Yes	No
(703) 979-4400	(703) 685-0051	(800) 426-6886	$$+	325	Yes	Yes
(202) 457-0565	(202) 331-9421	(800) 762-3777	$$$–	75	No	No
(703) 548-6300	(703) 684-7782	None	$$–	332	Yes	Yes
(703) 527-4814	(703) 522-7480	(800) 368-3408	$$$+	308	Yes	Yes
(202) 488-7500	(202) 488-0790	(800) 458-7500	$$$	203	Yes	Yes
(703) 734-2800	(703) 821-8872	(800) 336-3777	$$$–	301	Yes	Yes
(202) 393-3000	(202) 785-9581	(800) 424-2950	$$$$+	99	Yes	No
(202) 393-1000	(202) 639-5784	(800) HILTONS	$$$ $$$–	531	Yes	No
(202) 638-2626	(202) 628-4231	(800) 562-5661	$$$$+	197	Yes	No
(202) 234-3200	(202) 387-0085	(800) 964-5377	$$$	172	Yes	No
(202) 682-5300	(202) 371-9624	(800) 458-2817	$$$–	100	Yes	No
(202) 554-2400	(202) 863 1164	(800) 368-5668	$$$$–	100	Yes	Yes
(703) 247-3399	(703) 524-8739	(800) 221-2222	$$$–	126	Yes	No
(202) 289-5959	(202) 682-9152	(800) 221-2222	$$$$	197	Yes	No
(703) 642-3422	(703) 642-3422	(800) 435-6868	$$	148	Yes	Yes
(703) 922-9200	(703) 922-0132	(800) 999-7680	$$+	188	Yes	Yes

Hotel	Room Star Rating	Zone	Street Address
Connecticut Woodley Guest House	★	7	2647 Woodley Road, NW Washington, DC 20008
Courtyard Alexandria	★★★¹/₂	11	2700 Eisenhower Avenue Alexandria, VA 22314
Courtyard Crystal City	★★★¹/₂	11	2899 Jefferson Davis Highway Arlington, VA 22202
Courtyard Landover	★★★¹/₂	10	8330 Corporate Drive Landover, MD 20785
Days Hotel Crystal City	★★¹/₂	11	2000 Jefferson Davis Highway Arlington, VA 22202
Days Inn Alexandria	★★	11	110 S. Bragg Street Alexandria, VA 22312
Days Inn Camp Springs	★★¹/₂	10	5001 Mercedes Boulevard Camp Springs, MD 20746
Days Inn Connecticut Avenue	★★¹/₂	7	4400 Connecticut Avenue, NW Washington, DC 20008
Days Inn Downtown	★★¹/₂	3	1201 K Street, NW Washington, DC 20005
Doubletree Hotel National Airport	★★★★	11	300 Army Navy Drive Arlington, VA 22202
DuPont Plaza Hotel	★★★	6	1500 New Hampshire Avenue, NW Washington, DC 20036
Econo Lodge National Airport	★★	11	2485 S. Glebe Road Arlington, VA 22206
Econo Lodge West Arlington	★★¹/₂	11	6800 Lee Highway Arlington, VA 22213
Embassy Inn	★★¹/₂	6	1627 16th Street, NW Washington, DC 20009
Embassy Row Hotel	★★★★	6	2015 Massachusetts Avenue, NW Washington, DC 20036
Embassy Square Suites	★★★	6	2000 N Street, NW Washington, DC 20036
Embassy Suites Alexandria	★★★★	11	1900 Diagonal Road Alexandria, VA 22314
Embassy Suites Chevy Chase	★★★★	10	4300 Military Road, NW Chevy Chase, MD 20815
Embassy Suites Crystal City	★★★★	11	1300 Jefferson Davis Highway Arlington, VA 22202
Embassy Suites Downtown	★★★★	6	1250 22nd Street, NW Washington, DC 20037

Local Phone	Fax	800 Reservations	Rack Rate	No. of Rooms	On-site Dining	Pool
(202) 667-0218	(202) 328-3506	None	$$+	15	No	No
(703) 703-329-2323	Ext. 131	(800) 321-2211	$$$+	176	Yes	No
(703) 549-3434	(703) 549-7440	(800) 847-4775	$$$$	272	Yes	Yes
(301) 577-3373	(301) 577-1780	(800) 321-2211	$$$–	150	Yes	Yes
(703) 920-8600	(703) 920-2840	(800) 325-2525	$$$$–	247	Yes	Yes
(703) 354-4950	(703) 354-4950	(800) 325-2525	$$–	200	No	Yes
(301) 423-2323	(301) 702-9420	(800) 356-9630	$$+	125	Yes	Yes
(202) 244-5600	(202) 244-6794	(800) 952-3060	$$+	155	No	No
(202) 842-1020	(202) 289-0336	(800) 562-3350	$$$–	220	Yes	Yes
(703) 892-4100	None	(800) 222-TREE	$$$$–	632	Yes	Yes
(202) 483-6000	(202) 328-3265	(800) 841-0003	$$$+	314	Yes	No
(703) 979-4100	(703) 979-6120	(800) 234-4440	$$	160	No	Yes
(703) 538-5300	None	None	$$+	47	No	No
(202) 234-7800	(202) 234-3309	(800) 423-9111	$$$–	38	No	No
(202) 265-1600	(202) 328-7526	(800) 424-2400	$$$$$	196	Yes	Yes
(202) 659-9000	(202) 429-9546	(800) 424-2999	$$$+	250	Yes	Yes
(703) 684-5900	(703) 684-1403	(800) EMBASSY	$$$ $$$–	268	Yes	Yes
(202) 362-9300	(202) 686-3405	(800) 362-2779	$$$$$+	198	Yes	Yes
(703) 979-9799	(703) 920-5947	(800) EMBASSY	$$$$$+	267	Yes	Yes
(202) 857-3388	(202) 293-3173	(800) EMBASSY	$$$$ $$$–	318	Yes	Yes

Hotel	Room Star Rating	Zone	Street Address
Four Seasons Hotel	★★★★¹/₂	5	2800 Pennsylvania Avenue, NW Washington, DC 20007
Georgetown Dutch Inn	★★★¹/₂	5	1075 Thomas Jefferson Street, NW Washington, DC 20007
Georgetown Inn	★★★★	5	1310 Wisconsin Avenue, NW Washington, DC 20007
Grand Hotel of Washington	★★★★★	5	2350 M Street, NW Washington, DC 20037
Grand Hyatt Washington	★★★★	3	1000 H Street, NW Washington, DC 20001
Guest Quarters New Hampshire Avenue	★★★★	4	801 New Hampshire Avenue, NW Washington, DC 20037
Guest Quarters Pennsylvania Avenue	★★★★	5	2500 Pennsylvania Avenue Washington, DC 20037
Guest Quarters Suites Alexandria	★★★★	11	100 S. Reynolds Street Alexandria, VA 22304
Hampshire Hotel	★★★¹/₂	6	1310 New Hampshire Avenue, NW Washington, DC 20036
Hampton Inn Alexandria	★★★	11	4800 Leesburg Pike Alexandria, VA 22302
Harrington Hotel	★★	3	11th and E Streets, NW Washington, DC 20004
Hay-Adams Hotel	★★★★	3	One Lafayette Square, NW Washington, DC 20006
Henley Park Hotel	★★★★	3	926 Massachusetts Avenue, NW Washington, DC 20001
Holiday Inn Ballston	★★★	11	4610 N. Fairfax Drive Arlington, VA 22203
Holiday Inn Bethesda	★★★¹/₂	10	8120 Wisconsin Avenue Bethesda, MD 20814
Holiday Inn Camp Springs	★★¹/₂	10	4783 Allentown Road Camp Springs, MD 20746
Holiday Inn Capitol	★★★	2	550 C Street, SW Washington, DC 20024
Holiday Inn Central	★★★	7	1501 Rhode Island Avenue, NW Washington, DC 20005
Holiday Inn Chevy Chase	★★★	10	5520 Wisconsin Avenue Chevy Chase, MD 20815
Holiday Inn Crowne Plaza Metro Center	★★★★	3	775 12th Street, NW Washington, DC 20005

Local Phone	Fax	800 Reservations	Rack Rate	No. of Rooms	On-site Dining	Pool
(202) 342-0444	(202) 944-2076	(800) 332-3442	$$$$$ $$$$$–	196	Yes	Yes
(202) 337-0900	(202) 333-6526	(800) 388-2410	$$$+	47	Yes	No
(202) 333-8900	(202) 625-1744	(800) 424-2979	$$$$ $$$	95	Yes	No
(202) 429-0100	(202) 857-0127	(800) 848-0016	$$$$$+	263	Yes	Yes
(202) 582-1234	(202) 637-4781	(800) 233-1234	$$$$ $$$+	891	Yes	Yes
(202) 785-2000	(202) 785-9485	(800) 424-2900	$$$$+	101	No	Yes
(202) 955-6400	(202) 955-5765	(800) 822-4200	$$$$$–	239	Yes	No
(703) 370-9600	(703) 370-0467	(800) 424-2900	$$$$–	225	Yes	Yes
(202) 296-7600	(202) 293-2476	(800) 368-5691	$$$$	82	Yes	No
(703) 671-4800	(703) 671-2442	(800) HAMPTON	$$$–	130	No	Yes
(202) 628-8140	None	(800) 424-8532	$$$–	275	Yes	No
(202) 638-6600	(202) 638-2716	(800) 323-7500	$$$$ $$$+	143	Yes	No
(202) 638-5200	(202) 638-6740	(800) 222-8474	$$$$$+	96	Yes	No
(703) 243-9800	(703) 527-2677	(800) HOLIDAY	$$$+	221	Yes	Yes
(301) 652-2000	(301) 652-4525	(800) 638-5954	$$+	270	Yes	Yes
(301) 420-2800	(301) 735-5235	(800) HOLIDAY	$$+	149	Yes	Yes
(202) 479-4000	(202) 488-4627	(800) 465-4329	$$$$$–	529	Yes	Yes
(202) 483-2000	(202) 797-1078	(800) 248-0016	$$$$$–	213	Yes	Yes
(301) 656-1500	(301) 656-5045	None	$$$	216	Yes	Yes
(202) 737-2200	(202) 347-5886	(800) 448-9018	$$$$ $$$–	456	Yes	Yes

Hotel	Room Star Rating	Zone	Street Address
Holiday Inn Eisenhower Metro Center	★★★	11	2460 Eisenhower Avenue Alexandria, VA 22314
Holiday Inn Georgetown	★★★	7	2101 Wisconsin Avenue, NW Washington, DC 20007
Holiday Inn Governor's House	★★★	6	1615 Rhode Island Avenue, NW Washington, DC 20036
Holiday Inn Key Bridge	★★½	11	1850 N. Fort Myer Drive Arlington, VA 22209
Holiday Inn National Airport	★★★	11	1489 Jefferson Davis Highway Arlington, VA 22202
Holiday Inn Old Town	★★★	11	480 King Street Alexandria, VA 22314
Holiday Inn Silver Spring	★★★	10	8777 Georgia Avenue Silver Spring, MD 20910
Holiday Inn Thomas Circle	★★★	3	1155 14th Street, NW Washington, DC 20005
Hotel Anthony	★★★	3	1823 L Street, NW Washington, DC 20036
Hotel Lombardy	★★★½	4	2019 "I" Street, NW Washington, DC 20006
Hotel Washington	★★★½	3	Pennsylvania Avenue, NW at 15th Washington, DC 20004
Howard Johnson Downtown	★★	4	2601 Virginia Avenue, NW Washington, DC 20037
Howard Johnson National Airport	★★★	11	2650 Jefferson Davis Highway Arlington, VA 22202
Howard University Hotel	★★★	7	2225 Georgia Avenue, NW Washington, DC 20001
Hyatt Arlington	★★★	11	1325 Wilson Boulevard Arlington, VA 22209
Hyatt Regency Bethesda	★★★★	10	One Bethesda Metro Center Bethesda, MD 20814
Hyatt Regency Capitol Hill	★★★½	3	400 New Jersey Avenue, NW Washington, DC 20001
Hyatt Regency Crystal City	★★★½	11	2799 Jefferson Davis Highway Arlington, VA 22202
Inn at Foggy Bottom	★★★★	4	824 New Hampshire Avenue, NW Washington, DC 20037
J.W. Marriott Hotel	★★★★	3	1331 Pennsylvania Avenue, NW Washington, DC 20004

Local Phone	Fax	800 Reservations	Rack Rate	No. of Rooms	On-site Dining	Pool
(703) 960-3400	(202) 329-0953	(800) HOLIDAY	$$$+	202	Yes	Yes
(202) 338-4600	(202) 333-6113	(800) HOLIDAY	$$$–	296	Yes	Yes
(202) 296-2100	(202) 331-0227	(800) 821-4367	$$$+	152	Yes	Yes
(703) 522-0400	(703) 524-5275	(800) HOLIDAY	$$$+	178	Yes	Yes
(703) 521-1600	(703) 920-1236	None	$$$$–	306	Yes	Yes
(703) 549-6080	(703) 684-6508	(800) 368-5047	$$$+	225	Yes	Yes
(301) 589-0800	(301) 587-4791	(800) HOLIDAY	$$+	222	Yes	Yes
(202) 737-1200	(202) 783-5733	(800) HOLIDAY	$$$$–	208	Yes	Yes
(202) 223-4320	(202) 223-8546	(800) 424-2970	$$$–	99	Yes	No
(202) 828-2600	(202) 872-0503	(800) 424-5486	$$$	126	Yes	No
(202) 638-5900	(202) 347-4968	(800) 424-5900	$$$ $$$+	350	Yes	No
(202) 965-2700	(202) 965-2700	(800) 654-2000	$$$–	192	Yes	Yes
(703) 684-7200	(703) 684-3217	(800) IGOHOJO	$$$$	279	Yes	Yes
(202) 462-5400	(202) 667-0973	(800) 368-5729	$$$+	146	Yes	Yes
(703) 525-1234	(703) 875-3393	(800) 233-1234	$$$$$+	302	Yes	No
(301) 657-1234	(301) 657-6453	(800) 233-1234	$$$$$+	381	Yes	Yes
(202) 737-1234	(202) 737-5773	(800) 233-1234	$$$ $$$+	834	Yes	Yes
(703) 418-1234	(703) 418-1289	(800) 233-1234	$$$ $$$–	685	Yes	Yes
(202) 337-6620	(202) 298-7499	(800) 426-4458	$$$–	95	Yes	No
(202) 393-2000	(202) 626-6991	(800) 228-9290	$$$ $$$+	772	Yes	Yes

Hotel	Room Star Ratiang	Zone	Street Address
Jefferson Hotel	★★★★½	3	16th and M Streets, NW Washington, DC 20036
Kalorama Guest House	★★★	6	1854 Mintwood Place Washington, DC 20008
Latham Hotel Georgetown	★★★★	5	3000 M Street, NW Washington, DC 20007
Loew's L'Enfant Plaza	★★★★½	1	480 L'Enfant Plaza, SW Washington, DC 20024
Madison	★★★½	3	1177 15th Street, NW Washington, DC 20005
Manor Inn Bethesda	★★½	10	7740 Wisconsin Avenue Bethesda, MD 20814
Marriott Crystal City	★★★★	11	1999 Jefferson Davis Highway Arlington, VA 22202
Marriott Crystal Gateway	★★★★	11	1700 Jefferson Davis Highway Arlington, VA 22202
Marriott Hotel Bethesda	★★★	10	5151 Pooks Hill Road Bethesda, MD 20814
Marriott Hotel Key Bridge	★★★½	11	1401 Lee Highway Arlington, VA 22209
Marriott Tysons Corner	★★★★	11	8028 Leesburg Pike Vienna, VA 22180
Morrison House	★★★★	11	116 S. Alfred Road Alexandria, VA 22314
Morrison-Clark Inn	★★★★½	7	1015 L Street, NW Washington, DC 20001
Normandy Inn	★★½	6	2118 Wyoming Avenue, NW Washington, DC 20008
Omni Georgetown Hotel	★★★	6	2121 P Street, NW Washington, DC 20037
Omni Shoreham Hotel	★★★	7	2500 Calvert Street, NW Washington, DC 20008
One Washington Circle Hotel	★★★★	4	One Washington Circle, NW Washington, DC 20037
Park Hyatt (standard rooms)	★★★★½	5	24th Street at M Street, NW Washington, DC 20037
Park Hyatt (suites)	★★★★★	5	24th Street at M Street, NW Washington, DC 20037
Phoenix Park Hotel	★★★	2	520 N. Capitol Street, NW Washington, DC 20001

Local Phone	Fax	800 Reservations	Rack Rate	No. of Rooms	On-site Dining	Pool
(202) 347-2200	(202) 331-7982	(800) 368-5966	$$$$ $$$+	100	Yes	No
(202) 667-6369	(202) 319-1262	None	$$+	31	No	No
(202) 726-5000	(202) 337-4250	(800) LATHAM-1	$$$+	143	Yes	Yes
(202) 484-1000	(202) 646-4456	(800) 635-5065	$$$+	370	Yes	Yes
(202) 862-1600	(202) 785-1255	(800) 424-8578	$$$$$ $$$+	353	Yes	No
(301) 656-2100	(301) 986-0375	(800) 874-0050	$$$–	76	No	No
(703) 413-5500	(703) 413-0185	(800) 321-9879	$$$ $$$–	340	Yes	Yes
(703) 920-3230	(703) 979-6332	(800) 228-9290	$$$$ $$$–	700	Yes	Yes
(301) 897-9400	(301) 897-0192	(800) 228-9290	$$$$$–	407	Yes	Yes
(703) 524-6400	(703) 524-8964	(800) 327-9789	$$$ $$$–	585	Yes	Yes
(703) 734-3200	(703) 442-9301	(800) 228-9290	$$$$$–	390	Yes	Yes
(703) 838-8000	(703) 684-6283	(800) 367-0800	$$$$$	45	Yes	Yes
(202) 898-1200	(202) 289-8576	(800) 332-7898	$$$+	54	Yes	No
(202) 483-1350	(202) 387-8241	None	$$$+	75	No	No
(202) 293-3100	(202) 857-0134	(800) THE-OMNI	$$$$$+	294	Yes	Yes
(202) 234-0700	(202) 234-2500	(800) THE-OMNI	$$$$+	770	Yes	Yes
(202) 872-1680	(202) 887-4989	(800) 424-9671	$$$$+	151	Yes	Yes
(202) 789-1234	(202) 457-8823	(800) 233-1234	$$$$$+	224	Yes	Yes
(202) 789-1234	(202) 638-4025	(800) 824-5419	$$$ $$$+	224	Yes	Yes
(202) 638-6900	(202) 638-4025	(800) 824-5419	$$$	84	Yes	No

Hotel	Room Star Rating	Zone	Street Address
Pullman Highland Hotel	★★★½	6	1914 Connecticut Avenue, NW Washington, DC 20009
Quality Hotel Capitol Hill	★★½	3	415 New Jersey Avenue, NW Washington, DC 20001
Quality Hotel Central	★★★½	6	1900 Connecticut Avenue, NW Washington, DC 20009
Quality Hotel Downtown	★★½	6	1315 16th Street, NW Washington, DC 20036
Quality Hotel Silver Spring	★★½	10	8727 Colesville Road Silver Spring, MD 20910
Quality Inn College Park	★★½	10	7200 Baltimore Boulevard College Park, MD 20740
Quality Inn Iwo Jima	★★½	11	1501 Arlington Boulevard Arlington, VA 22209
Radisson Park Terrace	★★★½	7	1515 Rhode Island Avenue, NW Washington, DC 20036
Radisson Plaza at Mark Center	★★★½	11	5000 Seminary Road Alexandria, VA 22311
Ramada Hotel Bethesda	★★★½	10	8400 Wisconsin Avenue Bethesda, MD 20814
Ramada Hotel Old Town	★★★	11	901 N. Fairfax Street Alexandria, VA 22314
Ramada Hotel Tysons Corner	★★★½	11	7801 Leesburg Pike Falls Church, VA 22043
Ramada Inn Alexandria	★★½	11	4641 Kenmore Avenue Alexandria, VA 22304
Ramada Inn Downtown	★★★	7	1430 Rhode Island Avenue, NW Washington, DC 20005
Residence Inn Bethesda	★★★★	10	7335 Wisconsin Avenue Bethesda, MD 20814
Ritz-Carlton Washington DC	★★★★	6	2100 Massachusetts Avenue, NW Washington, DC 20008
Ritz Carlton Pentagon City	★★★★★	11	1250 S. Hayes Street Arlington, VA 22202
River Inn	★★★★	4	924 25th Street, NW Washington, DC 20037
Savoy Suites Hotel	★★★	7	2505 Wisconsin Avenue, NW Washington, DC 2000
Sheraton City Centre	★★★★	6	1143 New Hampshire Avenue, NW Washington, DC 20037

Local Phone	Fax	800 Reservations	Rack Rate	No. of Rooms	On-site Dining	Pool
(202) 797-2000	(202) 462-0944	(800) 424-2464	$$$$$–	145	Yes	No
(202) 638-1616	(202) 638-0707	(800) 638-1116	$$$	341	Yes	Yes
(202) 332-9300	(202) 328-7039	(800) 842-4211	$$$+	147	Yes	Yes
(202) 232-8000	(202) 667-9827	(800) 368-5689	$$$+	137	Yes	No
(301) 589-5200	(301) 588-1841	(800) 376-7666	$$$–	254	Yes	Yes
(301) 864-5820	(301) 864-5820	(800) 221-2222	$$	154	No	Yes
(703) 524-5000	(703) 522-5484	(800) 221-2222	$$$–	141	Yes	Yes
(202) 232-7000	(202) 332-8436	(800) 333-3333	$$$$–	219	Yes	No
(703) 845-1010	(703) 998-8759	(800) 333-3333	$$$$	500	Yes	Yes
(301) 654-1000	(301) 654-0751	(800) 331-5252	$$$–	160	Yes	Yes
(703) 683-6000	(703) 683-7597	(800) 333-3333	$$+	258	Yes	Yes
(703) 893-1340	(703) 847-8527	(800) 228-2828	$$$–	404	Yes	Yes
(703) 751-4510	(703) 751-9170	(800) 228-2828	$$$$–	193	Yes	Yes
(202) 462-7777	(202) 332-3519	(800) 368-5690	$$+	184	Yes	Yes
(301) 718-0200	(301) 718-0679	(800) 331-3131	$$$$$	187	No	Yes
(202) 293-2100	(202) 293-0641	(800) 241-3333	$$$$$ $$$+	206	Yes	No
(703) 415-5000	(703) 415-5061	(800) 241-3333	$$$$$+	345	Yes	Yes
(202) 337-7600	(202) 337-6520	(800) 424-2741	$$$+	127	Yes	No
(202) 337-9700	(202) 337-3644	(800) 944-5377	$$$–	150	Yes	No
(202) 775-0800	(202) 331-9491	(800) 526-7495	$$$ $$$+	351	Yes	No

Hotel	Room Star Rating	Zone	Street Address
Sheraton Crystal City	★★★¹/₂	11	1800 Jefferson Davis Highway Arlington, VA 22202
Sheraton National Hotel	★★★¹/₂	11	900 S. Orme Street Arlington, VA 22204
Sheraton Premiere Tysons Corner	★★★★¹/₂	11	8661 Leesburg Pike Vienna, VA 22182
Sheraton Suites Alexandria	★★★★¹/₂	11	801 N. St. Asaph Street Alexandria, VA 22314
Sheraton Washington Hotel	★★★★	7	2660 Woodley Road, NW Washington, DC 20008
St. James	★★★★¹/₂	4	950 24th Street, NW Washington, DC 20037
State Plaza Hotel	★★★¹/₂	4	2117 E Street & 2116 F Street Washington, DC 20037
Stouffer Concourse Hotel	★★★★	11	2399 Jefferson Davis Highway Arlington, VA 22202
Stouffer Mayflower Hotel	★★★★¹/₂	3	1127 Connecticut Avenue, NW Washington, DC 20036
Tabard Inn	★★★¹/₂	6	1739 N Street, NW Washington, DC 20036
Washington Court Hotel	★★★★	3	525 New Jersey Avenue, NW Washington, DC 20001
Washington Hilton	★★★¹/₂	6	1919 Connecticut Avenue, NW Washington, DC 20009
Washington Marriott Hotel	★★★★	6	1221 22nd Street at M Street, NW Washington, DC 20037
Washington Renaissance Hotel	★★★¹/₂	3	999 9th Street, NW Washington, DC 20001
Washington Vista Hilton	★★★★¹/₂	3	1400 M Street, NW Washington, DC 20005
Watergate Hotel	★★★★¹/₂	4	2650 Virginia Avenue, NW Washington, DC 20037
Westin ANA Hotel	★★★★¹/₂	5	24th and M Street, NW Washington, DC 20037
Willard Inter-Continental	★★★★¹/₂	3	1401 Pennsylvania Avenue, NW Washington, DC 20004
Windsor Park Hotel	★★¹/₂	6	2116 Kalorama Road, NW Washington, DC 20008
Wyndham Bristol Hotel	★★★¹/₂	5	2430 Pennsylvania Avenue, NW Washington, DC 20037

Local Phone	Fax	800 Reservations	Rack Rate	No. of Rooms	On-site Dining	Pool
(703) 486-1111	(703) 486-7248	(800) 862-7666	$$$+	220	Yes	Yes
(703) 521-1900	(703) 521-0332	(800) 468-9090	$$$+	417	Yes	Yes
(703) 448-1234	(703) 893-8193	(800) 572-ROOM	$$$$+	453	Yes	Yes
(703) 836-4700	(703) 548-4518	(800) 325-3535	$$$+	249	Yes	Yes
(202) 328-2000	(202) 234-0015	(800) 325-3535	$$$$ $$$	1,505	Yes	Yes
(202) 457-0500	(202) 659-4492	(800) 852-8512	$$$$–	196	No	Yes
(202) 861-8200	(202) 659-8601	(800) 424-2859	$$+	225	Yes	No
(703) 418-6800	(703) 418-3763	(800) HOTELS-1	$$$$$+	386	Yes	Yes
(202) 347-3000	(202) 466-9082	(800) HOTELS-1	$$$$$+	659	Yes	No
(202) 785-1277	(202) 785-6173	None	$$$$–	40	Yes	No
(202) 628-2100	(202) 737-2641	(800) 321-3010	$$$+	266	Yes	No
(202) 483-3000	(202) 265-8221	(800) HILTONS	$$$$$ $$$+	1,123	Yes	Yes
(202) 872-1500	(202) 872-1224	(800) 228-9290	$$$ $$$–	418	Yes	Yes
(202) 898-9000	(202) 789-4213	(800) 228-9898	$$$ $$$–	800	Yes	Yes
(202) 429-1700	(202) 785-0786	(800) 847-8232	$$$$+	399	Yes	No
(202) 965-2300	(202) 337-7915	(800) 424-2736	$$$ $$$+	235	Yes	Yes
(202) 429-2400	None	(800) 228-3000	$$$$ $$$–	415	Yes	Yes
(202) 628-9100	(202) 637-7314	(800) 327-0200	$$$$$$	340	Yes	No
(202) 483-7700	(202) 332-4547	(800) 247-3064	$$+	43	No	No
(202) 955-6400	(202) 955-5765	(800) 822-4200	$$$$$+	239	Yes	No

Index

If you would like to express your opinion about Washington or this guidebook, complete the following survey and mail it to:

Unofficial Guide Reader Survey
P.O. Box 43059
Birmingham, AL 35243

Inclusive dates of your visit: _____

How did you travel to Washington? ❑ Air ❑ Car ❑ Bus ❑ Train

Did you have a car during your stay? ❑ Yes ❑ No

Hometown: _____ State: _____

Number of Adults: _____ Minors: _____

Your age: _____ and Gender: M   F

The primary purpose of your visit: _____

Have you been to Washington before: ❑ Yes ❑ No

Where did you stay on your most recent visit? _____

Concerning your accomodations, on a scale with 100 the best and 0 the worst, how would you rate:

The quality of your room: _____
The value for the money: _____
Staff helpfulness: _____
How long did you wait to check in? _____ Check out? _____

Please list the restaurants where you ate, and rate your overall dining experience at each. Use the 100 = best, 0 = worst scale:

_____
_____
_____
_____